Human Behavior

J.B. LIPPINCOTT COMPANY
Philadelphia

Grand Rapids   *New York*   *St. Louis*   *San Francisco*
London   *Sydney*   *Tokyo*

Human Behavior

An Introduction for Medical Students

Edited by

Alan Stoudemire, M.D.

Associate Professor
Director, Medical Student Education in Psychiatry
Department of Psychiatry
Emory University School of Medicine
Atlanta, Georgia

24 CONTRIBUTORS

Acquisitions Editor: Lisa McAllister
Sponsoring Editor: Paula Callaghan
Project Editor: Tracy Resnik
Art Director: Susan Hess Blaker
Design Coordinator: Doug Smock
Designer: Doug Smock
Indexer: Ruth Elwell
Copy Editor: Mary Frawley
Production Manager: Helen Ewan
Production Supervisor: Kevin P. Johnson
Compositor: Circle Graphics
Printer/Binder: R.R. Donnelley
Cover Printer: NEBC

6   5   4   3   2

Library of Congress Cataloging in Publication Data

Human Behavior: an introduction for medical students/edited by Alan Stoudemire: with
    24 contributors.
        p.   cm.
    Includes bibliographical references.
    ISBN 0-397-50966-9
    1. Clinical health psychology.   2. Physician and patient.
3. Psychology.   4. Human behavior.   I. Stoudemire, Alan.
    [DNLM: 1. Behavior. BF 121 I615]
    R726.7.I57   1990
    616'.0019–dc20
    DNLM/DLC
    for Library of Congress   89–13552
                                                                              CIP

The authors and publisher have exerted every effort to ensure that drug selection and dosage set forth in this text are in accord with current recommendations and practice at the time of publication. However, in view of ongoing research, changes in government regulations, and the constant flow of information relating to drug therapy and drug reactions, the reader is urged to check the package insert for each drug for any change in indications and dosage and for added warnings and precautions. This is particularly important when the recommended agent is a new or infrequently employed drug.

Accompanying text:
Clinical Psychiatry for Medical Students
Edited by Alan Stoudemire, M.D.

This book is dedicated to my parents

CONTRIBUTORS

Bruce L. Ballard, M.D.

    Associate Dean
    Associate Professor of Clinical Psychiatry
    Cornell University Medical College
    New York, New York

Miron Baron, M.D.

    Professor of Clinical Psychiatry
    College of Physicians & Surgeons
    Columbia University
    New York, New York

Judith V. Becker, Ph.D.

    New York State Psychiatric Institute
    Professor of Clinical Psychology (in Psychiatry)
    College of Physicians & Surgeons
    Columbia University
    New York, New York

Peter J. Brown, Ph.D.

    Associate Professor and Chairman
    Department of Anthropology
    Emory University
    Decatur, Georgia

Steven A. Cohen-Cole, M.D.

    Associate Professor of Psychiatry
    Emory University School of Medicine
    Atlanta, Georgia

Pamela G. Dorsett, *Ph.D.*

> Clinical Assistant Professor of Psychiatry
> Emory University School of Medicine
> Atlanta, Georgia

Mina K. Dulcan, *M.D.*

> Associate Professor of Psychiatry
> Chief
> Child and Adolescent Psychiatry
> Emory University School of Medicine
> Atlanta, Georgia

Dwight L. Evans, *M.D.*

> Professor of Psychiatry & Medicine
> University of North Carolina School of Medicine
> Chapel Hill, North Carolina

Donald C. Fidler, *M.D.*

> Associate Professor of Psychiatry
> West Virginia University School of Medicine
> Morgantown, West Virginia

Joan Fiore, *Ph.D.*

> Adjunct Assistant Professor of Psychiatry
> Emory University School of Medicine
> Atlanta, Georgia

Mark G. Fuller, *M.D.*

> Assistant Professor of Psychiatry
> West Virginia University School of Medicine
> Morgantown, West Virginia

Robert N. Golden, *M.D.*

> Associate Professor of Psychiatry
> University of North Carolina School of Medicine
> Chapel Hill, North Carolina

Stephen A. Green, *M.D.*

> Clinical Associate Professor of Psychiatry
> Georgetown University School of Medicine
> Chevy Chase, Maryland

John J. Haggerty, Jr., M.D.

Associate Professor of Psychiatry
University of North Carolina School of Medicine
Chapel Hill, North Carolina

Lawrence B. Inderbitzin, M.D.

Associate Professor
Department of Psychiatry
Emory University School of Medicine
Training & Supervising Analyst
Emory Psychoanalytic Center
Atlanta, Georgia

Mark E. James, M.D.

Assistant Professor of Psychiatry
Emory University School of Medicine
Atlanta, Georgia

Nancy L. Kriseman, L.C.S.W.

Adjunct Associate
Department of Psychiatry
Emory University School of Medicine
Atlanta, Georgia

C. Michael Luke, M.D.

Clinical Assistant Professor of Psychiatry
Psychoanalytic Associate
Emory University School of Medicine
Emory Psychoanalytic Institute
Atlanta, Georgia

Richard P. Michael, M.D., Ph.D.

Professor of Psychiatry
Professor of Anatomy & Cell Biology
Emory University School of Medicine
Atlanta, Georgia

Cort A. Pedersen, M.D.

Assistant Professor of Psychiatry
University of North Carolina School of Medicine
Chapel Hill, North Carolina

Alan Stoudemire, M.D.

Associate Professor of Psychiatry
Emory University School of Medicine
Atlanta, Georgia

Troy L. Thompson, II, M.D.

Professor and Chairman
Department of Psychiatry
Jefferson Medical College
Thomas Jefferson University
Philadelphia, Pennsylvania

Bessel A. van der Kolk, M.D.

Lecturer in Psychiatry
Harvard Medical School;
Associate Visiting Professor
Rush Medical School
Chicago, Illinois
Director, Trauma Center
Massachusetts Mental Health Center
Harvard Medical School
Boston, Massachusetts

Thomas Wolman, M.D.

Director Coatesville-Jefferson Clinic
Clinical Assistant Professor of Psychiatry
Department of Psychiatry
Jefferson Medical College
Thomas Jefferson University
Philadelphia, Pennsylvania

Doris Zumpe, Ph.D.

Professor of Psychiatry (Ethology)
Emory University School of Medicine
Atlanta, Georgia

FOREWORD

It has become readily apparent during the past five years that there is a pressing national priority to increase the knowledge of mental disease among all physicians, to implement the understanding of psychiatric treatments and interventions, and to improve the skills of the majority of physicians who will undertake these treatments. The National Institute of Mental Health estimates that sixty percent of the thirty-two million people with mental disease in the United States receive their treatment within the primary care sector entirely. In fact, only one in five with mental illness receives care from the core mental health professionals, with psychiatrists providing only a portion of that care. There is also growing awareness that many nonpsychiatric physicians lack the motivation, the interest, or the conceptual framework that would permit them to provide state-of-the-art treatment to their many patients suffering from mental disorders.

What has been missing in medical education in psychiatry is the excitement and enthusiasm that is so evident in *Human Behavior: An Introduction for Medical Students,* edited by Dr. Stoudemire. The conceptual model that is offered is not peculiar to the behavioral sciences. The biopsychosocial model, in fact, will eventually permeate all of medicine. Beginning with this context and moving through the life cycle, the biological and psychological factors can be seen as the connecting links that support the scientific application of treatment approaches. This volume makes a most needed contribution to medical education and the eventual improvement of the medical care of the citizens of our nation.

Robert O. Pasnau, M.D.
Professor of Psychiatry
School of Medicine
University of California at Los Angeles
Los Angeles, California

PREFACE

The essence of the complete physician is the ability to integrate excellent medical treatment with compassionate psychological care of the patient. The primary emphasis, however, in medical training is devoted to assimilating a scientific knowledge base and practicing the technical aspects of medical diagnosis and treatment. Relatively little consistent attention is given to acquiring and developing the necessary knowledge and skills to understand and attend to the psychological and emotional needs of the medically ill. With rapid advances in medical science, diagnostic technology, and medical therapeutics over the past fifty years, medical students have been crushed by the amount of scientific information they must assimilate. The amount of time and attention devoted to teaching students fundamental principles of human behavior and the importance of psychological aspects of patient care is often given a low priority. The information barrage that students are subjected to, as well as a widespread tendency to track down a specialty choice early in medical school in an effort to limit the amount of information that must be mastered, further contributes to a trend toward narrowness in the training of physicians. In addition, compared to the "hard data" of other scientific disciplines, psychiatry often has appeared diffuse, amorphous, and out of the mainstream of traditional medicine.

There has been an enormous increase in the scientific knowledge base for psychiatry in all of its facets: biological, psychological, and sociological. The biochemistry of mental illness has gradually been elucidated from studies of aberrant neurotransmitter and receptor activity and molecular genetics. This emerging scientific knowledge has had profound influences on biological perspectives on mental illness. In addition, the field of psychopharmacology has made remarkable advances in providing specific treatments for certain psychiatric illnesses such as psychotic, mood, and anxiety disorders. Recent advances in neuroradiographic and neuroendocrine probes of the central nervous system have also provided remarkable new ways of measuring biological parameters of normal and abnormal mental functioning. Moreover, while these biological advances may appear to have supplanted the importance of psychoanalytic theories and the perspectives of developmental psychology in psychiatric illness, a fascinating body of information is accumulating to indicate that certain types of developmental traumas, deprivations, and stresses may have a lasting impact on the central nervous system, leading to altered social behavior, interpersonal relationships, affective states, and vulnerability to stress. Hence, intriguing scientific evidence is accumulating that may potentially link psychological theories of behavior with neurobiological perspectives that will enable a true integration of the behavioral sciences. Where pertinent, this text will point toward trends in this psychobiological body of knowledge.

Throughout this text, the term "biopsychosocial model" will be used. In its essence, this theoretical model for understanding behavior and illness emphasizes the importance of understanding behavior in health and illness from a systems perspective where multiple biological, psychological, and social systems interact and influence each other. To focus exclusively on either a biological, psychological, or sociological area while neglecting the others leads to a narrow—and mistaken—viewpoint. While in clinical situations necessity and urgency may lead the physician to focus on one given area initially (attending to a patient's acute myocardial infarction in the emergency room), one must nevertheless not lose sight of the psychological aspects of the illness (the patient's fears and emotional reactions to the heart attack) or the effects that the illness might have on other aspects of the patient's life (ability to work and financial affairs). Hence, this multi-dimensional biopsychosocial approach to patient care requires the physician to assess the multiple aspects of the patient's condition.

It is upon the general premise of the biopsychosocial model that this book is based, and it is this viewpoint that forms the predominant theme of the text. The text itself is divided into five sections that address different aspects of a biopsychosocial understanding of human behavior. The first section introduces the basic principles of the biopsychosocial model, its importance for patient care, and the scientific data to support the model. This chapter is followed by a review of sociocultural aspects of behavior, focusing on illness behavior and patterns of psychiatric symptoms viewed from a cross-cultural perspective.

Section II presents in some detail two major theoretical schools of psychology: psychoanalytic and behavioral theory. The reason to discuss primarily these two perspectives is addressed in the introduction to the chapter on psychoanalytic psychology, but basically involved a practical decision to cover principles in two major schools of psychological thought in some detail, rather than covering multiple viewpoints in a superficial manner, which would be of little practical use to the student. The important psychological principles of psychoanalytic and behavioral theory are presented as well as their importance for patient care.

In Section III, fundamentals of normal behavior are dealt with in a comprehensive manner from infancy to late life. While childhood and adolescent development have always received the most emphasis in psychiatry and psychology, the text has also incorporated an excellent discussion of *adult* developmental cycles that extends to issues of death and dying. The importance of the family system in development and adjusting to illness is also reviewed, as well as the physician's role in identifying and intervening in dysfunctional families. This section concludes with an intriguing discussion on one of the most exciting emerging areas in behavioral science, that is, the neurobiological effects of developmental stresses and emotional trauma, which as noted above, may serve to integrate psychological and biological perspectives on behavior and mental illness.

Neurobiological aspects of behavior are further discussed in Section IV, which addresses three areas relevant to the biological basis of behavior—ethology, neurobiology, and behavioral genetics. Contained in these chapters are data derived from basic neurochemical and genetic research that should intrigue and interest the most biologically oriented student, as well as provide fascinating evidence for the neurochemical influences on behavior.

In the final chapter, Green again draws upon the biopsychosocial model and attempts to integrate the principles discussed in previous chapters to demonstrate how they are useful and important in the psychological and emotional care of the patient. In this chapter, the specific types of emotional and psychological reactions that patients may have to illness will be discussed, as well as how they may be managed by physicians using the biopsychosocial model of medical care.

While this text briefly mentions and alludes to the significance of biological, psychological, and social factors in the development of psychiatric illness, specific psychopathological syndromes and the diagnosis and treatment of psychiatric disorders are not specifically addressed. Ideally, this text serves as the basis or entrée to the companion text in this series, *Clinical Psychiatry for Medical Students,* which does address fundamental principles of clinical psychiatry—and also takes an integrated approach to diagnosis and treatment of the major psychopathological syndromes in psychiatry.

As mentioned earlier in this introduction, the essence of the complete physician is the ability to practice excellent medicine while attending to the psychological and emotional needs of the patient in a compassionate manner. This is certainly not a new concept in medicine and has been the ideal of the profession for centuries. Nowhere has this ethic been more eloquently summarized as in the classic 1927 essay by Francis Peabody entitled "The Care of the Patient":

> Disease in man is never exactly the same as disease in an experimental animal, for in man the disease at once affects and is af-

fected by what we call the emotional life. Thus, the physician who attempts to take care of a patient while he neglects this factor is as unscientific as the investigator who neglects to control all the conditions that may affect his experiment. The good physician knows his patients through and through, and his knowledge is bought dearly. Time, sympathy and understanding must be lavishly dispensed, but the reward is to be found in that personal bond which forms the greatest satisfaction of the practice of medicine. One of the essential qualities of the clinician is interest in humanity, for the secret of the care of the patient is in caring for the patient.

Alan Stoudemire, M.D.

ACKNOWLEDGMENTS

This text could not have been completed without the tireless dedication, loyalty, and effort of my administrative assistant, Ms. Lynda Mathews. Her contribution to this book is greatly appreciated. In addition, I would like to thank Dr. Jeffrey Houpt, Chair of the Department of Psychiatry and Dean of Emory University School of Medicine, for his ongoing support and encouragement in my career development that has helped make this text a reality.

CONTENTS

1 The Biopsychosocial Model

1 The Biopsychosocial Model in Medical Practice

Steven A. Cohen-Cole

3

2 Culture, Ethnicity, and Behavior and the Practice of Medicine

Peter J. Brown and Bruce Ballard

31

2 Two Fundamental Psychological Theories of Human Behavior

3 Psychoanalytic Psychology

Lawrence B. Inderbitzin, C. Michael Luke, and Mark E. James

51

4 Behavioral and Social Learning Psychology

Pamela G. Dorsett

85

3 Human Development

5 Human Sexual Development and Physiology

Judith V. Becker

113

6 Childhood and Adolescent   131
   Development

   Mina K. Dulcan

7 Adult Development   178

   Thomas Wolman and Troy L. Thompson, II

8 The Family in Human Development   206
   and Medical Practice

   *Nancy L. Kriseman, Joan Fiore, and Alan
   Stoudemire*

9 The Behavioral and Psychobiologic   226
   Effects of Developmental Trauma

   Bessel A. van der Kolk

4 *Biological Basis of Behavior*

10 Ethology and Human Behavior   241

    Doris Zumpe and Richard P. Michael

11 Neurobiologic Aspects of Behavior   261

    *Cort A. Pedersen, Robert N. Golden,
    Dwight L. Evans, and John J. Haggerty, Jr.*

12 Behavioral Genetics   306

    Miron Baron

5 *Clinical Applications*

13 Supportive Psychologic Care of the   323
    Medically Ill

    Stephen A. Green

Appendix 1

A Problem-Oriented Method for   339
Teaching Human Behavior

Donald C. Fidler and Mark G. Fuller

Appendix 2

Audiovisual Guide   345

Donald C. Fidler

Index   363

The Biopsychosocial Model

1

The Biopsychosocial Model in Medical Practice

Steven A. Cohen-Cole

The following four postulates set forth the broad outlines of the biopsychosocial model of illness, which is the underlying philosophy for this textbook of human behavior:

1. Most illness, whether physical or psychiatric, is a biologic, psychologic, and social phenomenon.
2. Biologic, psychologic, and social variables influence the predisposition, onset, course, and outcome of most illnesses.
3. Physicians who are able to evaluate the relationships of biologic, psychologic, and social variables in their patients' illnesses will be able to develop more effective therapeutic interventions and to achieve better patient outcomes.
4. To evaluate and manage the psychosocial aspects of patients' medical problems adequately, physicians must be able to establish and maintain therapeutic doctor–patient relationships with many different types of patients.

Each chapter in this text will present a different perspective based on these postulates. This book will provide students with practical approaches to integrating these variables in patient care. Chapter 1 presents empirical and clinical data that support the four postulates described above, along with suggestions to help physicians use this approach in the care of their patients.

WHY SHOULD PHYSICIANS STUDY EMOTIONS, BEHAVIOR, OR SOCIAL PROCESSES?

Many medical students may wonder what a course in human behavior really has to do with their future practice of medicine. They may feel that they have come to medical school to learn about disease: how to diagnose and treat ailments of the body. These students may think that, while humanistic medicine (i.e., "caring for" and being "nice" or "understanding" to patients) is an important part of medical practice, the principles of a humanistic approach to medical practice are intuitive and self-evident and cannot or do not need to be "taught." In addition, many practicing clinicians and students acknowledge that patients with psychiatric problems often come to physicians for help, but they feel that such patients can be referred elsewhere for help with their psychiatric problems and that medical practice should focus on physical illnesses.

This view of disease and medical practice, which many physicians endorse, has been described as the "biomedical model of illness" (Engel, 1977). It argues that psychologic and social variables are of secondary importance in illness and the treatment process and that physician's major efforts should be primarily, if not exclusively, focused on the biologic aspects of physical illnesses.

This text disputes this position and advocates an integrated approach to patient care by use of a "biopsychosocial model of illness." This view endorses a multidimensional or systems approach to the practice of medicine, and conceptualizes illness and illness outcomes as determined by multiple biologic, psychologic, and social variables.

The biopsychosocial model maintains that emotional, behavioral, and social processes are implicated in the development, course, and outcome of illness. Medical students need to learn basic principles of psychosocial assessment and intervention to be able to practice this type of clinical medicine and to be able to provide adequate and comprehensive care for their patients. Physicians who can integrate the psychologic and social variables in their patients' illnesses will generally be able to develop more effective clinical interventions that will lead to better treatment outcome. In addition, physicians who endorse a biopsychosocial approach to medical practice will generally have better relationships with their patients, possibly fewer lawsuits, and will find the practice of medicine less stressful and more personally fulfilling.

After the following introductory case study, this chapter will then cover a wide range of topics related to biopsychosocial medicine including:

1. Psychologic and social factors related to the predisposition, onset, course, and outcome of physical illness;
2. The use of psychosocial treatments for physical illness;
3. A review of psychobiologic mechanisms that might mediate between psychosocial processes and biologic effects;
4. Recent findings in psychiatric epidemiology, particularly as they relate to the general practice of medicine;
5. Sociocultural influences on illness and illness behavior;
6. The applicability of the biopsychosocial model to traditional psychiatric illnesses.

The following case study will provide a basis to begin a discussion of biopsychosocial assessment and treatment. The case will be presented, and a model biopsychosocial formulation will be developed along with multidimensional treatment recommendations.

A CASE STUDY

Mr. RF is a 47-year-old married male with a 60-pack–year history of cigarette smoking (i.e., two packs a day for 30 years), who has a 5-year his-

tory of laryngeal cancer. He received several neck surgeries 5 years ago and now reports that his life has "never been the same" since that time. Physical problems include difficulty talking and swallowing, with unpredictable and uncontrollable episodes of coughing and vomiting. These episodes are extremely embarrassing to him and have led him to restrict his activities. He does not want to go out anymore and does not want to socialize with friends or family.

He and his wife report that he has been depressed for 5 years, but that the depression has gotten much worse in the last year or so. He does not want to do anything and derives almost no pleasure in living. He has frequent crying spells and has great difficulty sleeping at night. He usually can fall asleep without too much trouble, but often awakens in the middle of the night and cannot fall back asleep. He feels sad most of the time and feels that life is a burden. He often feels that he would prefer to be dead than to live in his current situation, but he says that he would not consider suicide. His appetite is poor, although he has not lost weight. He reports "no energy" and very low self-esteem. He is guilty about what he has done to his family as a result of this illness and blames himself for the illness because of his heavy smoking history. He has trouble making decisions and reports trouble concentrating, as exemplified in difficult keeping his mind on books, television programs, or conversations.

He reports a sudden cessation of sexual activity since his diagnosis of cancer. He has no libido and feels unattractive to his wife. He and his wife report the almost total absence of physical intimacy in their relationship during the last 5 years. They do not hug each other anymore. There is little overt conflict, and the patient feels grateful to his wife and feels that they have become "closer" since his illness. His wife, however, is very tearful in discussing the impact of the illness on her life. She feels guilty and responsible for her husband, but does not want to have to restrict her own life unreasonably. She feels that she has retained the ability to enjoy life and that if her husband cannot be motivated to go out, she has the right to go out without him. She spends time with her children and other friends.

Mr. RF and his wife are both worried about finances. Since his operations and his trouble talking, he has been unable to continue his work as a real estate agent. He has been denied Social Security disability payments. His wife works in retail sales, but her income is not sufficient to cover their household expenses, including the costs of their two children, a girl aged 14 and a boy aged 10. They are having trouble meeting the mortgage payments on their house, and they may need to sell the house and move into an apartment.

In addition, the patient is extremely worried about the impact of his illness on his children, especially because his own father died of lung cancer when the patient was 12. His mother, in addition, suffered from depressive illnesses, with two psychiatric hospitalizations for this problem.

He was referred for psychiatric evaluation. His internist felt that he was suffering from a rather severe depression and that his overall quality of life was more impaired than would be expected from the effect of the cancer itself.

CASE FORMULATION

Biologic Variables

The biologic variables are obviously the chief precipitants of Mr. RF's deteriorating condition. The cancer had a devastating impact on his life. He suffered from several difficult surgeries, and, after these surgeries, he could no longer function as well as he had previously.

Some new physical symptoms have been troublesome. His talking has become more dysarthric (slurred with poor enunciation). He has lost sensation on part of his tongue, and his coughing has become much worse. He is in the process of a new neurologic evaluation to determine whether he is suffering from a recurrence of his cancer. He has just learned that he is also suffering from hypothyroidism secondary to neck radiation for the cancer.

The hypothyroid condition can itself cause an organic mood disorder, which mimics major depression (O'Shanick et al, 1987). Similarly, the patient has been on the antihypertensive beta blocker, propranolol, which has also been implicated in organic mood disturbances (Hall et al, 1980). In addition, the patient's mother suffered from depressive illness. This family history suggests a biologically transmitted genetic predisposition to depression (see Chap. 12 on genetic vulnerability to psychiatric illness).

Psychologic Variables

Mr. RF's psychologic character traits play a prominent role in his current problems. He has always been a rather controlled, orderly person who has depended on his intellect and a thorough, rational approach to problems to help him cope with life's vicissitudes. He always disdained emotionality and felt that most of life's difficulties could be overcome if sufficient effort was put into working out practical solutions. He spent a great deal of effort organizing his work and his private life in order to arrange his affairs to be as predictable as possible. This personality style has been referred to as the "obsessive style" (Mackinnon and Michels, 1971) (see Chap. 3 for a discussion of ego defenses and personality style).

The cancer, by itself, presented a major threat not only to his life, but, by its very nature, to the predictability and certainty of his future. For a patient with an obsessive style of coping, the vagaries of cancer treatment and outcome present particularly troubling stresses. In addition, the patient's difficulty with eating and talking, as well as his unpredictable vomiting, compromised his control of his social circumstances and led to extremely embarrassing situations.

One episode on a trip to visit family was particularly disturbing. While eating dinner in an elegant restaurant, he suddenly and unpredictably vomited. This episode was so distressing to him, that he now phobically avoids all social situations. His depressive symptomatology has become much worse since then. The hopelessness, anhedonia (i.e., inability to experience interest or pleasure), and fatigue have gotten worse since then. He refuses almost all activities.

In addition to these difficulties, the patient is extremely guilty about his cigarette smoking and blames himself for his illness and the deleterious effect it is having on his family. He worries about the psychologic impact of the cancer on his children, especially if he should die from the disease. He cannot stop thinking about the death of his own father when he was young, and he is sad for himself and for his children at the same time.

Social Variables

The social variables are also prominent in this case.

First of all, the loss of the patient's income has had a very negative impact on the family. Worries about finances have introduced new stresses into the family, and they are facing the loss of their home. The loss of the job has also had a negative impact on the patient's self-esteem, in that he is no longer able to fulfill the "manly" role of "breadwinner" for the family.

In addition, the patient has cut himself off from several important sources of social support, which might contribute positively to his current quality of life. Because of extreme vulnerability to social embarrassment, the patient does not see friends or children as much as previously. He may go for weeks without any outside contacts.

His withdrawal has had very negative effects on his wife, and this has also affected their marital relationship. There is no more sexual intimacy. His wife is tearful in discussing this and the fact that there is no more physical contact (including hugging) of any kind in their marriage. As we discussed this, the patient said that it is very hard for him to express emotional issues and added that he feels very unlovable in his present condition.

Biopsychosocial Formulation

The biopsychosocial formulation must evaluate and integrate the impact of different variables on the clinical problem. The patient is clearly suffering from "major depression," which is itself a biopsychosocial illness. Neurochemical, endocrine, and neurophysiologic alterations are all part of this illness syndrome. Mr. RF's obsessive personality style makes adaptation to illness difficult, because good coping with cancer requires some ability to live with uncertainty as well as adequate self-esteem to cope with potentially embarrassing situations. His loss of his father at an early age may, in fact, predispose him to future depressive illness (see Chap. 9 for a discussion of developmental trauma as predisposing factors for future anxiety and depression).

His marriage and social contacts are also threatened by his illness and his response to the illness. The possibility of a recurrence of the malignancy presents a new challenge to a very unstable psychologic and social equilibrium.

It would be misleading, however, as well as dangerous to conclude that Mr. RF has "good reasons" to be depressed. He certainly has many good reasons to be "sad," but the syndrome of major depression does not uniformly result from significant physical illness or any severe stress. While the prevalence of psychiatric disorders is considerably higher in patients with chronic physical illness than in the general population (lifetime prevalence of 42% compared to 33%) (Wells et al, 1988), the majority of patients with terminal cancer do not, in fact, develop major depressive syndromes (Cohen-Cole and Stoudemire, 1987). Major depression is associated with physiologic and neurovegetative changes that occur in only a subset of individuals with severe physical illness (Cassem, 1988). When physical illness is complicated by a major depression, it should be vigorously recognized and treated. As Cassem (1988) has pointed out, "depression is a dread complication of physical illness." Physicians who suggest that patients may have "good reasons" to be depressed may do their patients a disservice because the incorrect assumption that depression is "normal" may lead to an acceptance of the syndrome without obtaining proper and effective treatment.

Biopsychosocial Management

Biopsychosocial management requires the integration of different therapeutic strategies along all three relevant dimensions.

Biologic Interventions

Biologic intervention for the cancer evaluation must proceed rapidly and without delay. The depression must be treated similarly. First of all, the patient must receive appropriate thyroid replacement therapy. It is possible that this intervention may make a major difference in the patient's symptoms of depression. Similarly, the physician should consider substituting another antihypertensive for the propranolol, which might be exacerbating his depression. (Chapter 11 discusses the biological influences on behavior, including mood regulation.)

If the patient does not respond rapidly to thyroid replacement or substitution of antihypertensives, biologic intervention for the major depression must be initiated. An antidepressant medication, such as doxepin or fluoxetine, should be prescribed to address the disruption in the patient's neurobiologic mood regulating and stress response system, and the drug should be monitored closely for effectiveness and side-effects (Cohen-Cole and Stoudemire, 1987).

Psychologic Interventions

Psychologic intervention is just as important. Several different forms of psychotherapy for major depression, including interpersonal and cognitive approaches, have been demonstrated to be as effective as pharmacotherapy. The short-term interpersonal approach would focus on the difficulties the patient has experienced in making the transition from his role as breadwinner to the "sick role." The interpersonal approach would also focus on the new stresses on the marriage because of the cancer (see Chap. 7 on adult lifecycles and the stressful effects of illness on the family).

In contrast, a cognitive approach would emphasize the unrealistic expectations

Mr. RF places on himself in the face of the devastating illness and help him maintain his self-esteem in spite of his new need to be more dependent on others (see Chaps. 3 and 4 for a general overview of psychodynamic and behavioral/learning principles in psychotherapy).

Formal psychotherapy would definitely be indicated for Mr. RF, but many such patients will not accept this form of treatment. They may believe that the need for psychotherapy points to a character "defect," and they defend themselves against this view by refusing psychotherapy. Other patients refuse psychotherapy because of the expense involved.

Primary physicians can help such patients accept formal psychotherapy by legitimizing the process of therapy. Physicians can point out that depression is, indeed, a medical illness that can be helped by expert treatment, including psychotherapy as well as medications. Physicians can also help patients accept psychiatric referral by offering to collaborate with the treating psychotherapist and to remain in contact with the patient during the treatment. It is also often helpful to discuss examples of other patients with similar problems who have benefited from psychiatric referral. (Chapter 8 lists techniques of referring patients and a formula for psychiatric evaluation and psychotherapy.)

Is there anything that the primary care physician can do with depressed cancer patients who do not accept psychiatric referral? There is, in fact, a great deal that can be done (see Chap. 13 on basic approaches to the psychologic care of patients). First of all, a solid interpersonal relationship must be established and maintained. This involves the use of good communication skills. *Careful listening* is essential, along with allowing the patient the opportunity to ventilate his/her feelings. Patients must be given *adequate opportunities to ask questions* as well. *Empathic comments,* which reflect the patient's feelings, can be quite helpful (e.g., "It is clear that you are especially worried about the impact that your illness may have on your children"). *Legitimizing* these feelings is also reassuring to patients (e.g., "I can certainly understand why you would find it so hard to think about the effect of your illness on your children"). Offering direct statements of support (e.g., "I will do what I can to help") as well as statements of partnership ("Let's try to work on this problem together") also can have a significant impact on patient's ability to cope. Lastly, *respectful comments that praise* the patient for actual coping efforts that have succeeded are usually very comforting (e.g., "I am really impressed with how well you managed to cope with your children's fears last week") (Cohen-Cole and Bird, 1986).

The most important communication skill is the *flexibility* required to observe the patient's response to different interventions and the ability and willingness to try interventions that will work for each patient. Some patients require more active support, while others prefer quiet listening. Physicians can learn these different approaches if they observe their patients closely and demonstrate the willingness to listen to their needs.

With respect to Mr. RF, physicians can help such obsessive patients by giving them as much control over their treatment as possible. Providing adequate information is essential, and questions must be answered directly and as specifically as possible. Commenting directly on the difficulty of loss of control is usually perceived as empathic by obsessive or worry-prone patients (e.g., "I can certainly understand why this unpredictable illness is so particularly stressful to you, since you have always been able to manage your affairs in an orderly, predictable way").

Similarly, obsessive patients usually are frightened and resistant to becoming dependent on anyone. Sometimes if this fear is acknowledged, physicians can help their patients by indicating that sometimes accepting dependency takes unusual strength (e.g., "I know that it is hard to have to depend on someone else to provide for your basic needs, but I want you to realize that it takes particular strength and courage to be able to ask for and accept help that you, in fact, really do need. You actually can do your friends and family a favor by accepting the help that they really do want to offer").

This patient may be reexperiencing the grief he suffered as a child as well as anticipatory grief over his own possible death. (Chapter 13 discusses in some detail the "grief model" of coping with illness, which relates directly to the type of supportive psychotherapy that the primary care physician may be able to accomplish.)

Social Interventions

Social intervention in this case is crucial. Vocational rehabilitation might be helpful in finding some productive employment for the patient. Social workers might help the patient find ways to appeal the Social Security decisions, and, if necessary, legal assistance could be considered to appeal disability decisions.

Mr. RF's marriage is quite stressed. There is loneliness for him and his wife, and they have not been able to talk to each other about their needs. A decrease in sexual activity is common after cancer diagnoses, but this decrease need not herald the end of all physical intimacy (e.g., hugging). Mr. RF and his wife need the opportunity to talk to each other about their needs. A primary care physician can be very helpful in this regard, simply by bringing up issues of intimacy and sexual relationships for open discussion. More open communication and ventilation of feelings are often sufficient to help resolve such problems. In more complicated cases, referral for sexual therapy can be essential (see Chap. 5 on human sexuality).

The children are probably quite anxious themselves and may be suffering from psychologic distress or even a psychiatric disorder. Every effort should be made to have them seen by the primary physician or by someone with special skills on the healthcare team. If indicated, individual or family therapy for the children may be important (see Chap. 6 on how children cope with illness).

Mrs. F has her own feelings of guilt, responsibility, and resentment, which have an impact on the overall quality of life of the couple as well as the family. She could benefit from a chance to explore and work through some of these feelings, either with the primary physician or with a psychotherapist.

Summary

Many of the interventions suggested above for the adequate management of Mr. RF involve sophisticated and extensive psychosocial interventions. In order for physicians to be able to provide this type of comprehensive patient care, they must develop the knowledge and skill necessary in the course of their medical training.

The psychosocial interventions described above do, in fact, require more time than a mechanical and narrowly biologic or "purely medical" approach, but they do not require the intensity or time demands of formal psychotherapy. It should be remembered that patients with chronic illness return to primary physicians many times and that a great deal can be accomplished through short supportive appointments spaced over longer periods of time.

Thus, in addition to the prescription of antidepressants, the adequate treatment of this patient necessitates numerous other psychologic and social interventions. The physician who is interested and sufficiently well trained to provide this comprehensive care can function efficiently and effectively in this role. Physicians should make it clear to such patients that a consultation with a psychiatrist may be necessary but would not disrupt their general medical care. In making a psychiatric (or other mental health referral), the primary physician should always indicate willingness and interest in staying involved in the care of the patient.

The prognosis for Mr. RF to obtain improved functioning and improved quality of life is quite good, assuming the patient complies with these multimodal treatment interventions.

THE BIOPSYCHOSOCIAL MODEL IN MEDICAL PRACTICE

Just as the biopsychosocial model of illness helps us understand and effectively treat patients like Mr. RF, who have concurrent major *psychiatric* disorders that are complicating their primary physical condition, the biopsychosocial approach is just as helpful for *medical patients*. In other words, evaluation and management of psychologic and social variables are critical in the care of the physically ill, *even if there is no major clinically significant psychiatric disorder present.* The following section will discuss the ways in which psychosocial variables have been shown to be significant in the predisposition, onset, course, and outcome of physical illness. Psychosocial interventions that lead to improved physical outcome and the psychobiologic mechanisms by which some of these influences may operate will also be cited. The section will conclude with suggestions for the practice of clinical medicine.

Psychologic and Behavioral Predisposition to Physical Illness

There are many psychologic, behavioral, and social variables that play a role in the development of physical illness. In fact, lifestyle and personal habits, such as tobacco use, alcohol and drug abuse, overeating, poor nutrition, lack of exercise, and so forth, account together for about 70% of all illness and death in the United States (Houpt et al, 1980). Obesity, for example, is related to heart disease, diabetes, and hypertension. Nicotine addiction from tobacco smoking is directly associated with lung cancer, emphysema, and coronary artery disease. Alcohol is related to cirrhosis of the liver, gastric ulcers, dementia, and half of the yearly fatal traffic accidents in the United States. The financial costs of these behaviorally related illnesses are staggering: the direct costs alone were approximately $250 billion dollars in 1983 (70% of a healthcare expenditure of $355 billion) (Kamerow et al, 1986). This figure does not even include an estimate of the indirect costs (e.g., lost productivity).

Personality factors have also been thought to be predisposing factors to certain physical illnesses. Probably the best known is the so-called Type A behavior pattern and its relationship to coronary artery disease. Coronary artery disease is now the leading cause of death in this country, and any knowledge about predisposing or other risk factors should help us design appropriate interventions. "Type A" individuals feel under relentless pressure of time and are usually under a competitive and hostile strain with other people. Such persons are usually quite serious and ambitious in their work. They often find it hard to relax and to enjoy interpersonal pleasures. In general, Type A individuals walk and eat rapidly, hurry others along in conversation, speak with a very strong emphasis, clench their hands and teeth, try to do two things at once, and experience great time pressure (Friedman, 1969)

Early studies found that people with strong Type A behavior patterns have two times the incidence of coronary artery disease compared with persons without this pattern (Type B individuals). Similarly, once someone experienced a heart attack, the presence of the Type A behavioral pattern was associated with five times the likelihood of experiencing a second heart attack. Furthermore, the presence of Type A behavior was associated with two times the likelihood of a heart attack being fatal (Rosenman et al, 1975).

There has been extensive controversy about the validity of the Type A behavior pattern and its hypothesized association with coronary artery disease. Some recent studies have failed to demonstrate the expected results (Ragland and Brand, 1988). Current conceptualization of the Type A behavior pattern now focuses more specifically on the dimensions of suspiciousness and hostility (Williams et al, 1980).

A major intervention study based on the Type A construct has recently lent some support to its validity. A 5-year controlled study examined the effects on cardiac recurrence of an elaborate stress-management intervention focused on reducing the strength of the Type A behavior pattern. At the end of the follow-up period, the recurrence rate for nonfatal infarcts in the intervention group was approximately half of that in the other groups. Moreover, within the treatment group itself, the rates of recurrence were lowest among those with the greatest reduction in Type A behaviors (Friedman et al, 1984). In general, despite recent skepticism, some elements of the Type A construct seem to describe a robust and persisting relationship to coronary artery disease and may still be considered as a possible risk factor for this disease (Dimsdale, 1988).

Onset of Illness

The most common psychosocial variable associated with illness onset has to do with the sometimes illusive concept of "stress." Everyone "knows" that stress is related to disease; the stress–illness connection is widespread in popular mythology and the media. The concept of stress provides the philosophic linkage between the mind and the body. It is a fascinating, controversial, and pervasive concept in medical care today.

Stress concepts are controversial because they are sometimes very loosely defined and oversimplified. Exaggerated claims that stress causes all illness in a rather straightforward, mechanistic manner have led to skepticism. However, careful definitions and well-designed research have led to some remarkable findings about the relationship of stress and illness.

Generally speaking, the term *stress* has been used to describe emotional distress, the situational conditions that appear to provoke such distress, or both. For the purposes of clarity in this chapter, "stress" will denote the subjective state of distress, and the conditions that provoke this arousal will be termed "stressors." In order for conditions to cause subjective stress, they generally must tax the adaptive capacity of the person.

Holmes and Rahe (1967) postulated that major events in a person's life requiring change of any kind, whether positive or negative, would require adaptive efforts and readjustment of the organism. They argued that these effects can be cumulative and that the more readjustment required by the person, the more likely the person would be to develop physical illnesses. Holmes and Rahe (1967) developed the Social Readjustment Rating Scale to measure the impact of cumulative life events on the person (Table 1-1). As can be seen, a number associated with hypothesized readjust-

Table 1–1 **Social Readjustment Rating Scale**

RANK	LIFE EVENT	VALUE
1	Death of spouse	100
2	Divorce	73
3	Marital separation	65
4	Jail term	63
5	Death of close family member	53
6	Personal injury or illness	50
7	Marriage	47
8	Fired at work	46
9	Marital reconciliation	45
10	Retirement	44
11	Change in health of family member	40
12	Pregnancy	39
13	Sex difficulties	39
14	Gain of new family member	39
15	Business readjustment	38
17	Death of close friend	36
18	Change to different line of work	36
19	Change in number of arguments	35
23	Child leaving home	29
24	Trouble with in-laws	29
25	Outstanding personal achievement	28
27	Begin or end school	26
29	Revision of personal habits	24
31	Change in work hours or conditions	20
32	Change in residence	20
33	Change in school	20
36	Change in social activities	18
39	Change in family get togethers	16
43	Minor violation of the law	11

(Adapted from Holmes TH, Rahe RH: The social readjustment rating scale. J Psychosom Res 11:213–218, 1967)

ment is assigned to each of 43 different but common life events. The higher the number, the more readjustment is usually required after the event. While there have been many methodologic criticisms of this instrument, hundreds of subsequent investigators using better instruments have also demonstrated an association between life event "scores" and future development of physical illnesses (i.e., the higher the current life events scores, the more likely persons have been to develop physical illnesses in the future; Cohen, 1981). The psychobiologic mechanisms through which life events or stressors can lead to illness are just beginning to be clarified and will be reviewed in a subsequent section.

Animal research has also been very illuminating in helping us understand the relationship of stressors to illness. A very large literature provides convincing data that a variety of stressors to animals (crowding, maternal separation, isolation, cold, immersion in water, electric shocks, rotation stress, and so forth) lead to increased incidence of hypertension, heart disease, ulcers, and decreased resistance to microbes, x-rays, and transplanted tumor cells (Ader, 1981; Cassel, 1974; Weiner, 1977; Weiner et al, 1981).

There are several lines of investigation linking stress and mortality. One of the most replicable findings about stressful life events has demonstrated the risk of grief. Widows and widowers suffer a significantly increased risk of dying in the year after the death of their spouses (Middleton and Raphael, 1987). A recent study published in the *New England Journal of Medicine* demonstrates that psychologic stress among patients with cardiac disease is associated with silent myocardial ischemia and ventricular dysfunction. This strongly suggests that stress is related to undesirable cardiac events and possibly cardiac death (Rozanski et al, 1988). Sudden cardiac death is often precipitated by emotional distress (Dimsdale, 1988).

Lack of social support also seems to be related to the occurrence of illness. One elegant epidemiologic study demonstrated in a prospective fashion that persons with low social support suffered from a significantly increased mortality 5 years later. This proved to be true even after controlling for the effects of smoking, health status, healthcare behavior, and all other health-related variables known to the investigators (Berkman and Syme, 1979).

Influence of Psychosocial Variables on the Course and Outcome of Illness

Numerous psychosocial variables have been shown to relate to the course and outcome of physical illnesses. In particular, an accumulation of significant life events can herald poor outcome. Social support in some circumstances has been shown to buffer the deleterious impact of high life events. A particularly ominous circumstance, then, is the combination of high life events without adequate social support to buffer these experiences. These two variables, particularly in combination, have been shown in numerous studies to predict poor outcome of physical illnesses.

High stress (as measured by the presence of many significant life events) and low social support was associated with four times the subsequent risk of death in patients with myocardial infarctions. This order of magnitude was identical to the relative risk associated with other cardiac complications such as arrhythmias, congestive heart failure, and so forth (Ruberman et al, 1984).

Similarly, obstetric patients with high life events scores and low social support have three times the rate of pregnancy complications (Nuckolls et al, 1972). Asthmatic patients experiencing high degrees of stressful life events and low social support are more likely to be using high dose steroid treatments (de Araujo et al, 1972).

Psychosocial Interventions Make a Difference in the Outcome of Physical Illness

The research indicating that psychosocial variables have an impact on illness predisposition, onset, course, and outcome becomes particularly important when it comes to the point of designing interventions. Prediction, by itself, has an importance in medical care, but psychosocial interventions that can be shown to improve the prognosis of physical illness might be able to lower morbidity and mortality.

Numerous studies indicate that psychosocial interventions do indeed affect health outcomes in a positive direction. A metaanalysis of 34 controlled studies examining the effects of a supportive, educational, or psychotherapeutic intervention on patients after myocardial infarctions or surgery demonstrated that such interventions were associated with improved physical outcome (less pain, temperature, infection, and so forth) as well as improved emotional outcome (less anxiety and depression). Furthermore, experimental subjects receiving the supportive interventions were discharged an average of 2 days earlier than control subjects (Mumford et al, 1982).

The study of cardiac patients with Type A behavior, discussed above, showed that behavioral intervention could halve the likelihood of experiencing future infarctions (Friedman et al, 1984). Providing a supportive companion to women in labor resulted in one half the complications compared with randomized control patients who did not receive this companionship. In addition, the women with the supportive companions achieved better bonding with their infants (Sosa et al, 1980).

Psychiatric treatment in patients with chronic physical illnesses, such as hypertension, diabetes, chronic respiratory illnesses, and so forth, has been shown to be associated with lower overall medical costs (Mumford et al, 1984). In addition, formal psychotherapy has also been shown to be effective in improving the physical outcome of patients with a wide range of physical illnesses (Cohen-Cole et al, 1986).

Psychobiologic Mechanisms

How does stress lead to illness? How does low support lead to poor physical outcome? How does psychosocial intervention improve physical outcome?

Most of the mechanisms through which psychosocial variables exert their specific effects on illness processes cannot yet be elaborated in molecular detail. However, many psychoendocrine, psychoneurologic, and psychoimmunologic pathways are beginning to be discovered and described.

The hypothalamus recognizes threatening circumstances and responds with the secretion of releasing factors, such as corticotropin releasing factor (CRF), which activate the anterior pituitary gland to release hormones, like adrenocorticotropic hormone (ACTH), which, in turn, act on the adrenal gland to stimulate the production of cortisol. Cortisol has widespread bodily effects, including effects on glucose utilization, metabolism, blood flow to large muscles, and so forth. Cortisol, in addition, suppresses many immune functions.

Selye (1976) was one of the early investigators to hypothesize the mechanism of hyperadrenal function as a mediator of the relationship between stress and disease. Other endocrine activation also seems stress related. Studies have demonstrated that prolactin, growth hormone, thyroid hormone, and androgens also increase with subjective stress (Sachar, 1980) (See also Chapter 11).

The autonomic nervous system is also implicated in the axis between stress and physical problems. Hypothalamic recognition of danger is the originator of the mechanism. Hypothalamic stimulation activates the autonomic nervous system with the elaboration of epinephrine and norepinephrine, which have widespread bodily effects including increased heart rate, blood pressure, and respiration. Such mechanisms may be related to the development of hypertension and related illnesses.

In addition to endocrine and nervous system responses, psychoimmunologic relationships may be implicated in the connection between psychosocial variables and illness outcomes. Grieving widows and widowers have been shown to have impaired lymphocyte responses to nonspecific mitogens. Persons under stress also show impaired natural killer cell activity (Dorian and Garfinkel, 1987). Numerous animal studies show the same associations linking stress with impaired immunity and increased illness outcomes (Dorian and Garfinkel, 1987).

Implications for the Practice of Medicine

The importance of psychologic and social variables in medical practice requires that physicians develop the knowledge and skills necessary to integrate these factors into general patient care. The skills necessary for this integration are complex and cannot be fully covered in this short introductory textbook.

The most important skill is the ability of the physician to communicate well with the patient. The doctor–patient relationship is the foundation of excellence in clinical medicine, and the interview is the building block of good relationships. Unfortunately, there is reason to believe that the general interviewing skills of physicians in practice are inadequate. One recent study demonstrated that physicians tended to interrupt their patients within the first *18* seconds of the interview. Patients did not get to tell their own stories, and physicians did not obtain an understanding of the most important problems of their patients (Beckman and Frankel, 1984). Other studies have shown that the empathic skills that students demonstrate in their early years of training tend to diminish as they advance in their education (Maguire and Rutter, 1976). Physicians do not educate their patients well, and 50% of patients do not follow physicians' recommendations (Meichenbaum and Turk, 1987). It is likely that physicians with better educational and motivational skills would lead to better informed patients who would adhere better to treatment recommendations. Such training has, in fact, been shown to lead to better patient outcome (Cohen-Cole and Bird, 1986b).

There are three basic functions to the medical interview:

1. To collect relevant data to develop and test hypotheses about illnesses.
2. To develop and maintain therapeutic relationships with patients.

3. To educate and motivate patients to adhere to treatment recommendations (Bird and Cohen-Cole, in press).

Each of these interviewing functions is best served by specific skills in communicating with patients. While these cannot be reviewed here, they are discussed in detail elsewhere, and, hopefully, medical students can get the opportunity to learn these skills in other settings (Cohen-Cole, in press).

The development of adequate interviewing skill is only the beginning of what is required to be able to integrate psychologic and social variables in medical practice. Physicians must also develop the disposition to collect relevant data concerning specific variables. For example, physicians should learn to ask patients about recent life stresses and levels of social support. Negative health habits, such as smoking, drinking, poor dietary habits, not wearing seat belts, and so forth, should be evaluated, and efforts should be made to educate patients and motivate them to change. Relevant knowledge of psychologic processes should be mastered. Possible psychosocial treatment interventions should be learned and implemented where relevant. The task for physicians is large and complex. This text provides a starting point in this important process.

EPIDEMIOLOGY OF PSYCHIATRIC DISORDERS IN GENERAL MEDICAL PRACTICE

Psychiatric Disorders in the Community

As discussed above, physicians need general psychosocial knowledge and assessment skills to be able to evaluate and appropriately manage relevant psychologic and social variables in patients with *physical* disorders. However, it is important for medical students to realize that similar skills are also needed for the recognition and management of frank *psychiatric* disorders that present in the general medical sector.

Almost 30 million Americans suffer from mental disorders, alcohol abuse, or other substance abuse in any 6-month period of time. These illnesses cause untold suffering, as well as enormous morbidity and mortality. The financial costs are staggering. The direct and indirect costs of these illnesses were estimated to be $218 *billion* dollars in 1983. Mortality from alcohol and drug abuse, substance abuse related accidents, and suicides related to other mental disorders all account for 108,000 deaths per year (Kamerow et al, 1986).

Patients with mental disorders tend to be high attenders of general medical clinics. These patients use about twice as many general healthcare resources as those without mental disorders. Interestingly, these general healthcare costs can be reduced by proper treatment for their substance abuse or mental disorder (Mumford et al, 1984).

The recently completed "Epidemiologic Catchment Area Study" (ECA) provides data from a household survey of 20,000 persons in five sites across the United States. About 20% of Americans have suffered from a clinically significant and diagnosable mental disorder in the preceding 6 months. Almost one third of Americans have suffered from a mental disorder at some time in their lives. Anxiety disorders (including phobias) are the most common mental disorders, followed by depression and alcohol and other substance abuse. Tables 1-2, 1-3, and 1-4 show the different prevalence rates of the major mental disorders by sex and age.

It is interesting to note that anxiety and depressive disorders are much more common in women and that substance abuse is more common among men. Overall, the total prevalence of mental disorders is about the same in men as in women, although women are much more likely to seek help for their problems than are men. Another important finding was that, contrary to expectations, mental disorders *do not* increase with age. In fact, they seem to decrease over the age of 65. The "baby boom" generation now seems to be suffering from a dramatically increased prevalence of mood disorders, in particular (Myers, 1984).

Besides the ECA study, there have been many other epidemiologic studies of psychiatric disorders, comparing prevalence in rural versus urban settings and in primitive versus more advanced societies. These studies were undertaken to test the

Table 1–2 **Selected Findings from the Epidemiologic Catchment Area Study**

	PREVALENCE (%)	
DISORDER	**Lifetime**	**6 Month**
Any disorder*	32.2	19.1
Schizophrenia	1.5	0.9
Mania	0.8	0.5
Major depression	5.8	3.0
Dysthymia	3.0	3.0
Substance abuse	16.0	6.0
Anxiety disorders	14.6	8.9
Somatization	0.1	0.1
Antisocial personality	2.5	0.8

* *Note:* The ECA study systematically underestimates the true prevalence of mental disorders because the survey instrument (the "Diagnostic Interview Scale") does not include a number of important psychiatric disorders including generalized anxiety disorder, posttraumatic stress disorder, somatoform pain disorder, hypochondriasis, conversion disorder, psychologic factors affecting physical condition, and all personality disorders other than antisocial personality.
(Data from Regier DA, Boyd SH, Burke JD Jr et al: One month prevalence of mental disorders in the United States. Arch Gen Psychiatry 45:977–986, 1988)

Table 1–3 **Selected Lifetime Prevalence by Sex**

	PREVALENCE (%)	
DISORDER	**Male**	**Female**
Any disorder	34	33
Major depression	3	6
Agoraphobia	3	8
Alcohol abuse	24	4.5
Antisocial personality	5	1

Table 1–4 **Selected Lifetime Prevalence by Age**

DIAGNOSIS	PREVALENCE (%)			
	18–24 yr	**25–44 yr**	**45–64 yr**	**65+ yr**
Major depression	6	9	5	1
Drug abuse	14	8	0.5	0.1

hypothesis that civilization and industrialization may be associated with increased rates of mental illness. While there are some small differences, the most impressive finding of crosscultural epidemiology has been the result that the prevalence of major mental disorders appears to be fairly stable across international boundaries (industrialized/nonindustrialized) as well as urban/rural boundaries (Murphy JM, 1988). There are some important exceptions, however, to these cross-cultural universals in the prevalence of the major mental disorders: schizophrenia is slightly *more* common in lower socio-economic classes (in the U.S.) and *less* common in less developed societies; schizophrenia tends to have a better outcome in less developed societies; economic and social instability are both associated with higher rates and poorer outcome of mental illness; bipolar disorder is slightly more prevalent in more socially advantaged classes; depression is somewhat more common in urban areas; depression is more likely to occur in relatively powerless women, without affective support and no outside employment (Kleinman, 1988; Boyd and Weissman, 1988; Murphy and Helzer, 1988). (Cultural issues are discussed in more detail in Chap. 2.)

Epidemiology of Psychiatric Disorders in Primary Care

Several recent studies (including the ECA study) confirm that one in every four general medical patients (25%) have a major psychiatric illness. It has been found that 6% to 10% of medical patients meet criteria for major depression and 3% to 6% meet criteria for panic disorder. At least 10% of all medical patients are likely to have an alcohol problem (Kessler et al, 1985; Von Korff et al, 1987). Among hospitalized medical–surgical patients, those patients with psychiatric comorbidity had significantly longer lengths of hospital stays (19 compared with 9 days) (Fulop et al, 1987). More than half of all these patients will *never* get help for their mental illnesses from mental health specialists. Their only chance for appropriate care will be from their primary care physician (Shulman et al, 1985).

Are these patients being appropriately recognized and treated by their primary physicians? The answer is an unequivocal *"no."*

Several studies that examined the ability of physicians to detect psychiatric disorders have concurred with the finding that only 10% to 50% (at the most) of major psychiatric disorders were detected. A recent study of major depression in the community determined that only 17% of patients with major depression were treated with an antidepressant medication, but over half were taking sedative hypnotic agents for insomnia and other nonspecific complaints (prescribed in most cases by their primary care physician) (Weissman et al, 1981). Only 8% of panic disorder patients were adequately treated. A recent study in Boston found that *none* of the patients who were diagnosed independently as meeting psychiatric criteria for alcohol abuse were recognized by the primary care physician (Borus et al, 1988). Most people who commit suicide visit their primary physician in the month before they actually kill themselves. Their psychologic distress is rarely recognized (Murphy GE, 1988).

Why is so much mental illness missed in the primary care sector? These problems result from a combination of factors that relate to both the patient and the doctor. First of all, patients do not usually go to their doctor complaining of a mental illness. They usually present with somatic complaints that require a high level of suspicion as well as diagnostic expertise on the part of the physician to diagnose accurately. Many patients also do not want to believe that they may be suffering from a mental disorder. Finally, physicians must be able to educate patients skillfully concerning the current psychobiologic understanding of mental illness in order to get them to accept proper treatment.

From the physician's point of view, psychiatric diagnoses are often missed because of time constraints, as well as limited knowledge and skills and lack of disposition to recognize such disorders (Cohen-Cole et al, 1982). Mental health training of primary care physicians is woefully inadequate. Residents in internal medicine receive an average of 8 hours/3 years of residency training in the management of mental disorders. This is true despite the fact that these problems occur in 25% of their patients (Strain et al, 1984). Family practice residents receive more than this, but almost no mental health training from psychiatrists (Goldberg et al, in press).

Psychiatric illnesses are among the most common and troubling disorders in the country and represent the major problem of 25% of all medical patients. Surveys of practicing physicians indicate that they feel undertrained in recognizing and treating these disorders. Current research indicates that physicians underrecognize psychiatric problems. The need for further education is clear.

SOCIAL EPIDEMIOLOGY AND ILLNESS BEHAVIOR: SOCIOCULTURAL INFLUENCES ON DISEASE, MEDICAL UTILIZATION, AND OTHER ILLNESS-RELATED BEHAVIORS

Social Epidemiology

Further arguments for the biopsychosocial model can be made from the standpoint of social epidemiology. Social epidemiology represents the field of study of relationships between social groupings and patterns of illness. Four variables—age, sex, race, and socioeconomic variables—have been studied most intensively.

Age

The incidence of illness is affected by age. Eighty-six percent of persons over 65 have one or more chronic medical conditions, most commonly arthritis, hypertension, and heart disease. Hearing impairments, diabetes, cataracts, and varicose veins are also common ailments of the elderly (Cockerham, 1978). Life expectancy has increased dramatically. In 1900, an American could expect to live to age 47, in contrast to a life expectancy over 70 now. Infant mortality has also declined dramatically from 16% in 1900 to less than 3%. These improvements result from two major factors: (1) the improved quality and quantity of healthcare services available and (2) the rise in the American standard of living (Cockerham, 1978).

Sex

The most striking sex difference in the United States in illness outcome is the strikingly higher life expectancy of females compared with males; male death rates exceed female death rates at all ages and for all causes except diabetes. The result is that, as of 1984, the average life expectancy of white females was 79 years compared with 72 years for white males. The same advantage applies to nonwhite females who in 1984 had a life expectancy of 74 years compared with 66 years for nonwhite males (Cockerham, 1978).

While mortality rates for American females have not risen, death rates for males, not counting military deaths in Vietnam, have increased since the 1960s. The rising mortality rates among young males can be attributed mostly to violent deaths, primarily automobile accidents, homicide, and suicide. In particular, the suicide rate among the young has shown an epidemiclike increase in the last two decades (Murphy GE, 1988).

This increased male mortality has led to a higher female : male ratio in the population. In 1910, because of immigration differences, there were 106 men for every 100 women. By 1940, the ratio was equal, and now there are about 95 men for every 100 women (Cockerham, 1978).

These differences are accounted for by both biologic and psychosocial processes. Males, in fact, do appear to be "weaker" physiologically in that their prenatal and neonatal death rates are higher. Psychosocial processes, however, may be related to higher accident and violent death rates as well as cultural pressures to succeed, which may lead to chronically stressful life circumstances. Female longevity can be a mixed blessing in that more females are now faced with the psychosocial problems of remarriage, employment after widowhood, and loneliness (Cockerham, 1978).

Race

There are major racial differences in illness and illness outcomes. The mortality rate for white infants is about half as high as that for black infants (1% compared with 2%; Cockerham, 1978). This difference is mostly attributable to social inequality, because there is no racial difference in infant mortality until the postnatal period begins. Nonwhite infant mortality rates are on a par with white infants at birth and increase threefold during the first 3 to 8 months of life (Cockerham, 1978).

Life expectancy, as discussed above, is lower among blacks than whites. Blacks are particularly vulnerable to hypertension. Although blacks represent 10% of the population, they account for 20% of the prevalence of hypertension. Between the ages of 25 and 44, hypertension kills black males 15 times more frequently than it does white males. The ratio of black to white females dying from hypertension in the same age category is 17 to 1. The increased morbidity and mortality from hypertension probably result from a combination of biologic, psychologic, and social variables, including genetic differences, stress, poor dietary habits, and decreased access to healthcare services (Cockerham, 1978).

Social Class

The uneven distribution of health among racial groups repeats itself when the distribution of health among socioeconomic groups or social class is considered. *On nearly every measure, membership in lower social classes carries health penalties similar to those of nonwhites.*

Numerous studies substantiate the relationship between poverty and lack of access to *quality* medical care. Despite evidence of more frequent visits to physicians made possible by Medicare and Medicaid, lower class persons are still treated within the framework of welfare medicine. Professional health practitioners prefer upper class patients and provide more personalized care to the middle and upper class sick. "The poor definitely get second rate medical care. This is self-evident to anyone who has worked either with them or in public medical facilities" (Cockerham, 1978).

The incidence of physical illness is affected by socioeconomic status (SES). SES represents a composite of income, education, and occupation. Persons in low SES groups are more likely to be afflicted with hypertension, arthritis, upper respiratory infections, speech difficulties, and eye diseases. There is a reduced life expectancy for lower SES persons, and longevity is correlated with higher SES in all age groupings (Cockerham, 1978). Coronary artery disease among middle and upper class men and breast cancer among middle and upper class women seem to be two notable exceptions to increased illness among lower SES persons. Most of the decreased life expectancy among blacks, in fact, can be accounted for by their lower SES (Cockerham, 1978).

Utilization and Related Illness Behaviors

Definitions

In order to more fully understand the importance of human behavior in medical practice, it is important to distinguish among the concepts of "disease," "illness," and "illness behavior." *Disease* refers to a disturbance in physiologic functioning of the organism. Such a disturbance can occur without the person's awareness. *Illness* refers to a state of poor health recognized by the person and usually treated by an expert. *Illness behavior* refers to the ways people respond to bodily indications and to the perceptions, values, attitudes, and interpretations that lead people to behave in particular ways in reference to their bodies (Kleinman et al, 1978).

From these definitions, it should be clear that disease and illness are not the same. Many patients may have "silent" disease. There may be some physiologic disruption of which they are not aware. Similarly, there are many people who have illnesses but who have no evidence of physiologic disease. Finally, the behaviors of persons may vary greatly according to whether or not they perceive themselves as ill, and their attitudes and values about how they should behave because of the presence of illness.

Physicians must deal as much with illness and illness behaviors as they do with disease itself. Physicians who understand something about cultural, social class, and personality differences in illness behavior will be able to provide more effective medical care. Patterns of illness behavior often make a great impact on the physical outcome of disease.

Decision Time: An Example of the Impact of Health Attitudes on Utilization and Outcome of Disease Processes

Deaths from myocardial infarction represent the number one killer of adult males from the ages of 30 to 60. Fifty percent of patients with myocardial infarction die before they ever reach a hospital (DiMatteo and Friedman, 1982). There is a great deal of variation, however, in the amount of time it takes such patients to reach the hospital. Fifty-six percent arrive within 4 hours after the onset of symptoms, 28% arrive within 4 to 14 hours after the onset of symptoms, and 16% arrive more than 14 hours after the onset of symptoms. Transportation issues only relate to about 10% of these cases. There are other factors that must be invoked to explain these great differences in how different persons respond to the initial awareness of chest discomfort. These variables account for the differences in decision time (DiMatteo and Friedman, 1982).

There are three general sets of factors that help explain differences in decision time.

Background Factors. Social class, age, sex, and ethnicity all have an impact on decision time. Persons of lower social class are less likely to seek medical help quickly. This may have to do with rather objective access and financial issues: They are less able to afford care, they may have more difficulty finding transportation, they may not feel as well-treated, and so forth.

Older patients are less likely to go for help quickly, and older females, in particular, are less likely to seek help quickly for symptoms of chest discomfort. This may relate more to the fact that females are less likely to think of cardiac events as explaining their chest symptoms than are men. Ethnic differences account for a great deal of variation in decision time. People of British descent have been trained to be more stoic about pain, and they are much less likely to seek help rapidly for symptoms of chest discomfort. Such differences can account for a great deal of the variations in decision times and can account for many of the variations in the lethality of the heart attack itself (DiMatteo and Friedman, 1982).

Psychologic Processes. Psychologic issues are extremely important in determining the response time of the person to physical symptoms. Patients must make a cognitive appraisal of the meaning of their perceived symptoms and then make judgments about what to do about it. Many persons misinterpret their initial cardiac symptoms. In fact, 70% of persons who first experience the pain of cardiac ischemia, originally consider the pain to result from abdominal indigestion or some source other than cardiac.

The psychologic defense of *denial* can play an important part in decision time. Mechanisms of defense are psychologic processes that enable persons to avoid the anxiety of facing certain issues. The defense mechanisms operate at an unconscious level, so that the persons are truly unaware of their operation. Denial is one very powerful mechanism through which the awareness of certain anxiety-provoking issues can be minimized or unrecognized. Because heart attacks are so terribly overwhelming, many persons do not want to face the anxiety of coping with this reality. The persons who are able to maintain steadfast denial for long periods of time after the onset of cardiac symptoms are the ones most likely to experience long decision times and are at more risk from the cardiac death before reaching the hospital (DiMatteo and Friedman, 1982).

Social Variables. The social context or situation of the patient also plays an important role in the amount of decision time it takes from the first awareness of chest discomfort to the arrival in the hospital for care. The day of the week seems to play a role as well. Persons are more likely to arrive at the hospital sooner if the pain episode occurs during the week, rather than on the weekend. Similarly, if the pain occurs at work, persons are more likely to seek care rapidly. It seems as if persons value their weekends and time at home and do not want to use this time in seeking medical help.

The presence of a spouse is also important. When the chest discomfort occurs in the presence of a spouse, the person is much more likely to get to medical help sooner. It seems much easier for persons to delay getting help if they are alone at the time the symptoms first occur.

In general, these variables—background, individual psychology or personality, and social variables—help determine the amount of time that a person takes from the time of first perception of chest discomfort to the time he/she decides to seek medical care. The seven most important variables all fall within these three categories:

1. Presence of the symptoms themselves.
2. Recognition of the symptoms.
3. Amount of social or physical disability.
4. Perceived seriousness.
5. Extent of cultural "stoicism."
6. Amount of relevant information or medical knowledge.
7. Availability of sources of help.

These variables all contribute to the decision time it takes a patient before he/she goes to the hospital. The most important of these variables are psychosocial in nature and account for a great deal of the ultimate variation in survival. For example, the mortality of "early" arrivals is about 10% compared with the mortality of late arrivals, which is about 27% (DiMatteo and Friedman, 1982).

Demographic, Cultural, and Sociopsychologic Variables Related to Utilization

The same type of variables that are related to the decision time to seek medical attention for chest pain symptoms are related to healthcare utilization in general.

Age and Sex. The findings for age and sex are fairly consistent: Utilization of health services is greater for females than for males and is greatest in the elderly. Despite the fact that males die at younger ages, females report higher morbidity and, even after correcting for maternity, have higher rates of hospital admissions. The female is sick more often than the male; or at least the act of defining one's self as ill and recognizing the symptoms of being sick seem to be more appropriate to the social role of the woman. Females tend to have higher rates of acute illnesses, chronic illnesses, and disability due to acute illnesses than males of the same age. Females also exhibit greater use of health services than males. In fact, the proportion of females in a household is causally linked to the number of physician visits: The greater the proportion of females in a household, the greater the demand or requirement for physicians (Cockerham, 1978).

Elderly persons, both males and females over the age of 65, visit physicians more often than younger persons. Physician visits are directly related to the availability of health insurance and the presence of physical disability (Cockerham, 1978).

Ethnicity, Social Networks, and Social Class. As discussed above in reference to decision time, medical utilization in general depends a great deal on the background characteristics of the person. Persons are socialized within a matrix that often endorses strong attitudes toward physical symptoms and the types of care that should be obtained for symptoms. Basically, ethnicity represents a social experience that influences how a particular person perceives his or her health situation.

Many cultural groups (e.g., Mexican-Americans, blacks) are suspicious of the modern healthcare system and avoid participating until disease becomes very severe. These groups often have a series of healthcare "options" ranging from family advisors to alternative forms of culturally sanctioned "healers." Other cultural groups rely strongly on modern medicine and visit the physician often for relatively minor complaints (Cockerham, 1978). Until recently, lower class persons visited a physician significantly less often than middle and upper class persons. With the advent of Medicaid and Medicare, financial obstacles to medical care seem less significant in determining utilization, and physician visits are now more equivalent across financial groupings (Cockerham, 1978).

Social–Psychologic Factors In Utilization. As discussed above in relation to decision time, individual psychologic factors play an important role in healthcare utilization. Unconscious denial of the significance of physical symptoms can delay life-saving medical intervention until too late.

In addition to the importance of mechanisms of psychologic defense, individual health beliefs will exert an impact of eventual utilization of medical resources. In order for a person to seek care, he or she must first decide that the symptoms represent an "illness." This usually depends on the amount of pain or discomfort he or she is experiencing and the amount of impairment in role functioning caused by the symptoms. Other symptoms or changes in the biologic state of the organism might also be seen as important depending on the knowledge of the person and the implications of these changes for future activities.

In addition to defining the symptoms as indicative of illness, the person must also believe that there is something that can be done for the symptoms by a physician. Even then, the person may not visit the physician if it is seen as too expensive, too painful or unpleasant, or too inconvenient.

Thus, decisions about medical utilization are made within the context of ethnic, social network, and social class matrices and modified by social–psychologic factors that weigh benefits and costs of treatment with an individual's personal health beliefs (Cockerham, 1978; DiMatteo and Friedman, 1982).

These same sociocultural variables apply to a patient's ability to accept or reject or adapt to the *sick role* (described below) and also have a great deal to do with the patient's ability or desire to adhere to the treatment recommendations made by the physician. The issue of adherence to medical regimens is central to overall outcome of medical care because most patients cannot be expected to recover from or avoid future disease complications unless they follow physicians' recommendations. Unfortunately, rates of nonadherence are extremely high: Hundreds of studies support the finding that about 50% of physicians' recommendations are *not* followed by their patients. This nonadherence cannot be explained by low education, low social class, or low intelligence. Ethnic, social network, social class, and health beliefs all seem more important (Meichenbaum and Turk, 1987).

In addition, other psychosocial factors are also critical, in particular the nature of the relationship between the doctor and the patient and the educational skills of the physician (Meichenbaum and Turk, 1987). This is yet another area where the communication skills of the physician are crucial to determining the illness outcome of the patient (Cohen-Cole and Bird, 1986b).

The Sick Role

Illness has a very well-defined role in our society, and being sick is associated with a relatively clear set of obligations and responsibilities, which have been clarified by the sociologist, Talcott Parsons.

There are eight basic dimensions of the "sick role" as described by Parsons:

1. A doctor must confirm the presence of sickness.
2. It is generally recognized that the *person* is not responsible for the sickness.
3. Sickness is generally accepted as an excuse or exemption from normal role responsibilities.
4. The sick person must seek legitimate medical assistance.
5. The sick role in general is "short term" (except for chronic illness).
6. The sick role is undesirable.
7. The patient must cooperate with efforts made to get well.
8. The patient must seek help (Cockerham, 1978).

These features of the sick role seem to describe our society's understanding of the meaning and implications of illness. Violations of any one of these expectations can lead to interpersonal problems for the patient or to tension in the doctor–patient relationship. For example, when patients are held responsible for their sickness (for example, alcoholism, smoking, sometimes psychiatric illness), physicians and society in general may blame the patients, and their access to medical care may be impaired. Tension in the doctor–patient relationship may result if the physician blames the patient for the illness.

To give another example, when patients do not act as if the sick role is undesirable, they may incur the resentment of family, fellow employees, as well as medical personnel. They may not receive the usual care and attention afforded to sick persons if the persons around them perceive them as enjoying the sick role.

Patients who do not cooperate with their treatment are also viewed negatively by the medical profession. Negative labels, such as "crock, troll, turkey, gomer," are often invoked to characterize such patients who do not fit into the traditional sick role model. Once patients get labeled in this manner, physicians often feel less obligated to follow through on the rest of their own responsibilities and obligations of taking care of the patient (Cohen-Cole and Friedman, 1983).

THE BIOPSYCHOSOCIAL MODEL FOR PSYCHIATRIC PATIENTS

This chapter has reviewed the many ways that patients with physical illnesses need to be seen in a biopsychosocial context in order to understand their needs and to care for them adequately. Conversely, the same biopsychosocial perspective needs to be followed for patients with primary psychiatric disorders and *no other clear physical illnesses*. It is becoming increasing clear that many, and perhaps most, major psychiatric disorders are characterized by biologic dysfunction (see Chap. 11). In some cases, this dysfunction has been proven to be genetically acquired (see Chap. 12), and in others, the biologic dysfunction can be linked to early environmental deprivations or stresses (see Chap. 9). Finally, biologic treatments have been shown to be remarkably effective for treating many psychiatric disorders and for returning disabled patients to active functioning.

While biologic psychiatry has made great strides in the last few decades, it is crucial to note that psychologic and social variables are also critical in the etiology and treatment of psychiatric disorders, even for those disorders with primarily biologic underpinnings. Social variables can predict course and outcome of many disorders and psychosocial interventions can have profound effects on the outcome of psychiatric disorders.

Thus, *it should be clear that psychiatric disorders are not qualitatively different from any other medical illness*. They are, in fact, *medical illnesses* just like any other medical illness. The historic disjunction between the mind and the body is no longer relevant for modern medicine. Biologic, psychologic, and social variables are crucial for determining the etiology, onset, course, and outcome of all illness. This is just as true for illnesses with primarily physical symptoms as well as for illnesses with primarily mental or behavioral symptoms.

SUMMARY

This chapter has presented and described the biopsychosocial model of illness, along with clinical and research findings that support its applicability to patients with physical as well as psychiatric symptoms. Physicians need to learn to integrate a wide variety of psychologic and social data into their work with patients in order to provide adequate and comprehensive care. In fact, when medical care has been expanded to include this biopsychosocial perspective, patient outcome has been shown to improve, as well as patient and physician satisfaction.

The remainder of this textbook provides a broad template for physicians to practice more integrated clinical medicine, according to these well documented biologic, psychologic, and social principles.

ANNOTATED BIBLIOGRAPHY

Balint M: The Doctor, His Patient and the Illness. New York, International University Press, 1957

    A classic text that discusses the role of the primary care physician in the management of psychologic problems of general medical patients.

Cassel J: Psychosocial processes and "stress": Theoretical formulation. Int J Health Serv 4:471–481, 1974

> This paper represents an elegant integration of research findings related to stress and makes a very sophisticated theoretic argument about the illness process as it relates to stressful situations.

DiMatteo RM, Friedman HS: Social Psychology and Medicine. Cambridge, Oelgeschlager, Gunn, and Hain, 1982

> This excellent text covers a wide range of issues related to social and psychologic issues in general medical practice.

Stoudemire A, Fogel B (eds): Principles of Medical Psychiatry. Orlando, Grune & Stratton, 1987

> This text represents the "state of the art" of psychiatric issues in medical disorders. Sophisticated and up-to-date.

Usdin G, Lewis JM (eds): Psychiatry in General Medical Practice. New York, McGraw-Hill, 1979

> This excellent source book for primary care physicians contains numerous excellent articles on many illnesses. Good discussions of doctor–patient relationship issues throughout. It is a little dated on psychopharmacology, however.

Weiner, H: Psychobiology and Human Disease. New York, Elsevier, 1977

> This book documents in exhaustive detail the research findings that demonstrate psychologic and social contributions to the predisposition, onset, course, and outcome of seven physical illnesses. Weiner also synthesizes current psychobiologic understanding of these etiologic relationships.

REFERENCES

Ader R (ed): Psychoneuroimmunology. New York, Academic Press, 1981

Beckman HB, Frankel RM: The effect of physician behavior on the collection of data. Ann Intern Med 101:692–696, 1984

Berkman LF, Syme SL: Social networks, host resistance, and mortality: A nine year follow-up of Alameda County residents. Am J Epidemiol 109:186–204, 1979

Bird S, Cohen-Cole SA: The 'three function model' of the medical interview: An educational device. In Hale M (ed.): Models of Teaching Consultation-Liaison Psychiatry, Basel, Switzerland, Karger, in press.

Borus JF, Howes MJ, Devins NP et al: Primary health care providers' recognition and diagnosis of mental disorders in their patients. Gen Hosp Psychiatry 10:317–321, 1988

Boyd JH, Weissman MM: Epidemiology of major affective disorders. In Michels R, Cavenar JO, Cooper AM et al (eds): Psychiatry, revised edition—1988, Vol 3. Philadelphia, JB Lippincott, 1988

Cassel J: Psychosocial processes and "stress": Theoretical formulation. Int J Health Serv 4:471–481, 1974

Cassem N: Depression secondary to physical illness. In Frances AJ, Hales RE (eds): Review of Psychiatry, Vol 7. Washington, APA Press, 1988

Cockerham WC: Medical Sociology. Englewood Cliffs, NJ, Prentice-Hall, 1978

Cohen F: Stress and bodily illness. Psychiatr Clin North Am 4:269–286, 1981

Cohen-Cole SA: The Medical Interview: The Three-Function Approach. St Louis, CV Mosby, in press

Cohen-Cole SA: Interviewing the cardiac patient. I. A practical guide for assessing quality of life. Quality of Life and Cardiovascular Care 2:7–12, 1985

Cohen-Cole SA: On teaching the new (and old) psychobiology. In Friedman C, Purcell EF (eds): The New Biology and Medical Education. New York, Josiah Macy Foundation, 1983

Cohen-Cole SA, Bird J: Interviewing the cardiac patient. II. A practical guide for helping patients cope with their emotions. Quality of Life and Cardiovascular Care 3:53–65, 1986a

Cohen-Cole SA, Bird J: Interviewing the cardiac patient. III. A practical guide to educate patients and to promote cooperation with treatment. Quality of Life and Cardiovascular Care 3:101–112, 1986b

Cohen-Cole SA, Bird J, Freeman A et al: An oral examination of the psychiatric knowledge of medical housestaff: Assessment of needs and evaluation baseline. Gen Hosp Psychiatry 4:103–111, 1982

Cohen-Cole SA, Friedman CP: The language problem: Integration of psychosocial variables into routine medical care. Psychosomatics 24:54–57, 1983

Cohen-Cole SA, Pincus HA, Stoudemire A et al: Recent research developments in consultation-liaison psychiatry. Gen Hosp Psychiatry 8:316–329, 1986

Cohen-Cole SA, Stoudemire A: Major depression and physical illness: Special considerations in diagnosis and biological treatment. Psychiatr Clin North Am 10:1–17, 1987

de Araujo G, Dudley DL, Van Asdel PP, Jr: Psychosocial assets and severity of chronic asthma. J Allergy Clin Immunol 50:257–261, 1972

DiMatteo RM, Friedman HS: Social Psychology and Medicine. Cambridge, MA, Oelgeschlager, Gunn, and Main, 1982

Dimsdale J, Ruberman W, Carleton R et al: Sudden cardiac death: Stress and cardiac arrhythmias. Circulation 76(Suppl 1):1198–1201, 1987

Dimsdale, JE: Research links between psychiatry and cardiology: Hypertension, Type A behavior, sudden death, and the physiology of emotional arousal. Gen Hosp Psychiatry 10:328–338, 1988

Dorian B, Garfinkel PE: Stress, immunity, and illness: A review. Psychol Med 17:393–407, 1987

Engel G: The need for a new medical model: A challenge for biomedicine. Science 196:129–136, 1977

Friedman M: Pathogenesis of Coronary Artery Disease. New York, McGraw-Hill, 1969

Friedman M, Thoresen CE, Gill JJ, et al: Alteration of Type A behavior and reduction in cardiac recurrences in post-myocardial infarction patients. Am Heart J 108:237–248, 1984

Fulop G, Strain JJ, Vita J et al: Impact of psychiatric comorbidity on length of hospital stay for medical/surgical patients: A preliminary report. Am J Psychiatry 144:878–882, 1987

Goldberg RJ, Novack DH, Fulton JP et al: A survey of psychiatry and behavioral science curriculum in primary care residency training. J Psychiatric Education, 9:3–11, 1985

Hall RCW, Stickney SK, Gardner ER: Behavioral toxicity of nonpsychiatric drugs. In Hall R (ed): Psychiatric Presentation of Medical Illness: Somatopsychic Disorders. New York, SP Medical and Scientific Books, 1980, pp. 337–353

Holmes H, Rahe RH: The social readjustment rating scale. J Psychosom Res 11:213–218, 1967

Houpt JL, Orleans CS, George LK et al: The role of psychiatric and behavioral factors in the practice of medicine. Am J Psychiatry 137:37–47, 1980

James M, Cohen-Cole SA: Major depression: Recent perspectives. Emory University Journal of Medicine, 3:110–119, 1989

Kamerow DB, Pincus HA, Macdonald DI: Alcohol abuse, other drug abuse, and mental disorders in medical practice. JAMA 255:2054–2057, 1986

Kessler LG, Cleary PD, Burke JD Jr: Psychiatric disorders in primary care: Results of a follow-up study. Arch Gen Psychiatry 42:583–587, 1985

Kleinman A: Rethinking Psychiatry: From Cultural Category to Personal Experience. New York, The Free Press, 1988

Kleinman A, Eisenberg L, Good B: Culture, illness, and care. Ann Intern Med 88:251–258, 1978

MacKinnon RA, Michels R: The Psychiatric Interview in Clinical Practice. Philadelphia, WB Saunders, 1971

Maguire GP, Rutter DR: Training medical students to communicate. In Bennett AE (ed): Communication Between Doctors and Patients. London, Oxford University Press, 1976

Meichenbaum D, Turk DC: Facilitating Treatment Adherence: A Practitioner's Guidebook. New York, Plenum Press, 1987

Middleton W, Raphael B: Bereavement: State of the art and state of the science. Psychiatr Clin North Am 10:329–345, 1987

Mumford E, Schlesinger H, Glass G: The effects of psychological intervention on recovery from surgery and heart attacks: An analysis of the literature. Am J Public Health 72:141–151, 1982

Mumford E, Schlesinger HJ, Glass GV et al: New look at evidence about reduced cost of medical utilization following mental health treatment. Am J Psychiatry 141:1145–1158, 1984

Murphy GE: Suicide and attempted suicide. In Michels R, Cavenar JO, Cooper AM et al (eds): Psychiatry, revised edition—1988, Vol 1. Philadelphia, JB Lippincott, 1988

Murphy JM: Cross-cultural psychiatry. In Michels R, Cavenar JO, Cooper AM et al (eds): Psychiatry, revised edition—1988, Vol 3. Philadelphia, JB Lippincott, 1988

Murphy JM, Helzer JE: Epidemiology of schizophrenia in adulthood. In Michels R, Cavenar JO, Cooper AM et al (eds): Psychiatry, revised edition—1988, Vol 3. Philadelphia, JB Lippincott, 1988

Myers JK, Weissman NM, Tischler GL et al: Six-month prevalence of psychiatric disorders in three communities; 1980 to 1982. Arch Gen Psychiatry 41:959–967, 1984

Nuckolls CB, Cassel J, Kaplan BH: Psychosocial assets, life crises and the prognosis of pregnancy. Am J Epidemiol 95:431–441, 1972

O'Shanick GJ, Gardner DF, Kornstein SG: Endocrine disorders. In Stoudemire A, Fogel BS (eds): Principles of Medical Psychiatry. Orlando, Grune & Stratton, 1987

Ragland D, Brand R: Type A behavior and coronary heart disease case-fatality. N Engl J Med 318:65–69, 1988

Regier DA, Boyd SH, Burke JD Jr et al: One month prevalence of mental disorders in the United States. Arch Gen Psychiatry 45:977–986, 1988

Rozanski A, Bairey N, Krantz D et al: Mental stress and the induction of silent myocardial ischemia in patients with coronary artery disease. N Engl J Med 318:1005–1012, 1988

Rosenman R, Brand R, Jenkins C et al: Coronary heart disease in the Western Collaborative Group Study: Final followup experience of 8 and a half years. JAMA 233:872–877, 1975

Ruberman W, Weinblatt E, Goldberg J et al: Psychosocial influences on mortality after myocardial infarction. N Engl J Med 311:552–559, 1984

Sachar EJ: Advances in Psychoneuroendocrinology. Psychiatr Clin North Am. Philadelphia, WB Saunders, 1980

Selye H: The Stress of Life, rev ed. New York, McGraw-Hill, 1976

Shulman RA, Kramer PD, Mitchel JB: The hidden mental health network: Treatment of mental illness by nonpsychiatric physicians. Arch Gen Psychiatry 42:89–94, 1985

Sosa R, Kennell J, Klaus M et al: The effect of a supportive companion on perinatal problems, length of labor, and mother–infant interaction. N Engl J Med 303:597–600, 1980

Strain J, Pincus HA, Houpt JL et al: Models of mental health training for primary care physicians. Psychosom Med. 47:95–110, 1985

Von Korff M, Shapiro S, Burke JD et al: Anxiety and depression in a primary care clinic. Arch Gen Psychiatry 44:152–156, 1987

Weiner H: Psychobiology and Human Disease. New York, Elsevier North-Holland, 1977

Weiner H, Hofer MA, Stunkard AJ (eds): Brain, Behavior, and Bodily Disease. New York, Raven Press, 1981

Weissman MM, Myers JK, Thompson WD: Depression and its treatment in a US urban community 1975–1976. Arch Gen Psychiatry 38:417–421, 1981

Wells KB, Golding JM, Burnam M: Psychiatric disorder in a sample of the general population with and without chronic medical conditions. Am J Psychiatry 145:976–981, 1988

Williams R, Haney T, Lee K et al: Type A behavior, hostility, and coronary atherosclerosis. Psychosom Med 42:539–549, 1980

2

Culture, Ethnicity, and Behavior and the Practice of Medicine

Peter J. Brown and Bruce Ballard

Disease and its treatment are only in the abstract purely biologic processes. Actually, such facts as whether a person gets sick at all, what kind of disease he acquires and what kind of treatment he receives largely depend upon social factors.

Erwin Ackerknecht

Culture is the fundamental source of the diversity in thought and behavior among different human groups. If you were to travel around the world, you would undoubtedly be struck by the cultural diversity you found—in food, architecture, religious beliefs, ideas about sex and marriage, and so on—and those differences would make the trip exciting and fun. But such cultural variation represents a challenge to the physician, because ideas about the etiology of illness and what to do when a person is ill also vary with culture. This chapter argues that sensitivity to cultural variation can have practical benefits for the effective delivery of healthcare. To a large degree, this argument builds upon the biopsychosocial model introduced in Chapter 1, particularly in terms of social variation in illness behavior.

Special consideration of the impact of culture and ethnicity on behavior is warranted because of a simple, but often unrecognized, fact that the United States is one of the most culturally heterogeneous nations. The ethnic diversity of patients who may come into a major metropolitan hospital is remarkable. We are a nation of immigrants, irrespective of a national ideology (the "melting pot" myth) that minimizes the importance of ethnic and class differences. For many medical students, clinical training is the first time they must regularly interact with people whose background is very different from their own. In the context of healthcare, a strict application of a biomedical model of disease also minimizes the importance of social diversity, because all cases (like all Americans) are expected to be alike.

But differences based on ethnicity or class are not simply "noise" that can be ignored. From an epidemiologic standpoint, ethnicity and class are clearly related to lifestyle patterns, for example, in diet or smoking or stress, as major causes of morbidity and mortality. As described in Chapter 1, basic elements of a patient's interaction with the medical system—for example, the interpretation of symptoms, the decision to seek care, or even the manner in which pain is experienced and reported—are largely determined by social and psychologic factors. Social science research suggests that patient noncompliance often arises from an incongruence between the patient's view of what is going on and the physician's view. There is a danger of *ethnocentrism* when one simply "explains away" noncompliance in terms of the personality of the patient. Understanding the patient's point of view and effectively communicating with patients from different cultural backgrounds represent an important challenge to those practicing medicine today.

In this chapter, we will briefly review some of the basic concepts that sociologists and anthropologists have applied to the understanding of illness behavior. Second, we will consider the relationship of culture and mental health, including some classic studies about social class and the prevalence of psychopathology. After a warning about the dangers of stereotyping, the third section describes some of the cultural beliefs and practices of a few major ethnic groups. When treating patients from cultural backgrounds different from your own, the application of the biopsychosocial model in the evaluation of patients can be supplemented with the suggestions for improved cross-cultural communication made in the conclusion of this chapter.

FUNDAMENTAL CONCEPTS

Human societies, unlike those of insects or animals, are distinguished by *culture*—learned patterns of thought and behavior. The ability to adapt through the nonbiologic mechanism of culture is the primary reason for the remarkable success of our species. Culture is transmitted from one generation to the next through the symbolic communication of language. It includes not only directly observable behaviors, like patterns of diet and social organization, but also an ideologic component, including beliefs and values. As such, culture provides a context of *meaning* to individuals. The function of culture is

> ...the preservation of a society by providing an overall consistency to a
> society's patterns and components. Every culture has a value system
> that classifies phenomena into good and bad, right and wrong, desirable
> and undesirable. (Favazza, 1985, p 247)

Anthropologists believe that the thousands of cultural variations in the world today reflect, in part, adaptations to local environmental conditions, yet are all evolutionarily derived from the original human lifestyle of hunting and gathering. Of course, cultural variation is constrained by some of the biologic universals of behavior (see Chap. 10) that predate the evolution of culture. There are not many universals of culture, but some, like the incest taboo, appear to be best explained in terms of sociobiologic theory (Wilson, 1978).

One important universal in human behavior is that all societies have medical systems that represent an attempt to combat the inevitability of disease and death. These systems include, at a minimum, three logically coherent elements: (1) a theory of the etiology of illness, (2) techniques for the diagnosis of illness, and (3) methods for appropriate therapy. In many societies, it is difficult to distinguish between the ethnomedical and religious systems. For a physician practicing in a multiethnic context, it is important to be aware of these preexisting medical beliefs and to avoid the fallacy of seeing patients as "empty vessels" waiting to be filled with biomedical knowledge (Polgar, 1963).

Culture Provides Explanatory Models of Illness

Ethnomedical systems provide both a categorization scheme for illnesses and, more importantly, explanations for their cause (Fabrega, 1974). From a cross-cultural perspective, Foster (1976) distinguished between *personalistic* and *naturalistic* medical systems based on the predominant orientation of their etiologic theory. This distinction is summarized in Table 2-1, although in complex societies like our own, elements of both types coexist. In personalistic systems, illness is thought to be the result of supernatural forces aimed at the patient for a particular reason, either through sorcery or spirit possession or because of a breach of taboo. In these systems, diagnosis and therapy largely involve shamanistic trance and ritual, aimed at correcting and counteracting the supernatural causes of illness; therapy is thought to be effective largely because of the belief of the patient in the power of the curer. Naturalistic ethnomedical systems, which include the traditional medicine of complex civilizations (India, China, Greece), are based on a principle of balance between elements of the body. Diagnosis based on the examination of symptoms and therapy involves the adjustment of humors to re-create the body's natural balance and health. A widely dispersed concept in naturalistic systems is the hot/cold theory of disease (discussed below for Hispanic patients).

In the context of modern medical care, it is effective for the clinician to be able to elicit the patient's "explanatory model" of illness (Kleinman et al, 1978) rather than to know the abstract details of an ethnomedical system. While lay explanatory models show significant individual variation, research indicates that ethnicity is an extremely important factor (Harwood, 1981). A patient's explanatory model can be learned through a few additional questions asked during the taking of a patient's history.

Table 2-1 **Typology of Ethnomedical Systems**

	PERSONALISTIC	**NATURALISTIC**
Causation	Active agent	Equilibrium loss
Illness	Special case of misfortune	Unrelated to other misfortune
Religion/magic	Intimately tied to illness	Unrelated to illness
Prevention	Positive action	Avoidance
Responsibility	Beyond patient control	Resides in patient
Societies	"Primitive" bands/tribes	State ancient "great traditions"

(Adapted from Foster GM: Disease etiologies in non-Western medical systems. Am Anth 78:773–782, 1976)

Table 2-2 **Questions for Eliciting a Patient's Explanatory Model**

1. What do you think has caused your problem?
2. Why do you think it started when it did?
3. What do you think your sickness does to you? How does it work?
4. How bad [severe] do you think your illness is? Do you think it will last a long time, or will it be better soon, in your opinion?
5. What kind of treatment would you like to have?
6. What are the most important results you hope to get from treatment?
7. What are the chief problems your illness has caused you?
8. What do you fear most about your sickness?

(Adapted from Kleinman A, Eisberg L, Good B: Culture, illness and care. Ann Intern Med 88:251–258, 1978)

Kleinman and colleagues (1978) have suggested eight questions (listed in Table 2-2) for eliciting such information. Some patients, however, viewing the physician as the ultimate expert on diagnosis and treatment, may find these questions inappropriate. These questions are, however, very useful for understanding why a particular patient with a particular constellation of symptoms is seeking medical care.

Culture Defines Normality

Members of all societies are *ethnocentric* in that they use their own arbitrary beliefs and values to judge people from another culture. What is considered "normal" and "abnormal," acceptable and unacceptable, moral and immoral interpersonal behavior varies from culture to culture and even within subcultures of society. Anthropologists have long observed that cultural patterns—including definitions of normal behavior—are generally "in fit" with local environmental conditions. In other words, culture has adaptive value.

For example, Favazza (1985) contrasts the cultural patterns of two tribes in Highland Papua New Guinea, the *Enga* and the *Fore*, in terms of sexuality, marriage, and mourning practices (see also Brown, 1978). The Enga, on one hand, face chronic overpopulation, and their cultural patterns function to limit population growth, which, if uncontrolled, would threaten group survival. Among the Enga, there are taboos against premarital sex; broad incest taboos in the patrilineal line, which limit available marriage partners; a high value placed on celibacy; and rules that prohibit the marriage of males less than age 30. Widows are strangled upon the death of a husband, and infanticide is practiced. It is reported that death was not considered a great cause for community anguish. In contrast, among the Fore tribe, who reside in an area of *underpopulation,* many elements of their cultural patterns may function to increase fertility, including liberal degrees of sexual experimentation, tribal ceremonies with erotic elements, encouragement of early marriage and "inheritance" of widows by the dead husband's male relatives. In contrast with the Enga, the Fore reportedly suffer considerable anguish over the death of one of their members. Hence, what is considered normal or "ethical" in terms of behavioral standards is relative to cultural and ecologic contexts.

An understanding of the patient's cultural norms is particularly important in the context of mental illness because what is considered a mental disorder should represent a significant deviation from local standards of expected behavior (Cockerham, 1986). Hence, societies vary as to what falls out of the realm of "normal" behavior and becomes "abnormal"—the latter often being labeled as some form of psychiatric or mental illness. While there is little doubt that social labels of abnormality can *function* as mechanisms of social control (Szaz, 1974), even as political tools, there appear to be boundaries on the relative range in which societies can define normality. Cross-cultural studies of the objective characteristics of "crazy" behavior, in societies as diverse as the Eskimo and the Yoruba of Nigeria, have been shown to be remarkably similar (Konner, 1989; Murphy, 1976).

Certain cultures have special manifestations of mental illness or aberrant behavior that have been described as "culture-bound syndromes" (Favazza, 1985; Simons and Hughes, 1985). There has been considerable debate concerning some of these culturally limited disorders, and it now appears many fit within DSM-III-R categories. Classic examples of these "culture-bound syndromes" include the conditions *koro* and *amok.*

Initially described in Southeast Asia (but also reported in Nigeria and the United States), koro is described as the perception that the penis is shrinking and retracting into the abdomen. There is a fear that death will occur once the penis has sunk into the abdomen. Amok ("running amok") is a syndrome first reported in Malaya and characterized by a period of brooding followed by extreme violence and homicidal attacks, ending with exhaustion and amnesia; this pattern has also been labeled the sudden mass assault taxon. Episodes of behavior resembling both syndromes have been reported in other areas of the world, and it now appears likely that these are "culturally constructed" rather than culturally limited. Although these syndromes sound bizarre, one would note that most "standards" for health and illness are also culturally constructed and dependent on the observer's own frame of reference and expectations. This is true for medical as well as mental health problems. In the social context where their prevalence is high, malaria, pinta, diarrhea, and kwashiorkor have all been described, and treated, in particular cultures as "normal" (Brown and Inhorn, 1989).

Culture Affects Personality Development

A large literature in anthropology examines the relationship between cultural practices, particularly early childhood experiences, and later adult personality. This area of study, begun in the 1930s and heavily influenced by psychoanalytic theory, led to descriptions of "national character," some of which had weaknesses of stereotyping. Cross-cultural comparative studies clearly show a covariance between a society's environmental circumstances and subsistence ecology, which, in turn, constrain the social learning contexts of childhood, adolescence, and, ultimately, an adult personality. Such a "modal personality" is ultimately reflected in the art, ritual, and religion of the society. For example, John and Beatrice Whiting (1975) have demonstrated how "husband–wife intimacy" (including sleeping arrangements and paternal involvement with children) is correlated with the degree to which a society is involved in war or its preparations.

The essential contribution of cultural factors to child development relates to the socialization and learning environment of the child (Favazza, 1985; Konner, 1989). That environment includes techniques of discipline, stressors the child may be exposed to, initiation rituals, behavioral expectations of the child, and skills of the parents and other caretakers. Children develop into adults, having had much of their values and standards of behavior transmitted to them by the family. The behavior and personality of the individuals along with the values inculcated by the family are absorbed from the cultural milieu and, thus, at least partially, determine how the individual interacts with society.

The relationship between culturally determined child-rearing practices and personality development includes three basic facts:

1. Excessive childhood deprivation (environmental, social, nutritional, emotional) is correlated with subsequent adult psychopathology.
2. Sharing of caretaking responsibilities by the mother may be beneficial.
3. Conflicts in the family system between love and hate, dependence and independence are more important for development than conflicts over bladder/bowel control or sexual behavior (Favazza, 1985, p 250).

Despite the wide variety in child-rearing practices throughout the world, including systems characterized by physical abuse or ritual homosexuality, most children grow up to be relatively well-adjusted adults.

In the past, cross-cultural research on child development forced the reconsideration of important concepts in psychiatry and psychology such as the universality of the childhood Oedipus complex (which, according to Malinowski (1927), does not fit the social dynamics of a matrilineal society like the Trobriands) or the universality of social stress related to sexuality in adolescence (which, according to Mead (1928), did not fit a permissive society like Samoa). In recent years both of these classic examples have been questioned (the Oedipus case by Spiro [1982] and the Samoa case by Freeman [1983]). Indeed, the entire model of early childhood influences on adult psychologic features has been seriously questioned in the work of Kagan (see Konner, 1989).

Nevertheless, there is little doubt that certain cultural and socioeconomic contexts may engender increased psychopathology as well as medical disease. Enormous stresses may be placed on persons when social processes change rapidly or situations are created whereby persons are subjected to situations that they have little or no ability to control. For example, in a classic study, Kardiner and Ovesey emphasized the impact of oppression and discrimination on the personality development of American blacks. They stated:

> The result of the continuous frustrations in childhood is to create a personality devoid of confidence in human relations, of an eternal vigilance and distrust of others. This is a purely defensive maneuver which purports to protect the individual against the repeatedly traumatic effects of disappointment and frustration. He must operate on the assumption that the world is hostile. (Kardiner and Ovesey, 1951, p 308)

The study was notable for its identification of how personality development could be affected by societal discrimination. Yet the observations may have over-emphasized psychopathologic findings while not adequately recognizing the adaptive strength of blacks to social oppression.

In a different context, in rural Western Ireland, Scheper-Hughes (1979) has described the cultural setting for unusually high prevalence of serious mental illness, particularly schizophrenia. Economic stresses in the region are severe and have resulted in female emigration and depopulation. The traditional pattern of land inheritance is linked to markedly delayed marriage ages for men and high rates of celibacy. The cultural context includes an ethos of severe sexual repression, as well as ridicule and scapegoating of children. In the historic past, the Irish tolerated eccentrics, including people who had visions, but today there is little such tolerance; this has resulted in high rates of hospitalization. Scheper-Hughes argues that these conditions contribute to the region's high prevalence of schizophrenia, as well as the specific symbolic themes in which disturbed thought patterns are presented by Irish patients.

THE IMPORTANCE OF SOCIAL CLASS

Medical sociology has made many significant contributions to our understanding of human behavior that are relevant to medicine. Two central concepts were introduced as part of the biopsychosocial model in Chapter 1: the disease/illness distinction and Parson's concept of the sick role. Sociologists tend to study both human behavior and mental disorders from the standpoint of larger groups and general trends in society (Cockerham, 1986). Special attention is given to socio-demographic variables such as race, age, sex, race, and socioeconomic status (or class) and their relationship to illness. Of all these social epidemiologic variables, social class appears to be particularly important because it is implicated in such a wide variety of diseases and disorders. The way in which social class or socioeconomic status is conceptualized and measured is an issue of considerable discussion. Moreover, the particular mechanisms that account for positive or, more commonly, inverse correlations between social class and illness (for example, diet, occupation, attitudes, stress, or access to medical care) are generally not well understood (Susser et al, 1985, Chap. 6). The role of social class in determining behavior is closely intertwined with ethnicity.

Just as socioeconomic factors may critically determine vulnerability to physical illness, several classic studies have examined socioeconomic factors in vulnerability to mental illness. Faris and Dunham (1939) studied mental disorder in a large Chicago community, noting that the highest rates of schizophrenia were found in slum areas. Hollingshead and Redlich (1958), in one of the most famous studies in the sociology of mental illness, studied such factors as race, ethnicity, religion, residence, occupation, and education in determining socioeconomic status and its relationship to mental illness; they, too, discovered that the lower the social class, the greater the prevalence of psychosis. The prevalence of schizophrenia was *eleven times* greater in the lowest social class as compared with the highest. In contrast, anxiety disorders were more prevalent in the upper socioeconomic strata. In addition, social class was found to be a

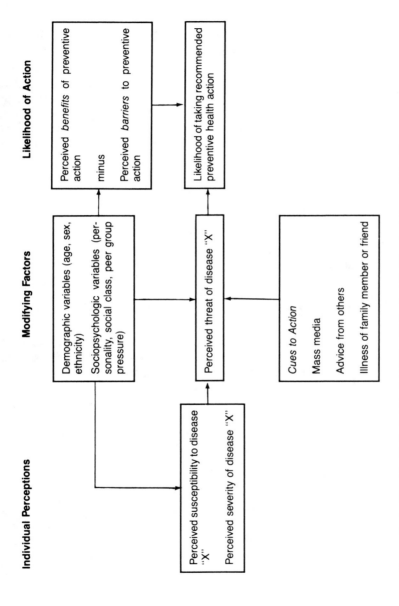

Figure 2–1. *The Health Belief Model. (After Wolinsky FD: The Sociology of Health. Belmont, CA, Wadsworth, 1988)*

major factor in determining whether care was received in a private or public psychiatric system, with services in the public system generally suffering from staff shortages and presumably inferior care. Srole and associates (1962) conducted another classic study, the *Midtown Manhattan study*, a sample of 1660 noninstitutionalized persons living in the midtown Manhattan area of New York City, and also found increased prevalence of disorders among lower socioeconomic groups. Similar results were found by Leighton and colleagues in the "Stirling County" (Nova Scotia) study (Leighton, 1963), a survey of a rural area in Canada.

The consistent finding that mental disorders are more common and severe in lower socioeconomic classes does not have a simple or uncontroversial explanation. It is generally considered that the concepts of *social stress* and *social selection* are both involved. The social stress hypothesis relates vulnerability of mental disorder to the adverse effects of poverty, particularly as it strains the family system. The social selection hypothesis holds that persons with mental disorders "drift downward" in the social order due to limited ability to function and be successful in society; this hypothesis is consistent with the notion of genetic predispositions to mental disorders.

In respect to other demographic variables in the U.S. population, gender-related associations include the observation that depression and anxiety disorders are more prevalent in women, while alcoholism is more prevalent in men. Married people, especially men, have fewer disorders than those who are single—possibly reflecting the "buffering" function and emotional support of marriage.

THE HEALTH BELIEF MODEL AND NONCOMPLIANCE

In recent years, medical sociologists have made important contributions to understanding human behavior in seeking healthcare, as well as the social organization of healthcare bureaucracies (Wolinsky, 1988). Of particular interest is Becker's (1974) *health belief model*, developed to understand the decision of people to adopt or reject disease-prevention behaviors. Noncompliance is considered a very serious problem; an estimated 50% of patients stop taking medications before they are supposed to (Zola, 1981). Four key factors are thought to be involved in this decision: (1) perceived susceptibility to the disease, (2) perceived seriousness of the disease, (3) perceived benefits and barriers to taking action, and (4) cues that motivate action (Fig. 2-1). This intuitively attractive model (and its standardized questionnaire) has spurred much research but has not been shown to have strong predictive power. One problem is that the link between attitudes and behaviors may not be causal at all. Moreover, the model focuses on attributes of the patient that cause noncompliance, almost in the spirit of blaming the patient, rather than examining critical features of physician–patient interaction. Zola (1981) contends that some of the structural features of physician–patient *interaction,* for example, in the authoritarian style of communication or the methods of patient reassurance, actually encourage noncompliance. When the patient's point of view is not understood, both the effectiveness of communication and the potential power of a "therapeutic alliance" between patient and provider are diminished (See also Eisenberg and Kleinman, 1981).

ETHNICITY AND MEDICAL CARE

In complex societies like our own, *ethnicity* is a fundamental source of cultural diversity and, for the medical practitioner, potential misunderstanding. The concept of ethnicity has three fundamental aspects: (1) it establishes ties by reference to common origins, (2) it implies that members of the collectivity share particular patterns of behavior and interpersonal interaction, and (3) it implies that ethnic groups participate with one another in a larger social system (Harwood, 1981). It is valuable to recognize that there is much variation in the degree to which members of ethnic groups share cultural standards or publicly express their ethnicity; this variation may be conceived as a continuum between "behavioral" and "ideologic" ethnicity.

Indeed, the concept of ethnicity brings with it a serious danger of *stereotyping*, the mistaken notion that all members of another group are alike. Even among recent immigrants there is much cultural variation based on regional, educational, and class differences in the country of origin. The length of time a person has been in the United States, his or her socioeconomic milieu, and language spoken at home, all make cultural stereotyping a dangerous enterprise.

It is important, nevertheless, that practitioners become culturally sensitized to the *range* of cultural beliefs and behaviors present in the ethnic groups they serve. This information can be clinically valuable in a medical setting, for example, in terms of interpreting a patient's complaints. In a classic study, Zborowski (1952) described ethnic variation in attitudes toward pain and cultural standards for communicating about their pain. Whereas both Jewish and Italian patients were described as having an "emotional" response to pain, the Italian-Americans in the sample were more concerned with the immediate relief from pain while Jewish patients were anxious about the implications of the pain in terms of the future health and welfare of the family. On the other hand, "WASP" patients reflected a cultural belief that it was "no use" to complain about pain and preferred to describe or report the experience. Patients from this cultural background attempt to avoid being a "nuisance" in the hospital setting, thinking of themselves as part of a team. A serious report of pain from this group, because it is based on different cultural standards about interpersonal communication of unpleasant things, must also be evaluated differently.

The experience of pain can only be communicated to the physician through the patient and his cultural beliefs and standards. The physician must be aware of both the danger of stereotyping and individual variation, and the characteristic health beliefs and behaviors of ethnic groups. The diversity created by the large number of black and Hispanic patients already present in the United States, as well as recent immigrants from Caribbean countries, Central America, and Southeast Asia has increased the importance of physicians evaluating the role of sociocultural factors that may influence disease vulnerability, attitudes toward illness and medical treatment, and, for our purposes, manifestations of presumed mental illness. With this in mind, a brief summary of some ethnic minorities in the United States is appropriate. (For more detailed discussions, see Clark, 1983; Harwood, 1981; or Spector, 1985, on general medical problems, and Gaw, 1982, for psychiatric disorders.)

Black American Patients

Urban black Americans comprise a very heterogeneous category, yet, as a group, they have been historically distinct, suffering from slavery in the past and recurrent racism to the present day. As a group, blacks suffer from a higher prevalence of a wide variety of disease, from hypertension and stroke to obesity, and consequently have higher age-specific mortality (Jackson, 1981; Polednak, 1987). The use of the term *race* in epidemiologic analysis, however, confuses the underlying issue by implying that differences in morbidity are the result of inherent biologic differences. It is valuable to recognize that population biologists abandoned the concept of "race" years ago. What is currently glossed as the effects of "race" in the literature is actually a complex interaction of social class, ethnicity, and, to a probably quite small degree, genetic differences. In most comprehensive analyses of sociomedical problems like infant mortality, it is social class that has the strongest impact. Emphasizing the heterogeneity among blacks, Spurlock, a psychiatrist, notes:

> Parallel to the recent emphasis on racism's generating social ills and im-
> paired health, there appears to be a pattern, in some clinical settings, of
> diagnosing the disturbed or disturbing behavior of many black children
> and adolescents as "adjustment reaction." In many such instances, clini-
> cians minimize or overlook, perhaps for complex reasons, intrapsychic
> factors and fail to recognize the diversity among Black people; that there
> is no one response of Black people to the stresses generated by racism.
> Parenthetically, the role of bias in patient assessment, whether of Black
> and other minority persons, or those from the dominant group, cannot
> be overemphasized. Implicit is the need to recognize the importance and
> effect of culture on the individual and, simultaneously, the need to per-
> ceive the patient as an individual having developed (with illness and
> health) within the culture. (1982, p 168)

Along these same lines of thought, Bradshaw (1978) observed that there were many "myths" about blacks, including notions that black families are matriarchal, in total disarray, and are "tangles of pathology." Similarly, he noted that issues of aggression in both patients and therapists must be understood from multiple perspectives, some adaptive and others maladaptive. Social support systems and communication styles in black patients are often misinterpreted and stereotyped, with some mental health professionals viewing blacks as not diverse but a homogenous social group (Acosta et al, 1982). It is difficult, however, to minimize the possible effects of widespread racism, and its consequent psychiatric stress, on medical conditions like hypertension and toxemia, which place both black mothers and their infants in jeopardy (Spurlock and Lawrence, 1979). It is interesting to note that the lay explanation for hypertension among many blacks is excessive stress due to racism, or "worriation" (Jackson, 1981).

An ethnographic study of the health beliefs and practices of urban, lower-class black Americans by Snow (1983) includes several useful observations for clinicians. The maintenance of good health, it is believed, requires a moderate lifestyle that involves protecting the body from cold, keeping it clean both inside and out, and eating a proper diet. Illnesses are classified as either "natural" or "unnatural"—from both causes, illnesses are thought to "attack" the body. Natural illnesses can be caused by cold, filth or dirt, or improper diet. An extremely important concern is the condition of the blood. Excessive cold is thought to be the cause of upper respiratory infection, "quick TB," and arthritis. Dirt and "impurities"—either from a failure to bathe, impeded menses, irregular bowel movements, or sexual excess—can cause a variety of illness. Use of laxatives, concern about interrupted menstrual flow, or attention to cleanliness are therefore health-enhancement measures. Improper diet is thought to cause two conditions that have clinical significance, "high blood" and "low blood." These indigenous folk concepts should not be confused with high and low blood pressure. "High blood" is the result of too much or too thick blood, which when suddenly going to the head can cause "falling out." The condition is thought to be the result of a diet of overly rich or red foods (particularly pork) and is treated with vinegar, bitters, or epsom salts, which should "thin out" the blood. "Low blood," conceptually allied to anemia, has the symptoms of weakness and fatigue, and treatment is through "building up the blood" with rich and red components of diet. The potential of confusion in these folk conditions in the treatment of hypertension is great (Snow, 1983).

Unnatural causes of illness include the "hex" (voodoo, hoodoo, "rootwork"), "power," and divine retribution for improper behavior. The hex can cause a wide variety of symptoms, particularly gastrointestinal problems, and is often thought to be the malign work ("root work") of a close relative or friend. The idea of hex can be a predominant theme in the presentation of psychiatric cases. Snow reports that many blacks believe medical doctors cannot help in the case of a hex, and patients seek the care of traditional religious healers with "the power" (Snow, 1983). Unless belief in rootwork is identified as part of the patient's presentation by the evaluating physician, extensive medical and psychiatric evaluation may prove to be frustrating. In general, however, blacks rely almost entirely on orthodox biomedicine for their care (Jackson, 1981).

Hispanic American Patients

The Spanish-speaking population of the United States is made up of a variety of ethnic groups, including people with cultural roots in Puerto Rico, Mexico, Cuba, as well as both Indian and Mestizo groups of Latin America. The cultural heterogeneity within this category is significant and important, yet there are several key commonalities. First is the obvious problems of language and problems of communication, which can be particularly critical in a healthcare setting. Other commonalities include general conditions of poverty and migration-associated stress; a cultural emphasis on the extended family; interactional norms linked with notions of respect and modesty for women; and some basic philosophic premises about the relationship of body and mind. The health beliefs and behaviors of these groups have been the subject of much social scientific research (Bauwens and Spicer, 1977; Schreiber and Homiak, 1981).

In respect to Mexican-Americans, Murillo (1972) notes that there is no specific Mexican-American family type but thousands of different families depending on regional, historic, political, socioeconomic, and acculturation factors. The Spanish language may or may not be spoken in the home. For example, some Mexican Americans have very little familiarity with Spanish, while others are bilingual and deal with differing nuances of communication, depending on the language being used. With the mixture of European Spanish and Indian influences, Mexican-Americans may have a range of religious beliefs; therefore it may be erroneous to assume, for example, that a patient is unduly influenced by Catholicism.

Research on the folk medical beliefs of all Hispanic groups indicates that both natural and supernatural causes of illness are thought to operate. Natural causes include drafts (*mal aire*), fallen fontanelle in children (*mollera caida*), intestinal obstruction (*empacho*), but most importantly an imbalance of hot and cold elements. The hot/cold theory of disease is based on traditional Hippocratic beliefs of four humors (the moist/dry distinction is essentially ignored in these folk beliefs). Illnesses, foods, and remedies are classified in the hot/cold system in terms of their essential character; illnesses represent either an excess or surfeit of hot or cold humors. Therefore cure, in this cultural conception, involves readjusting the body's humors to recreate a healthy balance. Harwood (1971, 1981) has shown that for Puerto Rican patients, the hot/cold theory can present problems of compliance when, for example, a "hot" illness like rheumatic fever is treated with a "hot" remedy like antibiotics. From the patient's perspective such an incongruence may defy their own cultural logic. Harwood shows, however, that the "principle of neutralization" in which the "hot" nature of an antibiotic can be balanced by taking the pill with a "cool" substance, like fruit juice or tea, can resolve the cultural incongruence and improve results (see Harwood, 1981, for detailed clinical suggestions). It is important to remember, however, that Puerto Rican and other Hispanic patients vary in the degree to which they give credence to the folk model, and, therefore, the clinician must try to determine, for individual patients, whether this folk conceptualization may affect treatment outcome.

Because of language problems, there may be mislabeling of some symptoms as "psychotic" in Hispanic patients, especially in patients who present with pseudohallucinations or the syndrome of *ataque* (also called Puerto Rican syndrome; see Harwood, 1977). The ataque syndrome includes anxiety, hyperventilation, and sometimes behavior resembling a seizure disorder; it is usually transient.

According to Harwood, the belief system of *espiritismo* (spiritism) is a common feature of Puerto Rican health culture in the Northeast. Espiritismo is a belief based on the reality and power of spirit possession, communication through mediums, and removal of harmful influences by spiritist specialists. It is practiced in neighborhood *centros*, which resemble a "clinic" with mediums and assistants. Patients are reported to present with a variety of somatic and anxiety-related symptoms, including nightmares and mood disturbances. The "therapy" of the patients is conducted by the medium, who communicates with a spirit who essentially conducts an exploratory psychotherapeutic interview with the patient to determine areas of emotional pain and conflict. Various types of malevolent spirits, which may possess the body, can control the patient. Harwood's work (1977) shows that spirits provide valuable mental health services to this underserved community and that their work can be successfully integrated with the biomedical approach.

Mention should also be made of the mental health conditions of *susto* (soul loss, or magical fright) and *nervios* (nerves). The symptoms of susto are similar to those of depression, although the condition is thought to be the result of the inadvertent separation of the soul from the body. The ritual cures of *curanderos* have been shown to relieve symptoms (Rubel et al, 1985). Hispanic ideas of curing appear to be linked to several philosophic premises (Table 2-3).

While the concept of good and evil spirits occupying and controlling one's body and behavior may sound primitive, it is quite similar to commonly held beliefs about spiritual life prevalent in early Christianity and that persist in many fundamentalist and Pentacostal Christians. Even psychoanalysis employs concepts of "good and bad objects" that are "introjected" or "internalized" from one's environment. Moreover, classic psychoanalysis have their own ritualistic aspects; psychotherapy and rituals and techniques of therapy are thus determined by cultural factors.

Other Ethnic Groups

Cultural summaries of health beliefs and behaviors relevant for clinical care are available for a wide variety of ethnic groups, including Chinese, Haitians, Italians, Navajos (Harwood, 1981), Philipinos, Japanese, Southeast Asians, Jamaicans, Pacific Islanders, Middle Easterners, Soviet Jews, and Alaskan Eskimos (Clark, 1983). Spector (1985) and Bauwens and Spicer (1977) provide similar discussions for lower-income whites.

Of particular note is Kleinman's (1980) work on traditional Chinese culture, aimed at understanding how cultural beliefs influence the experience of illness and the patient role. He has shown a general reticence of the Chinese to verbalize distressful affect and a tendency of anxiety and depression to be manifested in predominantly physical or somatic symptoms. The extent to which these characteris-

Table 2-3 **Latino Philosophic Premises about Health and Curing**

1. Illness can result from strong emotional states.
2. Illness can be caused by being out of balance with the environment.
3. Patients can be the innocent victims of malevolent forces.
4. The body and soul are separable.
5. Cure requires participation of the entire family.
6. The natural world cannot be distinguished from the supernatural.
7. Sickness of a member can bring a family closer.
8. A healer should be open and treat you with respect.

(Adapted from Maduro R: Curanderismo and Latino views of disease and curing. West J Med 139:64–71, 1983)

tics appear in Chinese Americans, including the effect of acculturation, is not clear. This same tendency to "somatize" dysphoric feeling states and for psychiatric disorders to present with predominantly physical symptoms is extremely common in primary care medical settings in the United States in both caucasion and black American patients.

DISCUSSION

Social and cultural factors are essential for understanding human behavior because they provide both context and meaning for action. Human thought and behavior encompasses such diversity between social groups because of culture. In childhood, all people learn their social group's beliefs about health, illness, and what to do when sick. Because such beliefs can influence the interpretation of symptoms and effective communication between the patient and physician, they are very important.

Learned cultural behaviors, for example, in diet or notions of "ideal body type," can influence the social epidemiologic distribution of disease. Higher prevalences of disease in minority ethnic groups, however, are better understood in terms of social class than culture itself. The social stresses of poverty have a large impact on physical and mental health.

Social and cultural practices of child care are thought to influence adult personality types. Cultural phenomena can have an impact on children's perceptions of the surrounding environment, that is, one's world view. Aspects of human development subject to cultural influence include the process of individuation from the family, identity formation and self-esteem, sexual behavior, values, the expression of aggression, and how one sees one's potential position within society. In the context of mental health, it is little surprise, then, that one sees in blacks and other minorities clinical phenomena such as major conflicts in self-esteem, intergenerational stresses within families due to disparities between traditional family values and changing external societal mores, and anger resulting from frustration from a perceived failure of society to allow for improvement in one's socioeconomic status due to discrimination.

Yet sensitivity to sociocultural issues in behavior must not be mistakenly converted into stereotyping patients and attributing unfortunate social circumstances of patients to "culture." Leighton states:

> Many of the deprived minority groups in North America . . . have to cope not only with minority status, but also with cultural differences, rapid culture change, varying degrees of sociocultural disintegration, and low socioeconomic class position. For the psychiatrist with a patient who is Black, Spanish speaking, Asian, or Native American it is important to think in terms of these multiple, interactive factors and not interpret from a cultural frame of reference only. (1982, p 233)

In most social situations, stereotyping is used to distance ethnic groups by creating barriers of misunderstanding between them. Physicians and other healthcare personnel must recognize the impact of their own sociocultural backgrounds on attitudes, perceptions, and prejudices that they may have toward persons of social, educational, racial, cultural, and lifestyle backgrounds different from their own. Physicians must be able to listen to the patient as well as respond in an empathic and nonjudgmental manner. It is also valuable to remember that the medical community itself has a culture—a set of values and beliefs about health and illness—which can simply be foreign and poorly understood by patients.

It is important to know and understand the cultural background of patients in both medical and psychiatric practice. Failure to do so will complicate understanding the patient's symptoms, making a correct diagnosis, and planning and communicating an effective treatment plan. Errors that may occur include stereotypic labeling of minority patients, drawing premature conclusions regarding the patient based on the patient's race and cultural and socioeconomic background, and failure to use interpreters when major language and cultural barriers exist between physician and patient (Favazza, 1985).

Suggestions for Improved Cross-Cultural Communication

If a physician is regularly dealing with patients from an ethnic group different from his or her own, it is valuable to be aware of the *range* of health beliefs and practices of that group; readings listed below contain coherent summaries. A multicultural clinical setting provides additional challenges to the practitioner. Berlin and Fowkes (1983) suggest the mnemonic *LEARN* (Table 2-4) to improve cross-cultural communication in the clinical setting. The first suggestion is the most important—*listen* to the patient's perception of the problem. This can be done by eliciting the patient's "explanatory model" through the questions indicated in Table 2-2. Research on patient satisfaction with physician consultation indicates that active verbal interaction, particularly the time spent listening to the patient, was the strongest predictor of satisfaction (Korsch and Negrete, 1972). When physicians explain their view of a patient's problem, it is important to use terms that can be understood. The acknowledgement of possible differences between the patient's and physician's views needs to be accomplished in such a manner that the patient's ideas are not demeaned but, rather, treated with respect. Such mutual respect, coming from both sides of a cultural boundary, can lead to a treatment plan that is acceptable to both patient and physician.

Table 2–4 **LEARN: A Guideline for Improved Communication**

L	**L**isten with sympathy and understanding to the patient's perception of the problem.
E	**E**xplain your perceptions of the problem.
A	**A**cknowledge and discuss differences and similarities.
R	**R**ecommend treatment.
N	**N**egotiate an agreement.

(Adapted from Berlin EO, Fowkes WC: A teaching framework for cross-cultural health care. West J Med 139:130–134, 1983)

ANNOTATED BIBLIOGRAPHY

Clark, MM: Cross-cultural medicine. West J Med 139: 1983

> This special edited issue contains excellent summaries on the health beliefs and behaviors of twelve different ethnic groups, as well as more theoretic summaries of issues surrounding culture and medicine.

Favazza AR: Anthropology and psychiatry. In Kaplan HI, Sadock BJ (eds): Comprehensive Textbook of Psychiatry, 4th ed. Philadelphia, William & Wilkins, 1985

> An in-depth review of cultural anthropology and psychiatry; a good treatment of cultural factors in psychodynamic processes, including curing. An interesting contrast to the more biocultural approach of Konner (1989).

Gaw A: Cross-Cultural Psychiatry. Boston, John Wright-PSG, 1982

> This book includes papers by a number of writers, elucidating aspects of psychiatry as applied to minority groups in the United States. It is useful for acquiring some general background information that is important in the clinical assessment of patients.

Harwood A: Ethnicity and Health Care. Cambridge, Harvard University Press, 1981

> An excellent collection of articles on major ethnic groups, their demographic and social epidemiologic characteristics and health beliefs. The article by Jackson on lower class urban blacks is particularly recommended.

Susser MW, Watson W, Hopper K: Sociology in Medicine. New York, Oxford University Press, 1985

> State-of-the-art discussion of medical sociology, including valuable treatments of social class and social mobility in relation to health.

REFERENCES

Acosta FX, Yamamoto J, Evans LA: Effective Psychotherapy for Low Income and Minority Patients. New York, Plenum Press, 1982

Bauwens E and Spicer EH: Ethnic Medicine in the Southwest. Tucson, University of Arizona Press, 1977

Becker M: The Health Belief Model and Personal Health Behavior. San Francisco, Society for Public Health Education, 1974

Berlin EO, Fowkes WC: A teaching framework for cross-cultural health care. West J Med 139:130–134, 1983

Bradshaw WH: Training psychiatrists for working with blacks in basic residency programs. Am J Psychiatry 135:1520–1524, 1978

Brown P: Highland Peoples of New Guinea. Cambridge, Cambridge University Press, 1978

Brown P, Inhorn M: Disease, ecology and human behavior. In Johnson TM, Sargent CF (eds): Medical Anthropology: A Handbook of Theory and Methods. New York, Greenwood Press, 1990

Clark, MM: Cross-cultural medicine. West J Med 139: 1983

Cockerham WC: Medical Sociology, 3rd Ed. Englewood Cliffs, NJ, Prentice Hall, 1986

Eisenberg L, Kleinman A: The Relevance of Social Science for Medicine. Dordrecht, Reidel Press, 1981

Fabrega H: Disease and Social Behavior: An Interdisciplinary Perspective. Boston, MIT Press, 1974

Faris REL, Dunham HW: Mental Disorders in Urban Areas. Chicago, University of Chicago Press, 1939

Favazza AE: Anthropology and Psychiatry. In Kaplan HI, Sadock BJ (eds): Comprehensive Textbook of Psychiatry, 4th ed. Baltimore/London, Williams & Wilkins, 1985

Foster GM: Disease etiologies in nonwestern medical systems. Am Anth 78:773–782, 1976

Freeman D: Margaret Mead and Samoa. Cambridge, Harvard University Press, 1983

Gaw A: Chinese Americans. In Gaw A (ed): Cross-Cultural Psychiatry. Boston, John Wright-PSG, 1982

Harwood A: Ethnicity and Medical Care. Cambridge, Harvard University Press, 1981

Harwood A: Rx—Spiritist as Needed: A Study of a Puerto-Rican Mental Health Resource. New York, Wiley, 1977

Harwood G: The hot-cold theory of disease: Implications for the treatment of Puerto Rican patients. JAMA 216:1153–1158, 1971

Hollingshead AB, Redlich FC: Social Class and Mental Illness. New York, John Wiley & Sons, 1958

Jackson JJ: Urban Black Americans. In Harwood A (ed): Ethnicity and Medical Care. Cambridge, Harvard University Press, 1981

Kardiner A, Ovesey L: The Mark of Oppression. Cleveland, World Publishing, 1951

Kleinman A: Patients and Healers in the Context of Culture. Berkeley, University of California Press, 1980

Kleinman A, Eisberg L, Good B: Culture, illness and care. Ann Intern Med 88:251–258, 1978

Konner M: Anthropology and Psychiatry. In Kaplan HI, Sadock BJ (eds): Comprehensive Textbook of Psychiatry, 5th ed. Baltimore, Williams & Wilkins, 1989

Korsch BM, Negrete VF: Doctor–patient communication. Sci Am 227(2):66–74, 1972

Leighton AH: Relevant generic issues. In Gaw A (ed): Cross-Cultural Psychiatry. Boston, John Wright-PSG, 1982

Leighton DC, Harding JS, Macklin DB, et al: The Character of Danger. New York, Basic Books, 1963

Maduro R: Curanderismo and Latino views of disease and curing. West J Med 139:64–71, 1983

Malinowski B: Sex and Repression in Savage Society. London, Routledge and Kegan Paul, 1927

Mead M: Coming of Age in Samoa. New York, Morrow, 1928

Murillo N: The Mexican-American family. In Wagner NN, Haug MJ (eds): Chicanos: Social and Psychological Perspectives. St Louis, CV Mosby, 1972

Murphy JM: Psychiatric labeling in cross-cultural perspective. Science 191:1019–1028, 1976

Polednak AP: Host Factors in Disease: Age, Sex, Race, and Ethnic Group. Springfield, CC Thomas, 1987

Polgar S: Health Action in Cross-Cultural Perspective. In Freeman HE, Levine S, Reader LG (eds): Handbook of Medical Scoiology. Englewood Cliffs, NJ, Prentice Hall, 1963

Rubel AJ, O'Nell CW, Collado-Ardon R: Susto, A Folk Illness. Berkeley, University of California Press, 1985

Scheper-Hughes N: Saints, Scholars and Schizophrenics. Berkeley, University of California Press, 1979

Schreiber JM, Homiak JP: Mexican Americans. In Harwood A (ed): Ethnicity and Medical Care. Cambridge, Harvard University Press, 1981

Simons RC, Hughes CC: Culture-Bound Syndromes: Folk Illnesses of Psychiatric and Anthropological Interest. Dordrecht, Reidel Press, 1985

Snow L: Traditional health beliefs and practices among lower class black Americans. West J Med 139:16–24, 1983

Spector RE: Cultural Diversity in Health and Illness. Norwalk, CT, Appleton-Century-Crofts, 1985

Spiro M: Oedipus in the Trobriands. Chicago, University of Chicago Press, 1982

Spurlock J: Black Americans. In Gaw A (ed): Cross-Cultural Psychiatry. Boston, John Wright-PSG, 1982

Spurlock J, Lawrence LE: The black child. In Noshpitz JD (ed): Basic Handbook of Child Psychiatry. New York, Basic, 1979

Srole L, Langer TS, Michael SI: Mental Health in the Metropolis: The Midtown Manhattan Study. New York, McGraw-Hill, 1962

Susser M, Watson W, Hopper K: Sociology in Medicine, 3rd Ed. Oxford, Oxford University Press, 1985

Szaz TS: The Myth of Mental Illness. New York, Harper and Row, 1974

Whiting JW, Whiting BB: Children of Six Cultures: A Psychocultural Analysis. Cambridge, Harvard University Press, 1975

Wilson EO: On Human Nature. Cambridge, Harvard University Press, 1978

Wolinsky FD: The Sociology of Health. Belmont, CA, Wadsworth, 1988

Zborowski M: Cultural components in response to pain. J Soc Issues 8:16–30, 1952

Zola IK: Structural constraints in the doctor–patient relationship: The case of non-compliance. In Eisberg L, Kleinman A (eds): The Relevance of Social Science for Medicine. Dordrecht, Reidel Press, 1981

Two Fundamental Psychological Theories of Human Behavior

2

Psychoanalytic Psychology

3

Lawrence B. Inderbitzin, C. Michael Luke, and Mark E. James

Section 2 (Chapters 3 and 4) will primarily discuss two major psychologic approaches that have been developed to understand human behavior: the *psychoanalytic* and *behavioral/learning* schools of psychology. The decision to present only these two major branches of psychology is based on (1) the practical limitations of space imposed by the length of this book; (2) the goal of focusing on the *essential* principles of understanding human behavior; (3) the fact that psychoanalytic and behavioral/learning approaches to behavior are fundamental in understanding other schools of psychology; and (4) the fact that these theories have received the most widespread application in understanding and managing the problems of psychiatric and medical patients.

Important psychologic concepts derived from other theories, however, are discussed and integrated into other chapters in the text. For example, the cognitive psychology of Jean Piaget is discussed in Chapter 6, family systems theory is discussed in Chapter 8, the life cycle developmental theory of Erik Erikson is discussed in Chapter 7, and theories of attachment behavior are elaborated in Chapter 9. Therefore, while Chapters 3 and 4 present the two most widely used *fundamental* theories for understanding human behavior, other important concepts are integrated throughout the text, emphasizing the importance of reading this text as a whole rather than in parts.

For a more thorough introduction to psychoanalytic concepts, the introductory texts by Brenner, Nemiah, Engel, and Malan are recommended (see Annotated Bibliography). Readers are referred to standard comprehensive textbooks of psychiatry for information regarding contributions to understanding human behavior by individuals such as Allport, Maslow, Lewin, Adler, Jung, Rank, Klein, Reich, Horney, Sullivan, Fairbairn, Balint, and Winnicott. We begin now with a comprehensive discussion of psychoanalytic theory followed by a discussion of behavioral and learning theory in Chapter 4.

PSYCHOANALYTIC THEORY

There are three fundamental aspects to psychoanalytic psychology: (1) a *method of investigation* of the mind; (2) a *general theory* of human behavior; and (3) a *method of treatment* for certain psychologic disorders. This chapter will discuss basic concepts primarily related to the latter two. Psychoanalysis grew from medical roots and was begun and initially developed by a neurologist, Sigmund Freud. From its beginning, psychoanalysis was oriented toward seeking the *origins* of psychologic disturbances and understanding how the biologically endowed infant developed in interaction with the environment. Contrary to popular belief, Freud emphasized the importance and interplay of *both* biologic and environmental influences throughout his writings (1905, 1916–1917), a view that is consistent with the general bio-psychosocial philosophy of this text.

While psychoanalytic concepts facilitate a comprehensive approach to understanding personality, they also have many practical applications in understanding the emotional reactions of patients during the stress of physical illness. For example, under the stress of physical illness, some patients will "regress" to more childlike behavior and have intense emotional reactions directed toward their physicians that often require specific interventions. The following case study demonstrates some of these principles.

A CASE STUDY

A 45-year-old woman was hospitalized for the evaluation of pelvic pain. She was eventually diagnosed with ovarian cancer in an early stage, and her physicians felt she was a good candidate for surgery. As the diagnosis and nature of her illness were explained, she listened quietly with a passive, bland facial expression. When asked if she had any questions, she said simply that there must have been a mistake "during all the testing," and that she was sure she did not have cancer because she could "just feel" that she did not. Over the next 24 hours, she began to insist that there would have been a clear message from "the Lord" directly to her if such a serious illness were present and that she could not allow surgical treatment for "something that isn't there anyway." She had been a religious woman in a traditional manner all her life and had not spoken of such direct communications from God in the past. She had no history of psychiatric illness and was described by her husband as "very strong and always in control of her emotions."

Her primary physician had several interviews with her over the next 2 days, listening patiently as she expressed her certainty that everything was "ok" and no treatment was needed. Without argument or confrontation, the physician calmly repeated his diagnostic impressions and recommendations at the close of each meeting. On one occasion, the patient became slightly tearful as she was assuring the physician that there had been an error in the tests. The physician remarked that it would be very frightening, in any case, to be told that one had cancer and needed an operation. The woman cried more deeply and apologized for "acting like a baby." As she felt permission to cry and to be afraid, she sobbed with the physician and then with her family as she began to agree that the evaluation had been carefully performed and the appropriate treatment should begin.

In the face of the extreme stress of learning she had cancer, this patient had regressed to a more primitive level of functioning. Her defensive denial was not characteristic of her previous personality style and represented her effort to maintain her sense of strength and emotional control. To acknowledge illness and fear was to "act like a baby" and might have felt like risking the loss of the love of her family members around whom she was always strong and in control. The physician was empathic and respectful of his patient's psychologic needs and conflicts. He tried to understand the feelings behind the patient's defenses, and he allowed the patient to maintain her defensive posture and resulting equilibrium until she felt safe and supported enough to accept the painful current reality.

As will be seen in the subsequent sections of this chapter, certain psychoanalytic concepts such as regression, defenses, ego strength, and transference can assist and deepen an understanding of the patient's behavior and facilitate the most effective way of helping a patient such as this through the course of an illness (see Table 3-1).

(*Text continues on page 56*)

Table 3–1 **Glossary of Key Concepts**

Adaptive point of view

The human organism has evolved to adapt to external reality; the ego has developed as an internal regulator of behavior and as an "organ" of adaptation.

Anal

This psychosexual stage occurs from 18 months to 3 years, during which anal sphincter control evolves and the child is aware of bowel function; pleasure is attained from anal and rectal stimulation through defecation and retention of feces; at this time, the child is involved with issues of mastery and autonomy, and conflicts emerge between obedience and defiance.

Character (personality) disorder

A disturbance of the personality involving habitual inflexibility of patterns of behavior without significant subjective discomfort; behavior is *ego-syntonic* in that the patient views it as appropriate, reasonable, and justified; yet the outcome of such behavior often results in problems for the patient.

Compromise formation

Activity or product of the functioning of the ego that balances the gratification of drives with the opposition against such gratification; although the instinctual drives and their associated unconscious wishes continually push for expression, this is opposed by the adaptation of the person to reality and by inner standards and morals; the ego allows for the gratification of drives in a disguised, substitute, or partial form, which is consciously unrecognizable as such; most mental events are the product of compromise formation; those that come to attention clinically are referred to as neurotic symptoms.

Conscious

Mental processes consisting of the ordinary stream of thoughts and emotions, which are actively experienced as they occur; these obey rational, secondary process logic; used as a noun or adjective.

(continued)

Table 3–1 **(continued)**

Countertransference

The feelings and attitudes of the therapist toward the patient, which may arise from activation of conflicts from the therapist's own past, or which may be a result of the patient's projections onto the therapist; countertransference may negatively impact the therapeutic approach toward the patient or may provide a source of data about unconscious processes occurring in the patient.

Defense mechanisms

Specific unconscious mental methods used by the ego to protect against the danger of conscious awareness of repressed drives or wishes associated with the real or imagined punishments of childhood.

Developmental point of view

Behavior is a product of both intrinsic factors and interaction of the person with the environment, but these change in an expectable sequence during the course of development; all behaviors form a continuum dating back to earliest infancy, and most symptoms relate to past experience during development.

Dynamic-motivational point of view

Psychoanalysis explains human behavior and mental phenomena as being motivated by goal-directed forces (wishes or needs inherent in the nature of humans), which may be in opposition to one another, resulting in conflicts and compromise formations.

Dynamic unconscious

The processes and contents of the "system unconscious" held out of conscious perception by the action of repression; they strive for discharge but are abhorrent or threatening morally, so this resulting conflict causes anxiety; if the repression fails, neurotic symptoms may result.

Ego

In Freud's structural model, it is the agency of the mind that mediates between id drives, external reality, and the prohibitions of the superego, working to facilitate maximal gratification while simultaneously adapting to external and internal moral standards; its complex set of functions includes reality testing, regulation of drives, relationships with other people and mental representations of others, thought processes (organizing perceptions, forming conclusions, re-membering, concentrating, learning, judgment, and so forth), defense mechanisms, autonomous functions (perception, motor function, intention, intelligence, language), and synthetic, integrating, and organizing functions.

Ego-ideal

Subgroup of superego functions that includes goals, ideals, and standards of exemplary achievement; it serves to regulate mood, behavior, and self-esteem through the generation of affects or shame.

Empathy

A special way of knowing or perceiving the emotional psychologic state of another; one person momentarily shares the quality of feelings possessed by another person.

Free association

The method of operation by the patient in psychoanalysis in which he or she thinks freely and reports everything that comes to mind without the usual selectiveness used in conventional discourse.

Id

In Freud's structural model, unconscious collection of drives, urges, and wishes that continually push for complete gratification despite reality.

Insight

The subjective experiential knowledge of formerly unconscious pathogenic mental content and conflicts that occurs during the process of psychoanalysis and is accompanied by adaptive behavioral changes.

(continued)

Table 3-1 *(continued)*

Instinctual drives

Innate inner stimuli that motivate the organism toward gratification, usually through another person; the two basic instinctual drives are the *sexual* and the *aggressive*.

Interpretation

Therapeutic intervention by the analyst to assist the patient to become aware of inner mental conflicts and ideas that had been excluded from consciousness, with the goal of accomplishing self-knowledge and symptomatic improvement.

Latency

This stage lasts from approximately age 5 to 12; the sexual drives and conflicts are less apparent as the major activities of this time period are learning and other socially approved channels of gratification; this is a period of considerable development of the ego.

Metapsychology

A highly abstract conceptual framework for organizing, systematizing, and orienting clinical data.

Neurosis

A mental disturbance involving abnormalities of thought, behavior, attitudes, and emotions; classic neuroses include hysteria, obsessions, phobias, and depression; the symptoms of neurosis are *ego-dystonic* (i.e., they are recognized by the patients as abnormal and alien to the self).

Object

A person or thing through which instinctual needs can be gratified or expressed; the inner mental schemas that conceptualize other persons are referred to as *object representations;* the area of study that explores the relationship of the self to inner objects is the theory of *object relations;* some include interpersonal relations in this definition.

Oral

The psychosexual phase during the first 18 months of life during which the mouth, lips, and tongue are the major source of sensual pleasure; because the infant is dependent on the mother during this stage, optimal development allows the infant to acquire a sense of trust and a sense that the world is safe and needs will be met.

Phallic–oedipal

The psychosexual stage occuring between the ages of 3 and 6; this phase begins as the penis or clitoris becomes the major source of sensual pleasure; the child develops an intense desire to possess exclusively the parent of the opposite sex and to eliminate the perceived rival other parent; the jealous conflict of a triangular relationship, with attendant fantasies related to castration, leads eventually to identification with the parents and the development of the superego.

Pleasure–unpleasure principle

The tendency of the mind to work toward achieving pleasure and avoiding unpleasure; according to Freud, this serves to reduce the amount of drive tension or mental stimulation, because pleasure represents a discharge of mental energy, and unpleasure represents an increase in undischarged mental energy.

Preconscious

In Freud's topographic model, psychic material not occurring as "deeply" in the mind as conscious or unconscious material; can be experienced consciously through attention.

Primary process

Type of thought occurring in the unconscious, characterized by irrationality, wishfulness, and domination by emotions and instinctual drives; the logic of primary process uses mechanisms seen in dreams such as displacement, condensation, and symbolization.

Psychic determinism

All psychologic events in the present are influenced and shaped by past experiences; nothing in mental life occurs solely by chance.

(continued)

Table 3–1 *(continued)*

Repetition compulsion

The tendency to repeat periodically the same, usually painful, experience; this is also referred to as the "neurosis of destiny"; because repetition compulsion is closely linked historically and conceptually with Freud's idea of death instinct, the more recent term "compulsion to repeat" may be preferable.

Resistance

The automatic opposition to free association that is activated to protect against the emergence of awareness of inner unconscious conflicts.

Secondary process

Rational, logical, controlled thinking that characterizes the ordinary conscious stream of thought.

Stages of psychosexual development

(See *oral, anal,* and *phallic*—the three stages.) Regular sequence of development of the instinctual drives; the expression of drives centers on and is organized around specific sensual anatomical regions (oral, anal, and phallic), which change in pleasurable emphasis in a specific inborn order as the infant grows and develops; multiple other developmental phenomena occur during these stages and are interwoven with the psychosexual phenomena during each phase. (See Fig. 3-1).

Structural model

Freud's later model (following topographic model) of psychic functioning, which categorizes three mental structures (see *ego, id,* and *superego*) defined as collections of psychological processes and functions.

Superego

In Freud's structural model, the group of mental functions that represent morals, standards (see also *ego-ideal*), prohibitions, and conscience, and generate the affects of guilt and shame; it is acquired through internalization of parental figures through identification.

Therapeutic alliance

The rational, nonneurotic, conscious relationship between patient and doctor based on the mutual agreement to work together for the patient's benefit.

Topographic model

Freud's first model (the structural model followed) of psychic functioning, which classifies three "regions" (see *conscious, preconscious,* and *unconscious*) of mental operations in terms of their relationship to consciousness.

Transference

The unconscious displacement of feelings, attitudes, and expectations from important persons in the patient's childhood to current relationships.

Unconscious

Everything in the mind outside of normal conscious awareness; processes here are irrational, obey primary process logic, and may be revealed through dreams, slips of the tongue (parapraxes), or free associations.

FUNDAMENTAL CONCEPTS

In developing psychoanalysis, Freud's methodology was essentially empiric. Because his theories were influenced by the science of his time (Helmholtz School), it is easily overlooked that the fundamental concepts are firmly rooted in clinical observations. In any scientific theory there is an interrelationship between the various hypotheses and concepts, with some being more basic and better established than others. In psychoanalytic theory, its various components are sometimes referred to as "points of view" (Rapaport, 1960).

The concept of *psychic determinism* provides the orienting attitude and groundwork on which everything else in psychoanalytic theory rests. It means that *all psychologic events are determined by antecedent ones and that nothing occurs by chance in mental life.* The *unconscious or topographic point of view,* like psychic determinism, is so well established that these two hypotheses have been described as "established laws of the mind" (Brenner, 1974, p 2). The term *unconscious* means *unnoticeable* and refers to mental processes and content that are significant and important in determining behavior but of which the person is *unaware.* Unconscious is used in psychoanalysis both as an adjective and a noun, and the latter refers to a portion of the mind sometimes called the *dynamic unconscious,* which contains drives, feelings, and ideas held out of conscious awareness by countering forces.

Freud's first theory of the mind and of intrapsychic conflict was the *topographic model* in which the mind was divided into *conscious, unconscious* (repressed), and *preconscious* (the preconscious being capable of becoming conscious under directed attention). The *conscious* province of the mind was governed primarily by what was referred to as *secondary process* (rational, logical thinking). The unconscious, on the other hand, was governed by different laws referred to as *primary process*—irrational thought processes that defy Aristotelian logic and are closely linked to emotional states; primary process includes the type of symbolic thought that characteristically occurs in dreams.

Freud (1900) wrote *The Interpretation of Dreams* within the framework of the topographic model, which subsequently (Freud, 1923) became subordinate to the *structural model* (discussed later). Freud's monumental discoveries about the meaning of dreams also served to confirm the significant findings from his earlier research with hysteria, such as the importance of the unconscious, the instinctual drives, and the influence of past developmental experiences on the present. His understanding of dreams led to the formulation of a new general psychology.

Dreams

In respect to dream theory, current evidence indicates that dreams serve a variety of purposes, including information storage, problem solution, expression of fantasied outcomes in interpersonal relationships, and provision of insight into ongoing experiences. One of the most important functions of dreaming, according to psychoanalytic theory, is the expression, fulfillment, or gratification of unconscious infantile wishes or impulses in a disguised or difficult to recognize form. Put simply, the dream is a coded message and *represents a wish-fulfillment.*

On awakening, the dream that is consciously remembered is referred to as the *manifest dream.* It is never what it seems to be, but rather, is a product of the action of dream activity on the *latent dream content,* which consists of unconscious infantile urges, wishes, and conflicts. The dream is also shaped by one's ongoing daily concerns, known as the *day residue,* and by any physical sensations occurring during sleep, such as discomfort or noise.

The mental activity that transforms the latent dream content into the manifest dream is referred to as the *dream work*. Unconscious impulses, memories, day residue, and physical sensations are reworked, disguised, and distorted during the dream work by specific mechanisms described by Freud. *Condensation* is the process by which a large amount of unconscious material is combined and expressed in a single event or image in the manifest dream. Often one thing in the manifest dream represents the simultaneous expression of multiple unconscious urges, conflicts, or thoughts and feelings. *Displacement* is the mechanism that changes the accent of meaning in the dream by changing the object toward which the impulse is directed or the feeling is attached. This results in the strange or illogic quality of dream imagery. The emotional energy belonging to an important latent idea is transferred to a more neutral or innocuous manifest image. Foreground material in the manifest dream may then represent less significant latent content, whereas some of the lesser events in the manifest dream may be associated with more important latent content. *Symbolism* is the mechanism by which an unconscious idea is represented metaphorically in the manifest dream by something else. Finally, in the *dream work*, the various distorted themes and images are woven into a relatively coherent story line, a process known as *secondary elaboration*.

In psychoanalysis, dream analysis can lead to insights about defensive processes and resistances, the state of the transference, and important childhood events in addition to unconscious instinctual strivings (wishes). In early psychoanalytic history, dreams were considered *the* "royal road to the unconscious," in contrast to the current view that dreams are *one* important and unique source of data for analysis.

The Dynamic Point of View

The description of the unconscious and the topographic model continues with the *dynamic or motivational point of view*. Freud's belief that behavior is in part determined by *wishes* or *needs* ("instinctual drives" in psychoanalytic theory) that are biologically derived was based on two familiar observations: (1) that behavior is *not always triggered by external stimulation* but often occurs without it, as though spontaneously; and (2) behavior, in general, may be observed to have causally determined goal-directed components (Rapaport, 1960, p 48).

Experienced as an inner pressure, the instinctual drives in Freud's theory aim toward satisfaction, guided by the compass of "the pleasure–unpleasure principle leading toward activities that provide gratification and away from those that provide pain" (Cooper et al, 1989, p 2). Instinctual drives require something (usually termed *object* in psychoanalytic theory) through which or in regard to which they can achieve their aims, and the coordination between drive and object are now assumed to be guaranteed by evolution (i.e., the infant's need to nurse at the mother's breast).

It is important to note that the instinctual drives of humans differ significantly from the instincts of other animals. *"Instincts" refers to innate, biologically inherited propensities to respond in stereotypic ways that have individual or species survival value.* Certain complex behaviors of animals, such as mating rituals and migrations of birds, have survival value and are *unlearned* (see Chap. 10). The instinctual drives of humans, while they may have great compelling force, do not always *necessarily* have survival value. In addition, because of intelligence factors, humans have a great capacity for learning and problem solving (an *ego* capacity in psychoanalytic terms) that, coupled with a long and complex process of social and emotional development, leads to extensive plasticity and adaptability.

Two basic drives are most often emphasized by psychoanalysts, the *sexual* and the *aggressive*. Although Freud defined sexual in a broad way, equating it with sensual or pleasurable (1905), the term sexual drive has continued to be *erroneously* used as a synonym for sex and/or for sexual intercourse.

In most of the manifestations of the drives that we can observe, the sexual and the aggressive components are intermingled. Although part of our constitutional endowment, the instinctual drives undergo a complex development (psychosexual development) and will be described later in conjunction with the *developmental point of view.*

The **adaptive point of view** in psychoanalytic theory refers to external reality as a source of stimuli, and this thesis has undergone greater change in psychoanalytic psychology than any other (Rapaport, 1960). Of central importance are the contributions of Hartmann (1939, 1948, 1958). The human organism from this point of view is considered to be a product of evolution and is born preadapted to reality. The ego develops as an internal regulator of behavior and becomes the human's "organ of adaptation." Reality and adaptation "are the matrix of all behavior" (Rapaport, 1960, pp 60–61).

The **developmental hypothesis,** or the *genetic point of view* (the term *genetic* referring here to a process of development—not in the sense of cell biology) was implicit even in Freud's earliest work. From this point of view, every behavior is the product of two basic interacting factors: (1) intrinsic forces, which are *antecedent* to and *independent* of experience; and (2) *experiential* factors, which are based on learning or other forms of environmental influence. In this conception, all behaviors are part of a continuum extending back to earliest infancy. Furthermore, development is not a straight line process forward but rather occurs in a series of progressions and regressions. The clinically important concepts of regression and fixation are interrelated and are intrinsic aspects of the developmental hypothesis.

Regression, mentioned earlier as a frequent behavioral reaction observed in patients during the stress of both physical and psychiatric illness, refers to the *turning back* from a more mature pattern of behavior to a more immature or childlike state of feeling and thinking. The process of regression often serves a self-protective or defensive purpose. The following case history is illustrative of this process.

A CASE STUDY

A 55-year-old university professor was transferred to the oncology unit after being diagnosed with colon cancer. After surgery that resulted in a colostomy, he became increasingly withdrawn and uncommunicative. He told his physician that he was certain his wife of 30 years no longer loved him, and he wondered if she would continue to visit. He became apathetic and uninvolved in his treatment, even though his physicians were optimistic about his prognosis. He began to depend on the nurses for bathing and feeding, acting as if he were physically incapable of managing himself. A formerly proud, independent, and dignified man, his behavior became more dependent and helpless. He complained, whined, and became angry when his demands were not immediately met.

This patient "regressed" to an earlier mode of functioning in reaction to the diagnosis of cancer. Such regression of ego functioning is often associated with the development of depression, increased dependency needs, and preoccupation with the fears characteristic of early childhood. In this case, the patient subsequently revealed that he experienced his surgery not only as a mutilation of his body but was ashamed and embarrassed by the loss of control of his bowels imposed by the colostomy. He also felt helpless, afraid, and had an intense need to be cared for, but hated these feelings of dependency at the same time.

The concept of *fixation* refers to an arrest or failure in the developmental process. There is a tendency for areas of development that are not fully mastered to retain a component of continued or unresolved emphasis in the person's behavior that plays a role in later personality functioning. The concepts of fixation and regression are strongly linked to each other, because under stress there is a tendency of patients to *regress* to stages of developmental immaturity in which they may be *fixated*. In Freud's thinking, the degree of *regression* was determined in part by the level of the patient's developmental immaturity or "point of fixation" in psychosexual development. These ideas were central in his thinking about the etiology of neurosis. The following elaboration of the developmental hypothesis will help to clarify these concepts further.

PSYCHOSEXUAL DEVELOPMENT

Based on evidence from adult and childhood analyses as well as child observations, Freud postulated an inborn developmental sequence of *psychosexual stages* according to which areas of the body progressively achieved primacy in regard to certain pleasurable sensations and activities. He termed these modes of functioning *oral, anal,* and *phallic.* Under normal circumstances Freud postulated that there is a more or less orderly progression from one "zone" to the next, with each phase merging into the next as psychosexual development proceeds. However, conflicts at any stage of development could result in fixation and regression to an earlier unmastered developmental phase.

The *oral stage* of psychosexual development in this theory occurs approximately during the first year and a half of life. During this stage, the mouth, lips, and tongue are the primary areas of pleasurable sensations and gratification; and the majority of the child's activities and relationships to others occur principally through the oral cavity and mucosa. The prototype of oral pleasure is the baby nursing at the breast. This is a period of absolute dependence on the mother for nourishment, pleasurable sensation, and a secure atmosphere. A sense of trust should develop that the world is a safe place and that the child's basic needs will be met.

Evidence of difficulties encountered during the oral period of development are sometimes revealed in the personalities of adults, especially during times of stress, as in the following case.

A CASE STUDY

A 30-year-old woman was followed as an outpatient in a general medical practice. She tended to be unusually clinging and dependent on the physician for reassurance, although she recognized that she was basically physically healthy. She was extremely sensitive to the slightest delay and sometimes remarked that her physician was not "warm enough," never gave her enough time, and probably "really didn't care." She often made demands for medication and had a tendency to become dependent on tranquilizers and sleeping pills. In expressing her need for a secure, consistent, and dependable caretaker, she was both clinging and needy but, at the same time, was unable to trust her physician and was silently resentful toward him. Exploration of her early family life revealed evidence of a cold, inconsistent, and neglectful mother who gave little emotional nurturance to her children, leaving them with unmet yearnings to be cared for, nurtured, and protected.

Such personality traits and modes of interpersonal behavior may result from fixation at and/or regression to the oral phase of development. This period of infancy is marked by feelings of helplessness, dependency, and need for nurturance and protection. Children who are neglected, deprived, or abused, either physically or emotionally during this period of development may experience a lifelong unmet intense "hunger" for love and may feel a sense of insecurity accompanied by a basic mistrust of others; they often both expect and fear that they will be hurt or rejected in interpersonal relationships. These difficulties with trust, attachment, and commitment may be complicated by a sense that they are unlovable or not worthwhile. When unmet needs of love, mixed with fear of rejection and feelings of anger, frustration, low self-esteem, and depression become intrinsic parts of the personality makeup, there are often also difficulties establishing stable adult relationships. This stage of development is also discussed in the context of attachment theory in Chapter 6 and Eriksonian psychosocial theory in Chapter 7. The neurobiologic effects of developmental trauma in this phase of development are discussed in Chapter 9.

The *anal stage,* which Freud termed *sadistic–anal* to emphasize the importance of the *aggressive* drive in this stage, occurs from about *18 months to 3 years.* The anal and rectal mucosa, as well as the feces themselves, are a main source of both pleasurable and unpleasurable sensations, which become a focus of the child's interest. During this period, anal sphincter control develops, and the child acquires a sense of mastery and autonomy. Struggles for control often ensue as the child has more freedom to produce or withhold bowel movements. The child simultaneously begins to experience some degree of independence and a new sense of control over other aspects of life.

Developmental issues at this stage are marked by struggles over control versus lack of control, obedience versus defiance, protest versus submission, and giving versus withholding, leading to the unfortunate labeling of this period as the "terrible two's." The frequent use of the word "no" is not necessarily a sign of defiance and stubbornness but a way of the child to assert his or her own needs and wishes, resist unwanted intrusion of the parents, and protect one's own self interests independent of the wishes of the parents. It is a time when the child is testing his or her assertion, aggression, and independence, and represents an effort to exert some degree of independent control. Problems during this stage of development are often associated with family environments that are strict, rigid, overly controlling, critical, and emotionally constricted. Children's early attempts at expressing anger and assertiveness are sometimes responded to with severe criticism and punishment in such settings, resulting in the perception that certain emotions are bad, dangerous, or unacceptable. The resentment and frustrations of being unable to express their own angry feelings are then repressed and may require rigid personality defenses to maintain a sense of control. Such persons as adults may appear to be emotionally rigid, aloof, and constrained, and have difficulties expressing affectionate as well as angry feelings. In psychiatric terminology these traits are characteristic of *obsessive-compulsive* personalities.

A critical, demanding, perfectionistic family atmosphere may contribute to smoldering resentment. This situation, combined with a fear of expressing their feelings, makes the core problem of obsessive compulsive patients one of unresolved anger and fear of both punishment and loss of the parent's love and approval. Attempts to gain parental love by achieving and being "perfect" may become a driving force in the personality. Hence, the person's self-esteem becomes overly dependent on productivity and approval from external sources. The following is illustrative.

A CASE STUDY

A 40-year-old businessman was admitted to the hospital for evaluation of abdominal pain. He was polite, but his manner was formal, tense, controlled, and emotionally distant. While undergoing diagnostic procedures, he appeared constantly indecisive, demanding a thorough and logical explanation for each step in the diagnostic process. He was stubborn at times and submitted slowly and reluctantly to the most routine recommendations and requests. He experienced the medical workup as an issue of control and as being "forced" into something he did not want to do.

This patient's behavior indicated a central conflict over the childhood issue, "Should I obey or say 'No'?" If the physician respects this sort of patient's need for control and independence and provides careful detailed explanations, "power struggles" and treatment failures can often be avoided.

According to Freud, the *phallic,* or the *phallic–oedipal* stage, is next to occur and extends from about age 3 to age 6. The leading organ of pleasure during this stage is the phallus (the penis for the boy and the clitoris for the girl), and masturbatory stimulation results in pleasure that more closely approaches the usual sense of the word "sexual" (see also Chap. 5).

Freud considered the *Oedipus complex,* which occurs during this stage of development, to be of central importance in both normal and pathologic psychologic development. The central defining features of the Oedipus complex relate to the attitude of the child toward the parent of the opposite sex. From the little boy's perspective, he wishes to possess mother exclusively and eliminate father; from the little girl's perspective, the wish is to eliminate mother and take her place with father. In order to fully understand and appreciate the Oedipus complex and its decisive influence on subsequent development and functioning, several factors need to be further emphasized.

By the age of 4 or 5, the child has reached a level of development of conceptual thinking characterized by a *qualitative* as well as a *quantitative* difference in perceptual and cognitive capacities. Children are able to fantasize and to recognize within themselves the existence of feelings of love, hate, jealousy, and fear, much as they occur in later life. Furthermore, they are able to perceive their parents not only in terms of their sexual differences but also in terms of the parents having some kind of relationship including a sexual one, from which the child is excluded. This *triangular* relationship is characteristic of the oedipal phase and differentiates it from the "preoedipal" child's relationships, which are predominantly dyadic or "two-wayed." In addition, the intensity of the feelings associated with the Oedipus complex is comparable to the most passionate love affair in adult life. The child's situation may be further complicated by the fact that the jealously hated rival—the parent of the same sex—is also someone who is loved. Wishes to eliminate the feared and hated rival may result in intense fears of punishment for these hostile wishes but also the threat of the loss of the parent's love.

As the little boy enters the oedipal phase, his primary attachment is already to his mother, and his developing mental fantasy life begins to center around wanting to possess her exclusively in some sexual way, which is still poorly defined in his mind. The stirrings within him are expressed in wishes such as to look at her, touch her, and marry her. He may show increasing jealousy and hostility toward his father, who is viewed as a rival for mother's affections, that culminate in wishes to get rid of father in some way. Resultant fears that father will find out about his wishes and retaliate by punishing him, possibly by even castrating him, combined with his wishes to maintain his loving relationship with his father, lead him to renounce his wishes for mother and to strengthen his *identification* with father. It is as if the little boy says to himself, "I can't have Mommy, so I'll give up my wishes for her and grow up to be like Daddy and marry someone like Mommy."

The situation with the little girl is more complicated and also extremely controversial. Freud (1925) thought that the little girl's first "phallic" impulses were directed toward the mother just like the little boy's, and her attention was focused on her clitoris much like the little boy's is focused on his penis. Thus, the little girl's oedipal phase *begins* with masculine strivings. When the little girl discovers the little boy's penis, she feels that her clitoris is "inferior" and experiences this as a "narcissistic injury," a degrading humiliation that leads both to "penis envy" and a blaming of her mother for the plight. According to classic Freudian theory, this leads to a relinquishing of mother as the primary source of love and a turning to the father in hopes that he will provide her with a penis or a baby as a substitute. In the little girl's mind, her mother now becomes the jealous rival. Freud (1925, p 256) thought, *"Whereas in boys the Oedipus complex is destroyed by the castration complex, in girls it is made possible and led up to by the castration complex."* The oedipal conflict in girls is resolved eventually through repression due to fears of genital damage and loss of the mother's love.

Freud believed, then, that feminine identification is a developmental by-product of a primary sense of *genital inferiority*, and that *penis envy*, the discontent with one's own genitals and the desire to possess a penis or other masculine qualities, persists unconsciously as a core determinant of personality in women. This theory emphasized only what the little girl does not have rather than what she does have. Although many psychoanalysts have reported findings from selected patients that tended to confirm Freud's view of female sexual development, others such as Stoller (1968, 1976), Blum (1976), and Kleeman (1976) have reported evidence of a girl's *primary femininity* as had been proposed much earlier by Horney (1926), Jones (1927), and Fenichel (1945). Current theory derived from clinical work and observation of children (Chehrazi, 1986) indicates that early in development girls recognize and form mental representations of their genitals, and experience them in a positive and pleasurable way. Identifying with the mother and expressing wishes for a baby occur prior to the oedipal conflict. The recognition of anatomical differences is an important event for both sexes. Some girls may experience curiosity and envy for the penis as a transient phase specific reaction, which is normally worked through and resolved. Derivatives relating to conflicts at this stage of development have been observed to reemerge in some women in the context of regression, neurosis, or narcissistic character pathology, and is evidenced by hostile rivalry toward men with feelings of inadequacy and sexual dysfunction. Freud also suggested that the development of the superego, which occurs as a consequence of resolving the Oedipus complex, is inadequate in women. However, this component of his theory has been discarded, and, in contemporary theory, the female superego is not inferior to the male counterpart but differs in content. Obviously, these theories of female development have incited controversy and severe criticism.

Resolution of the Oedipal Stage

Eventually, for both boys and girls, reality dictates that an exclusive relationship with the parent of the opposite sex is not possible, resulting in the so-called "oedipal defeat." Sexual identity becomes crystallized as identifications with the parent of the same sex are solidified. The wish to possess the parent of the opposite sex and the intensely competitive feelings toward the parent of the same sex become repressed. A variety of possible traumas during this period (such as disturbed family interactions; emotional, physical, or sexual abuse; loss of a parent; and illnesses and operations) may contribute to neurotic pathology.

Disturbances in development prior to the oedipal stage often distort the oedipal situations. For example, if a girl has a cold, unavailable, or rejecting mother, she may turn to the father prematurely and intensely for nurturance and support, resulting in an overly sexualized attachment to him in the oedipal period. Anger toward the rejecting mother may persist with an inner core of unmet needs for love and acceptance. In an effort to get father's attention and compete with mother, the prototypical theatric, dramatic, attention-seeking, seductive "little girl" routine may become a persistent and ingrained personality trait. While these persons may be "seductive" in a sense, they use their feminity and sexual attractiveness primarily to gain love and attention to compensate for the frustrating relationship with their mother. Hence, adult sexualized relationships have as a fundamental goal securing maternal nurturance and closeness.

In boys, another variant of the oedipal conflict results when a cold, rejecting, or unavailable father provides an untenable model for identification. The boy, therefore, becomes intensely involved with mother and also identifies predominantly with her, leading to the so-called effeminate male or male hysteric. Special problems may result if the father is demeaning, humiliating, or abusive, thereby compounding the sense of anger and frustration in the child through further injuries to his sense of self-esteem. Hence, little boys who are subjected to intense teasing, criticism, and humiliation by their fathers (where the father is competitive with their son for the wife's attention) may develop painful self-doubts about their basic masculinity, adequacy, and competence. The hypermasculine "macho" personality sometimes represents an attempt to compensate for and deny traumatic shame and humiliation experienced during the phallic–oedipal stage of psychosexual development. These persons are recognized in adulthood as always needing to prove their masculinity in various types of hyperaggressive, hypersexual, and risk-taking behaviors.

One classic example of behavior that indicates unresolved oedipal issues in both adult men and women is the repetitive pattern of becoming intensely attracted to persons of the opposite sex whom they "cannot have" or who are in some way unavailable or inappropriate. This is a repetition of the effort to competitively secure love of the unavailable parent of the opposite sex, which was never resolved. The typical dilemma for such persons is that, even if they are eventually able to secure the love of their longed-for romantic object, they may soon lose interest and move on to another "conquest" in an effort to again win love, approval, and affirmation of their self worth.

There are many other variations on the oedipal theme. Personality characteristics that are often evidence of unresolved oedipal-related issues in adults include intense concerns over competitiveness, envy, rivalry, jealousy with underlying feelings of insecurity, excessive guilt, and conflicts about success.

Massive trauma in psychosexual development can occur if children are subjected to overt sexual molestation, abuse, or incest, or if the parent is covertly and overtly sexually seductive with the child. While sexual abuse was once thought to be a rare event, it has been estimated that as many as 10% to 25% of female children may have been subjected to some form of sexual abuse, with alcoholism in the family being a primary risk factor. While a discussion of the pervasive impact that sexual abuse may have on children's psychosexual development and their later interpersonal and sexual relationships is beyond the scope of this text, one may say that the effects are often devastating and cause lasting problems if psychotherapeutic treatment is not received.

THE DEVELOPMENT OF THE EGO
AND THE STRUCTURAL MODEL

We now turn from the subject of the stages of psychosexual development to the concept of the *ego*. In Freud's earliest work, the term *ego* stood for the person, self, or consciousness, which, in turn, was equated with "the dominant mass of ideas" (Freud, 1893–1895, p 116). *Defenses* or *ego defense mechanisms* were associated with consciousness, and the unconscious was used to refer to that part of the mind in which unacceptable wishes, feelings, and ideas were sequestered from conscious awareness.

As Freud developed his psychoanalytic techniques with an increasing emphasis on free association, and his clinical experience expanded, he observed that psychologic defenses against forbidden or painful unconscious material were also unconscious. Furthermore, he recognized that self-punitive tendencies could also be outside of awareness (such as unconscious sense of guilt). These observations led to Freud's elaboration of the *structural model* in 1923. "Structure" is not being referred to here in a physical or anatomic sense; in psychoanalytic theory "structures" are defined as those determiners of behavior whose rate of change is slow; therefore, they have a relatively stable, enduring, or permanent quality. The "structures" of the structural model are *hypothetic constructs* that are defined by their psychologic functions in mental life. The three major components of the structural model are the *id, ego,* and *superego,* which are discussed below.

The *id* is closely tied to biologic endowment and is considered the source of motivation (instinctual drives). Wishes are considered to be derived from the drives. The id functions unconsciously and in accordance with the *pleasure principle;* that is, it strives for immediate and complete gratification without regard for reality.

The *superego,* which also functions in a largely unconscious manner, includes the moral values, standards, and prohibitions that are internalized in the course of development. The superego or conscience prohibits and is punitive (i.e., by guilt). The superego also includes the *ego ideal,* which embodies the goals and aspirations of the person and is important in the regulation of self-esteem and mood. It originates during early development to compensate for the loss of primary narcissism and is modified during subsequent developmental phases as the idealized qualities of significant others are internalized. Although major internalization of the ego ideal occurs as the oedipal conflict is resolved, this structure reaches its definitive quality during late adolescence (Blos, 1974).

Some analysts consider the ego ideal to be a substructure of the ego rather than the superego, and others think it is an altogether separate mental structure. One major function of the ego ideal is protection against narcissistic injury (damage to self-esteem) because a person can compare his or her thoughts and behavior against internal standards rather than with idealized others. Pathology of the ego ideal contributes to disorders of self-esteem regulation as observed in patients with narcissistic personality disorder and depression (Bibring, 1953). Conflict of the ego with the superego produces the emotion of guilt.

Although most analysts agree that the superego as an autonomous, structured, functional entity is established in conjunction with the resolution of the Oedipus complex, its development does not begin nor end at this point. The superego is developmentally closely linked to the ego, and both agencies evolve through processes known as *identification* and *internalization.* The external prohibitions and restraints of the parents are transformed into internal regulators by the child because of fear of punishment and need for the parent's love (to offend or displease the parent would bring about rejection). Thus, precursors to the superego begin during the anal stage of development, if not even earlier, and are evidenced by a change from pleasure in messiness and rebellion to pride in cleanliness and control. The postoedipal (approximately ages 6 to 8—early latency) superego is characteristically harsh and severe but not fully reliable in controlling behavior. This severity of superego tends to decrease in late latency (ages 8 to 12). Further transformation in the superego based on new identifications with peers and cultural standards during adolescence result in more autonomy and the ability to make one's own decisions and regulate self-esteem internally. Hence, one begins to make choices based more on one's own value judgment and moral standards rather than being controlled by the dictates of the internalized parental superego developed during childhood. The ego's functions include those that relate to reality (i.e., reality testing and adaptation to reality), regulation of drives and feelings, defensive reactions, relationships to other people, intellectual synthesis and integration, and autonomous activities (perception, cognition, and motility, and so forth). All of these functions undergo a gradual development beginning in infancy. Although some of the ego's functions are conscious, many are unconscious. No sharp line can be drawn between id and ego; they exist on a continuum and cannot be separated except in situations of conflict (Freud A, 1966).

THE ROLE OF ANXIETY IN PSYCHOANALYTIC THEORY

In conjunction with the structural theory, Freud described the *central role of anxiety* in mental conflict in another of his major works, *Inhibitions, Symptoms, and Anxiety* (1926). The concept of anxiety is inextricably linked to his theories of neurosis. In two classic psychoanalytic case studies ("Little Hans" and the "Wolf Man"), he recognized that anxiety causes repression (forcing of ideas and feelings into the unconscious) and related the development of anxiety to *four typical danger situations,* each characteristic of a particular stage of development. Freud postulated that when more stimuli occur than can be adequately mastered by the immature ego, the situation becomes traumatic for the child, and anxiety develops.

The first danger situation is loss of the nurturing or caretaking parent, the primary "object" of the child's dependency and love (*loss of the object*). In this situation, the fear is loss or abandonment of the mother. The next danger situation is fear of the *loss of the parent's love.* By the third or fourth year, the fear is loss of the penis or *castration* in the boy and the analogous fear of *genital damage* in the girl. The fourth danger, according to Freud, occurrs in conjunction with the resolution of the Oedipus complex and is the fear of disapproval or punishment by the superego (*guilt*).

An additional aspect of Freud's theory of anxiety is the ego's ability to *anticipate* a danger situation and actively produce a small alerting amount of anxiety, which he called *signal anxiety.* Other feelings, such as depression, can also function in a warning capacity. This signal not only warns of danger but initiates psychologic defensive activities to regulate, control, and ward off the threat from conscious awareness and protect against further disturbing feelings.

THE MECHANISMS OF DEFENSE

In the structural theory, intrapsychic conflict and anxiety are central. According to the *principle of multiple function,* all behavior serves several functions, is responsive to many pressures, or is a solution for many tasks. Thus, for the psychoanalyst, no behavior is *only* what it manifestly seems to be. Instinctual drives, defenses, unpleasurable affects (including guilt from the superego) are the components of psychic conflict that combine to form what Brenner has referred to as *"compromise formations"* (Brenner, 1982). All compromise formations are overdetermined (i.e., more than one wish or defense is represented simultaneously in all behaviors).

Ego *mechanisms of defense* are various automatic, involuntary, unconsciously instituted psychologic activities that are activated in response to signals of anxiety or other unpleasurable feelings. Defenses are among the processes by which the ego contributes to compromise formation. The term *mechanism* is somewhat misleading and is best understood as an action of the ego in response to signal anxiety. As previously noted, signal anxiety alerts the ego to a conflictual situation, which may lead to a danger situation or a combination of danger situations. The term *defense* indicates the ego's opposition to other components of the conflict, such as unacceptable instinctual wishes, painful affects, or self-punitive impulses. The ego's action may be conscious or unconscious and may result in observable behavior or in an inhibition and absence of expected behavior.

The ego may also defend against painful affects such as depression, guilt, or shame. It is important to note that both the objects of defense and the defensive actions are numerous and diverse. For example, one feeling can be used to defend against another—an angry contempt toward someone to ward off a sense of admiration and envy. There may be denial of an aspect of internal reality, such as sexual longing, or denial of external reality, such as the death of a loved one. The complex nature of conflict and the principle of multiple function described earlier make it impossible to categorize defenses completely.

The phenomenon of *repression* is considered the primary ego defense, and Anna Freud (1936), in her influential book, *The Ego and the Mechanisms of Defense,* describes other "mechanisms of defense" used by the ego, such as identification, isolation of affect, reaction formation, regression, undoing, projection, reversal, turning against the self, and sublimation (Table 3-2). She also notes defenses are often mistakenly equated with psychopathology, even though they are a necessary and adaptive aspect of personality development and functioning.

Table 3–2 **Defense Mechanisms**

Delusional projection
Frank delusions about external reality, usually of a persecutory type.
Denial (psychotic)
Denial of external reality.

(continued)

Table 3–2 *(continued)*

Distortion

Grossly reshaping external reality to suit inner needs.

Projection

Attributing one's own unacknowledged feelings to others.

Schizoid fantasy

Tendency to use fantasy, autistic retreat, and imaginary relationships for the purpose of conflict resolution and gratification.

Hypochondriasis

The transformation of reproach toward others arising from bereavement, loneliness, or unacceptable aggressive impulses into first self-reproach and then complaints of pain, somatic illness, and neurasthenia.

Passive–aggressive behavior

Aggression toward others expressed indirectly and ineffectively through passivity.

Acting out

Direct expression of an unconscious wish or impulse in order to avoid being conscious of the affect or the ideation that accompanies it.

Dissociation

Temporary but drastic modification of one's character or of one's sense of personal identity to avoid emotional distress.

Repression

Seemingly inexplicable naivete, memory lapse, or failure to acknowledge input from a selected sense organ.

Displacement

The redirection of conflicted feelings toward a relatively less important object than the person or situation arousing the feelings.

Reaction formation

Conscious affect and/or behavior that is diametrically opposed to an unacceptable instinctual (id) impulse.

Intellectualization

Thinking about instinctual wishes in formal, bland terms that leave the associated affect unconscious.

Altruism

Vicarious but constructive and instinctually gratifying service to others.

Humor

Overt expression of feelings without individual discomfort or immobilization and without unpleasant effect on others.

Suppression

The capacity to hold all components of a conflict in mind and then to postpone action, emotional response, or worrying.

Anticipation

Realistic anticipation of or planning for future inner discomfort.

Sublimation

Indirect or attenuated expression of instincts without adverse consequences or marked loss of pleasure.

(Adapted from Vaillant GE (ed): Empirical Studies of Ego Mechanisms of Defense, pp 105–117. Washington DC, American Psychiatric Press, 1986)

Defenses develop in an approximate chronology, and empiric studies demonstrate that defensive styles correlate with independent measures of mental health and certain diagnostic categories (Vaillant, 1986). This has led to systems of classifying defenses (immature, neurotic, and mature) that tend to be oversimplified and perhaps misleading. The most mature person uses "immature" defenses at times and vice versa (see Table 3-2). If defenses that are "normal" in early childhood, like denial, projection, and splitting, persist into later years, severe psychopathology may result, such as that seen in patients with borderline personality disorder discussed later in this chapter.

THEORY OF NEUROSIS

The psychoanalytic theory of neurosis is grounded in the structural model. The basic tenet of this theory is that intrapsychic conflict leads to *compromise* among the agencies of the mind. The extent to which the compromise is "neurotic" is determined by the degree of anxiety or other painful affect involved and the amount of maladaptive behavior entailed.

Any time the ego is confronted with impulses that, if gratified, would lead to psychic danger, the ego signals a conflict. It allows a small discharge of anxiety to initiate defenses against the threatening impulse, and accommodates to the pressure of the drives, superego, and external reality with a compromise. It is the success of such compromises in terms of feelings and behavior that determines the health and stability of the person. Ideally, anxiety should be experienced primarily in its *signal function*, (i.e., as an appropriate signal to possible danger), and the person's conduct should afford pleasure while being generally acceptable to others. A defense against an impulse can also help satisfy the impulse in a more acceptable way (e.g., displacement or sublimation). In cases of pathologic guilt, the aggressive drive may be involved in superego acts of self-punishment. Every compromise has aspects of drive satisfaction, moral values, and accommodation to reality.

In what is known as a *symptom neurosis*, the compromise is felt as painful and maladaptive, and although the person may feel unable to alter the pattern, there is conscious acknowledgment of suffering and motivation to change. In *character neuroses*, the situation is somewhat different. The essence of character is in the repetitive and incessant use of certain defenses that gives the person a particular "stamp." Although character traits and defenses may be rigid and automatic, they often are relatively comfortable to the person and are termed *ego-syntonic*, indicating that they are not a source of distress. For these reasons, conflicts stemming from maladaptive character defenses may be more difficult to treat, and efforts to change such mechanisms are met with a great deal of resistance. From the patient's point of view, these characteristic compromises are familiar and sensible and may be described as "part of the way I am." The reasons for interpersonal conflicts are externalized and are believed to be due to the faults of others. An important insight from the study of character is the need to transform such defenses into *ego-dystonic* experiences with a subsequent motivation to change.

MODERN EGO PSYCHOLOGY

A comprehensive and integrated psychoanalytic theory of the person's adaptation to reality and the nature and pattern of relationships with other people ("object relations") was not fully present in psychology before 1937 (Rapaport, 1959). Hartmann and his collaborators (1939, 1946, 1952) and Erikson (1937) recognized a gap in the theory—that the basic concepts of drive, defense, and conflict did not, in themselves, provide a comprehensive or sufficient view of psychic development. "The newborn infant is not wholly a creature of drives; he has inborn apparatuses [perceptual and protective mechanisms] which [later] we attribute . . . to the ego" (Hartmann 1939, p. 49). These apparatuses which serve adaptation are present from the beginning of life. Basic ego or personality capacities primarily involve aspects of the developing human such as *perception, motility,* and *memory.* Thus, Hartmann proposed the concept of the *conflict-free* aspect of the ego that existed independently of instinctual drives and psychic conflict. He also conceptualized that these ego capacities were geared toward making adaptations to the environment as biologically endowed and were present prior to conflict and not a product of conflict solution (Rapaport, 1959, p 12). The tremendous biologic endowment of the human infant in such areas as perception, temperament, feelings, cognition, motivation, and perception have been supported by a wealth of formal childhood development research. Some of these concepts are discussed from the standpoint of child development in Chapter 6, from the ethologic perspective in Chapter 10, the neurobiologic viewpoint in Chapter 11, and the genetic in Chapter 12.

Structures of the conflict-free sphere have *primary autonomy* (i.e., from drives and conflict). Hartmann (1939) also described how components of conflict (drive and defense) can achieve *secondary autonomy* through a *change of function.* For instance, a function that originally served a defensive purpose may through development become independent of its connection with a drive and serve some other function, such as adaptation.

OBJECT RELATIONS DEVELOPMENT

The term *object* first appeared in psychoanalytic theory as an essential aspect of the definition of drive. Freud defined the term *object* as the thing toward which a drive is directed, and there could be no drives without objects. The term is often used to describe real people existing as a part of external reality, as well as images of those people within the mind. A multiplicity of object relations theories have evolved, and there are great differences, even among object relations theorists, as to how the term *object* or *object relations theory* should be defined.

In this presentation, we distinguish interpersonal relations, which refer to relationships with people in the real world, from internalized object relations, which is our main focus. The child's earliest experiences have dyadic (self-object) features even before there is clear differentiation between the self and object.

We have chosen to present the work of Spitz and Mahler to illustrate how the earliest structures of the psychic apparatus are built up during specific stages of development through the process of internalization of object relations. Their work is strongly empirically based and consistent with the important clinical and theoretic contributions of Jacobson and Kernberg. It must be remembered, however, that there are other, very different approaches to object relations theories, such as those of Fairbairn, Guntrip, and Klein.

Renee Spitz (1965) was probably the first major psychoanalytic investigator who used direct observations of the early mother–child relationships to study the development of object relations. (The term *object relations* in psychoanalytic terms usually refers to the relationship of the infant to anything other than him- or herself, which is at least initially the mother, then father, and later other "objects" of the person's attention and desire.)

Although Spitz was not the first investigator to note the smile of the infant that appears at around 6 weeks, he placed it in the context of social significance and considered it the *first organizer* of the psychic structure (Spitz, 1965). Spitz believed that during the first few weeks of life, neonates lived in a relatively undifferentiated, disconnected state, primarily perceiving only internal stimuli and little beyond their own bodies. This phase of development between birth and about 1 month of age was described similarly by Mahler, who called this period the *normal autistic phase* (Mahler et al, 1975). The mother's attuned responses to the child's needs are provided in such a way as to promote a sense of safety and to protect the infant from any excessive internal and external stimulation, stress, or discomfort.

Awareness of something other than oneself—initially the mother—who satisfies one's needs begins at about the second month of life, the beginning of the phase called *normal symbiosis.* As a result of the mother's helpful ministrations, infants begin to retain mental representations of her associated with reduction of tension and with pleasurable sensations such as satiety and cuddling. The infant's perception of mother, however, is still only fragmentary and not clearly differentiated from his or her own sense of self. It was postulated that infant and mother identities "share a common boundary" and sense of fusion or merger (symbiosis). The term *part-object* was used to designate that, at this time, the mother is only "partly" recognized in terms of her nurturing and/or frustrating functions, which could at times be perceived by the infant as inconsistent. "Good-mother" representations become associated with the all-fulfilling, nurturing, and pleasurable aspects of mother, and "bad-mother" representations become associated with aspects of mother that may be frustrating or do not meet the infant's demands for immediate gratification or are punitive or rejecting. Ideally, the child would integrate these separate aspects and responses of mother into a coherent unified mental representation so that the child realizes that one and the same mother can be both gratifying but occasionally frustrating as well. In addition, the child would also realize that seemingly conflicting emotions (anger and love) could be felt toward the same person at alternating times or that these two emotions could be experienced simultaneously (ambivalence).

The two earliest stages of relative nondifferentiation between infant and mother (normal autism and normal symbiosis) end at about 5 months in this model of development, and the formal phase of *separation–individuation* proper begins (Mahler et al, 1975; see Table 3-3 and Fig. 3-1).

Table 3-3 **The Separation-Individuation Process**

PHASE/AGE	COMMENT
Normal autistic (Birth–1 month)	No differentiation of inside versus outside, "me" versus "not me."
	Experience of need-satisfying activities of mother blend with the experience of needs themselves.
	Establishment of physiologic homeostatic equilibrium in new postpartum conditions.
Normal symbiotic (1 month–5 months)	Increased attention and interest in outside world.
	Dawning awareness of mother and establishment of specific bond with her (or primary caretaker).
	Specific smiling response.
Subphases	
A. Differentiation (5 months–7 months)	Increasing manual, tactile exploration of mother's face.
	Efforts to push back to take a look at mother.
	Comparison of mother with "other," familiar and unfamiliar (comparative scanning).
	Curiosity and wonder about external world with frequent "checking back to mother."
	Development of stranger anxiety.
B. Practicing (7 months–16 months)	"Early" practicing period with motility away from mother by crawling, climbing, and righting self.
	Practicing period "proper" heralded by free, upright locomotion.
	Rapid development of autonomous ego functions in close proximity to mother.
	Active exploration of environment with mother as "home base" and frequent trips back to her for "emotional refueling."
	Development of separation anxiety.
	Beginning of representational intelligence and first level of self-identity.
C. Rapprochement (16 months–24 months)	Toddler more aware of loss of "ideal sense of self" when separated from mother.
	Experience of separateness as relative helplessness.
	Efforts made to regain union with mother by bringing and sharing objects with her, seeking attention and "wooing."
	Wish to be helped and soothed by mother immediately when needed while simultaneously wishing to retain autonomy and self-control (ambitendency).
	Frequent "no-win" situations for mother as she tries to foster autonomy and also provide safety and assistance for child.
D. Object constancy (24 months–36 months)	Establishment of self-representation as predominantly positive in spite of child's imperfections and limitations.
	Internal representation of mother as basically "good" and reliable, even though occasionally frustrating and disappointing.
	Recognition of mother as a separate person with wishes and preferences of her own.
	Increasing tolerance of separations and more trusting of adult substitutes.
	Continued development of a variety of ego functions allowing greater frustration tolerance, understanding of limits, and ability to obey simple rules for personal safety.

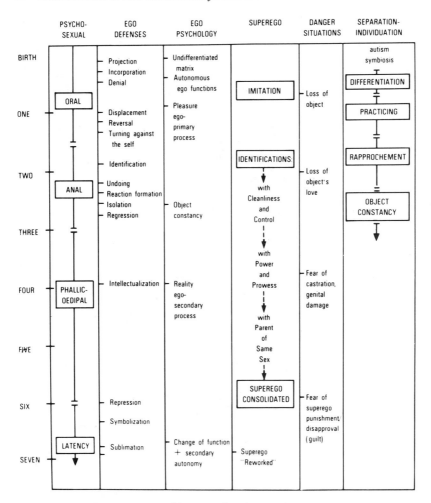

Figure 3–1. *Parallel lines of human development.*

The period of 6 to 36 months is a critical stage of development when a discrete self-concept and identity are developed based on a sense of awareness of separateness from mother. Patients with so-called *borderline* personality disorders have been associated with major developmental difficulties at this stage of development.

There are four *subphases* of separation–individuation. The first is called *differentiation* (5 to 7 months). It is heralded by the tendency of the increasingly alert child to push himself or herself back from the usual position of molding to the mother's shoulder and "take a look." This early deployment of physical measures to "push back" from mother and scan and explore her visually is labeled the *hatching process.*

Practicing, the second subphase, encompasses a period of 7 to 16 months. It is evidenced by a dramatic maturation of motor function. The child can now crawl and explore and exhibits the joy of discovery. Toddlers at this stage feel omnipotent and oblivious to harm as they experience a "love affair with the world." Children during this phase often become so absorbed in and delighted with their activities that they are oblivious to mother, only occasionally needing to return to her for "refueling" and reassurance that she is consistently there to protect and nurture them as the need arises.

Rapprochement is the third phase of separation–individuation. It extends from about 16 months until 18 to 24 months. Mother is no longer taken for granted by the child. The child's increased awareness of being separate and having her own limitations in meeting all the child's needs threatens the child with a traumatic loss of self-esteem. For example, if the child is upset, hurt, or unable to carry out a task, he or she may be torn between wishes to be near mother and be comforted by her and a compulsion to move away from her and function independently. There may be periods of increased irritability and an increase in stranger and separation anxiety during this time. Mahler referred to the rapprochement period as a "crisis" because of the deep ambivalence and conflict within the toddler about dependence–independence issues. The mother, at this time, is confronted with frequent "no-win" situations. The resolution of this phase depends in large part on her ability to allow the child sufficient separation and autonomy while still being flexibly available for support "on demand." Difficulties in negotiating this period of great vulnerability have been associated with serious personality problems in adults. The following example illustrates the rapprochement phase.

A CASE STUDY

A 20-month-old boy was admitted to the pediatric unit for an asthma attack. This was his fourth admission in 5 months, and it was evident that there were problems with his taking medication at home. The mother felt that her son had become "impossible to handle." She stated, "He wants to take the medicine himself, but he spills it, and, when I try to help, he resists and spits it out." The nurses observed that the mother quickly limited the child's appropriate explorations of the ward and was overly protective, and the child was frequently seen trying to free himself from her "hugs."

In this characteristic rapprochement phase conflict of separation–individuation, the mother needed to be supported in her efforts to do things for her son that he could not safely do alone, while also loosening the restraints on his explorations, curiosity, and attempts at independence.

In the third year of life, the fourth and final subphase unfolds, and the child ideally obtains what is known as *object constancy.* A secure sense of self is developed with differentiation between the self and a stable mental representation of the mother who can be seen as a distinct person with wishes and preferences of her own and experienced as "good" even when she is frustrating or disappointing.

The term *object constancy* has been used in two different ways, which has led to some confusion. In the cognitive sense, the term has been used to refer to the capacity to maintain a stable inner image of a person even when the person is not present. This use is derived from Jean Piaget's (see Chap. 6) concept of "object permanence" and is a prerequisite for the establishment of object constancy. Object constancy, which should solidify during the third year of life, refers to the ability to maintain an inner image or representation of the mother, the thought of which enables the child to experience a sense of safety, comfort, and love even in the mother's absence. Problems in the adult personality stemming from difficulties in attaining "object constancy" during separation–individuation are exemplified by the following case.

A CASE STUDY

A 25-year-old man was admitted to intensive care after taking an over-dose. When he was alert, he described taking the pills "on impulse" after a fight with his girlfriend precipitated by her wish to leave him. His history revealed a pattern of self-destructive actions, particularly after frustrations and disappointments in close relationships. His relationships were usually stormy and chaotic, with frequent outbursts or rage when he felt rejected or disappointed by the other person. Although the young man saw people frequently and had a number of superficial friends, none of the relationships endured, and he usually felt painfully empty and depressed when alone. He was intolerant of the shortcomings of others and the inevitable disappointments in human relationships. He appeared to be unable to maintain an idea of another person as basically "good" when he felt that his needs were not being totally met. His emotional reactions to such frustrations alternated between rage and despair, and, characteristically, his aggression became directed toward himself in a self-destructive manner.

In medical settings, persons of this sort often oscillate between idealizing and devaluing their physicians, depending on how thoroughly they feel their needs are being met at any given moment. It can be very difficult for the physician who is feeling unfairly attacked by an ungrateful patient to avoid responding by retaliating, by becoming angry, or by rejecting the patient. Some physicians will acquiesce to unreasonable demands to avoid feeling guilty in response to provocations, thereby avoiding the full blast of the patient's anger. The general pattern of alternating between idealization and devaluation of others is a general characteristic of borderline personalities. Separation–individuation theory will again be discussed in Chapters 6, 7, and 8.

SELF THEORY AND THE DEVELOPMENT OF THE SELF

Another psychologic theory that has developed out of the general framework of the psychoanalytic tradition is *self psychology.* It offers some important insights into certain aspects of personality development. The primary focus of self psychology as elucidated by Kohut (1971) is on the development and psychopathology of the core sense of self. Kohut defined and used the terms *self* and *narcissism* in a way that differed from other psychoanalysts. He considered the self to be a psychic structure, but not one of the "agencies" of the mind such as the ego or superego as described by Freud.

In attempting to understand patients with narcissistic personality disorders, Kohut observed and described specific kinds of psychologic reactions, known as *transferences,* that emerged during his treatment of such patients. First, he described an "idealizing" transference that corresponds to the patient's image of the idealized parent; second, he described a "mirroring transference" that represents a component of the patient's own self-aggrandized image. Developmentally, Kohut postulated that the child's "grandiose" sense of self is the equivalent of "I am perfect; look at me"; the idealized image of the parent is "You are perfect and I am a part of you." From these two structures, Kohut postulated a *separate developmental line* for the development of one's sense of "self." For example, the grandiosity, sense of invincibility, and exhibitionism often seen in children (hence, the popularity of and identification with "super hero" cartoon characters) are the forerunners of initiative, ambition, and healthy self-esteem in the adult when developmental disturbances do not seriously interfere.

Kohut placed great emphasis on the need for the mother to be *empathic* with the child for the development of a healthy sense of self. The mother must provide "mirroring" or approving responses of pleasure and excitement to the child's exhibitionism and prevent sudden severe traumatic disappointments when the inevitable frustrations of reality are met and children painfully realize their own limitations. Thus he emphasized the mother's functions as a necessary regulator, modulator, and protector of the child's self-esteem through empathic responsiveness. The failure of the mother to help the child attenuate the infantile grandiosity and transform it into a healthy sense of self-esteem leads to pathology of the self as evidenced by a retention of archaic grandiosity in the adult.

Persons with narcissistic personalities may display an air of haughty grandiosity and entitlement. Their lives are a desperate search for power, attention, or money to shore up their sense of self and their basic sense of value. Patients with narcissistic personality disorders are often characterized by egocentricity, self-importance, grandiosity, selfishness, and arrogance in varying degrees. They tend to relate to other people in an exploitive manner and use others to embellish or meet their own needs.

Kohut considered the development of the self as *the* central issue in psychic development and thought the sexual and aggressive drives, so crucial in classic Freudian theory, were by-products of disturbed development of the self. His theory of psychopathology emphasizes defects in the development of self rather than intrapsychic conflicts. Classic Freudian analytic approaches based on resolving intrapsychic conflict are not necessarily incompatible with Kohut's emphasis on empathy and healing of the self in the therapeutic process. Empathy on the part of the therapist has always been an intrinsic part of traditional psychoanalytic treatment. Kohut's contributions not only emphasize the importance of empathy, but also focus attention on narcissistic psychopathology and personality types who are considered unlikely to benefit from traditional psychoanalytic approaches.

PSYCHOANALYTIC THEORY AND THE PHYSICIAN–PATIENT RELATIONSHIP

Now that the basic concepts in psychoanalytic theory have been reviewed, how may they be practically helpful in clinical medicine? One may begin to address this question by examining the nature of the physician–patient relationship.

The therapeutic importance of the relationship between the physician and patient has been known and emphasized throughout recorded medical history. Hippocrates insisted that the physician know the patient "as an individual and [know] all the relevant circumstances of his life" (Hutchins, 1952 p. 117). However, the remarkable technologic advances in medicine, which have greatly increased our knowledge about diseases, make it easy to forget that for each patient the experience of illness is different, depending on the person's specific circumstances.

Psychoanalysts, beginning with Freud, considered the physician–patient relationship to be a subject for explicit study. The phenomenon of *transference* is an essential and extremely valuable concept that explains various aspects of the physician–patient relationship that may appear to be inexplicable and unreasonable.

The term *transference* is defined as unconsciously applying feelings, attitudes, and expectations from important persons in one's *past* to people in one's *current* life. Freud first learned about the role of transference in the psychoanalytic situation in a manner that would be ultimately helpful for all practicing physicians in caring for their patients. His singular focus on the interesting psychopathology of his patient Dora (1905), led to his overlooking an important aspect of the physician–patient relationship, the *transference,* aspects of which were subsequently responsible for failure of her treatment. Freud described it this way: "Owing to the readiness with which Dora put one part of the pathogenic material at my disposal during the treatment, I neglected the precaution of looking out for the first signs of *transference,* which was being prepared in connection with another part of the same material—a part of which I was in ignorance.... In this way the transference took me unawares, and because of the unknown quantity in me, which reminded Dora of Herr K., she took her revenge *on me* as she wanted to take her revenge *on him,* and *deserted me* as she believed herself to have been *deceived and deserted by him"* (Freud, 1905, pp 118–119). This unrecognized part in which the patient "transferred onto" and "repeated" with Freud a particularly painful and problematic aspect of a past relationship with Freud led Dora to rejecting Freud as a therapist as once she had been rejected by Herr K; thus the treatment failed.

Transference reactions stem from early childhood experiences with the parents and include a broad range of dependent, sexual, and aggressive feelings and wishes. Transference occurs, to some extent, in all human relationships and forms the substrate for one's emotional reactions to other people throughout life. Transference often develops with special intensity between patient and physician due to the dependency on the physician that often develops in the context of painful and anxiety-provoking medical illness. Transference feelings may lead to childlike expectations for the physician to protect and nurture the patient back to health as would a parent.

Freud divided transference into positive and negative (hostile) types and further subdivided positive transference into an "unobjectionable" positive transference and the "erotic" transference. Negative transference and erotic transference function as resistances to the psychoanalytic treatment process. However, the "unobjectionable" positive transference was considered by Freud to be necessary and especially useful in the physician–patient relationship (Freud, 1911–1913, p 139).

Countertransference refers to the displacement *onto the patient by the therapist or physician* of feelings, wishes, and attitudes derived from the therapist's or the physician's own early childhood experiences. Hence, countertransference may be thought of as the physician's own transference to the patient.

It is not uncommon for patients to have or develop transferences to their physicians, and the vast majority of such reactions are positive if patients are capable of basic trust in other people and are capable of forming a cooperative relationship with the physician. Evidence of problematic (negative) transference reactions are evidenced by patients who appear unreasonably suspicious, hostile, litigious, antagonistic, provocative, excessively dependent or clinging, or even sexually seductive. Hence, a mistrustful patient may have been traumatized or hurt in early stages of life when especially vulnerable to a person on whom he or she sought help or were dependent—usually a parent figure. This mistrust and anger can be transferred on the physician because the patient may react to the physician (unconsciously) in a similar manner. Problematic erotic transferences can also seriously disrupt the doctor-patient relationship.

Likewise, physicians may suddenly experience intense, seemingly inappropriate reactions to patients—either hostile, affectionate, or sexual—if the patient comes to represent a conflicted significant figure from their own life. Awareness that such reactions on either the patient's or physician's part may be complicating the physician–patient relationship should give rise to self-inspection on the part of the physician and possibly a psychiatric consultation (formal or informal) to gain an objective view of the situation. Problematic transference reactions in the medical setting are usually most pronounced when patients are severely regressed under the stress of a medical illness or the patient (or physician) has evidence of a preexisting personality disorder.

The Treatment Alliance

Another aspect of the physician–patient relationship derived from psychoanalytic therapy applicable to the medical setting is the *treatment alliance,* which is also referred to as the therapeutic alliance or working alliance. In general, these terms all refer to the rational, conflict-free, conscious relationship between the patient and physician, which is based on their agreement to work together for the patient's benefit. It is probably based in part on the existence of a positive transference.

In general, an attitude of concern, respect, honesty, and courtesy combined with empathy and protection of privacy and confidentiality will foster a positive relationship in any physician–patient relationship. Studies indicating why therapist/physician–patient relationships fail have tended to confirm this observation. If the physician is able to convey a genuine interest in being helpful to the patient, and there is a congruence between the patient's own current, crucial interests and the interests of the physician, the treatment, medical or psychiatric, is most likely to continue on a positive track and not be prematurely interrupted by the patient (Inderbitzin, 1990; Nicholi, 1978).

Illness, and especially hospitalization, tend to create a situation of *forced dependency* and certain types of regressive behavior in patients, which may pose a threat to the physician–patient relationship and the ongoing treatment. The specific nature of the patient's reaction in such instances is determined by a variety of factors, including the circumstances of the current situation (such as the nature and severity of the illness), the current state of the physician–patient relationship, and previous experiences with caretakers in similar situations. A major determinant, however, is the nature of the underlying personality structure of both the patient and physician.

The applications of psychoanalytic concepts and psychodynamic-based therapy in the care of the medically ill patient are discussed further in Chapter 13.

PSYCHOANALYSIS AND PSYCHOANALYTIC PSYCHOTHERAPY

Psychoanalytically oriented psychotherapy is a method of treatment based on psychoanalytic theory and technique and is the most widely practiced form of psychotherapy in the United States (Henry et al, 1973; Parloff, 1979). It is most often described in terms of comparisons and contrasts with its parent discipline, classic Freudian psychoanalysis. As described first by Freud (1911–1913), psychoanalysis is the treatment of choice for patients who suffer from chronic symptoms or characterologic problems reflecting intrapsychic conflict, developmental arrests or deviations, and/or structural deficits not inconsistent with growth potential. Psychoanalysis is particularly preferable over other treatment methods if chronic symptoms have not improved or are not likely to improve with briefer, less intense forms of psychotherapy. Furthermore, if some other treatment would provide temporary relief but with high risk of recurrence of the chronic symptoms, psychoanalysis should be considered. In addition to these criteria for psychoanalysis, patients must also fulfill certain criteria for analyzability, which include the capacity to form a treatment relationship, maintain it in the face of a therapeutic regression, and then ultimately relinquish it.

The overall goal of psychoanalysis is to foster the greatest change in personality structure that is possible. Psychotherapeutic goals vary widely, but an overall goal is the resolution of symptoms and some degree of behavioral change. Patients suffering from acute symptoms, even if they reflect evidence of intrapsychic conflict, are treated more appropriately with psychotherapy than psychoanalysis, unless the symptoms are embedded in a rigid character structure, or there is evidence of developmental distortions or arrested development. The psychoanalytic treatment situation is designed in such a way as to intensify the transference relationship and center the patient's infantile neurotic conflicts around the person of the analyst. Although this may occur also in other forms of treatment, *it is not an aim* of routine psychotherapy; some psychotherapies, such as brief psychotherapy, are designed to minimize transference manifestations. Patients who show evidence of not being able to distinguish between transference reactions to the analyst and reality should, in general, be treated by psychotherapeutic rather than psychoanalytic methods. In psychoanalytic technique, the analyst tries to avoid becoming a model for the patient and uses interventions primarily intended to promote insight. The psychotherapist, however, sometimes deliberately tries to provide a model for the patient and offers suggestions and other supportive measures.

Psychoanalysis requires four to five sessions per week, use of the couch, and is open-ended with a usual duration of at least 3 years. The technique of free association is central to the methodology of classic psychoanalysis (Kris, 1989). The psychoanalytic situation is structured in such a way (including the analyst's neutrality and relative anonymity) to foster a temporary therapeutic regression, allowing intrapsychic conflicts to be observed by analyst and patient. The analytic situation is, in a sense, artificially contrived to enable patients to reexperience and remember in the here and now as much of their painful and problematic past as is possible and to bring past experiences to the conscious surface where insight can be used for change. In his or her interventions, the psychoanalyst is guided primarily by the manifestations of transference and resistance (Freud, 1914), and *interpretation* is the primary technique applied to gain insight and foster change in the intrapsychic balance.

Modifications of classic psychoanalytic technique and the development of other psychoanalytically oriented psychotherapies resulted from efforts to shorten psychoanalytic treatment and adapt it to a wider range of patients, including those too disturbed to tolerate classic psychoanalysis. Insight-oriented (expressive) psychotherapy and so-called supportive psychotherapy are not dichotomous methods of treatment. Supportive elements exist even in the most insight-oriented classic psychoanalysis, and, at times, interpretations, which are usually thought of as an expressive therapeutic technique, can be the most effective supportive intervention. Recent books by Luborsky (1984) and Werman (1987) emphasize that supportive and expressive therapies exist on a continuum, and these authors illustrate the flexible application of psychoanalytic concepts to different kinds of patients with various types of goals and at different stages of treatment.

Although psychotherapy has been shown to be effective for a wide variety of problems and disorders (Bergin and Lambert, 1978; Luborsky et al, 1975; Smith et al, 1980), there are many unanswered questions and remaining problems. We need to learn much more about "What therapy, administered by what therapist, is effective for which patients with what conditions?" (Luborsky, 1984, p xv). Like any other effective treatment in medicine, psychotherapy has the potential of causing great harm as well as much benefit to patients. It is essential that an experienced clinician who is knowledgeable about both psychopathology and various treatment modalities perform a careful diagnostic evaluation and assess the need for medical and neurologic evaluation and the possible need for psychopharmacologic agents before any form of psychotherapy is recommended. Many authors, such as Levine (1952) and Malan (1979), have emphasized the crucial role of diagnosis and have described diagnostic evaluation processes that begin with a clinical psychiatric diagnosis but necessarily go far beyond that. Such a diagnostic process always includes a psychodynamic understanding of the conflicts within the patient and between the patient and his environment, as well as how these conflicts developed out of the patient's past. Study of the precipitating factors of the present illness are particularly useful in this endeavor. Furthermore, it is necessary to know about the patient's strengths and highest level of functioning, weaknesses and most severe disturbances, and the balance between the two. Only the clinician who is able to grasp empathically the patient's inner world and way of being in the world is able to prescribe effectively. Many of the principles and practices of psychotherapy that are especially helpful in understanding and practically helping patients with emotional difficulties in coping with medical illness are discussed in Chapter 13.

ANNOTATED BIBLIOGRAPHY

Brenner C: The Mind in Conflict. Madison, CT, International Universities Press, 1982

> In this work, Brenner elaborates on the theory of psychic conflict—how infantile wishes come into conflict and lead to various compromise formations. Along the way he reviews his own revisions of important psychoanalytic concepts.

Brenner C: An Elementary Textbook of Psychoanalysis, rev ed. New York, International Universities Press, 1973

> This book is a widely recommended comprehensive introduction to the fundamental concepts of classic psychoanalytic theory. Brenner discusses the fundamental hypotheses, the drives, psychosexual stages of development, the topographic and structural models, ego functioning, object relations, parapraxes, wit, dreams, psychopathology, and psychic conflict.

Engel G: Psychological Development in Health and Disease. Philadelphia, WB Saunders, 1962

> This is a distillation of George Engel's thinking about human psychologic functioning derived from many years of teaching medical students and residents. The development of the psychic apparatus is described as resulting from the interaction of biologic, psychologic, and social processes. Engel also discusses how psychologic adaptations affect body functions in health and disease. The first half of the book delineates the stages of development in considerable detail; the second half presents a unified concept of health and disease, explaining the role of psychologic processes in medical and psychiatric illnesses.

Freud A: (1936). The Ego and the Mechanisms of Defense, rev ed. New York, International Universities Press, 1966

> This classic work by Anna Freud, originally published in 1936, advanced the theory of the role and functioning of the ego. It examines various ego defense mechanisms, including how and why they operate, and is illustrated with many clinical examples from the author's psychotherapeutic work with children.

Levy S: Principles of Interpretation. New York, Jason Aronson, 1984

> This book is concerned with the technical theory of interpretation used in psychoanalytically oriented psychotherapy. Levy describes how the interviewer or therapist listens to the productions of the patient, and then formulates and verbalizes interventions that best facilitate the therapeutic process. Many clinical vignettes illustrate the technical points described.

MacKinnon R, Michels R: The Psychiatric Interview in Clinical Practice. Philadelphia, WB Saunders, 1971

> The authors provide a discussion of basic principles of the psychodynamic interview, then focus on how these are applied in the interviewing and psychotherapy of patients with specific types of psychopathology. Their discussions describe the core psychodynamic issues present in these patients, how these will manifest in the interview, and how the interviewer can therapeutically intervene.

Malan D: Individual Psychotherapy and the Science of Psychodynamics. London, Butterworths, 1979

> Malan describes the principles and techniques of intensive psychotherapy, beginning with basic psychoanalytic principles. He stresses the observational data and the psychodynamic formulations that can be generated to explain the data and test the hypotheses. This book is structured around many illustrative case examples and explains a method of brief psychotherapy as well as long-term therapy. The theoretic orientation of the author includes attention to object relations and the role of the vicissitudes of infantile experience in shaping adult psychopathology.

Nemiah J: Foundations of Psychopathology. New York, Oxford University Press, 1961

> This book reviews the basic concepts of psychoanalysis, then provides an explanation of the psychodynamic bases of various types of psychopathology. It is strongly empiric in its approach, and the concepts are richly illustrated with many clinical cases, which clearly demonstrate the applicability of psychoanalytic principles in the management of medical and psychiatric patients. Especially useful is the emphasis on the role of fantasy in mental life.

Waelder R: Basic Theory of Psychoanalysis. New York, International Universities Press, 1960

> The author reviews many fundamental concepts of psychoanalysis, with elaboration on the topics of the sexual and aggressive instincts, anxiety, ego psychology, and basic principles of psychotherapy. Waelder effectively addresses many of the criticisms that have been leveled at psychoanalysis over the years.

Zetzel E, Meissner W: Basic Concepts of Psychoanalytic Psychiatry. New York, Basic Books, 1973

> This book reviews psychoanalytic theory, including discussions of anxiety, repression, developmental theory, primary and secondary process, narcissism, ego functions and development, object relations, identity formation, neurosis, and therapy. Like most of the books on this list, it evolved out of years of teaching these principles to residents and medical students.

REFERENCES

Bergin A, Lambert M: The evaluation of therapeutic outcomes. In Garfield S, Bergin A (eds): Handbook of Psychotherapy and Behavioral Change: An Empirical Analysis. New York, John Wiley & Sons, 1978

Bibring E: The mechanism of depression. In Greenacre P (ed): Affective Disorders. New York, International Universities Press, 1953

Blos P: The genealogy of the ego ideal. Psychoanal Study Child 29:43–88, 1974

Blum G: Masochism, the ego ideal, and the psychology of women. J Am Psychoanal Assoc 24(Suppl):157–191, 1976

Brenner C: The Mind in Conflict. New York, International Universities Press, 1982

Brenner C: An Elementary Textbook of Psychoanalysis, rev ed. New York, Doubleday, 1974

Chehrazi S: Female psychology: A review. J Am Psychoanal Assoc 34:141–162, 1986

Cooper A, Francis A, Sacks M: The Psychoanalytic Model. In Michels R, Cavenar J, Cooper A et al (eds): Psychiatry, vol 1. Revised New York, Basic Books; Philadelphia, JB Lippincott, 1989

Erikson E: Configurations in play-clinical notes. Psychoanalytic Quarterly 6:139–214, 1937

Fenickel O: The Psychoanalytic Theory of Neurosis. New York, W.W. Norton, 1945

Freud A: (1936). The Ego and the Mechanisms of Defense, rev ed. New York, International Universities Press, 1966

Freud S: Inhibitions, Symptoms and Anxiety. SE 20, 1926

Freud S: Some Psychical Consequences of the Anatomical Distinction Between the Sexes. Vol 19, 1925

Freud S: The Ego and the Id. Vol 19, 1923

Freud S: General Theory of the Neuroses. Vol 16, 1916–1917

Freud S: On the history of the psycho-analytic movement. The Standard Edition of the Complete Psychological Works of Sigmund Freud, vol. 14, 1914.

Freud, S. Papers on Technique. Vol 12, 1911–1913

Freud S: Fragment of an Analysis of a Case of Hysteria. Vol 7, 1905

Freud S: The Interpretation of Dreams. Vols 4 & 5, 1900

Freud S: Studies on Hysteria. Vol 2, 1893–1895

Hartmann H: (1939). Ego Psychology and the Problem of Adaptation New York, International Universities Press, 1958

Hartmann H: The mutual influences in the development of the ego and id. Psychoanal Study Child 7:9–30, 1952

Hartmann H: Comments on the psychoanalytic theory of instinctual drives. Psychoanal Q 17:368–388, 1948

Hartmann H, Kris E, Loewenstein R: Comments on the formation of psychic structure. Psychoanal Study Child 2:11–38, 1946

Henry W, Sims J, Spray S: Public and Private Lives of Psychotherapists. San Francisco, Josey-Bass, 1973

Horney K: The flight from womanhood: The masculinity complex in women as viewed by men and women. Intl J Psycho-Analysis 7:324–339, 1926.

Hutchins R (ed): Great Books of the Western World. Chicago, University of Chicago Press, 1952

Inderbitzin L: Treatment alliance in acute schizophrenia. In Levy S, Ninan P (eds): Schizophrenia: Treatment of the Acute Psychotic Episode. Washington, DC, American Psychiatric Press, 1990

Jones E: The early development of female sexuality. In Papers on Psycho-Analysis. London, Balliere, Tindall and Cox, 1948

Kleeman J: Freud's views on early female sexuality in the light of direct child observation. J Am Psychoanal Assoc 24(Suppl):3–28, 1976

Kohut H: Analysis of the Self. New York, International Universities Press, 1971

Kris A: Psychoanalysis and psychoanalytic psychotherapy. In Michels R, Cavenar J, Cooper A et al (eds): Psychiatry, vol 1. Revised New York, Basic Books; Philadelphia, JB Lippincott, 1989

Levine M: Principles of psychiatric treatment. In Alexander F (ed): Dynamic Psychiatry. Chicago, University of Chicago Press, 1952

Luborsky L: Principles of Psychoanalytic Psychotherapy. New York, Basic Books, 1984

Luborsky L, Singer B, Luborsky L: Comparative studies of psychotherapies: Is it true that "Everybody has won and all must have prizes"? Arch Gen Psychiatry 32:995–1008, 1975

Mahler M, Pine F, Bergman A: The Psychological Birth of the Human Infant. New York, Basic Books, 1975

Malan D: Individual Psychotherapy and the Science of Psychodynamics. Boston, Butterworths, 1979

Nicholi A: The therapist–patient relationship. In Nicholi A (ed): The Harvard Guide to Modern Psychiatry. Cambridge, The Belknap Press of Harvard University Press, 1978

Parloff MB: Can psychotherapy research guide the policymaker? A little knowledge may be a dangerous thing. Am Psychol 34:296–306, 1979

Rapaport D: The Structure of Psychoanalytic Theory. Psychological Issues 2(2). New York, International Universities Press, 1960

Rapaport D: A historical survey of psychoanalytic ego psychology. Introduction in Erikson E: Identity and the Life Cycle. Psychological Issues 1(1). New York, International Universities Press, 1959

Smith M, Glas G, Miller T: The Benefits of Psychotherapy. Baltimore, Johns Hopkins Press, 1980

Spitz R: The First Year of Life. New York, International Universities Press, 1965

Stoller R: Primary femininity. J Am Psychoanal Assoc 24(Suppl):59–78, 1976

Stoller R: Sex and Gender. New York, Science House, 1968

Vaillant G: Empirical Studies of Ego Mechanisms of Defense. Washington, DC, American Psychiatric Press, 1986

Werman D: The Practice of Supportive Psychotherapy. New York, Brunner/Mazel, 1987

Behavioral and Social Learning Psychology

Pamela G. Dorsett

The preceding chapter was an overview of the basic principles of psychoanalytic psychology and its application to the care of patients. In this chapter, the contributions of behavioral and learning theory will be discussed. While the concluding section of this chapter compares psychoanalytic with behavioral theory and therapy, no attempt will be made to reconcile or integrate psychoanalytic and behavioral/learning theory, although serious efforts have been made to do so (Marmor and Woods, 1980). It is the position of this text that both perspectives have value. The two approaches are presented recognizing that appreciation of diverse models may facilitate selection and use of the most appropriate techniques for each given patient's needs.

BASIC CONCEPTS OF BEHAVIORAL THEORY

The philosophy of the science of human behavior called behaviorism has evolved from a rich albeit brief history. There are, however, several basic characteristics and assumptions common to most positions within behavioral psychology.

First, the subject matter for study is *objectively measurable behavior*, particularly the relationship between behavior and the environment. Behaviors may be external and directly observable (e.g., the eye blink or social interactions) or internal and monitored through instrumentation (e.g., the physiological responses of brain wave activity or blood pressure). Some theorists argue, however, that private, inaccessible, or "covert" events such as cognitions and emotions should also be studied.

A second characteristic of behavioral psychology is a commitment to *experimentation* and the empirical method. Behavior is defined objectively and in such a way that it can be measured reliably. The nature of the relationships between behavior and the environment are explored, described, and analyzed by means of experiments using methodology similar to that employed in the study of the natural sciences. Through experimentation, general laws or principles of behavior can be discovered such that behavior can be predicted and controlled.

Third, *learning* is emphasized. Further, it is assumed that adaptive and maladaptive behaviors are acquired in basically the same ways. The behavioral perspective rejects the notions of traits and underlying processes (e.g., conflicts) in explaining behavior. Personality development, whether "normal" or "abnormal," is seen as the result of the unique contributions of learning experiences and genetic endowment. Maladaptive behavior that is not learned can be affected by learning principles, and significant environmental factors can be changed to alter this behavior. As such, the behavioral view is optimistic regarding change.

Additional assumptions could be included, depending on the position on private events, because it is here that individuals are most likely to disagree. Specifically, the issue entails (1) the role of private events in explaining behavior, and (2) the inclusion versus exclusion of such events in experimentation. An overview of the development of the behavioral movement will facilitate appreciation of these issues.

MAJOR CONTRIBUTIONS TO THE BEHAVIORAL MOVEMENT

Many figures have made significant contributions to the behavioral movement (Table 4-1). Space allows only some of these to be presented briefly. (See Kazdin, 1978, for a complete history of the behavioral psychology movement.)

Ivan Pavlov (1849–1936) and two other neurophysiologists in Russia, Ivan Sechenov (1829–1905) and Vladimir Bechterev (1857–1927), played significant roles

Table 4–1 **Major Contributions to the Behavioral Movement**

Ivan Sechenov (1829–1905)	Proposed that behavior was reflexive to external stimuli and advocated the use of experimental methodology for the study of behavior.
Vladimir Bechterev (1857–1927)	Focused on aversive stimuli and reflexes with humans and other species. Attempted to apply principles of reflexology to psychiatric disorders. Advocated objectivism, empiricism, and experimentation in psychology.
Ivan Pavlov (1849–1936)	Formulated principles of classical (respondent) conditioning. Advocated objectivism, empiricism, and experimentation in psychology.
John B. Watson (1878–1958)	Advocated objectivism, empiricism, and experimentation in psychology with observable behavior as the subject matter. Publicized the behavioral position. "Father of Behaviorism." Extended application of the classical conditioning model to the development of emotions in humans.

(continued)

Table 4-1 *(continued)*

Edward L. Thorndike (1874–1949)	Studied patterns of behavior in trial-and-error learning. Formulated the Law of Effect and emphasized the consequences of behavior.
Edward C. Tolman (1896–1961)	Maintained that behavior is purposive and referred to subjective states in accounting for behavior. Proposed that reinforcement serves as information and not to strengthen behavior directly.
B. F. Skinner (1904–)	Shifted focus of explanations for behavior from stimuli to consequences. Formulated principles of operant conditioning. Advocated a methodological approach for studying behavior called the experimental analysis of behavior. Presented the radical behaviorism position. Helped distinguish operant and respondent (classical) conditioning. Had great impact on the development of behavior modification.
Joseph Wolpe (1915–)	Employed an animal model to study the development of emotional reactions and ways of treating such problems. Developed treatment techniques based on the principle of reciprocal inhibition. Techniques generated research and contributed to the development of behavior therapy.
Albert Bandura (1925–)	Emphasized reciprocal determinism and cognitive and self-regulatory processes. Elucidated variables affecting observational learning.

in the development of behaviorism. Their major contributions included (1) application of the experimental method to the study of psychological phenomena including direct, objective observation and measurement of specific behaviors; (2) explaining behavior objectively in terms of observable, controlled manipulations or operations; and (3) elucidation of the principles of classical or respondent conditioning (Table 4-2).

Pavlov studied digestion and developed a surgical technique that made it possible to obtain secretions directly from the glands and, therefore, to observe and measure the secretions outside the animal's body. He had already begun to direct his research toward elucidation of the variables affecting the acquisition and elimination of "psychic secretions" (i.e., gastric secretions elicited by stimuli such as the sight of food rather than by direct physical stimulation) when he received the Nobel Prize in 1904 for his work in digestion. His initial attempts to explain the secretions on the basis of "expectancies" were not productive, so he set about the task of analyzing the nature of the responses and their relationship to other events.

Table 4–2 **Classical or Respondent Conditioning**

TERM	DEFINITION	EXAMPLE
Unconditioned stimulus (UCS)	Elicits an unconditioned response or reflex.	Blast of air into eye causes eye blink.
Unconditioned response (UCR)	Reflex elicited by an unconditioned stimulus.	Eye blink in response to blast of air.
Conditioned stimulus (CS)	Previously neutral stimulus that comes to elicit an unconditioned response through pairings with an unconditioned stimulus.	Tone presented immediately before blast of air into eye. Tone alone comes to elicit eye blink.
Conditioned response (CR)	Response elicited by the conditioned stimulus.	Eye blink in response to tone.
Discrimination	The conditioned response is elicited by some stimuli similar to the conditioned stimulus but not by others.	Tones of a particular frequency range elicit the eye blink but others do not.
Generalization	Stimuli similar to the conditioned stimulus elicit the conditioned response.	Tones most similar to the original one elicit the eye blink.
Extinction	Conditioned stimulus loses the power to elicit the conditioned response by no longer being paired with the unconditioned stimulus.	After repeated presentations of the tone without the blast of air, the tone alone no longer elicits the eye blink.

CLASSICAL OR RESPONDENT CONDITIONING

Pavlov found that by repeatedly pairing a stimulus that elicited the salivation reflex, the previously neutral stimulus would also elicit a reflexive-type response. For example, a tone would not elicit salivation. However, if the tone was presented with food for several conditioning trials, then, when presented alone, the tone did elicit salivation. In this paradigm, the food is called an *unconditioned stimulus* (UCS), and the response it elicits is called an *unconditioned response* (UCR) or reflex. The tone, a previously neutral stimulus which comes to elicit salivation through conditioning or pairing with the UCS, is called a *conditioned stimulus* (CS). The response it elicits is a *conditioned response* (CR).

Pavlov determined that the CS loses its power to elicit a CR if it is no longer paired with the UCS, a process called *extinction*. After some period of time has elapsed following extinction, the presentation of the CS may again temporarily elicit the CR. This phenomenon is called *spontaneous recovery*.

Pavlov demonstrated that, once a CS had been established, similar stimuli also elicited the CR, a phenomenon called *generalization*. Tones of similar though different frequencies, for example, elicited a salivation response. However, if *different* tones were presented *without* being followed by the food and only *one* tone was paired with the UCS, then only *one stimulus* elicited the *CR*. This is the process of *discrimination*.

From a behavioral viewpoint, classical conditioning is the basis for the emotional responses we have to events, objects, situations, or people. John B. Watson (1878–1958) extended application of the model to study and to demonstrate the development of emotions in humans.

Watson believed that all learning occurred according to the principles of classical conditioning, including emotions, which he saw as physiological responses to observable stimuli. He and his assistant experimentally demonstrated that a phobia could be developed by means of classical conditioning (Watson and Rayner, 1920). In a classic experiment, 9-month-old Albert was presented with a white rat and initially showed no indications of fear but rather approached and touched the animal. The child was then presented the rat as a metal bar was banged loudly, resulting in a startle response. After several conditioning trials, Albert cried at the sight of the rat and would not approach or touch the rat. Additionally, the fear generalized to other similar, white furry objects, such as a rabbit, dog, fur coat, and a ball of white wool. Unfortunately, Albert's mother left the hospital before Watson could decondition Albert's fear.

Although such an experiment would not be conducted today because of obvious ethical problems, it remains a classic study. It demonstrated that an emotional response and related maladaptive behavior, in this case a phobia, could be acquired through a relatively simple learning process rather than being the result of underlying processes and conflicts that can be neither observed nor studied experimentally.

Watson published a paper called "Psychology as the Behaviorist Views It" in 1913 and promulgated the behavioral position (Watson, 1913). He proclaimed that the methodology of psychology should be objective and experimental like the natural sciences and that the subject matter should be observable behavior and environmental stimuli. The goal of psychology, he advocated, should be the prediction and control of behavior.

Edward L. Thorndike (1874–1949) investigated trial-and-error learning with cats in puzzle boxes. Thorndike's focus was different from other investigators in two major ways. First, he studied a sequence or pattern of behavior over trials rather than very specific responses such as Pavlov. Second, he emphasized the importance of the *consequences* of behavior and formulated the *Law of Effect:* A behavior that is followed by a satisfying state of affairs will be strengthened, while one that is followed by an annoying state of affairs will be weakened.

Edward C. Tolman (1896–1961) also employed the experimental method for study of animal behavior. In contrast to others discussed so far, Tolman referred to subjective states and intervening variables in his interpretation of behavior. He maintained that behavior is purposive or goal-directed and that consequences serve only an informational function.

B. F. Skinner's (1904–) approach was to study discrete and easily measured behavior of the individual subject intensively over time. He designed his own apparatus and recording devices. The "Skinner box" consists of a soundproofed box with a lever and food magazine. Depressions of the lever close a circuit, which automatically records lever pressing over time and which also results in the delivery of food according to a preprogrammed schedule. A discrete, easily measured and recorded response, such as the lever press, facilitates investigation of variables and their relationships to behavior. For example, by manipulating the *contingencies* for delivery of food, Skinner observed reliable, distinctive patterns of behavior specific to the particular contingencies implemented. The methodology he developed for studying behavior is called the *experimental analysis of behavior.*

Skinner's contributions to the field are impressive. He formulated through his writings the philosophy of science called radical behaviorism. This philosophy recognizes private events such as cognitions and emotions as important but also defines these experiences as behaviors that are affected, as are observable behaviors, by environmental events. Private events *do not cause* other behaviors, according to Skinner.

Skinner also shifted the focus of explanations for behavior from stimuli and classical or respondent conditioning to consequences and a type conditioning he named *"operant."* He did a great deal to clarify the distinction between the two types of learning. Skinner developed a program of research in *operant conditioning* that resulted in the formulation and elucidation of basic principles that govern behavior and the extension of these principles, discovered in the animal laboratory, to applications to human behavior. Of all learning theorists, Skinner has had the most significant impact on the development of behavior modification, the application of the principles of behavior to address human problems (cf Kazdin, 1978).

OPERANT CONDITIONING

In *operant conditioning,* an animal or person "operates" on the environment and produces a change, a consequence for the behavior. As such, the organism is viewed as *active* rather than passive, as is the case with respondent conditioning in which responses are *elicited* by stimuli. An operant is *emitted* in the presence of certain stimuli and produces consequences that affect the future probability of the behavior. For example, a food-deprived rat in an operant chamber ("Skinner box") depresses a lever, which results in delivery of a food pellet. The animal's response (the lever press) produces a change in its environment—the response closes the circuit and food is delivered. The delivery of food contingent on occurrence of the lever press affects the likelihood of the response occurring again. In the case of respondent conditioning, presentation of the CS produces a CR. However, occurrence of this response does not produce a consequence or change in the situation. It is the stimulus that controls the behavior.

Consequences are defined in terms of their effect on behavior. If the effect is to *strengthen* or *increase* behavior, the event is *reinforcing.* When the behavior is *decreased* or *weakened* by the event, it is *punishing.* (Table 4-3).

The critical feature of the consequence is not whether it is judged to be "pleasant" or "unpleasant." It is the *effect* of the consequences on behavior that is important. Similar consequences may, therefore, have very different effects on the behavior of various individuals. Two children, for example, may each be scolded contingent on their teasing the family pet. One child may engage in the behavior less frequently as a result of the scolding while a second child may tease the animal more often. In the former case, the scolding has the function of punishing or weakening the behavior, but, in the latter situation, scolding is, in fact, a reinforcer for the child's

Table 4–3 **Operant Conditioning—Consequences**

TERM	DEFINITION	EXAMPLE
Positive reinforcement	Increasing the probability of a behavior by presenting a positive reinforcer following occurrence of the behavior.	Patient is praised for adhering to diet restriction 1 week and continues to do so for a second week.
Negative reinforcement	Increasing the probability of a behavior by terminating or avoiding an aversive event or the loss of a positive reinforcer following the occurrence of the behavior.	Patient adheres to diet and exercise regimen in order to discontinue daily insulin.
Contigent presentation	Decreasing the probability of a behavior by presenting a punisher following occurrence of the behavior.	Patient is reprimanded for smoking and stops for several days.
Contingent withdrawal	Decreasing the probability of a behavior by removing a positive reinforcer or the opportunity for positive reinforcement following occurrence of the behavior.	Patient is not seen for an appointment when he/she arrives more than 15 minutes late, and frequency of tardiness decreases.
Extinction	Decreasing/eliminating a behavior by withholding reinforcement for the behavior.	Excessive patient requests for mood-altering medications are decreased by refusing to comply with such requests.

behavior. The child may receive little parental attention, and negative attention to the child may be better than no attention at all.

Reinforcement

Reinforcement refers to the procedure of increasing the probability of a behavior by the contingent delivery of a reinforcing event that follows the behavior. The event that strengthens the behavior is called a *reinforcer.* Reinforcers may be *positive* or *negative* depending on whether the consequence entails the presentation or removal of some event. Take, for example, the behavior of compliance with requests. One child may be praised by a parent or teacher for complying with a request to put his or her toys away after playing. Subsequent to the praise, the child puts the toys away more frequently. Praise is being "added" or presented in this case and is a *positive reinforcer.*

A second child may comply more frequently with parental requests to put toys away in order to *terminate* or *avoid a scolding,* an *aversive* event. In these situations, compliant behavior is *negatively reinforced.* Behavior that is strengthened because it avoids contact with an aversive event is called *avoidance behavior.* When the behavior results in termination or removal of the aversive event, it is referred to as *escape behavior.*

Consider a second example involving compliance with a medication regimen.

One patient may take medication as ordered because doing so is associated with improved physical condition, attention and praise from the physician, or other events that occur after the medication is taken. The behavior is positively reinforced. Another patient may comply with the physician's order because taking the medication results in the termination or avoidance of aversive physical symptoms. This is an example of behavior maintained by *negative reinforcement*. Patients may stop taking the medication once their symptoms have ceased and only resume the regimen when unpleasant effects reoccur, an example of *escape behavior.*

There are several different types of reinforcers. The reinforcing properties of *primary reinforcers* seem to be more biologically based rather than being dependent on learning. Examples include *food, sex,* and *water.* Other types of reinforcers acquire their reinforcing properties through pairing with other established reinforcers. These are called *conditioned reinforcers.* An example of a *conditioned reinforcer* is praise, which is frequently paired with other reinforcers. *Generalized reinforcers* are events that acquire and maintain their reinforcer effectiveness through pairing with many other reinforcers. Money, for example, can be exchanged for numerous and diverse objects, events, and so on, which are reinforcing for the person. Money would cease to be reinforcing if it were no longer paired with other reinforcers. *Conditioned* and *generalized* reinforcers can be particularly useful in bridging the delay between occurrence of a behavior and delivery of more powerful, but delayed, reinforcers. For example, receiving a letter of acceptance for a manuscript with positive feedback may function to strengthen writing behavior pending publication.

Tokens are a special type of generalized reinforcer that can be exchanged for various objects, events, and so forth, called *backup reinforcers.* They allow for behavior to be reinforced immediately and for a variety of reinforcers to be exchanged so as to decrease the probability of satiation and to increase the possibilities for identifying multiple reinforcers.

Token systems have been effectively implemented and used in schools, prisons, and institutions for the mentally retarded (Kazdin, 1977). Economic principles are employed in setting up these systems. The tokens have a particular exchange value, the backup reinforcers vary in cost, and it is essential that there be opportunities to earn adequate numbers of tokens so backup reinforcers are attainable.

Several factors influence reinforcer effectiveness. First, the reinforcer must be presented *contingently.* That is, it should be delivered contingent on the occurrence of desirable behavior. Second, the most effective procedure is *immediate presentation* of the reinforcer after the behavior has occurred. Third, it is also important to consider the difficulty of performing the behavior, how much behavior is required, and the amount of the reinforcer. Although the general rule is "more reinforcer means greater effectiveness," too much reinforcer can result in *satiation* or a decrease in reinforcer effectiveness associated with recent consumption or exposure to the reinforcer. Generally, the greater the deprivation or limits on contact with the reinforcer, the more effective the reinforcer will be for altering behavior.

Developing New Behavior

Contingencies can strengthen behaviors once they occur. However, particular behaviors may not be in the person's repertoire. In such cases there are no opportunities to reinforce the response because it is not likely to occur. For example, if the goal is to teach language to a nonverbal child, one would not be successful in helping the child to speak if reinforcers were contingent only on emission of words. In these cases, it is necessary to *shape* the behavior. The starting point is to identify behavior that is already occurring that resembles the desired behavior. For example, assume one is interested in teaching a child to say "eat." A reinforcer might initially be given immediately after the occurrence of *any* vocalization sounds *approximating* the sounds of the word "eat" while *other dissimilar sounds* are *not* reinforced. Once the child imitates the sound "ee," then other vowel sounds would subsequently not be reinforced. Only "ee" would be reinforced, and, hence, "ee" would occur more frequently. This is *differential reinforcement,* and the result is *response differentiation.* The requirement for reinforcement would then also include the consonant sound as well. The procedure of *differentially reinforcing* closer and closer approximations to the final target behavior is called the *method of successive approximations.* Completely new behavior is produced through *shaping.*

Complex behaviors or skills, whether desirable or undesirable, are often developed originally from simple behaviors through the process of shaping. Skills such as playing an instrument or carrying on a conversation are examples of complex behaviors that are shaped. Loud and persistent demands of children (or adults) are also behaviors that can be developed by means of shaping albeit adventitiously.

Imitation

Obviously all new skills do not require shaping. We acquire a great deal of complex behavior by observing others and imitating their behaviors. *Modeling* is a very powerful means of learning new behavior.

Albert Bandura's classic studies demonstrated very clearly that children can learn behaviors by observing others (Bandura et al, 1963). Modeling has been successfully employed to reduce fear and anxiety in adults and children. For example, Melamed and Siegel (1975) had children about to be hospitalized for surgery observe a film of a child coping with hospitalization, with a resultant decrease in anxiety.

Characteristics of the model as well as the consequences of the behavior for the model affect the likelihood of imitation by an observer. Imitative behaviors can become intrinsically reinforcing. The young ballet dancer diligently practices barre exercises such as the grand battement en vant so as to "match" the method of the teacher. Performance of the behavior itself is reinforcing. Further discussion of observational learning is presented within the context of social learning theory.

Extinction

In *extinction,* the reinforcer that has maintained a response no longer follows the behavior and the behavior decreases and is eliminated. Once the response no longer occurs, we say that it has been extinguished.

Wolf and associates (1970) eliminated vomiting in a 9-year-old mentally retarded girl in a residential setting. The child's vomiting resulted in the teacher returning her to the dormitory. The extinction procedure entailed keeping the child in class. In addition, social reinforcement for behaviors other than vomiting was applied. Vomiting, an escape behavior, was extinguished.

Chronic pain patients, for example, may complain excessively about physical discomfort for which there is no medical cure. Such complaints are frequently maintained, at least in part, by the attention and sympathy they evoke from others. The behavior may be decreased by withholding attention and sympathy when complaining occurs (an extinction procedure) and also socially reinforcing the patient's talk about any subject other than pain (e.g., the weather, how well he or she feels, recent activities, and so forth) with attention and praise.

It is typical to see a temporary increase in the intensity, rate, or duration of a behavior when an extinction procedure has been implemented. In the case described above, for example, patient complaints would, in all likelihood, increase initially in frequency and intensity. The time it takes for the behavior to be eliminated depends on the schedule of reinforcement that has maintained the behavior.

Schedules of Reinforcement

The *schedule of reinforcement* is the rule that specifies the time and response requirements for a reinforcer to be delivered. The rate and pattern of the behavior as it is maintained and/or extinguished are determined by the schedule. When there is only one schedule operating in a situation, it is called a *simple schedule.* Such schedules can be *continuous* or *intermittent.*

Continuous reinforcement (CRF) means that every occurrence of the behavior is immediately reinforced. If a response has been reinforced continuously, then it will extinguish more rapidly than if it has been reinforced on an intermittent basis. We say that behaviors maintained by intermittent schedules are more *resistant to extinction.*

Some intermittent schedules are *response-dependent* only. That is, the reinforcer is delivered contingent on the number of times the behavior has occurred. *Fixed-ratio* (FR) and *variable-ratio* (VR) are two such schedules.

A second type of schedule is both *response-dependent* and *time-dependent.* Interval schedules can be *fixed* (FI) or *variable* (VI). Table 4-4 further clarifies the simple schedules.

Punishment

We have already discussed the extinction procedure as one way to eliminate behavior. However, it is not always possible to identify the reinforcer(s) maintaining a behavior nor is it always feasible to control reinforcement for some behaviors. For example, a teacher is more likely to ignore misbehavior of a school-age child than are his or her peers. *In order to extinguish a response, any reinforcer maintaining the behavior must be consistently withheld.* There are also situations in which extinction of a particular behavior would be dangerous or unethical. For example, attention may well be the reinforcer maintaining self-injurious behavior in a mentally retarded child. However, the child could seriously injure himself or herself if allowed to self-abuse while attention was withheld. Extinction can also be fairly lengthy at times, particularly if the behavior has been maintained on a lean intermittent schedule of reinforcement. In such cases, it may be more appropriate to use procedures that rapidly suppress behavior.

Table 4–4 **Definitions of Four Simple Schedules of Reinforcement and Descriptions of the Patterns of Behavior Generated by Each**

REINFORCEMENT	RULE	PATTERN OF BEHAVIOR
Response-Dependent		
Fixed ratio (FR)	Reinforcer is delivered after a specified number of responses (e.g., FR5 means after each fifth response the reinforcer is delivered).	Rapid emission with minimal hesitation between responses. Occurrence of postreinforcement pause once the ratio is completed but before another is begun. The larger the ratio, the longer the pause.
Variable ratio (VR)	Reinforcer is delivered after a variable number of responses which equal some average (e.g., VR5 means an average of five responses must occur before delivery of the reinforcer).	High rates of behavior with minimal hesitation between responses. No postreinforcement pause occurs. Produces greatest resistance to extinction.
Response- and Time-Dependent		
Fixed interval (FI)	Reinforcer becomes available after a fixed interval of time has elapsed. A response must then occur in order for the reinforcer to be delivered (e.g., FI5 means that the reinforcer becomes available after 5 minutes but a response must then occur to produce the reinforcer).	Period of time in the beginning of the interval with no responding. Responses gradually increase in rate until a very high, fast rate is observed at the end of the interval.
Variable interval (VI)	Reinforcer becomes available after variable intervals of time have elapsed, which equal some average. A response must then occur in order for the reinforcer to be delivered (e.g., VI5 means that the reinforcer becomes available after an average of 5 minutes has elapsed, but a response must then occur to produce the reinforcer).	Rate is not particularly high or fast, but it is consistent.

A *punisher* is an event that decreases the behavior it follows. Punishment may entail the *contingent presentation* of some event or the *contingent withdrawal of a positive reinforcer* for weakening behavior. Suppose 7-year-old Tom frequently hits his 4-year-old brother Bill. Tom's parents decide that only explaining the consequences of his behavior is not effective in decreasing the hitting so they search for more efficacious consequences.

In such a situation, it is important to remember that punishment produced by contingent presentation or stimulation entails decreasing a behavior by "adding" or presenting some event, such as scolding or spanking. Tom's parents appropriately and wisely reject physical punishment as an alternative for several reasons. An obvious, serious difficulty is that physical punishment involves modeling aggressive behavior. Second, behavior may be suppressed by physical punishment, at least partly, because emotional responses are elicited by the aversive stimulation, which are incompatible with other behaviors. For example, a child who is very hurt and frightened by physical punishment may be temporarily "immobilized" by these emotional responses, which compete with performance of other behaviors—both undesirable and desirable ones. Third, because aversive stimulation does elicit physiological (emotional) responses and activity of the sympathetic division of the autonomic nervous system, these responses can become conditioned to previously neutral and/or positive stimuli in the punishing situation. A child who is beaten with a belt, for example, may develop emotional reactions, such as fear of belts, or the child who is physically punished in a particular room may become fearful of the room and avoid it. The emotional reactions can also become conditioned to the punishing agent as well, such that he or she is feared and avoided. Physical punishment should not be used with children—*period.*

Most of these problems can be avoided by decreasing the frequency of the behavior by withdrawing a freely available reinforcer contingent on occurrence of the behavior. This is not the same thing as withholding the reinforcer for a behavior in an extinction procedure. In extinction, the response no longer produces the reinforcer. Punishment by contingent withdrawal entails removing a reinforcer that is already available contingent on occurrence of the behavior.

Look at how extinction and punishment by contingent withdrawal might work to reduce Tom's hitting behavior. Assume that the reinforcer maintaining the hitting is the attention Tom receives from his parents when he strikes Bill. Extinction would entail ignoring the hitting, with a resultant reduction and elimination of the behavior. For the reasons outlined earlier, however, this may not be the best strategy. Tom's hitting behavior may be dangerous to Bill. One would also be concerned about the temporary increase in the frequency and/or intensity of the hitting during extinction. The alternative would involve decreasing hitting by removing Tom to an area where there were no reinforcers for some brief period of time (*timeout from reinforcement*) or removing a freely available reinforcer when hitting occurred. For each instance of hitting, Tom might have to sit by himself for 7 minutes (1 minute per year of age), or he might lose the opportunity to play with a preferred toy for a few minutes.

A major factor to be considered when employing punishment is that such a procedure suppresses behavior, often rapidly but also temporarily. *It does not teach appropriate behavior.* In order for punishment to be maximally effective, it is essential that appropriate behavior, incompatible with the undesired response, be reinforced. In Tom's case, for example, the desired alternative to hitting Bill might be playing with him, sharing toys, helping his younger brother, and so forth, with no occurrences of hitting. The children's parents could praise Tom and show him affection for these behaviors, first on a continuous schedule of reinforcement and then gradually requiring more and more behavior for reinforcement.

There are additional factors that influence the effectiveness of *punishers*. The punisher should be *contingent* on occurrence of the behavior and should be *delivered immediately*. The person should be *deprived* with respect to the punisher. Noncontingent aversive stimulation and/or withdrawal of positive reinforcers, as well as frequent use of punishers, will decrease their effectiveness and possibly result in increased emotional behavior, which can compete with performance of appropriate, alternative behaviors. There are data indicating, for example, that excessive aversive consequences and noncontingent reinforcement are employed by parents of children with conduct disorders (Snyder, 1977). The children learn aggressive behavior through modeling and are also taught that there is no relationship between their behavior and consequences.

As is the case for reinforcers, there are also different types of punishers. *Primary punishers* do not require association with other punishers to be effective, although effectiveness is diminished through adaptation. *Conditioned punishers* must be paired with other punishers to be effective. Threats of punishment, for example, may deter behavior but only if followed by punishment if the behavior is performed. *Generalized punishers*, such as social disapproval, are associated with many other punishers.

Antecedents

So far we have discussed the importance of consequences for operant behavior. The antecedents of behavior are also significant variables in explaining behavior (Table 4-5). People behave in the presence of certain stimuli or stimulus situations.

We learn to engage in different behaviors depending on the situation. This is accomplished by means of *discrimination training:* in the presence of some stimuli a particular behavior is reinforced and in the presence of different stimuli the behavior is extinguished. A small child may learn, for example, that one parent ignores tantrums while the other gives the child what he or she wants and, therefore, reinforces the tantrum. The parent who reinforces the tantrums becomes a *discriminative stimulus* (S^D) for tantrums (i.e., the presence of this parent signals that reinforcement is forthcoming if the behavior does occur). The other parent is associated with nonreinforcement of tantrums and is called an S^Δ (ess-delta) if the behavior occurs less frequently in his or her presence than in the presence of the S^D. When the tantrum behavior is more likely to occur in the presence of the S^D than its absence, we say that *stimulus control* over the tantrum behavior has been established. The behavior is called *discriminated behavior.*

In clinical medicine, a person with a chronic pain problem may be observed to emit more pain behaviors when another person is present to observe and respond to the behaviors than when no one is near or when someone who does not attend to the pain behavior is present. In this situation, there is stimulus control over the pain behavior. (However, this does not mean that the patient is "intentionally" or consciously behaving in such a way. One need not be aware of the contingencies in order for one's behavior to be affected by them.)

Table 4–5 **Operant Conditioning—Antecedents**

TERM	DEFINITION	EXAMPLE
Discrimination training	In the presence of certain stimuli or stimulus situations, a behavior is reinforced, and, in the presence of others, the behavior is extinguished.	A medical student gets credit for labeling an event that increases the behavior it follows a "reinforcer" but not for labeling it anything else.
Discriminative stimulus (S^D)	Signals that reinforcement is forthcoming if the behavior occurs in its presence.	Giving a correct definition in response to the question "What is a positive reinforcer?" results in credit for a correct answer.
S^Δ	Signals that reinforcement is not forthcoming if the behavior occurs in its presence.	Giving the definition for a punisher in response to the question "What is a positive reinforcer?" results in no credit for the answer.
Discriminated behavior	Behavior that is more likely to occur in the presence of the S^D than in its absence.	Giving the definition for positive reinforcer is more likely to occur when asked "What is a positive reinforcer?" than when some other question is asked.
Stimulus control	Achieved for a behavior when it is more likely to occur in the presence of the S^D than in its absence.	The question comes to control the response of the definition.
Fading	Stimulus is gradually removed or faded so that another stimulus presented with it will control the response.	Initially a verbal prompt may be required to facilitate the response of giving the definition but is gradually removed so that the question only controls the response.
Generalization	Behavior occurs in the presence of different and/or novel stimuli or stimulus situations.	Given one example of a positive reinforcer, the student is able to identify others.

In order to facilitate the development of discriminated behavior, two stimuli are sometimes presented together. One stimulus is then gradually removed or *faded* so the other controls the response. For example, modeling may be initially paired with verbal instructions but faded over time.

It is frequently desirable for a behavior to occur in the presence of different and/ or novel stimuli or situations. Such an occurrence is called *generalization.* This is accomplished by *generalization training,* which entails reinforcement of the behavior in the presence of other stimuli until all members of a stimulus class are associated with occurrence of the behavior. For example, a person may be working to improve his or her assertiveness skills and begins practicing with one family member. The person practices with more and more family members until eventually he or she is responding assertively with the group (or stimulus class) of family members.

Applied Behavior Analysis

Applied behavior analysis is a branch of science that uses the methodology of the experimental analysis of behavior to address human problems. In the first issue of *Journal of Applied Behavior Analysis* published in 1968, Baer and associates defined applied behavior analysis (Baer et al, 1968). The science entails the systematic application of techniques derived from behavioral principles to change socially important behaviors. Experimental designs in which the person serves as his or her own control are employed to demonstrate that the intervention was responsible for the behavioral changes observed and measured. These changes should be clinically (and not merely statistically) significant and generalize to other behaviors and situations and also be maintained over time.

WOLPE AND THE PRINCIPLE OF RECIPROCAL INHIBITION

Joseph Wolpe (1925–) employed an animal model to study the development of emotional reactions or "experimental neuroses" and ways of treating such problems once acquired. Cats were shocked while in cages and sometimes as they approached food. The "experimental neuroses" consisted of behaviors indicative of anxiety associated with the cage where shocked and lack of feeding behavior despite severe food deprivation. The behaviors generalized to similar situations and were more intense in situations that more closely resembled the experimental cage, room, and so forth. Wolpe reasoned that given the inhibition of feeding by anxiety, then anxiety might also be inhibited by eating. Wolpe reduced the "neurotic symptoms" in the cats by inducing feeding in the original room or in rooms that resembled the original room. Once the cat fed in the original room without signs of anxiety, it was placed in the cage as well. Wolpe considered the "neurosis" eliminated once the cat ate in the experimental cage without indications of anxiety. He maintained that the animal could not be fearful or anxious and feed simultaneously. That is, anxiety and feeding are *reciprocally inhibiting,* the occurrence of one inhibits the other.

Wolpe extended the treatment procedures based on laboratory work with animals to applications with humans. He developed an abbreviated version of Jacobson's (1938) progressive muscle relaxation procedure and initially employed relaxation to inhibit anxiety and fear in the presence of actual anxiety-provoking stimuli. Basically, he sought a method more convenient than gradual *in vivo* (real life) exposure and decided to try imagined scenes. *Systematic desensitization,* as he called it, entails pairing deep muscle relaxation with imaginal scenes in a graded fashion from the least to most anxiety-provoking. The responses to anxiety-provoking stimuli are "reconditioned" with relaxation replacing or "inhibiting" the anxiety. Wolpe also used assertive responses and sexual arousal to inhibit anxiety.

Wolpe's work constituted a bridge between animal experimentation in the laboratory and the development of treatment procedures for human problems. Behavioral techniques developed by Wolpe, such as systematic desensitization, were based on the principle of reciprocal inhibition formulated from experiments. Much research was generated by his work, particularly related to systematic desensitization, and this contributed significantly to the development of behavior therapy.

COGNITIVISTS

The methodological behaviorism of Watson ignores private events in explaining or studying behavior. Radical behaviorists, such as Skinner and applied behavior analysts, recognize cognitions as important but do not ascribe causal properties to such events in explaining behavior; cognitive events are other behaviors to be explained by environmental events. Wolpe proposes unobservable mechanisms in his accounts for behavior but rejects the proposition by some that all fears are mediated by faulty cognitions.

Cognitivists, however, relegate private events, particularly cognitions, to causal status. Some purport that cognitions mediate between environmental events and behavior. Social learning theory and the *cognitive* and *cognitive–behavioral* therapies focus on such mediators in accounting for behavior and behavior change.

Social Learning Theory

The foremost theorist and researcher in the area of social learning is Albert Bandura (1925–). It is Bandura's contention that not only is the behavior of the person affected by the environment, but that the person's behavior affects future consequences. Cognitive processes of the person also mediate behavior and the effects of the environment on behavior. The term *reciprocal determinism* refers to the interaction of behavior, cognitive variables such as expectancies, and the environment. Individuals can also influence their own behaviors and are capable of self-direction.

A great deal of learning occurs as a result of observing others. According to Bandura (1977), *modeling* is mediated by a number of component processes.

First, one must attend to the model or modeling stimulus in order for observational learning to occur. There are several aspects of the *attentional processes.* Both characteristics of the observer and the model affect what will actually be observed. For example, models who are more attractive or pleasing to the observer are more likely to be observed than those without these characteristics. With respect to observer characteristics, the person must have, for example, adequate sensory capacities for attending.

Second, the person must remember the observed behavior by means of *retention processes.* These include, for example, symbolic coding or having verbal labels or descriptions for the behavior. Symbolic (mental) or motor rehearsal are additional processes that may be employed to retain what was observed.

Motor reproduction processes have to do with reproducing the information retained into specific behavior. The physical capabilities of the observer, for example, determine whether the observed behavior can be performed.

Finally, *motivational processes* determine *if* the observed behavior will be performed. The processes include, for example, vicarious reinforcement, or reinforcement observed for the model's behavior. Bandura posits that the person who sees the model's behavior reinforced will likely expect that his or her own matching or imitative behavior will also be followed by such consequences. Other motivational processes include the nature of self-evaluation and feedback and self-reinforcement.

Bandura's contributions in the area of observational learning are highly significant. As indicated earlier, his classic studies demonstrated very clearly that children learn aggressive behavior from observing aggressive models (Bandura et al, 1963). *Subsequent research has shown that one of the best predictors of aggressive behavior in children is aggressive behavior by the parents* (Pfeffer et al, 1983). As discussed earlier, empirical demonstrations of such modeling effects lend further support to arguments against the use of corporal punishment.

Cognitive and Cognitive–Behavioral Therapies

Meichenbaum (1977) maintains that the same principles that govern observable behavior can also be applied to modify private events, such as cognitions. By altering cognitions, such as self-talk, behavior and emotions can also be changed. Other cognitivists such as Beck (1976) and Ellis (1962) identify faulty cognitions as the primary problem and focus their efforts on directly altering irrational thoughts.

Meichenbaum and other researchers have sought to evaluate empirically the effectiveness of "cognitive–behavior modification techniques" such as self-instructional training. Fewer controlled studies have investigated Beck's "cognitive therapy" or the "rational–emotive therapy" developed by Ellis. Hollon and Beck (1986) have recently reviewed experimental evaluations of the efficacy of cognitive and cognitive–behavioral therapies. They concluded that the data do not indicate that these interventions are any more effective than strictly behavioral interventions. Additionally, the studies have not shown conclusively that cognitive changes that occur are associated with these techniques alone.

APPLICATIONS OF PRINCIPLES TO HUMAN PROBLEMS

Behavior therapy or modification entails the application of laboratory-based psychological principles for changing behavior. A great deal of research has been and continues to be generated in evaluation of treatment techniques derived from principles of operant and respondent conditioning.

It is important to note that procedures are not applied like a "behavioral bag of tricks" or in a "cookbook" fashion. The approach entails individualized treatment that can consist of multiple interventions. The person's problems need not be narrowly circumscribed, such as a simple phobia, in order for behavioral interventions to be appropriate and effective. With these points in mind, a brief presentation of a few behavioral techniques follows. (See, for example, Garfield and Bergin, 1986, and Gentry, 1984 for more complete descriptions of behavioral interventions and research regarding effectiveness.)

Contingency management entails the manipulation of consequences to affect changes in behavior. For example, token systems have been implemented to increase treatment compliance in an elderly cardiac patient (Dapcich-Miura and Hovell, 1979) and in pediatric hemodialysis patients (Magrab and Papadopoulou, 1977). Parent training programs entail instruction in the use of contingency management techniques for dealing with children's behaviors (Forehand and McMahon, 1982; Patterson and Guillion, 1976). These programs focus on teaching parents a number of behavior management skills including how to (1) identify specific behaviors to change; (2) increase positive interactions with the child and decrease commands and criticisms; (3) provide positive reinforcers such as praise, affection, points, and so forth for desirable behavior; (4) use timeout and loss of points for negative behaviors. The same principles of behavior apply to younger and older children (and adults), but the ways in which they are implemented may vary.

Contingency contracting is a strategy that can also be employed for children, adolescents, or adults to address diverse problem behaviors. The contingency contract specifies behaviors and their consequences in explicit detail and is most effective when negotiated with all parties having input and agreeing on the contingencies. For example, Taylor and associates (1980) decreased a patient's unnecessary overuse of medical services by making visits to two health professionals contingent on not seeing others without permission. Contingency contracting has also been successfully used for treating marital problems. Boelens and associates (1980) found that comparable levels of marital satisfaction were reported by couples receiving either system-theoretic counseling or "reciprocity counseling" (contingency contracting) but that the latter intervention was associated with greater maintenance of improvements at 6-month follow-up.

Establishing *appropriate stimulus control* over behavior is frequently indicated. Sometimes there are too many S^D's for a behavior, as is the case for overeating. For an obese person, numerous environmental cues may control eating behavior. One goal is to reduce the number of stimuli associated with eating by restricting activities that occur concurrently with eating. Behavioral treatment programs for obesity address this problem and include interventions to help alter stimulus control for eating behavior, among other interventions such as contingency contracting.

Social skills training entails systematic instruction and training in an area of communication using behavioral principles. Global skill areas such as assertiveness or conversational skills are broken down into specific, teachable units of behavior. The social skills training model consists of (1) describing the specific behavior to be learned along with a rationale for its acquisition; (2) modeling the behavior; (3) having the person practice the skill in role-plays; and (4) giving feedback for the performance. The steps are repeated until each skill is mastered. The social skills training model has been employed to teach many different skills to diverse populations, such as friendship-making skills with children (Oden and Asher, 1977), conversational skills with adolescents (Minkin et al, 1976), and social inadequacy in adults (Trower et al, 1978), to name only a few.

Although there is debate regarding *how* it works, *in vivo exposure* to fear-provoking stimuli is the current treatment of choice for most phobic disorders (Emmelkamp, 1986). *Gradual in vivo exposure* to fear-provoking stimuli may be self-paced or arranged by a therapist. The patient works through an anxiety hierarchy by working with a therapist and exposing himself or herself to real life stimuli. More severely impaired persons likely require more therapist involvement (Barlow, 1988).

Flooding in vivo entails abrupt, prolonged exposure to the fear-producing stimuli. The patient is accompanied to the situation, as in the case of agoraphobia, or may be presented the stimuli in the office by a therapist. The person stays in the situation until there is a significant reduction in anxiety. The procedure is repeated until the anxiety is eliminated. A treatment package consisting of *in vivo exposure* with *response prevention* of rituals has been shown to be more effective for decreasing anxiety and ritualistic behavior associated with obsessive–compulsive disorder than either component alone (Foa et al, 1980).

Imaginal flooding entails indirect exposure in an abrupt and prolonged fashion. The patient is instructed to imagine the anxiety-provoking scenario by the therapist and continues to do so until there is significant reduction in anxiety. Self-report, overt behavior, and physiological responses (e.g., pulse rate and blood pressure) are assessed to evaluate level of anxiety. Imaginal flooding has been employed for treatment of posttraumatic stress disorder associated, for example, with combat experiences (Fairbank et al, 1983).

Relaxation techniques can be employed as a primary treatment component for patients with diverse problems ranging from essential hypertension and Raynaud's disease to chronic pain and insomnia. Progressive muscle relaxation (PMR; Jacobson, 1938) entails learning to relax deeply the muscles of the body by systematically tensing each of several muscle groups and abruptly releasing the tension. This helps increase awareness of the differences in the sensations of tension and relaxation and also how to produce relaxation. Eventually, patients are able to induce a state of deep relaxation without the tension–release cycles.

Heart rate, blood pressure, brain waves, penile erections, body temperature, and muscle activity are all responses that have been employed in *biofeedback*. Electrical signals from the particular response are measured, amplified, and then converted to visual or auditory information for the patient. This objective, observable feedback about a particular system or function of the body helps the patient to learn how to exert control over the response. Some examples of clinical applications include electromyographic (EMG) biofeedback for neuromuscular recovery in cardiovascular accident patients, for fecal incontinence caused by sphincter weakness, and for chronic pain problems. Biofeedback is most often used in conjunction with relaxation training.

Most of the techniques described above can be employed to address numerous and diverse problem areas in medicine including, to name only a few, pain management, treatment compliance, anorexia, asthma, anxiety, hypertension, patient management, obesity, sexual dysfunction, and cardiovascular disease. *Behavioral medicine* involves the application of behavior principles and technology to medical or health-related problems. Table 4-6 lists a few practical clinical applications of behavior therapy to the problems of medical patients as summarized by Abel and Associates (Abel et al, 1987).

Table 4–6 **Objective Behavioral Approaches to Diagnosis, Treatment, and Patient Compliance**

	OBJECTIVE CRITERIA FOR DIAGNOSIS	TREATMENT APPROACH	OBJECTIVE CRITERIA FOR COMPLIANCE WITH TREATMENT APPROACH
Anorexia nervosa	Weight lost, observation of eating behavior	Contingency management	Weight recording by therapist
Bulimia nervosa	Patient's tape recording of bulimic episode	Covert sensitization	Listening to audiotaped treatment sessions
Type A behavior	Psychophysiologic assessment of electromyography	Progressive muscle relaxation, EMG biofeedback	Psychophysiologic assessment of electromyography
Hyperventilation	Hyperventilation provocative test	Controlled breathing	Direct observation of patient's breathing by therapist
Shy bladder	Inability to void in public rest rooms	Extinction of avoidance behavior and exposure	Direct observation of voiding training
Drop attacks	Direct observation of motor skills performance	Muscle relaxation and ambulation skills training	Observation of ability to ambulate, use of pedometer

(Abel GG, Rouleau J-L, Coyne BJ: Behavioral medicine strategies in medical patients. In Stoudemire A, Fogel BS (eds): Principles of Medical Psychiatry, pp 329–345. Orlando FL, Grune & Stratton, 1987)

COMPARISONS OF THE BEHAVIORAL AND PSYCHOANALYTIC MODELS

A comparison of behavioral and psychoanalytic models for explaining and changing human behavior yields multiple differences (Table 4-7). There is, however, at least one similarity of these two diverse schools of thought, namely *determinism.* Psychoanalysts and behaviorists both posit *causes* for behavior that do not include the notion of free will.

At this point, the two approaches diverge. Major differences have to do with the nature of the causes, the significance of behavior itself, and the focus of interventions to produce change. Psychoanalytic theory proposes the behavior is symbolic of underlying, intrapsychic processes and is a symptom of unconscious conflict. The focus of treatment is, therefore, on the underlying processes rather than on the behavior or symptoms. Early experiences are highly significant from a psychoanalytic perspective in which treatment entails bringing unconscious material and conflicts into consciousness.

The behavioral position is that the behavior of the individual is the focus of treatment. Behavior is seen as being determined, not by intrapsychic processes, but by reinforcement history, current contingencies, and genetic endowment. Observable environmental events such as antecedents and consequences, the current contingencies, are analyzed. As such, the behavioral approach emphasizes contemporary rather than historical factors in explaining and changing behavior. Behavioral interventions consist of applying principles of operant and/or classical conditioning to change the behavior itself.

Table 4–7 **The Behavioral and Psychoanalytic Models**

BEHAVIORAL MODEL	PSYCHOANALYTIC MODEL
1. Behavior is determined by current contingencies, reinforcement history, and genetic endowment.	Behavior is determined by intrapsychic processes.
2. Problem behavior is the focus of study and treatment.	Behavior is but a symbol of intrapsychic processes and a symptom of unconscious conflict. The underlying conflict is the focus of treatment.
3. Contemporary variables, such as contingencies of reinforcement, are the focus of the analysis.	Historical variables, such as childhood experiences, are the focus of the analysis.
4. Treatment entails application of principles of operant and/or classical conditioning.	Treatment consists of bringing unconscious conflicts into consciousness.
5. Objective observation, measurement, and experimentation are the methods employed. The focus is on observable behavior and environmental events (antecedents and consequences).	Subjective methods of interpretation of behavior and inference regarding unobservable events (e.g., intrapsychic processes) are employed.
6. Theory is based on experimentation.	Theory is predominantly based on case histories.
7. Tenets can be formulated into testable hypotheses and evaluated through experimentation.	Many tenets cannot be formulated into testable hypotheses to be evaluated through experimentation.

There are also significant differences in the two models from the standpoint of methodology. Psychoanalysis is subjective, and the focus, as well as the mechanisms of change, are largely unobservable. Inference and interpretation are employed by the analyst. Additionally, psychoanalytic theory was developed from case histories, and tenets of the theory are quite difficult to evaluate empirically and validate.

The behavioral approach, on the other hand, is objective and based on the empirical method. Behavioral theory has been formulated and tested by means of experimentation. Also, the approach entails a commitment to empirical evaluation of behavioral treatment interventions.

CRITICISMS OF THE BEHAVIORAL MODEL

One criticism of the behavioral model is that explanations for human behavior are oversimplified and ignore emotions and cognitions. There are two aspects of the response to such criticism. First, simple principles established in the animal laboratory can be employed to account for complex behaviors. Current applications of behavior therapy are often comprehensive and address multiple problems of the person. The second issue raised in this criticism is related to the role of private events in explaining behavior. Although all behaviorists do not ascribe a causal role to internal events in explaining behavior, few deny that thoughts and feelings are important and should be considered. Behavioral, physiological, cognitive, and emotional factors may all be dealt with in treatment depending on the nature of the primary problem. Treatment of posttraumatic stress disorder (Fairbank and Keane, 1982), for example, entails assessment of behavioral, physiological, and self-report indices of fear or anxiety.

A second criticism is based on an assumption that if the person's behavior is determined by principles of operant or respondent conditioning, then the person is passive and does not himself or herself affect the environment. While this may apply in the case of respondent conditioning, in operant conditioning the person operates on the environment and produces a change. There is, therefore, an interactive relationship with the surroundings, not a passive one.

Some critics maintain that changes produced by behavioral procedures are not maintained over time or do not generalize to the natural environment. This is an important issue for all psychological interventions, regardless of theoretical perspective. Maintenance and generalization are aspects of treatment outcome that are addressed in evaluations of behavioral interventions. These data show better results for some types of interventions than others. For example, follow-up data for behavioral treatment of agoraphobia are generally more impressive than the maintenance of weight loss produced by behavioral intervention.

A fourth issue raised by critics of behavioral approaches is that of "symptom substitution." The notion is that elimination of a problem behavior or "symptom," without dealing with the underlying cause, will result in the reappearance of the behavior or the development of another problem behavior (i.e., one symptom will be substituted for another if the intrapsychic conflict is not resolved). The concept is based on assumptions about the nature of maladaptive behavior and inferences regarding unobservable processes that stem largely from psychoanalytic theory and its basis in a "closed hydraulic system" model of psychic energy but influenced Freud. It is difficult to investigate "symptom substitution" empirically due to the lack of specificity by those who propose the argument regarding the nature of the symptoms, the conditions under which it is likely to occur, or the length of time posttreatment that elapses prior to appearance of the "substitute" symptom (Bandura 1969). Research does not support the argument for symptom substitution. There are situations in which a behavior may be only temporarily suppressed as in the case of punishment for a response without reinforcement for a desirable incompatible behavior. This does not mean that symptom substitution has occurred. It can mean that empirically derived and validated procedures have not been properly implemented.

A related criticism of a behavioral approach by some is that it is superficial and does not focus on promoting insight and self-understanding. From a behavioral perspective, the focus is on changing behavior, setting specific goals that can be objectively defined and assessed. The difficulty in setting similar goals involving insight or self-understanding are apparent. Moreover, behavior change does not necessarily follow insight regarding the causes of the behavior. Self-understanding may, however, be a collateral of behavior change.

Many criticisms are actually misconceptions about behaviorism and behavioral interventions, and some are briefly summarized (and corrected) in Table 4-8. More complete discussions of misconceptions and criticisms can be found about radical

Table 4–8 **Misconceptions About Behaviorism and Behavior Therapy**

MISCONCEPTION	CORRECTION
1. Genetic endowment is ignored in accounting for behavior.	Behavior is explained in terms of current contingencies, reinforcement history, *and* genetic endowment.
2. Individual uniqueness is not considered.	Although principles of behavior are applicable for all persons, the specific contingencies in effect and the learning history are unique for each individual. These factors must be considered for each person. Also, intensive, systematic study of the person over time has been promoted and used by behaviorists as an experimental methodology.
3. The approach is mechanistic and dehumanizing, and behavior therapists are cold and not empathic.	The approach is objective and systematic. The goals are humanistic and include alleviation of human suffering. Research suggests that behavior therapists display warmth and empathy comparable to therapists with different orientations (Sloane et al, 1975).
4. Behavioral techniques are appropriate for only some groups (e.g., children, the mentally retarded) and for very circumscribed problems (e.g., phobias).	Behavioral principles apply across groups and problem behaviors. Research indicates that some treatment procedures are more effective than others for specific problem behaviors or disorders.

behaviorism in Skinner's (1974) *About Behaviorism* and about behavior therapy in Bellack and Hersen (1980) or Wolpe and Wolpe (1988).

CONTRIBUTIONS OF THE BEHAVIORAL APPROACH

Contributions of the behavioral model are primarily related to the major features of the approach, namely objectivity, commitment to experimentation and the empirical method, and an emphasis on learning and environmental contributions to behavior. These features of the approach are important for both clinical practice and research.

The behavioral approach entails formulation of specific, individualized goals for treatment, which consist of objectively defined and measurable behaviors. Treatment focuses on current conditions and is also described objectively and precisely so as to allow for reporting and replication by others. Progress toward treatment goals and evaluation of the intervention involve measurement of target behaviors during baseline, treatment, and follow-up periods. Such features of the model are particularly significant from the standpoint of accountability in clinical practice as well as the practical utility of specificity in formulating treatment goals and objectivity in assessing progress toward these goals.

Behavior therapy is self-evaluative; empirical demonstration of the effectiveness and identification of the limits of interventions is a commitment of the field. Intensive study of the individual allows for investigation of the types of problems and persons for whom a particular intervention is most effective. Important aspects of treatment effectiveness such as maintenance of effects over time and generalization to other situations and behaviors are evaluated, and clinical research efforts are increasingly focused on programming and facilitating positive outcomes in these areas. This commitment to evaluation increases the likelihood that the individual patient receives the most appropriate and effective treatment and that the body of knowledge about interventions will continue to grow.

Interventions are often implemented and effectiveness is assessed in the person's natural environment. Because paraprofessionals and nonprofessionals can be trained to implement programs designed by professionals expert in the behavioral approach, the feasibility and cost-effectiveness of intervening in the natural environment are enhanced. This, in turn, enhances generalization and maintenance. Behavior therapy techniques are frequently less time-consuming and less expensive than other approaches and are as effective or more effective than most of these.

ANNOTATED BIBLIOGRAPHY

Bandura A: Social Learning Theory. Englewood Cliffs, NJ, Prentice-Hall, 1977

The reader interested in Bandura's theoretical position and more information about observational learning would likely find this original work useful and easy to understand.

Barlow DH (ed): Clinical Handbook of Psychological Disorders. New York, The Guilford Press, 1985

The purpose of this edited handbook is to provide professionals with illustrations of how to implement behaviorally oriented interventions for a number of disorders such as agoraphobia, depression, obesity, and sexual dysfunction.

Cooper JO, Heron TE, Heward WL: Applied Behavior Analysis. Columbus, OH, Merrill Publishing, 1987

> This is an excellent resource for the person interested in learning about operant conditioning and the application of the principles to human problems.

Garfield SL, Bergin AE (eds): Handbook of Psychotherapy and Behavior Change, 3rd ed. New York, John Wiley and Sons, 1986

> This is the third edition of a superb reference for current psychotherapy practice and research. The reader is referred, in particular, to chapters dealing with the practice and evaluation of behavior therapy and behavorial medicine.

Gentry WD (ed): Handbook of Behavioral Medicine. New York, The Guilford Press, 1984

> This edited handbook is especially useful for learning more about medical and health-related applications of behavioral interventions.

Hatch JP, Fisher JG, Rugh JD (eds): Biofeedback: Studies in Clinical Efficacy. New York, Plenum Press, 1987

> Clinical applications and current research in the area of biofeedback are presented in this edited volume. Examples of some of the problem areas addressed are gastrointestinal disorders, Raynaud's syndrome, chronic pain, and hypertension.

Hersen M, Van Hasselt VB (eds): Behavior Therapy with Children and Adolescents: A Clinical Approach. New York, John Wiley & Sons, 1987

> Readers interested in more information about behavioral applications for diverse problems of children and adolescents may find this a useful resource.

Kazdin AE: History of Behavior Modification: Experimental Foundations of Contemporary Research. Baltimore, University Park Press, 1978

> Kazdin's presentation of the history of behavior modification is thorough, organized, and readable. A great deal of information about key figures of the behavioral movement and their respective contributions is available in the book.

Marmor J, Woods JM: The Interface Between Psychodynamic and Behavioral Therapies. New York, Plenum Medical Books, 1980.

> The authors discuss how behavior therapy can be integrated or used in parallel with psychodynamically oriented approaches.

Skinner BF: About Behaviorism. New York, Vintage Books, 1974

> Skinner presents a lucid, interesting discussion of the philosophy of science called radical behaviorism and addresses numerous misconceptions about radical behaviorism and the experimental analysis of behavior.

Skinner BF: Science and Human Behavior. New York, The Free Press, 1953

> Skinner's discussion of punishment in this book is worthwhile reading. He argues cogently against the use of punishment and for a number of alternative strategies to decrease behavior.

Wolpe J, Wolpe D: Life Without Fear: Anxiety and Its Cure. Oakland, CA, New Harbinger Publications, 1988

> Wolpe and his son present a behavioral account of anxiety and its treatment for the lay audience. The book is nontechnical and easily read and understood.

REFERENCES

Abel GG, Rouleau J-L, Coyne BJ: Behavioral Medicine Strategies in Medical Patients. In Stoudemire A, Fogel BS (eds): Principles of Medical Psychiatry, pp 329–345. Orlando, Grune & Stratton, 1987

Baer DM, Wolf MM, Risley TR: Some current dimensions of applied behavior analysis. J Appl Behav Anal 1:91–97, 1968

Bandura A, Ross D, Ross S: Imitation of film-mediated aggressive models. J Abnorm Social Psychol 66:3–11, 1963

Bandura A: Principles of Behavior Modification. New York, Holt, Rinehart and Winston, 1969

Bandura A: Social Learning Theory. Eglewood Cliffs, NJ, Prentice-Hall, 1977

Barlow DH: Anxiety and Its Disorders: The Nature and Treatment of Anxiety and Panic. New York, The Guilford Press, 1988

Beck AT: Cognitive Therapy and the Emotional Disorders. New York, International Universities Press, 1976

Bellack AS, Hersen M: Introduction to Clinical Psychology. New York, Oxford University Press, 1980

Boelens W, Emmelkamp P, MacGillavry D et al: A clinical evaluation of marital treatment: Reciprocity counseling vs system-theoretic counseling. Behav Anal Modif 4:85–96, 1980

Dapcich-Miura E, Hovell MF: Contingency management of adherence to a complex medical regimen in an elderly heart patient. Behav Ther 10:193–201, 1979

Ellis A: Reason and Emotion in Psychotherapy. New York, Lyle Stewart, 1962

Emmelkamp PMG: Behavior therapy with adults. In Garfield SL, Bergin AE (eds): Handbook of Psychotherapy and Behavior Change, 3rd ed. New York, John Wiley & Sons, 1986

Fairbank JA, Gross RT, Keane TM: Treatment of posttraumatic stress disorder: Evaluating outcome with a behavioral code. Behav Modif 7:557–568, 1983

Fairbank JA, Keane TM: Flooding for combat-related stress disorders: Assessment of anxiety reduction across traumatic memories. Behav Ther 13:499–510, 1982

Foa EB, Steketee G, Milby JB: Differential effects of exposure and response prevention in obsessive–compulsive washers. J Consult Clin Psychol 48:71–79, 1980

Forehand R, McMahon RJ: Helping the Noncompliant Child: A Clinician's Guide to Parent Training. New York, Guilford Press, 1982

Garfield SL, Bergin AE (Eds.): Handbook of Psychotherapy and Behavior Change, 3rd ed. New York, John Wiley & Sons, 1986

Gentry WD (Eds.): Handbook of Behavioral Medicine. New York, The Guilford Press, 1984

Hollon S, Beck AT: Research on cognitive therapies. In Garfield SL, Bergin AE (eds): Handbook of Psychotherapy and Behavior Change. New York, John Wiley & Sons, 1986

Jacobson E: Progressive Relaxation. Chicago, University of Chicago Press, 1938

Kazdin AE: The Token Economy. New York, Plenum, 1977

Kazdin AE: History of Behavior Modification: Experimental Foundations of Contemporary Research, Baltimore, University Park Press, 1978

Magrab PR, Papadopoulou ZL: The effect of a token economy on dietary compliance for children on hemodialysis. J Appl Behav Anal 10:573–578, 1977

Marmor J, Woods JM: The Interface Between Psychodynamic and Behavioral Therapies. New York, Plenum Medical Book, 1980

Meichenbaum DH: Cognitive Behavior Modification. New York, Plenum, 1977

Melamed BG, Siegel LJ: Reduction of anxiety in children facing hospitalization and surgery by use of filmed modeling. J Consult Clin Psychol 43:511–521, 1975

Minkin A, Braukmann CJ, Minkin BL et al: The social validation and training of conversational skills. J Appl Behav Anal 9:127–140, 1976

Oden S, Asher SR: Coaching children in social skills for friendship making. Child Dev 48:495–506, 1977

Patterson GR, Guillion ME: Living with Children: New Methods for Parents and Teachers, rev ed. Champaign, IL, Research Press, 1976

Pfeffer C, Plutchik R, Mizruchi M: Predictors of assaultiveness in latency age children. Am J Psychiatry 140:31–35, 1983

Skinner BF: About Behaviorism. New York, Vintage Books, 1974

Sloane RB, Staples FR, Cristol AH et al: Psychotherapy versus Behavior Therapy. Cambridge, Harvard University Press, 1975

Snyder JJ: Reinforcement and analysis of interaction in problem and nonproblem families. J Abnorm Psychol 86:528–535, 1977

Taylor CB, Pfenninger JL, Candelaria T: The use of treatment contracts to reduce medical costs of a difficult patient. J Behav Ther Exp Psychiatry 11:77–82, 1980

Trower P, Yardley K, Bryant BM et al: The treatment of social failure: A comparison of anxiety-reduction and skills-acquisition procedures on two social problems. Behav Modif 2:41–60, 1978

Watson JB: Psychology as the behaviorist views it. Psychol Rev 20:158–177, 1913

Watson JB, Rayner R: Conditioned emotional reactions. J Exp Psychol 3:1–14, 1920

Wolf MM, Birnbrauer J, Lawler J et al: The operant extinction, reinstatement, and re-extinction of vomiting behavior in a retarded child. In Ulrich R, Stachnik T, Mabry J (eds): Control of Human Behavior, vol II. Glenview, IL, Scott Foresman, 1970

Wolpe J, Wolpe D: Life Without Fear: Anxiety and Its Cure. Oakland, CA, New Harbinger Publications, 1988

Human Development

5

Human Sexual Development and Physiology

Judith V. Becker

Because human life begins with procreative activity, it may be appropriate that this section on normal human development begins with an overview of human sexuality. Human sexuality is an integral part of life from birth until death and concerns about sexuality are an issue throughout the lifecycle. Many factors can affect sexual development and sexual functioning, such as genetic endowment, biologic factors, interpersonal development, and cultural background. Consequently, physicians should be knowledgeable about human sexuality from a variety of perspectives, including biologic, psychologic, cultural, and behavioral, particularly because they are often called on to advise patients regarding sexual matters and assess sexual dysfunction in almost all areas of medical and surgical practice.

Clinicians universally report that the majority of patients seen in clinic or hospital settings are uncomfortable discussing issues related to sexuality. Patients tend to rely on physicians and other healthcare professionals to broach the subject first. It is important that the physician be aware of and sensitive to the patient's reticence, but it is equally important that physicians be aware of *their own* relative comfort or discomfort in assessing matters of sexuality in their patients. A solid understanding of all aspects of sexual development and physiology will facilitate the clinician's skills in this regard and decrease whatever anxiety physicians themselves may experience dealing with the sexual problems of their patients. This chapter will cover basic aspects of human sexuality including genetic and hormonal factors in determination of genital gender expression, an overview of basic developmental considerations, and the normal human sexual response cycle. Other developmental, biologic, and cultural factors as they affect the expression of human sexual behavior are discussed in other chapters of this text. This chapter provides a basic introductory overview of sexuality. Human sexuality and human sexual development will be discussed more extensively in Chapter 6. Hormonal influences on sexual behavior will be discussed in Chapter 11.

PRENATAL SEXUAL DEVELOPMENT

Of the 23 pairs of chromosomes in each cell in the human body, one pair, the sex chromosomes, are responsible for sexual development. The genetic sex of a person is established at conception. The sperm cell contributes either an x or y chromosome, and the ovum contributes an x chromosome. The outcome of the pairing of chromosomes in the majority of cases is either female (xx) or male (xy). Chromosomal abnormalities can occur, however, and involve either the loss or addition of a chromosome (Table 5-1). For example, when an additional chromosome is added (xxy), the resulting pattern is Klinefelter's syndrome, the most common sex chromosome disorder. Such individuals develop a male body type; during adolescence, sexual development may be delayed because of a testosterone deficiency. The characteristics of Klinefelter's are apparent by adulthood with atrophic testes and infertility (Kolodny et al, 1979). The xyy genetic pattern is another variation, which has on occasion been associated with impulsive and aggressive behavioral problems.

The absence of a chromosome, such as in Turner's syndrome (xo), produces a female body type and external genitalia, however, ovaries are absent. Short statue and amenorrhea characterize this disorder. Females born with an xxx pattern have diminished fertility.

During the first 6 weeks of life, male and female embryos appear identical; the as yet undifferentiated pair of gonads will differentiate to become either ovaries or testes. If the y chromosome is present in the embryo, the gonads will differentiate into testes. A substance referred to as the H-Y antigen is responsible for this transformation. In the absence of the y chromosome or H-Y antigen, the gonads develop into ovaries.

If the gonads differentiate into testes, fetal androgen (testosterone) is secreted and male genitalia (epididymus, vas deferens, ejaculatory ducts, penis, and scrotum) develop. In the absence of fetal androgen, female genitalia (fallopian tubes, uterus, clitoris, and vagina) develop.

If fetal androgen is present in the body of a genetic female (adrenogenital

Table 5-1 **Summary of Chromosomal Abnormalities in Sex Differentiation**

DISORDER	CHROMOSOMAL PATTERN	PHYSIOLOGIC–BEHAVIORAL CHARACTERISTICS
Klinefelter's syndrome	47, XXY	Sexual development may be delayed because of testosterone deficiency. Atrophic testes and infertility.
Turner's syndrome	45, XO	Short stature, amenorrhea, ovaries absent.
	XYY	Occasionally associated with impulsivity and aggressive behavioral patterns.
Female adrenogenital syndrome	46, XX	Excessive fetal androgen present and external genitalia masculinized. Tomboyishness in childhood.
Androgen insensitivity syndrome	46, XY	Genetically male, however, androgen receptors defective, consequently, external female genitalia develop. Raised as females.

syndrome), the effect is that the external genitalia are masculinized. In some cases, the clitoris is enlarged. In others, there is a fully developed penis and scrotal sac (absent the testes). If in a genetic male androgen is missing or androgen receptors are defective (androgen insensitivity syndrome), female genitalia will develop.

SEXUAL DEVELOPMENT IN THE INFANT

Upon birth, the sexual development and differentiation, which had been controlled in utero by genetic and hormonal factors, are then subject to both social and cultural influences (Money and Ehrhardt, 1972). During the first year of life, the child experiences pair-bonding. The infant's needs are to be nourished, touched, and held. Because it is usually the mother who primarily meets these needs, the first bond of attachment is to her. The "oral" stage of infant development includes not only the sucking and swallowing reflexes to achieve nourishment but all aspects of bodily contact including cuddling and touching (Higham, 1980). (See also Chap. 3.)

Male and female children manifest behavioral differences in the first few years of life. Maccoby and Jacklin (1974), in a review of research on sex differences, conclude that males and females differ in four primary areas: (1) girls have greater verbal ability, (2) boys have greater visual-spatial and (3) mathematic abilities, and (4) boys are more aggressive. These authors note that biologic factors may be implicated in aggression, while the sex differences observed in the other three areas are influenced by social pressure. (Biologic and hormonal factors in development and human behavior are discussed at some length in Chaps. 10, 11, and 12.)

Genital responses occur in infancy. Male infants have spontaneous erections on occasion, and newborn females have vaginal lubrication. These early sexual physiologic responses are inborn reflexes as opposed to learned events (Kolodny et al, 1979).

Male and female children touch and explore their genitals as early as 6 to 12 months of age. Masturbation to orgasm has been reported to occur in young infants. Kinsey and his associates (1948) noted the occurrence of orgasm in some male children younger than 1 year of age. Bakwin (1974) described masturbation to orgasm in female infants. Affectionate behavior in children, including hugging, touching, and kissing, can be observed by age 2.

Researchers agree it is critical that an infant be assigned a gender status in accord with their external genital status, because gender identity is imprinted on the child during the first 24 to 36 months of life and, once established, is highly resistant to change. In the majority of cases, gender status is assigned at birth; the physician at delivery observes the genitalia and announces the sex. In those cases where individuals are born with ambiguous genitalia or a defect of the sex organs, there may be a delay in assigning gender status. Parental counseling is imperative to facilitate the assigning of gender status in ambiguous anatomical cases.

Developmentally by age 3 and sometimes earlier, children develop an awareness of sex roles. Modeling and reinforcement of sex roles occur within the family environment and to some extent may be influenced by cultural and social factors. Gender disorders can occur early in life. Girls appear to be less susceptible to gender disorders than are boys. For example, the ratio of males to females applying for transsexual surgery is 4:1. Furthermore, males are more likely to develop paraphilias. Paraphilias are characterized by sexual fantasies or arousal to sexual objects or behaviors that are not considered normative. For example, arousal or sexual urges involving nonhuman objects, children, or nonconsenting partners, suffering or humiliation (pedophilia, sadism, fetish, exhibitionism).

Sexual interest is displayed during early childhood. Three-year-olds have been shown to evidence an awareness of genital differences. By age 4, children may begin to exhibit some sexual play ("show and tell" or "doctor and nurse" games). Four-year-olds also show an interest in where babies come from and how they get into or out of their mothers. Also at age 4, children begin to show the need for privacy in dressing habits and bathroom behavior. However, they continue to be curious about their own bodies and the bathroom behaviors of others.

At age 5, children become more modest about exposing their bodies and, in general, are more self-contained. Six-year-olds display a greater awareness and interest in sex differences. The 6-year-old may also use slang vocabulary and joke about elimination functions. By age 7, children feel more self-consciousness about their bodies and body exposure.

The middle (prepubertal) years of childhood have historically been labeled the "latency" period, because it was believed that sex drive was suppressed. However, more recent studies of childhood sexuality contradict this belief. Kinsey (1953) reported that sex play with peers occurred equally with same and opposite sex playmates. Furthermore, the number of girls and boys who had experienced orgasm showed a gradual increase in the prepubertal years.

PUBERTY

Puberty is a period marked by profound anatomical and physiologic changes in males and females. Reproductive capacity is reached during this period. The biologic changes seen in the female include breast development and the growth of pubic hair. Menstruation usually begins between the ages of 11 and 13. Internal sexual structures, including the uterus, grow and mature during this period. Endocrine changes that occur during the normal menstrual cycle are seen in Figure 5-1.

Males experience growth of pubic hair, penile and testicular enlargement, and ejaculation. The prostate and seminal vesicles develop and enlarge during this period.

Both males and females experience growth in height and weight. In general, boys experience their growth spurt about 2 years later than girls. There is a wide variation in the timing of pubertal events, related to genetic as well as environmental factors (Tanner, 1975). For girls, breast budding may begin anywhere from age 8 to age 13; the onset of menarche usually occurs between the ages of 10 and 16.5. For boys, penile and testicular growth begins between the ages of 10.5 and 14.5 (Marshall and Tanner 1969, 1970).

In Western societies there has been a decrease in the age of onset of puberty. Over the past 150 years, the age of onset menarche has dropped from age 17 to 13 (Tanner, 1975). This is probably related to complex changes in nutrition, social conditions, and public health (Meyer-Bahlburg, 1980).

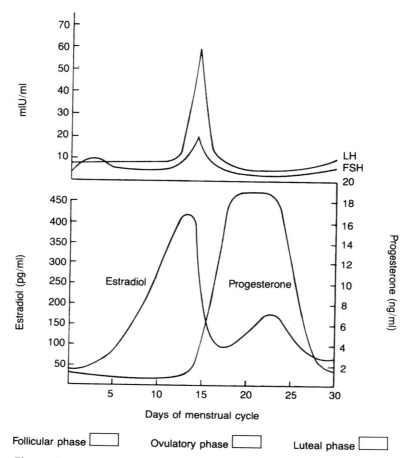

Figure 5–1. *Hormone changes during a typical menstrual cycle. (Reproduced with permission from Benson RC (ed): Current Obstetric and Gynecologic Diagnosis and Treatment, 3rd ed. Copyright 1980 by Lange Medical Publications, Los Altos, CA)*

The physiologic events that occur during puberty can extend over a period of 3 to 4 years in females and for a longer period in males. The period of adolescence is a critical period of transition between childhood and adulthood. Psychologically, this period is one of identity formation and involves emotional conflict and role confusion (Erikson, 1963).

Although adolescents become capable of reproduction during puberty, the adolescent girls' first couple of menstrual cycles may not involve ovulation. For male adolescents, ejaculation may occur before sperm are viable.

During the period of adolescence, males and females may engage in self-stimulatory sexual behavior as well as sexual behavior with their peers. Masturbation to orgasm occurs more frequently in males than females. Hunt (1974) reported that

63% of the males in his study sample had masturbated to orgasm by age 13, compared to 33% of the female sample. Hunt also reported that adolescents masturbate at an earlier age than reported by the Kinsey studies. Hunt (1974) found that 93% of males and 63% of females masturbate at some time in their lives. Even though masturbation is a common practice, unfortunately many adolescents are embarrassed about it.

Sex play, including mutual masturbation, may occur during prepuberty and puberty. About 10% of boys and 5% of girls engage in sexual relations with a same sex peer during adolescence.

Adolescents today engage in intercourse at an earlier age and more frequently than did previous generations of adolescents. Seventeen percent of boys and five percent of girls age 15 reported having had intercourse at least once; by age 18, 64% of boys and 44% of girls had had intercourse (Zelnick, Kantner, and Ford, 1981; National Research Council, 1987).

Because adolescence is a period of sexual maturation, the adolescent may have concerns about his or her changing body and sexual drive. Adolescents often face sexual issues related to masturbation, sexual anatomy, sexual identity, premarital sex, contraception, pregnancy, abortion, and sexually transmitted diseases, including AIDS. For adolescents to resolve these issues successfully, they need to have a knowledgable, caring, and supportive adult available to listen and provide guidance. The role of the physician is particularly critical because the physician may be the person the adolescent seeks out for assistance with these issues. Consequently, it is important that the physician be nonjudgmental. If, for ethical reasons, the physician feels that he/she cannot be nonjudgmental in regard to some issue (abortion, contraception), then referrals should be made to other individuals or agencies. In Chapter 6, development aspects of human sexuality will be discussed in some detail from infancy through adolescence.

ADULTHOOD

Once individuals reach adulthood, they are faced with a plethora of choices in every aspect of life, including marriage, childbearing, and lifestyle. Sexual conflicts and problems may arise during this period, often brought on by pressure to conform to peer influence, societal and sexual norms. Individuals may experience problems with pair bonding. For some people, infertility may present a problem; for others pregnancy may put a stress on a couple's sexual relationship. The presence of a child or children may reduce the time couples have to spend alone with each other. It is crucial that couples be able to communicate with one another to solve any problems that may arise.

Middle age is a period during which persons begin to adapt to the aging process. For some people, this period is one of liberation (children leave home, more time for leisure activities); others experience feelings of anxiety and despair. Sexually, physiologic changes are seen in both men and women. For women, menopause is brought about as a result of lower levels of sex hormones. As the ovaries age, circulatory levels of estrogen and progesterone gradually decrease. Age of menopause can vary from the late thirties to late fifties. As a result of these lowered hormonal levels, the following changes occur: shrinking of the vaginal wall, labia majora, uterus, and fallopian tubes. The reduction of vaginal lubrication in the expansion of the vagina can make intercourse uncomfortable. Estrogen replacement can be used to treat these problems if medically safe. There is no evidence of increased psychiatric morbidity during the menopause (such as depression) contrary to popular belief, although flushing, "hot flashes," and some degree of transient emotional lability may be seen because of fluctuation of estrogen levels.

Physiologic changes also occur in males. However, these changes in endocrine and reproduction functions are more gradual and occur somewhat later than in women. Androgen levels, which are relatively constant after puberty, show a gradual decline until the midforties when they drop to 55% to 60% of what they were earlier. By age 65, levels are 30% of what they were at age 30 (Silny, 1980). As the male ages, a number of behavioral changes in sexuality occur: penile erection is slower, the erectile refractory period following ejaculation increases, morning erections and noctural emissions occur less frequently, and there is a decline in ejaculation force and amount of ejaculate (Silny, 1980).

THE ELDERLY

The capacity for sexual enjoyment is present at all ages as is the need for love and intimacy. Persons who are in good health and have willing and cooperative sexual partners can continue active sex lives until their nineties or older. It is almost a universal phenomenon among physicians to assume that old people are not interested in sex, are generally sexually inactive, or believe that it is not necessary to inquire about sexual matters in the elderly. (See also Chapter 7.)

IMPACT OF LIFE EVENTS ON SEXUALITY

Persons at any age may undergo a life experience that can affect their sexual functioning. It is important that physicians be aware of these events; they include: sexual assaults, illness, trauma (spinal cord injuries), surgical procedures (mastectomy, hysterectomy, enterostomy), medication (antihypertensives, psychotropics), sexually transmitted diseases (HIV infection, herpes, and so forth). The effects of medical illness on sexual functioning may be reviewed elsewhere (Fagan and Schmidt, 1987).

HUMAN SEXUAL RESPONSE

Human sexual response represents a complex interaction of the nervous, vascular, and endocrine systems, which interact to produce sexual desire, arousal, and orgasm. In order to understand the sexual response cycle, it is necessary to have an understanding of its anatomical and physiologic determinants.

Male Genital Anatomy

Male sexual anatomy consists of external organs (the penis, scrotum, and testes) and internal organs (the prostate, vas deferens, seminal vesicles, and Cowper's glands).

The penis consists of the glands penis, the corona, the corpora cavernosa, and corpus spongiosum (which also contains the urethra). The corpora spongiosum and cavernosa contain erectile tissue. The corpora cavernosa diverge at the base of the penis to form the crura, which are attached to the pelvic bone (Figs. 5-2 and 5-3).

The testes are located within the scrotum. The principal functions of the testes are sperm production and production of testosterone. Sperm are produced within the seminiferous tubules.

The major function of the internal organs is the transportation of sperm. The sperm produced in the testes are mixed with fluids from the prostate, seminal vesicles, and Cowper's glands.

Female Genital Anatomy

As in the male, the female sexual anatomy consists of external organs, including the mons, labia, clitoris, the perineum, and the internal organs, which consist of the vagina, cervix, uterus, ovaries, and fallopian tubes. The mons is the area of fatty tissue

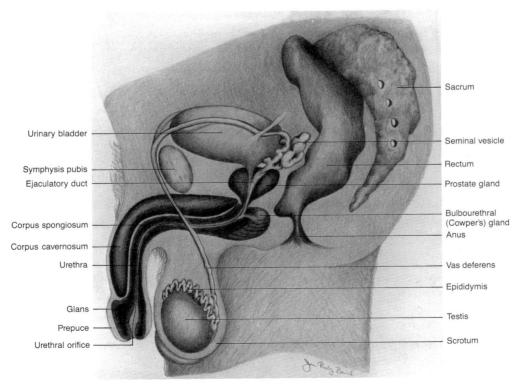

Figure 5-2. *Internal side view of the male reproductive system.*

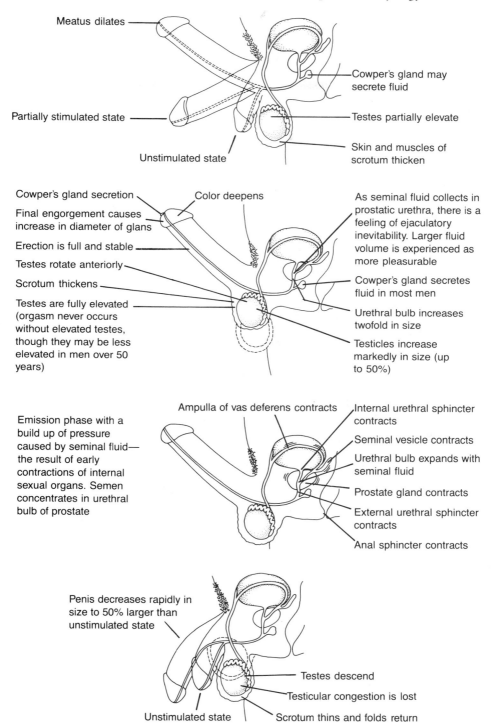

Meatus dilates

Cowper's gland may secrete fluid

Partially stimulated state

Testes partially elevate

Skin and muscles of scrotum thicken

Unstimulated state

Cowper's gland secretion

Color deepens

Final engorgement causes increase in diameter of glans

Erection is full and stable

Testes rotate anteriorly

Scrotum thickens

Testes are fully elevated (orgasm never occurs without elevated testes, though they may be less elevated in men over 50 years)

As seminal fluid collects in prostatic urethra, there is a feeling of ejaculatory inevitability. Larger fluid volume is experienced as more pleasurable

Cowper's gland secretes fluid in most men

Urethral bulb increases twofold in size

Testicles increase markedly in size (up to 50%)

Ampulla of vas deferens contracts

Internal urethral sphincter contracts

Emission phase with a build up of pressure caused by seminal fluid—the result of early contractions of internal sexual organs. Semen concentrates in urethral bulb of prostate

Seminal vesicle contracts

Urethral bulb expands with seminal fluid

Prostate gland contracts

External urethral sphincter contracts

Anal sphincter contracts

Penis decreases rapidly in size to 50% larger than unstimulated state

Testes descend

Testicular congestion is lost

Unstimulated state

Scrotum thins and folds return

Figure 5–3. *External and internal changes in the male sexual response cycle.*

and hair that cover the pubic bone. From the bottom of the mons extend the labia majora, which merge with the perineum. Within the labia majora are the labia minora. The labia minora enclose the clitoris, urethral opening, and vaginal opening (Figs. 5-4 and 5-5).

The clitoris, which consists of the glans and shaft, is covered by the clitoral hood. The clitoral shaft, like the penis, contains the corpora cavernosa and the corpus spongiosum. The base of the shaft forms the crura, which are attached to the pelvic bone. The perineum is the area between the posterior boundary of the labia and the anus.

The vagina has been described as a "potential space." The vagina has the capacity to contract and expand, and is lined with squamous epithelium cells, which are responsible for vaginal lubrication.

At the top of the vagina is the cervix, which is a passageway between the vagina and uterus. The uterus is a muscular structure comprised of three layers.

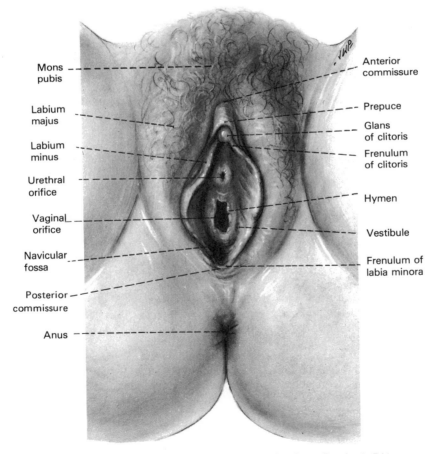

Figure 5–4. *The vulva. (Reprinted with permission from Danforth DN, Scott JR: Obstetrics and Gynecology, 5th ed. Philadelphia, JB Lippincott, 1986)*

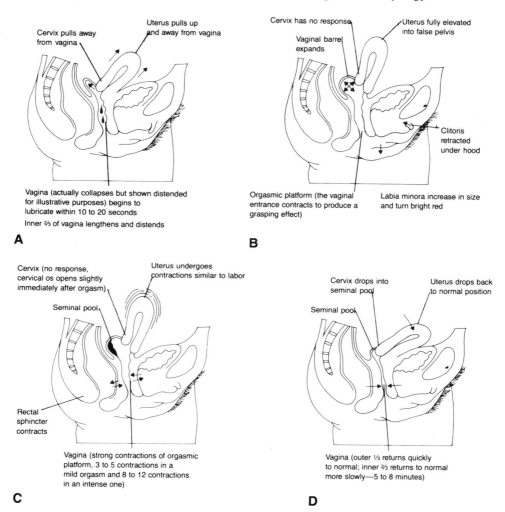

Figure 5–5. *Internal changes in female sexual response cycle. (A) Excitement stage, (B) plateau stage, (C) orgasm stage, and (D) resolution stage. (Reprinted with permission from Reeder JR, Martin LL: Maternity Nursing, 16th ed. Philadelphia, JB Lippincott, 1987)*

The ovaries are located on either side of the uterus. The ovaries secrete the hormones progesterone and estrogen, and release ova, which are transported from the ovary to the uterus by the fallopian tubes.

Human Sexual Physiology

Sexual response is not limited to the functions of the genitalia. To fully understand sexual response, the role of sexual stimuli and the response of the nervous system must also be examined.

Weiss (1972) suggests that sexual stimuli can be divided into two categories:

reflexogenic (direct tactile stimulation of erogenous zones) and psychogenic (thoughts, images, fantasies, sights, smells, sounds, tastes, and so forth). The source of sexual stimulation in many instances is a combination of both. There is tremendous variability in what serves as sexual stimulation for people. Learning and conditioning play a major role in determining what a particular person will find arousing.

The nervous system serves as the communication system to the body to facilitate the sexual response. In this interaction both the central nervous system and the peripheral nervous system are involved. When a person is exposed to sexual stimuli, a message is sent from the brain or spinal cord through the peripheral nervous system (to either the autonomic or somatic branches). Stimulation of the somatic branch is responsible for the muscle tension that occurs during sexual stimulation. Stimulation by the autonomic nervous system is responsible for penile erection and vaginal lubrication.

The autonomic nervous system has two branches, the parasympathetic and sympathetic. These two branches are seen as antagonistic, in that the parasympathetic branch releases acetylcholine and is dominant during periods of relaxation, whereas the sympathetic branch releases adrenaline and noradrenaline and responds during periods of stress. These systems work in concert during sexual arousal. The *parasympathetic* nervous system is responsible for the expansion of the arterial blood vessels and the concomitant erection of the penis in males and vaginal lubrication in females. As arousal increases, the sympathetic nervous system plays a greater role, as evidenced by an increase in heart rate and blood pressure. Ejaculation is triggered by discharge of the sympathetic branch. This discharge creates an imbalance in the autonomic nervous system and is compensated by the release of acetylcholine from the parasympathetic branch. With this release comes the sensation of relaxation and warmth after orgasm (Rosen and Rosen, 1981) in both men and women.

As mentioned previously, sexual experience can vary tremendously from individual to individual. Responses to sexual stimulation can be influenced by a number of factors. Byrne and Byrne (1977) describe three components that serve to influence a person's response to sexual stimulation; these are informational, emotional, and imaginal. The *informational* component represents a person's beliefs and expectations regarding sexuality. The *emotional* component consists of perceptions and feelings about sexual stimuli. For example, a person may experience happiness, joy, anxiety, or guilt in response to sexual stimuli. The *imaginal* component refers to the images or fantasies a person experiences when faced with sexual stimuli.

The endocrine system plays a crucial role in sexual response. The hormones responsible for sexual and reproductive functions are produced by the endocrine glands under the supervision of the hypothalamus. The hypothalmus is responsible for sending messages to the autonomic nervous system as well as regulating hormone levels. The endocrine glands involved in sexual functioning include the anterior pituitary, adrenal glands, and gonads (testes or ovaries). The sexual hormones secreted by the anterior pituitary include follicle-stimulating hormone (FSH), luteinizing hormone (LH), and prolactin. These hormones, called gonadotropins, stimulate the gonads to produce hormones. Estrogen and progesterone are produced and secreted by the ovaries, testosterone by the testes. Prolactin is responsible for progesterone production and the stimulation of the mammary glands to produce milk after childbirth.

The role of the vascular system is equally as important. In the male, penile erection is achieved through vascular engorgement of erectile tissue in the cavernous and spongy corpora of the penis. There is controversy, however, over the specific neurovascular mechanisms involved. There is also controversy over the role nervous mechanisms and arteriovenous shunts play in the control of tumescence.

In females, data suggest that precapillary arterial dilation accompanies the early phases of vasocongestion and shift to arterialized blood flow, and increased venous output occurs as arousal increases (Wagner and Ottesen, 1980).

The Sexual Response Cycle

A number of models of the sexual response cycle have been proposed, ranging from a two-stage model to a four-stage model. Ellis (1906) proposed a two-stage model, which involved the processes of tumescence and detumescence. Kaplan (1979) describes a three-stage model including *desire*, produced by activation of a specific neural system in the brain, *excitement*, produced by reflex dilatation of blood vessels, and *orgasm*, reflex contractions of certain genital muscles.

Masters and Johnson (1966), based on their psychophysiologic laboratory studies, describe a four-stage model. The four stages are *excitement, plateau, orgasm,* and *resolution* (Fig. 5-6).

Excitement is characterized by the onset of sexual feelings. During this stage, blood pressure and heart rate increase, breathing becomes faster and deeper, and skin "mottling" occurs. In males, erection is experienced, the scrotum thickens, the scrotal sac flattens, and the testes begin to elevate. In females, the breasts begin to swell, nipples become erect, and vaginal lubrication occurs. Some women experience vasocongestion of the clitoris. The uterus enlarges and begins to rise from the pelvic floor. The vagina begins to enlarge.

The *plateau* stage is characterized by a more advanced state of arousal. The penis is distended, and the testicles have thickened and elevated. Reflex contraction of the cremasteric muscles cause the testes to move upward toward the body. The testes may increase as much as 50% from their basal size.

Females experience a marked vasocongestion of the outer third of the vagina during the plateau stage. Masters and Johnson have labeled this the *orgasmic platform.* The vasocongestion causes the labia minora to become larger and thicker, and it may change in color to dark red or purple. During the plateau stage, the uterus has ascended from the pelvic floor.

Orgasm is a reflex brought about by the vasocongestion and myotonia that occur during arousal. The buildup of muscle tension during sexual arousal is a major factor in triggering the orgasmic response. In the male, ejaculation occurs. During the first stage (emission) of ejaculation, semen is moved to the urethra. Masters and Johnson have labeled the sensations that occur during the emission phase as the period of "ejaculatory inevitability." The ejaculatory phase (expulsion) is characterized by semen being expelled from the urethra. The contractions of the bulbocavernosus muscles create the expulsion. Following ejaculation the male experiences a

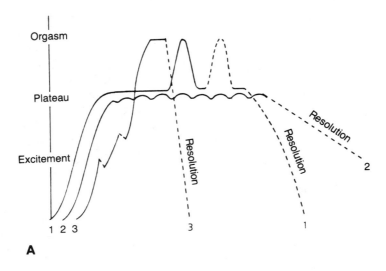

A

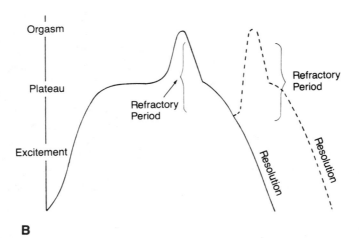

B

Figure 5–6. The sexual response cycle. **A:** Three representative variations of female sexual response. Pattern 1 shows multiple orgasm; pattern 2 shows arousal that reaches the plateau level without going on to orgasm (note that resolution occurs very slowly); and pattern 3 shows several brief drops in the excitement phase followed by an even more rapid resolution phase. **B:** The most typical pattern of male sexual response. The dotted line shows one possible variation: a second orgasm and ejaculation occurring after the refractory period is over. Numerous other variations are possible, including patterns that would match 2 and 3 of the female response cycle. (Masters WH, Johnson VE: Human Sexual Response. Boston, Little, Brown & Co., 1966. © 1966 by William H. Master and Virginia E. Johnson)

refractory period (a certain length of time must elapse before he can ejaculate again). The length of the refractory period varies from male to male. In general, it is correlated with age, in that the older the person, the longer the refractory period.

For the female, orgasm is characterized by rhythmic contractions of the perineal, bulbar, and pubococcygeal muscles, and the muscles of the perineal floor. Females do not experience a refractory period, and thus multiple orgasms are possible within a relatively short period of time.

The final stage, *resolution,* is characterized by the body returning to its basal state.

Rosen and Beck (1988), commenting on these various models, note that, while it is important to formulate and specify sexual arousal in terms of a model, the existing models are incomplete and potentially biased. These authors further propose that the three- and four-stage models are little more than elaborations of the biphasic model. Further research addressing the key psychophysiologic concepts is necessary. As noted in Figure 5-6, multiple patterns of sexual response may occur particularly in women. About 5–10% of women rarely or never experience orgasm, yet experience marked sexual pleasure. Many, if not most, women usually require additional clitoral, non-coital stimulation (i.e., by manual methods) to achieve orgasm during sexual activity.

DISCUSSION

The overview that has been presented relates to sexual functioning in an intact individual. Sexual dysfunctions occur when there are disruptions in the psychologic, physiologic, or anatomical processes involved in the process. It is important for physicians to be aware that sexual problems can arise in both heterosexual and homosexual relationships. The physician should not assume that the patient is in a heterosexual relationship. When taking a sexual history, use the phrase "sexual partner" so that the patient is free to disclose, if she or he chooses, whether the partner or partners are male, female, or both. It is important in providing good patient care that physicians be aware of their own attitudes regarding sexuality and sexual preference and are nonjudgmental in providing services to patients whose sexual preference is different than their own.

A discussion of the specific sexual types of sexual dysfunction and their treatments is beyond the scope of this chapter, but the sexual dysfunctions as described in DSM-III-R include Hypoactive Sexual Desire Disorder, Sexual Aversion Disorder, Female Sexual Arousal Disorder, Male Erectile Disorder, Inhibited Female Orgasm, Inhibited Male Orgasm, Premature Ejaculation, Dysparennia, and Vaginismus.

It should be emphasized, however, that sexual concerns and dysfunction occur quite commonly in the general population, especially in the context of medical illness. Physicians have an essential educational and therapeutic role in helping patients with sexual matters, and, therefore, the importance of a sound knowledge for physicians in both normal and abnormal sexual functioning cannot be overemphasized.

Finally, it should be emphasized again that sexuality must always be understood and assessed in the context of each individual patient's psychologic, physical, and social matrix. The approach to assessing a patient's sexual functioning or dysfunctioning will be determined by the patient's developmental stage; age; social situation; sexual orientation and preferences; medical status; and cultural, religious, and ethical considerations. In an era when sexual behavior and attitudes toward sex have undergone profound changes in all areas of society—including the healthcare sector—special challenges are presented for physicians in providing medical care, education, counseling, and treatment for their patients.

The techniques and format for taking a medically oriented sexual history from a patient are beyond the scope of this introductory text and are covered in the companion text to this volume on clinical psychiatry (Fagan and Schmidt, 1990). Table 5-2, however, lists the essential areas that should be covered in this type of interview, whether it is taken as a separate examination or part of a comprehensive medical history. Of equal importance as *what* is asked is *how* the interview is conducted. Patients should be reassured that such questions are a routine part of the medical interview and confidential and given the opportunity to voice any general concerns or questions regarding their sexual life in an open-ended manner before the structure interview questions are asked. Depending on the response to this open-ended question, the clinician might then ask questions about the areas listed in Table 5-2 in a

Table 5–2 **Basic Sexual History (modified to age of patient and clinical circumstances)**

Introductory comments about why the interview is being conducted and its routine or special nature given the clinical situation at hand; reassurance about confidentality
Open-ended question, to give the patient an opportunity to voice any areas of special worry or concern regarding this part of the interview or sexual concerns in general
Source of information about sex in growing up
Attitudes of the parents toward sex
Age of onset of puberty
Age of menarche and menstrual history in women
Age of first intense romantic or sexually oriented relationship
History of childhood molestation or incest
History of venereal diseases
Attitudes about masturbation and frequency
Age of first intercourse; number of partners
General pattern of attraction to person of the opposite or same sex; general patterns of heterosexuality or homosexuality
Abortions, miscarriages, pregnancies; complications of pregnancies
Method(s) of birth control
Frequency of current sexual activity
Physical discomfort with sexual activity:
    Men: Problem with arousal or achieving and maintaining erection, ejaculation control; ability to achieve orgasm; physical comfort with intercourse
    Women: Problems with arousal, lubrication, achieving orgasm, physical comfort with intercourse
Conflicts in relationship, or marriage over sexual matters: frequency, methods of birth control, sexual dysfunction
Medications or illness that seem to affect negatively sexual desire or functioning
Issues regarding decision to avoid or achieve conception and have children
Risk factors for AIDS or other concerns regarding this disease

systematic manner. Patients should be reassured that if there are areas they would "rather not talk about" for any particular reason, that question could be deferred to a later date, or if they are uncomfortable with discussing a particular area, they may be asked what is the nature of their concern. It goes without saying that the interview is modified according to the age of the patient and general clinical circumstances at hand in deciding what areas to explore in some depth or what questions may not be clinically relevant. For more information about sexual assessment and indications for referral for sexual dysfunction therapy, see Fagan and Schmidt, 1990. For more details regarding sexual development, physiology, and the diagnosis and treatment of specific sexual dysfunctions, see selected articles in the Annotated Bibliography. In this text, aspects of human development will be discussed in Chapter 6.

ANNOTATED BIBLIOGRAPHY

Becker JV, Kavoussi RJ: Sexual Disorders. In Talbott J, Hales R, Yudofsky S (eds): Textbook of Psychiatry. Washington DC, American Psychiatric Press, 1987
> An overview of sexuality and sexual dysfunction from the standpoint of clinical psychiatry.

Fagan PJ, Schmidt CW: Psychosexual Disorders. In Stoudemire A (ed): Clinical Psychiatry for Medical Students. Philadelphia, JB Lippincott, 1990

Fagan PJ, Schmidt CW: Sexual dysfunction in the medically ill. In Stoudemire A, Fogel BS (eds): Principles of Medical Psychiatry. Orlando, Grune & Stratton, 1987
> An excellent overview for medical students of basic approaches to assessing and treating sexual dysfunctions most commonly encountered in general medical practice.

LoPiccolo J, Stock WE: Treatment of sexual dysfunction. J Consult Clin Psychol 54:158–167, 1986
> Presents a review of current knowledge on treatment of sexual dysfunctions.

Masters WH, Johnson VE, Kolodny RC: Human sexuality. Boston, Little, Brown & Co, 1982
> Good introductory level text on topic of human sexuality.

Money J, Ehrhardt A: Man and Woman, Boy and Girl. Baltimore, Johns Hopkins Press, 1974
> Comprehensive presentation of the differentiation and dimorphism of gender identity from conception to maturity.

REFERENCES

American Psychiatric Association: Diagnostic Manual of Mental Disorders, 3rd ed rev. Washington, DC, American Psychiatric Association, 1987

Bakwin H: Erotic feelings in infants and young children. Medical Aspects of Human Sexuality 8:200–215, 1974

Byrne D, Byrne L: Exploring Human Sexuality. New York, Thomas Crowell, 1977

Ellis H: Studies in the Psychology of Sex. New York, Random House, 1906

Erikson E: Childhood and Society. New York, WW Norton and Co, 1963

Fagan PJ, Schmidt CW Jr: Sexual Dysfunction in the medically ill. In Stoudemire A, Fogel BS (Eds.) Principles of Medical Psychiatry. Orlando, Grune & Stratton, 1987, pp. 307–327.

Fagan PJ, Schmidt CW: Psychosexual Disorders. In Stoudemire A (ed): Clinical Psychiatry for Medical Students. Philadelphia, JB Lippincott, 1990

Higham E: Sexuality in the infant and neonate: Birth to two years. In Wolman BB, Money J (eds): Handbook of Human Sexuality, pp 16–27. Englewood Cliffs, NJ, Prentice-Hall, 1980

Hunt M: Sexual Behavior in the 70's. New York, Dell, 1974

Kaplan HS: Disorders of Sexual Desire. New York, Bruner/Mazel, 1979

Kinsey AC, Pomeroy WB, Martin CE: Sexual Behavior in the Human Male. Philadelphia, WB Saunders, 1948

Kinsey AC, Pomeroy WB, Martin CE et al: Sexual Behavior in the Human Female. Philadelphia, WB Saunders, 1953

Kolodny RC, Masters WH, Johnson VE: Textbook of Sexual Medicine. Boston, Little, Brown & Co, 1979

Maccoby E, Jacklin C: The Psychology of Sex Differences. Stanford, CA, Stanford University Press, 1974

Marshall WA, Tanner JM: Variations in the patterns of pubertal changes in boys. Arch Dis Child 45:13–23, 1970

Marshall WA, Tanner JM: Variations in patterns of pubertal changes in girls. Arch Dis Child 44:291–303, 1969

Masters WH, Johnson VE: Human Sexual Response. Boston, Little Brown & Co, 1966

Meyer-Bahlburg H: Sexuality in early adolescence. In Wolman BB, Money J (eds): Handbook of Human Sexuality, pp 62–82. Englewood Cliffs, NJ, Prentice-Hall, 1980

Money J, Erhardt A: Man and Woman, Boy and Girl. Baltimore, Johns Hopkins University Press, 1972

National Research Council: Risking the Future. Washington, DC, National Academy Press, 1987

Rosen RC, Beck JG: Patterns of Sexual Arousal. New York, Gilford Press, 1988

Rosen R, Rosen LR: Human Sexuality. New York, Alfred A. Knopf, 1981

Silny AJ: Sexuality and Aging. In Wolman BB, Money J (eds): Handbook of Human Sexuality, pp 124–146. Englewood Cliffs, NJ, Prentice-Hall, 1980

Tanner JM: Growth and endocrinology of the adolescent. In Gardner LI (ed): Endocrine and Genetic Diseases of Childhood and Adolescence, pp 14–64. Philadelphia, WB Saunders, 1975

Wagner G, Ottesen B: Vaginal blood flow during sexual stimulation. Obstet Gynecol 56:621–624, 1980

Weiss HD: The physiology of human erection. Ann Intern Med 76:793–799, 1972

Zelnik MD, Kantner JF, Ford K: Sex and Pregnancy in Adolescence. Beverly Hills CA, Sage Publications, 1981

6

Childhood and Adolescent Development

Mina K. Dulcan

This chapter reviews the basic principles and theories of normal human development from conception through adolescence. Significant milestones in physical, cognitive, language, emotional, and social growth will be covered. In the discussion that follows, the roughly 20 years of development will be divided into prenatal, infant (the first year), toddler (1 to 3 years), early childhood (3 to 6 years), school age (6 to 12 years), and adolescent periods. In each period, development in *physical, cognitive, language, affective,* and *social* domains will be described, as well as special topics applicable to that age group. At each stage, interactions between developmental status and physical illness or hospitalization will be highlighted. Important aspects of family functioning at different developmental stages will also be discussed.

WHY STUDY HUMAN DEVELOPMENT?

Knowledge of the normal development of children and adolescents provides an essential framework for understanding adult development and child and adult psychopathology. Childhood developmental factors may influence the pathogenesis of mental illness at any age. Knowledge of the developmental process and its phases also facilitates the medical care of young persons and adults and their families by making understandable their phase-specific reactions to illness at each stage of the life cycle.

Different Views of Development

There are two basic ways of discussing development. One may take a cross-sectional view, describing all aspects of a particular age, or describe each area longitudinally from a particular theoretic perspective. This chapter will take the cross-sectional option in an attempt to integrate the various developmental theories and capabilities at each developmental stage, because this is the way patients present in the medical setting. (See Figs. 6-2 and 6-3 for a graphic summary of parallel lines of human development from several theoretic perspectives, similar to the schemata presented in Table 3-1.)

What is Normality?

Although this may seem like a question with an obvious answer, there are widely discrepant definitions of what constitutes "normality." The term may be used to describe data that fit a normal or gaussian frequency distribution, with a symmetric distribution of scores, and a mean that coincides with the median. In this case, the mean plus or minus two standard deviations encloses 95% of the contents. The term "normal" is then applied to persons who score within this 95% range on a particular measure. "Normal" height and weight are typically determined in this way. A related use of the term "normal" refers to a statistical norm or average, which, of course, is tied to the original population from which the data were gathered.

Alternatively, "normal" may refer to what is socially or culturally acceptable (to a particular group). Cultural aspects of normality and psychopathology are discussed in Chapter 2. "Normal" may also be used to describe individual-specific response patterns (i.e., what is normal or usual for a given person) in an attempt to distinguish stable unusual characteristics from those that represent a change or deviation.

"Normal" may also be used to mean healthy, without pathology, or ideal. In the context of preventive medicine and psychiatry efforts, normality implies that the individual or group carries no excess risk of future disease or psychopathology.

Development has many aspects, including physical, cognitive, and emotional, with finer subdivisions in each of these three areas. It is important not only to assess in which areas a person's development is normal or abnormal, but also to evaluate the evenness or synchrony of development across different domains.

Developmental Theories

This chapter will present multiple theories of development, because at present no single theory is sufficiently comprehensive. Multiple perspectives, all with some degree of inherent value, must be invoked to provide an integrated and balanced view of the many factors that influence human development.

Each developmental theory identifies stages that unfold in an orderly progression, each phase building on the previous one, becoming more complex and differentiated, and then launching the next phase. Developmental theories identify the maximum expected capabilities at each stage. A profile can be constructed for each person, marking progress compared to expected norms in each developmental area. In both normal children and those with psychopathology, development may progress at different rates in different areas. There are times when apparent regression to an earlier stage of development is not only normal, but facilitates subsequent growth.

Psychoanalytic, object relations, and behavioral and learning theories of development are described in Section 2 of this text, and psychosocial (Eriksonian) theory is discussed in Chapter 7. Current knowledge about neurobiologic aspects of behavior is summarized in Section 4.

This chapter will focus primarily on observable developmental milestones or landmarks, physiologic and neurologic aspects of development, cognitive theories of development, beginning with Piaget, and interactions between the child and the family, as development proceeds. An attempt will be made to apply findings from clinical observations and research in developmental psychology to the child, adolescent, and family as they are likely to present in the medical setting.

Developmental Milestones

Arnold Gesell, a pediatrician working at the Yale Clinic of Child Development, and his colleagues (Gesell et al, 1940), through their objective observation of behaviors and capabilities in large numbers of children at various ages, made a major contribution to pediatrics and child development. Their data identified "milestones" by which to measure the intactness of the child's abilities, as determined by interaction between biologic endowment and environment. Areas assessed include the motor, personal–social, adaptive (use of motor abilities to interact with the environment), and language domains. The widely used Denver Developmental Screening Test (Fig. 6-1) graphically displays the age at which each milestone is attained by 25%, 50%, 75%, and 90% of normal infants and children (up to 6 years of age).

Piagetian Cognitive Development

Jean Piaget, a Swiss cognitive psychologist working in the early and mid-1900s, became intrigued by the *wrong* answers given to questions on intelligence tests by children of different ages. He devoted his career to the study of *epistemology*, or how thought is transformed into a body of knowledge. Unlike Freud, whose theories were developed primarily by retrospective extrapolation from neurotic adults, Piaget's conception of cognitive development was based on the direct observation of his own three children, starting in infancy. He viewed children as active participants in learning, rather than passive recipients.

Piaget believed that four factors influence cognitive behavior:

1. Maturation of the nervous system.
2. Experience.
3. Social transmission of information, or teaching.
4. *Equilibration:* The innate tendency for mental growth to progress toward increasingly complex and stable levels of organization.

Piaget also defined four major stages of cognitive development, *sensorimotor, preoperational, concrete operations,* and *formal operations.* These are not uniformly attained, but appear within a rather wide range of ages (Fig. 6-2 and 6-3). Each child's rate of development is determined by his or her intelligence and the above factors.

Certain definitions are essential to understanding Piaget (Piaget and Inhelder, 1969). A *scheme* is an organized pattern of behavior that is repeatable and generalizable (e.g., sucking, reaching for a mobile hanging in the crib). Piaget believed that development proceeds through certain processes that are basic tendencies in human beings.

1. Active seeking of stimulation.
2. *Organization:* The tendency to arrange processes into coherent systems.

(Text continues on page 137)

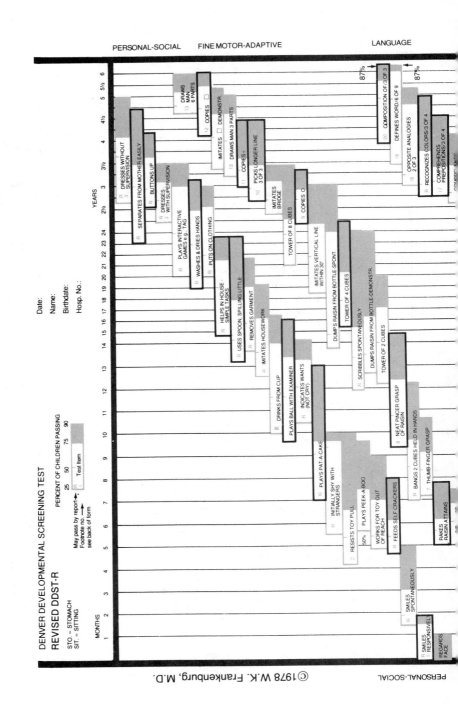

DENVER DEVELOPMENTAL SCREENING TEST
REVISED DDST-R

STO = STOMACH
SIT. = SITTING

PERCENT OF CHILDREN PASSING

25 50 75 90

May pass by report
Footnote no.
see back of form

Test Item

Date:
Name:
Birthdate:
Hosp. No.:

© 1978 W.K. Frankenburg, M.D.

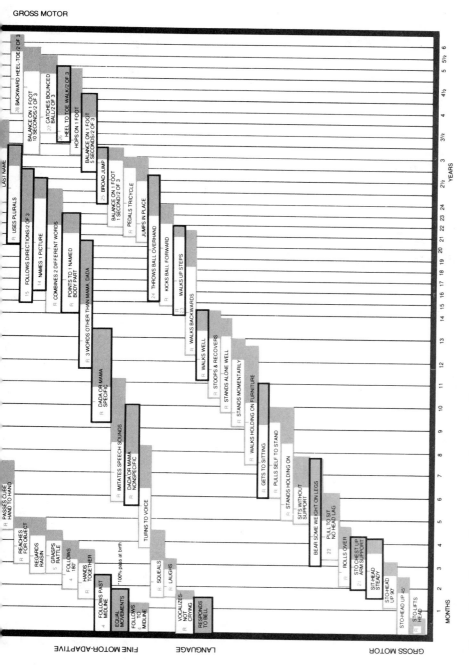

Figure 6-1. *Denver Developmental Screening Test.*

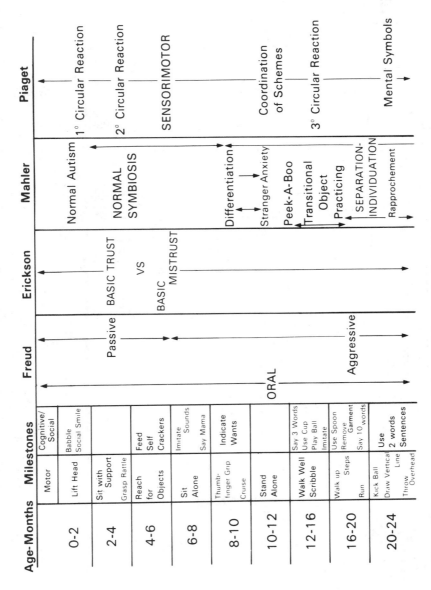

Figure 6-2. *Correspondence of stages of development—birth to 2 years.*

3. *Adaptation:* A dynamic process combining *assimilation* and *accommodation.*
   Assimilation: The tendency to use current schemes to deal with the environment, in both familiar and new situations.
   Accommodation: The modification of cognitive structures according to environmental pressures.
4. The need for action to precede intellect.

Despite his small and select database, and methods that would be considered primitive by today's standards, Piaget's theories have been highly influential in the study of child development. Although subsequent research has found that, under the proper conditions, children can solve problems much earlier, and developmental stages are far more flexible, less discrete, and more responsive to context and affect than Piaget believed, his notion that thought and reasoning change *qualitatively* as well as *quantitatively* with development has remained important in our understanding of intellectual development.

PRENATAL DEVELOPMENT

The prenatal period is an important one, for both parents and fetus. The child's endowment at birth depends on both his/her genetic makeup and the prenatal environment. Subsequent influences include the birth process, medical interventions, and later social, emotional, and physical factors in the environment. Even in utero the fetus's heart rate responds to chemical, auditory, and emotional stimuli to the mother, and habituates to repeated exposure to these stimuli.

Risks to the Fetus

Prematurity
Some of the causes of prematurity include multiple pregnancy, fetal abnormalities, and structural or endocrine abnormalities in the mother. Obstetricians and neonatologists are increasingly able to prevent or treat prematurity and its sequelae, such as respiratory distress syndrome and hemorrhage into the central nervous system.

Intrauterine Growth Retardation
These babies are born small for their gestational age, and may be delayed in other areas as well. Contributing factors include maternal malnutrition, drugs taken by the mother (including alcohol and nicotine), placental abnormality, infection, and maternal disease such as hypertension.

Genetic Abnormality
Genetic counseling prior to pregnancy or new methods of prenatal diagnosis can reduce the incidence of babies born with a chromosomal aberration (e.g., Down's syndrome) or inherited abnormality of a single gene (e.g., Tay-Sachs disease). Neona-

tal screening has significantly reduced the sequelae of other genetic disorders, such as phenylketonuria.

Maternal Disease

Early and thorough prenatal care reduces the risk to the fetus by identification and medical management of maternal diabetes, hypertension, or other disorders. Immunization protects the fetus from the often devastating effects of maternal rubella infection. Intrauterine infection with the AIDS virus, transmitted across the placenta from an infected mother, is a rapidly increasing problem.

Maternal Ingestion of Substances Harmful to the Fetus

The science of teratology is concerned with the effects on the baby of maternal cigarette smoking, and use of alcohol, drugs, or prescribed or over-the-counter medications. Fetal alcohol syndrome, the best studied, is characterized by varying degrees of pre- and postnatal growth retardation, dysmorphic features, other physical malformations, below normal intellect, and attentional and learning disabilities (Steinhausen and Spohr, 1986).

Babies born to mothers addicted to narcotics have low birth weights and show a neonatal abstinence syndrome consisting of extreme irritability, lability, and overreactivity to environmental stimuli. Evidence is increasing of long-term effects on behavior and intelligence. As cocaine and "crack" abuse has reached epidemic proportions, the number of infants affected in utero continues to increase.

Emotional Factors

Emotional stress during pregnancy has been implicated in the genesis of birth defects and complications of pregnancy and delivery, as well as in later abnormalities. Animal data suggest that the mechanism is by way of alterations in levels of steroid hormones.

Complications in the Newborn Period

Sophisticated medical care in the newborn period can avert or moderate the harmful effects of birth injury, prematurity, hypoxia, hyperbilirubinemia, hypothyroidism, and infection.

Outcome

Although problems during pregnancy, birth, and the neonatal period may have physical, cognitive, and/or emotional sequelae, many studies of high-risk infants, especially those with uncomplicated premature birth, have shown considerable improvement with time, resulting in far less impairment than originally expected.

The ability of "intelligence" testing in infancy to predict results of testing of intellectual functions at school age is controversial. Changes have been attributed to both the remarkable resiliency of the central nervous system of the human infant and the marked differences in types of abilities able to be tested at different ages. At best, scores on specific tests in infancy account for 50% of the variation among children in specific cognitive and language abilities at age 2 (Siegel, 1981). Accuracy of predicted IQ decreases as the time interval increases, in part because the caretaking environment can powerfully exacerbate or ameliorate early damage.

Mental Retardation

Mental retardation is defined by a score on a standardized intelligence test (Table 6-1) that is significantly below average (i.e., IQ score below approximately 70), together with significant impairment in adaptive functioning, which has its onset in childhood. Mental retardation has a wide variety of causes, summarized in Table 6-2.

Mild mental retardation (IQ from 50–55 to 70), by far the most common category, is not usually attributable to a known medical cause, but rather to a combination of factors including inheritance from parents whose genetic endowment is below average, lack of cognitive stimulation, malnutrition of mothers and children, inadequate prenatal and pediatric medical care, and environmental toxins such as lead. *Primary prevention* (reduction in the numbers of retarded children) includes such efforts as improved family planning and prenatal care, and education of mothers, as well as larger societal efforts to reduce poverty. Immunization against rubella, genetic counseling, prenatal diagnosis through such techniques as ultrasound and

Table 6–1 **Tests of Intelligence**

Standard IQ Tests

Kaufman Assessment Battery for Children (K-ABC)
   age 2½ to 12½
   Less dependent on culturally based information and schooling
Stanford–Binet
   Age 2 to adulthood
   Heavily language based
Wechsler Preschool and Primary Scale of Intelligence (WPPSI)
   Age 4 to 6½
Wechsler Intelligence Scale for Children—Revised (WISC-R)
   Age 6 to 16
Wechsler Adult Intelligence Scale (WAIS)
   Age 16 and over

Tests for Specialized Uses

Bayley Scales of Infant Development
   Age 3 to 30 months
   Estimates cognitive developmental level in very young children
Leiter International Performance Scale
   Nonverbal test for use with children who are deaf, autistic, or do not
      speak English
   Not as well standardized as other IQ tests
Peabody Picture Vocabulary Test (PPVT-R)
   Brief test of receptive language abilities, often used as screening test of
      IQ

Table 6–2 **Significant Causes of Mental Retardation**

Genetic Factors

Chromosomal abnormalities
Down's syndrome
Cri-du-Chat syndrome
Many other rare named syndromes
*Single gene abnormalities—inborn errors of metabolism**
Phenylketonuria (PKU)
Maple syrup urine disease (Menkes' disease)
Homocystinuria
Tyrosinemia
Galactosemia
Hypothyroidism
Genetic endowment at the lower end of the distribution

Prenatal Factors

Maternal chronic illness
Diabetes mellitus
Anemia
Emphysema
Hypertension
Malnutrition
Maternal infection passed to fetus
Rubella (German measles)
Cytomegalic inclusion disease
Syphilis
Toxoplasmosis
AIDS
Maternal ingestion of toxic substances
Alcohol
Narcotics
Cocaine/Crack cocaine
Nicotine

Obstetric Complications

Acquired Cognitive Deficit in Infancy or Childhood

Severe malnutrition
Infection
　Encephalitis
　Meningitis
Head trauma
Lead intoxication
Asphyxia
Brain tumors

Environmental and Sociocultural Influences

* *Note:* newborn screening techniques are available to permit early identification and
treatment, which will prevent sequelae of these six disorders.
(Data from Kaplan HI, Sadock BJ: Synopsis of Psychiatry, 5th ed. Baltimore, Williams &
Wilkins, 1988)

amniocentesis, and newborn screening for disorders such as phenylketonuria can reduce the incidence of more severe forms of mental retardation.

Secondary prevention focuses on early identification and intervention, to reverse or minimize developmental delays. *Tertiary prevention,* minimizing complications and maximizing adaptive functioning, requires specialized treatment and rehabilitative services.

Parental Response to Physical Illness or Handicap in the Newborn

The parents of an ill or damaged infant must go through a process of mourning the loss of their expected healthy child. The stages are similar to those following a death: anger, denial, and grief (see also Chapter 7). Parents must resign themselves to the loss of their fantasies of an ideal child and begin to adapt their expectations to the child's realistic potential.

Medical problems in an infant may be viewed by the parent (and others) as a negative reflection on the parent. Parental guilt is an additional factor, especially for genetic diseases or complications, which may be attributed (rightly or wrongly) to maternal behavior. The parents' anger, resentment, guilt, and/or denial may interfere with their ability to work together with the pediatric team. Parents may find it difficult to relate to an infant with medical problems, especially if the baby's survival is in question.

Realistic additional caretaking and financial burdens may stress parents beyond their ability to cope. Parents with unresolved negative feelings, overwhelming stressors, insufficient emotional or material support, and/or inadequate understanding of the medical situation may be unable to comply with medical regimens once they take the baby home. Marriages may break down under the stress of the multiple demands of caring for a physically or mentally handicapped child. The importance of the primary physician in providing ongoing emotional support and assistance in obtaining appropriate services cannot be overemphasized.

INFANCY: THE FIRST YEAR

The neonate is much more competent than previously thought, although there is considerable variation among normal infants. Historically, the infant was viewed as passive. In the earliest psychoanalytic theories, the child was seen as acted upon by instinctual drives. Behaviorists saw the baby as shaped by external stimuli and contingencies, or consequences. It is now recognized that babies are active participants in developing relationships and in influencing their environment with strong biogenetic endowments that are heterogenous. Even in the first days of life, the newborn has considerable sensory, motor, intellectual, communicative, and affective abilities, which progress rapidly in the next 12 months.

Physical Development in Infancy

Neurologic

As neurons sprout multiple, branching dendrites, cortical synapses develop rapidly in the first year of life, to a number greater than in adults. Excess synapses are subsequently "pruned" to reach adult numbers.

Even newborns have remarkable sensory abilities. Visual fixation is possible within a few hours after birth. For the first month, babies are able to focus on objects only at a distance of about 8 inches. By age 4 months, they are able to accommodate visually as well as an adult.

The 1-week-old infant can distinguish and prefers complex visual patterns and movement. Infants seem to be genetically programmed to pay attention to complex patterns such as the human face, and can not only visually fix on, but even follow with their eyes and head, a drawing that resembles a human face. Within the first month of life, the infant can use visual information to modulate motor responses such as reaching and grasping.

Neonates can search with their eyes for the source of an interesting sound, especially speech. Within a week of birth, infants can distinguish their mother's voice and the smell of her breast milk from that of another woman. The pattern of the infant's sucking indicates preference for sweet liquids.

The senses of proprioception, pressure, and touch are all functional at birth. Despite evidence that the neonate perceives pain, it has been an unfortunately common practice to perform circumcision or even major surgery *without* anesthesia!

Gross motor

At birth, the neonate is unable to reach or grasp purposefully, and has primitive motor reflexes. By 16 weeks, the infant can hold up his/her head. The child sits with support at 28 weeks, and sits alone, creeps, and pulls to stand by 40 weeks. Standing alone is achieved around 48 weeks. By 12 months of age, the child is walking with support (called "cruising").

Sleep

Most infants sleep through the night (or at least do not fuss when they waken) by 6 to 9 months of age. Up to half of all infants, however, have irregular sleep patterns and occasional or persistent night wakening throughout the first year.

Physiologic

The first year is a period of rapid physical growth, with an increase in weight of approximately 300%.

Cognitive Development in Infancy

Piaget's first stage, the *sensorimotor,* covers approximately the first 2 years of life. In the first 4 months of age, the infant begins with *primary circular reactions,* which are motor reflexes or habits centered on his/her body. These are initially quite simple (e.g., putting the thumb in the mouth and sucking), but become increasingly complex as the baby uses trial and error to attempt to repeat an interesting but accidental result. At this stage children are able to turn toward sounds, engage in mutual imitation of sounds, and to follow a moving object.

Secondary circular reactions emerge in the 4- to 10-month-old, as schemes are extended to the external environment to reproduce interesting chance events (e.g., shaking legs makes the crib mobile jiggle). The baby is able to follow the expected path of a moving object that disappears, and to recognize an object, even if parts are hidden. By 10 to 12 months, babies begin to combine secondary schemes to reach a goal. At this age, the infant can overcome simple obstacles, perceive a connection between events, and anticipate the next in a familiar series. The child learns that an object exists even when out of sight (*object permanence*) and searches actively for an object that disappears. This is facilitated by the rapid enhancement of memory between 8 and 12 months of age.

Communication in Infancy

In addition to cries stimulated by pain, hunger, fear, and so forth, babies engage in crying that seems to serve the function of discharge of tension. This type of crying occurs at discrete, regular periods of the day, most often in the late afternoon and evening, for up to 2 to 3 hours. It can be distinguished from other crying, and the usual means of comfort are unsuccessful. It is most noticeable from 3 to 10 weeks, corresponding to "3-month colic." All normal babies demonstrate this type of crying to some extent, although there is wide variation in duration and intensity. Anticipatory guidance can help parents deal with the anxiety and tension these fussy periods cause, and avert the development of more serious problems (Brazelton, 1962).

Between 5 and 10 months, the infant begins to babble and play with sounds, both alone and together with an adult.

Affective Development in Infancy

Attachment

In exploring the development of the infant's relationship with the mother, it has become increasingly clear how powerfully the infant can influence adult behavior. The term *attachment* is used to describe the infant's behaviors, feelings, and cognitions directed toward mother (or mothering figure). Attachment is an affectional or emotional tie formed between one person and another, which endures over time and leads to seeking physical closeness to the important figure. Attachments are highly specific, although the infant may form an attachment to more than one person. *Attachment behavior* promotes proximity or contact. *Bonding* is a term unfortunately used rather indiscriminately, but should be reserved for the mother's positive feelings and behaviors toward the infant.

John Bowlby and his colleague, James Robertson, became interested in attachment by way of their work with children separated from their parents by World War II, or for briefer periods by hospitalization or foster care. Bowlby (1969) drew from his own observations as well as from ethology (see Chap. 10), evolutionary theory, psychoanalysis, cognitive–developmental theory, and systems theory in his conceptualization of the purpose and mechanisms of attachment formation. He took a

Darwinian view that the inborn behavioral systems characteristic of a species enhance survival, and proposed that the biologic function of attachment behavior is protection from environmental danger, by ensuring parental interest and proximity. In the human infant, he observed behaviors that are initially reflexive (e.g., following with the eyes, clinging, sucking, and smiling). These behaviors, maintained and promoted by cognitions and feelings, are used increasingly in a social interactive context with the parent.

As early as the first hours of life, the parents and child can engage in a reciprocal interaction, which initiates the development of attachment. At 6 to 8 weeks of age, the infant achieves a true "social smile" when he/she selectively recognizes the mother's smile and smiles in response, producing a powerful affective response in the mother. The strength of these tendencies, their likely neurobiologic underpinnings, and the remarkable adaptability of the human infant can be seen in blind babies, who show a specific smiling response to their mother's voice. Other infant behaviors that signify and strengthen attachment include crying, vocalizing, looking, greeting, and clinging, which are selectively directed at the mother (or other primary attachment figure).

Although the process can begin soon after birth, attachment is not instantaneous, but develops over time. In order to develop a stable attachment, the infant must have sufficient contact with a mothering person, the ability to distinguish the mothering person, and at least the beginning of the conception that a person has an independent existence even when not present. Once the first attachment has formed, the infant can generalize to a small number of other people. Illness or handicap in the child, physical or emotional illness in the parent, or parental lack of sensitivity to the needs of the baby can all impair attachment formation.

The realization that attachment and bonding can begin immediately after birth has been influential in humanizing hospital maternity procedures and in increasing opportunities for parental contact with premature and ill newborns. In many circles, however, there has been an unfortunate overemphasis on the "critical period," a very brief period of time immediately following birth after which formation of attachments and parenting ability were said to be impaired. This notion has added to the stresses on adoptive parents and parents of ill babies. There is a lack of objective data to support this so-called critical "sensitive period" in the *first hours* of life or the necessity for extended immediate contact with the neonate in order to establish a secure affective relationship between the baby and either mother or father.

Goldberg (1983) summarizes the evidence and its implications:

> Even among those who feel that early contact has been overrated, there are few who would argue that it is unimportant. Initial contacts are one phase in an ongoing process, and parents should be supported in this phase as well as others. Therefore, when not medically contraindicated, the opportunity for early interaction in the delivery or recovery room should be offered in order to make the experience of birth more humane, more positive, and more rewarding for parents.
>
> Second, individual differences in enthusiasm for immediate or even extended contact are normal. Insofar as possible, it is desireable to offer or allow contacts to occur when comfortable and convenient for the par-

ents. The mother who wants or needs time to rest before holding her baby should not be made to feel that she is abnormal for not wanting to do so immediately. The mother who does not prefer rooming in or who does not keep the baby in her room as much as possible should also be made to feel comfortable with her decision.

Finally, the notion of early contact as critical rather than potentially beneficial needs to be dispelled. The emphasis on "early bonding" has already created an expectation on the part of many parents that if they do not have this experience they have somehow failed and will never be fine parents (p 1379).

Erickson identified the establishment of *basic trust* as the primary affective task of this developmental period (see Chap. 7). This period roughly corresponds to the current "oral stage" of development discussed in Chapter 3.

Early Attachment Behavior and the Effects of Deprivation in Infancy

Rene Spitz's pioneering work on *hospitalism* and *anaclitic depression* identified the devastating effects on infants of separation from their mother when compounded by lack of stimulation (Spitz, 1945, 1946). Absence of a suitable mothering figure prevents or disrupts the formation of attachments. Severe maternal deprivation can lead to a decrease in intelligence, impaired ability to trust or to form meaningful interpersonal relationships, and even death. *Failure to thrive,* caused by insufficient or inappropriate mothering, is a syndrome characterized by lack of growth despite adequate access to food, listlessness, and delayed cognitive, social, and motor development.

Mary Ainsworth pioneered in identifying and measuring attachment behaviors as indicators of the strength and security of attachment. She and others have found that insecure, anxious, or weak attachment may predict developmental problems later in childhood. A *securely attached* infant experiences separation anxiety when left by the mother. The baby seeks proximity and contact with the mother, especially when frightened or in a new situation. When with the mother, the baby is able to play and explore comfortably. When left, the infant protests or follows.

There are several types of *insecure attachment,* which are believed to have negative implications for the development of trust and healthy relationships, even into adulthood. A phenomenon Ainsworth called *anxious resistant attachment* is believed to be promoted by parental inconsistency. The parent is available and helpful at some times but not others. There are frequent separations. Threats of abandonment are used to control the child, leading to uncertainty and separation anxiety in the child. Children demonstrating what Ainsworth calls *anxious avoidant attachment* expect to be rejected by others. This pattern is believed to result from constant rebuffs from the mother when approached for comfort or protection. Problems in attachment are seen clinically as a spectrum from mild to more serious and is most extreme in the case of severe abuse, neglect, or prolonged institutionalization. Mothers of insecurely attached infants have been observed to be less attuned to the baby's needs, often not giving assistance when needed, or intruding with help when the child did not need it. Others discourage the infant's efforts at exploration and autonomy. The pattern of attachment seen in the first year has been correlated with observations at age 3½ and 6 years (Bowlby, 1988).

Problems in attachment phases of development may be manifested clinically in later childhood, adolescence, and adulthood by persons who have difficulty in forming close, lasting emotionally intimate relationships. Such persons may have "learned," by way of the inconsistency of the mother, to anticipate rejection and the emotional distress and pain that accompanies it. Hence, closeness with other people may be viewed as an inherently risky proposition from the emotional standpoint where the chances of rejection or disappointment are always present. Anxiety over being rejected or abandoned emotionally may lead to a defensive posture of maintaining one's emotional distance, avoiding intimacy and commitment to avoid the feelings that accompany rejection and disappointment.

Stranger anxiety develops between 9 and 18 months, not only in response to strangers but to anyone other than the mothering adult(s). At this age, the infant can remember the mother's face, compare it with the stranger, and realize the difference and the absence of the mother.

It is clear that the first year is a crucial time for forming the first attachment, after which the process is much more difficult. This has important implications for the care of young children who must be placed outside of the home.

Attachment behavior is exaggerated under stress from physical discomfort, fear, or separation from the mother. Bowlby (1975) described the sequence of the baby's emotions on separation: first *protest*, with acute distress and crying; then misery and grief, which he termed *despair;* followed by apparent apathy and disinterest, or *detachment.* Brief separations are benign, but as separations become longer, repeated, and/or accompanied by other stressors, the likelihood of emotional sequelae increases.

A favorite baby game, "Peek-a-boo," demonstrates the child's egocentric cognitive perspective (if I can't see something, it isn't there) used in the practicing of separation from the parent. To the infant, he or she is making the adult come and go, thereby gaining control of the experience and of the anxiety about being left alone.

Many of the details of attachment theory need to be rethought in view of the current rarity of "traditional" families (i.e., two married parents, with the mother as full-time homemaker and the almost exclusive caretaker of the baby). Recent data from a middle class sample demonstrate that 1-year-old infants of mothers who worked full time in the first year of life were as likely to be securely attached to their mothers as infants whose mothers did not work outside the home (Zimmerman and Bernstein, 1983).

Although infants and children may show remarkable resistance to developmental problems related to attachment, probably due to the infant's genetic endowment or compensating factors elsewhere in the family system, developmental trauma in this period may have lasting effects on the personality and vulnerability to childhood and adult psychiatric illness. In Chapter 9, van der Kolk discusses the scientific evidence for the lifelong consequences of developmental trauma during this stage of life.

Separation–Individuation

Mahler's theory of separation–individuation is covered in detail in Chapter 3. Wolman and Thompson, in Chapter 7, describe how the thematic paradigm of separation–individuation can be repeated throughout the life cycle. More recent data about infant behavior and capabilities, however, have cast serious doubt about some of the details of the stages, particularly the stage of so-called normal autism popularized by psychoanalytic object relations theorists.

The Transitional Object

By the end of first year, many children have chosen what Winnicott called a *transitional object:* a toy, blanket, pillow or piece of clothing, usually soft, to which the child is very attached, and uses to comfort him/herself, most often at times of separation or going to sleep. It represents both the child and the mother. Whether or not a child uses a specific transitional object has not been found to have prognostic significance.

Temperament

Children are born with general temperaments that appear to be genetically endowed. The concept of temperament, the "how" or style of behavior, was developed by Thomas and Chess (1986). Their New York Longitudinal Study followed 133 children from 85 middle class families from infancy through young adulthood. Nine relatively stable dimensions or traits could be identified in infancy.

1. Activity level.
2. Rhythmicity (regularity and predictability of biologic functions).
3. Approach or withdrawal to novel stimuli.
4. Adaptability to environmental change.
5. Intensity of reaction.
6. Threshold of responsiveness (intensity of stimulation required to evoke a response).
7. Quality of mood (positive, neutral, or negative).
8. Distractibility.
9. Attention span and persistence.

Many of the children studied were found to demonstrate clusters of these variables (Table 6-3). The *easy* child is a delight to parents, and usually at low risk for emotional or behavior problems. *Difficult* children are at highest risk (70%) of developing behavior problems. In the New York Longitudinal Study, difficult children were 10% of the total sample, but constituted 23% of the children with behavior problems. Children characterized as *slow to warm up* are also at risk, which can be significantly reduced by sensitive management by parents and teachers.

Especially significant is the temperamental "match" or "goodness of fit" between the child and the parent's own temperament, expectations, and child-rearing

Table 6-3 **Temperamental Clusters**

Easy

Positive mood
Regular biologic rhythms
Adaptable
Low intensity
Positive approach to novelty

Difficult

Negative mood
Irregular biologic rhythms
Slow to adapt
Intense reactions
Negative response to novelty

Slow to Warm Up

Negative responses to new stimuli
Mild intensity
Gradual adaptation after repeated contact

(Data from Thomas A, Chess S: Temperament in Clinical Practice. New York, Guilford Press, 1986)

style. Continuity of temperament is found when there is a stable pattern of interplay between the child and the environment. With a less fixed pattern, temperamental characteristics can change for the better or worse.

Chess and Thomas's work has inspired a substantial body of additional research in the measurement and properties of temperamental characteristics. Twin studies suggest a substantial genetic component to both temperament and to other personality variables. Children identified at age 2 as extremely inhibited, quiet, and restrained in unfamiliar situations tend to remain shy and socially avoidant at age 7. They tend to have greater sympathetic reactivity than outgoing children, as measured by heart rate acceleration and early morning salivary cortisol levels. Two-year-olds who are uninhibited tend to remain fearless and outgoing (Kagan et al, 1988).

Response of Child and Family to Physical Illness in Infancy

When infants less than 6 months old are hospitalized, they are most upset by change in the usual routine. It is helpful to have the parents do as much of the care as possible, and to arrange for consistency of nurses. For the older infant who has formed strong differential attachments, separation may be traumatic, especially in the foreign hospital environment and when accompanied by physical discomfort and medical procedures. Stranger anxiety adds to the baby's distress. The infant's immature cognitive development exacerbates the problem, because explanations are of no use. The constant presence of a parent is extremely important. In the absence of an attachment figure, the baby's thrashing, refusal to eat, and inability to sleep may have serious medical consequences. Fortunately, most pediatric hospital settings not only permit, but encourage parents to "live in" while their young child is hospitalized.

Green and Solnit (1964) have described a *vulnerable child syndrome*, occurring after a child survives a potentially fatal illness. The family may have completed anticipatory mourning, and have difficulty reintegrating the child. Alternatively, the child may subsequently be overprotected and underdisciplined, with resulting immaturity and difficulty with age-appropriate separation and development.

THE TODDLER: AGES 1 TO 3

Figures 6-2 and 6-3 summarize development in this period along multiple lines.

Physical Development of the Toddler

Gross Motor

By 30 months, the child not only stands, but walks and runs with ease.

Fine Motor–Adaptive

During this period, there is a rapid increase in fine motor abilities, such as using a crayon, and in eye–hand coordination. Young toddlers show increasing interest in feeding themselves, first with fingers, then using utensils. The child's reduced nutritional needs, resulting from much slower physical growth than in the first year, compounded by increasing interest in activity and in the environment, lead to dramatic decreases in appetite. The parent who views this with alarm and focuses excessively on eating can promote a feeding problem. It is important to avoid turning mealtime into a power struggle. The child who consumes excessive quantities of milk or of "empty calorie foods" can develop serious deficiencies in iron or other essential nutrients. Overindulgence in highly sweetened foods can result in obesity and/or tooth decay.

Toilet Training

Toilet training usually occurs between ages 2 and 3. Prerequisites include regularity of bowel and bladder function, the ability to sense bladder and rectal fullness, the ability to control the sphincter muscles, the psychologic ability to delay, the wish to imitate adults and to please the parents, and the ability to communicate the need to use the toilet. A child reported to have been trained earlier is usually a very regular child whom the parent has learned to "catch," by putting him/her on the potty at predictable times of elimination. When toilet training is started too early, the resulting learning process is longer, and often more difficult. Capitalizing on the child's wish to imitate adults and using rewards such as praise and small treats can facilitate learning. Punitive or threatening methods of training should not be used under any circumstances. Most children establish control of urination during the day by age 2½ and at night by age 3½ to 4. Approximately 10% of 6-year-olds (predominately boys)

Age-Years	Milestones	Freud	Erickson	Mahler	Piaget
2	Solitary play / Toilet Trained	Anal			
3	Copy Circle. Parallel Play / Know First and Last Names	Urethral / Phallic	Autonomy vs. Shame & Doubt		
4	Copy Cross Know Primary Colors Cooperative Play	Oedipal	Initiative vs. Guilt	Firm Object Constancy	Preoperational
5	Draw 3 part Man / Copy Square				
6	Draw 6 part Man / Print Name				
7	Copy Diamond / No Longer reverse Letters	Latency	Industry vs. Inferiority		
8	Jump Rope, Tie Shoes / Ride 2 Wheel Bike				Concrete Operations
9	Define abstract words				
10					
11	Puberty-Girls		Identity vs. Diffusion		
12					Formal Operations
13	Puberty-Boys	Adolescence			
14					
15	Repeat 6 digits forward and 5 digits backward				
16					
17					

Figure 6-3. *Correspondence of stages of development—2 to 18 years.*

however, still wet the bed. Late attainment of nocturnal control tends to be familial. Almost all children have achieved bowel control by age 4.

Sleep

A recent study of sleep habits in middle class 1 to 3-year-olds found an average daily sleep total of 12 hours, including a 2-hour nap (Crowell et al, 1987). In 1 week, 10% of the children reported a nightmare, and 7% experienced a *night terror (pavor nocturnus*—see below). Twenty-one percent of 18 to 23-month-olds awakened during the night. Thirty-one percent of the 24 to 29-month-olds took more than 30 minutes to fall asleep on more than three nights in a week. Children aged 30 to 36 months were most likely to have difficulty settling (16%) and to express fears of the dark (24%). All children in this age group tend to use a nightlight.

Cognitive Development of the Toddler

Piaget's Stages

The *sensorimotor stage* continues. In the first half of the second year, the *tertiary circular reaction* develops. This is the attempt to produce novelty for its own sake, by extending existing schemes to a variety of objects. The *preoperational stage* begins in the third year (see section entitled "Early Childhood" for description).

Object permanence, the conviction that an object continues to exist even when out of sight, is solidified around 18 to 20 months of age. Children understand this about persons, especially their parents, before things.

Milestones

Eighteen-month-olds can recognize themselves in mirrors and pictures. By the latter half of the second year, the child is able to retain and use mental symbols, a necessary precursor to the use of language.

Increased interest in the environment and ability to explore, in the absence of judgment or understanding of consequences, put toddlers at extremely high risk for accidents. Parents must avoid overly restricting the child's exploration or responding punitively to inadvertent damage of objects, while ensuring safety. Systematically childproofing the house and using tactics that distract the child into other activities and projects can reduce both danger and parental power struggles.

Speech and Language of the Toddler

Development

At 1 year of age, most children use two or more words besides mama and dada, and understand simple commands. Over the next 6 months, toddlers make extensive use of jargon (i.e., sounds that resemble speech, but are unintelligible). Most 2-year-olds have a 300-word vocabulary, use phrases and two-word sentences, and can point to body parts when named. Around 30 months, most children can use pronouns correctly. In all children, comprehension precedes expressive abilities.

Some *echolalia* (repetition of overheard words or phrases) is normal into the third year. Developmental dysfluency or repetition of words or phrases is normal between ages 2 and 4. This should be differentiated from *stuttering,* which includes blocking and repeating of sounds, with motor and subsequent emotional tension, and eventual severe anxiety about speech.

Normal children vary widely in their rate and style of language acquisition. A hearing test and a language assessment are indicated, however, if an 18-month-old uses no words or just "mama" and "dada," and doesn't point to what he/she wants. Although a few normal children are simply late talkers, such a delay could be caused by deafness, aphasia, mental retardation, or autistic disorder. Concern is warranted if a 2-year-old is not putting two words together, has a vocabulary of less than 20 words, has speech that is unintelligible to the parents, or does not understand commands or questions without gestures.

Affective Development of the Toddler

Object Relations
In the first half of the second year, a phenomenon that Emde and colleagues have called *social referencing* appears, in which the infant looks to the parent for emotional cues about a novel event.

Mahler's description of this period is discussed in detail in Chapter 3. To briefly recapitulate, as the *practicing subphase* continues (12 to 18 months), the toddler moves away from the parent to explore. The child then tends to return frequently to "refuel" (i.e., to establish emotional contact and to refresh his/her internal image of the mother). A securely attached child will be able to use the mother as a base from which to investigate the environment. In the *rapprochement subphase* (16 to 24 months), children's growing realization of their separateness, physical ability to move away from the parent, and their own helplessness leads to intense ambivalence about their attachment and dependency needs. Many toddlers increase clinging to parents, tantrums, thumb or finger sucking, and need for their transitional object. The third year sees *consolidation* and resolution, as the child becomes comfortable with brief separations. (Variations on the separation–individuation pattern in development may be repeated in later life cycle stages of development such as adolescence and early adulthood [see Chap. 7].)

The third year is marked by the child's struggle for autonomy and separateness from the parents. This may be seen in the form of negativity and tantrums, as children practice making decisions and asserting themselves, but become overwhelmed by feelings that are unable to be expressed verbally. The middle of this year is the height of the "terrible twos," although the duration and intensity vary greatly among children. Some degree of negativism is essential in the child's development of a sense of independence and individuality. Children benefit from consistent, firm, but sympathetic limits. Tantrums should be ignored, and *never* rewarded, to avoid transforming an expression of frustration into a device for manipulating adults. Whenever possible, direct confrontations should be avoided. It is helpful if parents can avoid taking the toddler's obstinant behavior as a personal affront and not take a punitive or rigidly overly controlling approach to prove "who's boss." The most effective means of handling defiant behavior is usually by brief periods of "time out" or in the case of tantrums, by ignoring. Corporal or physical punishment should not be used (see Chap. 4).

Emotions and Mechanisms of Defense

In the third year of life, a sense of *empathy* for others begins to emerge. The child also has a growing understanding of emotions and their correspondence with verbal labels. *Reaction formation* is a defense mechanism that typically appears in this period, as seen in children who have recently been toilet trained and become excessively upset by messiness. This is presumed to protect the child against wishes to urinate and defecate at will. The development of defense mechanisms is discussed in a psychoanalytic framework in Chapter 3.

Fears

The toddler's lack of experience, small size, and helplessness compared to adults foster the development of fears, such as loud noises, animals, the dark, and separation from parents. Another common fear is of the bathtub, exacerbated by toddlers' inability to judge relative sizes and determine that they could *not* actually fit down the drain.

Gender-Related Issues

Core morphologic or gender identity is the usually unshakable conviction of being a male or a female, which develops through a complex interaction of physiologic and environmental factors (Money, 1987). It can be seen around 18 months, or even earlier, and is often established by 24 to 30 months. Absolute integration of gender identity can be expected by age 3. While psychologic and sociocultural factors play an important role in shaping gender identity, for most persons, biologic gender is the determinant of identity as a male or female.

In utero, sexual differentiation proceeds in the female direction in the absence of masculinizing hormones (androgens). Androgens alter the development of the central nervous system, as well as the genitalia. Normally, all of the child's gender-related characteristics are consistent: chromosomes, prenatal hormones, gonads (ovaries and testes), internal and external genitalia, postnatal hormones, and secondary sex characteristics (developing at puberty). (See also Chap. 5.)

Cultural factors are extremely important in the development of *gender role behavior*: behavior that is considered by society to be appropriate for one sex or another. Examples for children include speech, physical mannerisms, gait, clothing, play activities, and playmates. Adults treat boys and girls differently from infancy (Shepherd-Look, 1982). Boys are picked up more as newborns, are handled more roughly than girls, and are more frequently engaged in rough-and-tumble play. Mothers talk more to girls than to boys. Adults offer different toys to boys and girls, and by age 1, toy preference along stereotypic gender lines is established. Beginning in the second year, fathers pay significantly more attention to boys than to girls. By age 2, boys show a clear preference for their fathers over their mothers (Hodapp and Mueller, 1982). Differential treatment and expectations continue throughout the course of development.

It has now been recognized that masculinity and femininity are not polar opposites, but orthogonal (independent) variables, each being found in varying amounts in both males and females. The interaction of physical and environmental factors in the development of gender identity and role behavior is complex. Some hints can be gleaned from the study of children with inconsistent gender-related factors. For example, girls whose mothers were treated with masculinizing progestogens during pregnancy are more likely to be tomboys, preferring intense outdoor play and male peers and avoiding doll play, but they are not more likely to become transsexual or homosexual.

Genetic females with congenital adrenal hyperplasia, a defect in cortisol synthesis that leads to pre- and postnatal excess of androgenic hormone precursor, are born with masculinized external genitalia and normal female internal organs. Clear, early gender assignment with consistent medical and surgical treatment can result in stable gender identity as *either* a male or a female, depending on initial assignment. Reassignment attempts fail if carried out after 18 months to 3 years.

Androgen-insensitivity syndrome (testicular feminization) in XY genetic males is characterized by insensitivity of all body cells to testosterone, leading to female-appearing external genitalia. These children are usually reared as females. Histologically normal but nonfunctional testes are removed to avoid virilization and increased risk of malignancy. If the child is treated as a normal girl, she will usually develop female gender identity, stereotypically feminine role behavior, and, in adolescence, sexual interest in males.

Tentative evidence from children prenatally exposed to treatment with estrogen and progestogen (to avoid loss of pregnancy) shows demasculinization of males and increased feminization of females.

Social Development of Toddlers

Early in this period, children are curious about other children. The first half of the third year sees the development of *parallel play* (i.e., solitary unrelated play conducted in pairs). Over the next 6 months, children begin to engage in *associative play*, with pairs or small groups of children, doing the same thing side by side, but not really interacting. Toddler play is based on sensorimotor activity: opening and shutting, emptying and filling, with more interest in the process than the product.

Response to Illness and Hospitalization During the Toddler Phase

Hospitalized toddlers react primarily to separation from their parents. They may react by rejecting parents when they visit, being aggressive toward parent surrogates (e.g., nurses), regressing in their toilet training, and/or refusing to eat. If parents are absent, children may develop depression, sleep disturbance, diarrhea, or vomiting. Fortunately, virtually all hospitals allow and encourage parents to stay with young children. The presence of a transitional object or other familiar items from home may be helpful.

Children with preexisting problems in development or in the parent–child relationship have more sustained difficulty, although a child who is weakly attached may have less immediate distress on separation. A neglected child may be indiscriminately eager for adult attention and stimulation.

Toddlers are also concerned about the intactness of their bodies, as seen in their great interest in bandages. Some children believe that body contents can leak out through a cut in the skin.

EARLY CHILDHOOD: AGES 3 TO 6

Physical Development in Early Childhood

Gross Motor

Most 3-year-olds can stand on one foot, jump, run smoothly, and climb stairs with alternate feet. They are beginning to show hand preference, and to be able to ride a tricycle. Four-year-olds should ride a tricycle well, climb on a jungle gym, and throw a ball overhand. By age 5, balance is better, and the child should be able to skip smoothly.

Fine Motor–Adaptive

The 3-year-old can build a tower of nine or ten blocks. By age 4, most children can button and lace, feed themselves neatly, pour from a pitcher, dress, and wash. Drawing ability progresses from copying a circle (3 years) to copying cross and drawing simple man with head, eyes, and legs (4 years) to copying a square and a triangle, and drawing a recognizable man with basic body parts (eyes, nose, mouth, body, arms, legs, and feet). The 5-year-old plans pictures in advance, and may include elaborate scenes or complex events.

Most children are dry at night by the latter half of the fourth year. They are able to use the toilet independently in the daytime, at least in familiar places.

Cognitive Development in Early Childhood

Piaget's Stages

The *preoperational stage* of intellectual development extends from approximately 2 to 7 years of age. The child learns to classify, to place objects in order (by trial and error), and to construct sets equivalent in number by matching one to one. The preoperational child is unable to deal with more than one dimension at a time, or to recognize that a person or thing conserves its identity when it undergoes minor variations in appearance. Problem solving is by trial and error, rather than by planned strategies.

The use of nonverbal mental symbols, followed by language, gives the child the ability to transcend space and time. This ability can be seen in the child's deferred imitation of actions, drawing scenes clearly based on memory, and meaningful use of words. *Symbolic play* appears. This is pretend or imaginative play with toys or acting out roles and stories. Toys are used to symbolize the real objects they resemble.

Private speech, which is egocentric and has a social intent but fails to communicate, precedes true social speech. The child still has private meanings for some words. Toddlers often use pronouns without referents, as if the listener knew to whom the pronoun referred without being told. The preoperational children are normally *egocentric* (i.e., children tend to relate everything to themselves). Piaget believed that the child was unaware of the point of view of the listener or even that the listener may have another point of view or different knowledge. More recent work has shown that 4-year-olds do speak differently to adults than they do to 2-year-olds, indicating an awareness of differences in ability. They are able to show some understanding of another's perspective, if the task is carefully designed.

Children this age often have difficulty understanding cause-and-effect relationships. Thinking tends to be *concrete*, with explanations often based on past experience, whether or not it is relevant. Reasoning is often *transductive* (attributing causality to juxtaposition in time or space) rather than *inductive* (from the particular to the general) or *deductive* (from the general to the particular). Piaget called this *phenomenalistic causality*.

Young children are *animistic* (i.e., they believe all events can be explained by the action of some humanlike agency or force, which wills things to happen for its own purposes). Words and actions are not fully differentiated. *Magical thinking*, the belief that words, thoughts, and wishes can cause events in the external world, is typical of the child in the preoperational stage. One may clearly see persistence of these childlike forms of thinking in adults who appear to have progressed beyond these stages to analytic and deductive forms of reasoning in approaching experience and life problems.

Four-year-olds have difficulty distinguishing truth from fiction. Even for 7-year-olds, wishes distort their thinking and perception of reality, which may be misinterpreted by adults as lying. A child who desperately wishes he had not broken his mother's vase may actually convince himself that he or she did not. This phenomenon may be seen in older children and even adolescents who are cognitively or emotionally immature or under great stress.

Moral development in the 3 to 6-year-old is characterized by *moral realism*: the belief in immanent justice, and the inevitability of punishment. Physical misfortunes and accidents are seen as punishment for wrongdoing (present at some time in all children, at least in thought). Piaget termed the morality of this stage *objective* (i.e., guilt is determined solely by the amount of damage, not the intent or motivation). For example, from the child's moral viewpoint, someone who spills a whole bottle of ink while trying to help set the table is more guilty than a person who spills a drop of ink while playing with a pen which he or she has been forbidden to touch. Young children are absolute in their judgment of right and wrong, and are unable to see positive and negative aspects of the same person or event.

Preoperational children do not know or follow the real rules of games, but nevertheless insist that they do. They believe that rules are originated by a godlike absolute authority, and are unchangeable. Children are more likely to follow parents' rules if they are highly identified with them (e.g., admire them, believe they take after them, and want to grow up to be like them). Hence, the ethical examples set by the parents in their own behavior is probably much more important that all of the externally imposed rules, prohibitions, and punishments that most parents traditionally emphasize in trying to train their children in moral behavior.

Milestones

Four-year-olds have little understanding of past and future. By age 5, there is a better understanding of yesterday and tomorrow, and an ability to carry over play activities from one day to the next. There is a beginning understanding of clock and calendar time. Five-year-olds can identify simple similarities among the differences between objects. Children at this age believe that death is reversible, like sleep.

Speech and Language in Early Childhood

Language permits mastering negative feelings by learning to put them into words instead of acting on them, yielding improved impulse control and ability to delay gratification.

Vocabulary develops at the average rate of nine new words per day until the age of 6! Three-year-olds ask constant questions for the sake of talking. They play with words, and use and understand prepositions like "in," "on," "under." Four-year-olds' articulation is still somewhat immature, but their speech should be largely intelligible in context. Word play includes crude puns. Complex parts of speech, such as adverbs, and more difficult prepositions and conjunctions appear. By 5 years old, articulation should be clear and correct, answers to questions more succinct and relevant, and questions fewer, more direct, and more meaningful. Correct finished sentences can be constructed, including hypothetical and conditional clauses. In this period, language development is ahead of the ability to understand concepts. Adults must be cautious not to assume that children understand more than they actually do.

Affective Development in Early Childhood

Object Relations

Mahler proposed that firm emotional *object constancy*, the ability to maintain a positive inner image of an important person despite the level of need or satisfaction, is established by around 36 months (see Chap. 3). There is variation, however, depending on previous experience and the character of the mother–child relationship. Under a stress such as hospitalization, previously attained object constancy can be temporarily lost.

Day Care

As changing societal expectations for women and economic necessity lead to ever-increasing numbers of working mothers, the issue of day care becomes more crucial. In 1986, 7.8 million preschool children in the United States had mothers working outside the home; the projected number for 1990 is 10 million (US Bureau of the Census, 1987). It is anticipated that by 1990 75% of all American mothers with children at home will be in the work force, with the most rapidly increasing group the mothers of children under 1 year old (Zigler and Hall, 1988). In 1986, only 30% of preschool children were cared for in their own homes, with 41% cared for in someone else's home, and 15% in group day care (US Bureau of the Census, 1987).

The effects of day care are difficult to study because of the inability to form appropriate control groups by randomly assigning children to care by their mother or various forms of day care. Mothers who choose (or are able) to stay home are different in many ways from those who are employed outside of the home. A recent summary of research on day care (Zigler and Hall, 1988) found that outcome depended on the amount of time spent in day care, and the quality of the day care setting, especially the staff : child ratio and stability of caretakers. Other important factors were the mother's feelings about working and about her job, maternal stress, family financial status, parental absence, stability in the home, the quality of the child's attachment, and the child's temperament. Individual children vary in their response to day care. Some studies have found children who have been in group day care to be more social, assertive, and aggressive (especially boys). On the other hand, some children may become anxious. Children have not been found to be more likely to become primarily attached to the day care provider rather than the parent. There are, however, indications that some children in out-of-home care prior to the age of 1 are more likely to be insecurely attached to their mothers and to show a higher degree of oppositionality and noncompliance at age 2.

Fears
Normal fears include the dark, animals, bodily harm, monsters, ghosts, and death. Cognitive development at this age does not permit the use of sophisticated psychological defenses to control anxiety in the face of perceived danger.

Gender-Related Issues
The learning of gender roles and societally determined gender role behavior starts in the toddler period. By age 3, children can identify some tasks and possessions as masculine and others as feminine. Cultural influences are strong and can overcome even parental and day care center determination to avoid teaching stereotypical masculine and feminine behavior. Even kindergarten children know the sex-role stereotypes of Western culture, aspire to stereotypical sex-appropriate occupations, choose same-sex friends, and evaluate the work of same-sex adults and children more highly than those of the opposite sex.

Each child has an individual balance of masculine and feminine characteristics, influenced by temperamental factors and parental modeling and expectations. There is no evidence that having a homosexual or transsexual parent *necessarily* leads to disturbances of sexual or gender identity in the child.

Cross-gender behavior is normal in boys until age 5. Cultural expectations for gender role behavior in girls are much more flexible, so tomboyish behavior is generally not abnormal at any age, unless it is accompanied by a rigid avoidance of all feminine clothes and activities. Boys are more aggressive than girls as early as age 2, continuing through adolescence.

Sexuality
Three-year-olds are aware of sex differences, but are prone to primitive theories regarding sexuality and pregnancy. Boys are increasingly aware of sensations in the penis. The fear of loss of or damage to the genitals may be accentuated by viewing female genitals and by punitive threats made by parents in response to masturbation. Detumescence of the penis after an erection may reinforce fears of castration.

Belief in oral impregnation (encouraged by jokes about swallowing watermelon seeds) may lead to irrational attitudes toward food. Children begin to demonstrate behavior that suggests fantasies about or observation of or listening to sounds associated with sexual intercourse, which may be initially confused with some form of physical attack, fighting, or wrestling. Sex education is important, geared to the level of the child's curiosity and understanding. Preoccupation with or detailed knowledge about sexual behavior may suggest inappropriate exposure to sexual activity or even sexual abuse.

Imaginary Companions

Up to one fifth of 3 to 6-year-olds have an imaginary companion, a fantasy person or animal to whom the child gives a name, an appearance, and a character. The child may or may not disclose this to his/her parents. The phenomenon is most often seen in imaginative children of above-average intelligence. At various times the companion serves as scapegoat, playmate, and protector. By 10 years of age, the imaginary companion is usually given up.

Dreams

Until about 5 years of age, the child believes that dreams are real events. Children may be frightened by their angry or aggressive feelings toward their parents and project them onto monsters, who then appear in nightmares. A phenomenon often confused with nightmares is the *night terror* or *pavor nocturnus*. Unlike "nightmares," which occur during REM sleep as a part of normal dream activity and are often remembered, the night terror occurs during non-REM sleep stage 3 to 4. The child appears terrified, screaming, confused, with dilated pupils, sweating, rapid pulse, and hyperventilation, and does not respond to comforting. When alert, a feeling of terror and/or dream fragments are rarely recalled. There is a rapid return to sleep and morning amnesia for the episode. This phenomenon is most common in children age 3 to 6, and does not indicate psychopathology. It is usually much more upsetting to parents than to the child.

Family Relationships

Toward the end of this period, children begin to recognize the discrepancy between reality and their idealized image of their parents. This leads to the "family romance," the fantasy that the child has other, real parents, who are far better than those with whom he/she lives. This stage may be particularly difficult for adopted children and their parents.

Even those who do not accept Freudian developmental theory observe that many 3 to 6-year-olds show exaggerated romantic behavior toward the parent of the opposite sex, coupled with disinterest in, or even rivalry toward the parent of the same sex. Freud interpreted this behavior as part of the Oedipal crisis (see Chap. 3). As this stage passes, the child moves from a dyadic preoccupation with the parent of the opposite sex to a more balanced relationship and identification with both parents, and a readiness to invest energy outside of the family into relationships with friends.

Social Development in Early Childhood

Three-year-olds are able to play alone (*solitary play*) or side by side with another child (*parallel play*) for longer periods of time. Four-year-olds are more able to engage in *cooperative* or small group play. They are beginning to be able to share, but are often bossy, and have difficulty understanding the feelings of another child. By 5, most children can engage in the planning and execution of group projects, and participate in elaborate dramatic play. Empathy and leadership are beginning to appear.

Play serves a critical defensive function, enabling children to regain a sense of control by playing out scenarios in which they have been passively acted on (e.g., by a doctor) by taking an active role in the play. Libidinal and aggressive impulses can be discharged through symbolic or fantasy play. Play is also used to develop mastery of both skills and emotions and to prepare for adult roles. The need for "playful" activity obviously persists throughout life.

Preschool: Ages 3 to 6

The time from age 3 to 6 is often called the preschool period. The child who has been cared for at home by the parent(s) often has his/her first experience with major separation at entry to nursery school (age 3 or 4) or kindergarten (age 5). A temporary regression, with crying, clinging to the parent, wetting or soiling, refusal to eat, or sleep disturbance, is not unusual. In an otherwise well-adjusted child, if the separation is handled sensitively by teacher and parent, the child soon returns to his/her previous level of functioning, or even makes a jump ahead. For children who have not mastered previous stages of separation–individuation or for the child whose parents are reluctant to separate, the first signs of separation anxiety disorder or school phobia may be seen at this stage. Children whose prior exposure to peers has been limited may have more difficulty adjusting to the preschool experience. This is also the age at which oppositional defiant disorder or attention-deficit hyperactivity disorder may first become apparent, as the child is expected to function as a member of a group and follow rules, and is observed by the teacher, who has a wider experience with normative child behavior than the parents.

Prevention and Early Intervention

Head Start is an ambitious preschool program for disadvantaged children aged 3 to 6, established with federal funding in 1965. This and other intervention programs for young children and their parents aim to counteract the effects of poverty and deprivation, which lead to impaired performance in school and, eventually, in adult life. While the Head Start program itself has been difficult to evaluate due to political controversy, wide disparity among local programs, and lack of appropriate control groups, long-term follow-up of children enrolled in other preschool prevention and intervention projects finds that children show gains in IQ and other cognitive measures during the first year of the program, with cognitively structured curricula producing greater change than play-oriented programs. Some programs also produce improvement in adjustment to school and in social skills. Unless intervention, including parent involvement, continues after the child's entry into regular school, IQ declines to the lower 90s and below, especially in the most deprived children. Programs that focus simultaneously on parent and child, especially those beginning with

1 and 2-year-olds, yield substantial gains in IQ for both the target child and younger siblings, which are maintained at least through the first grade. For the most severely intellectually and economically disadvantaged families, intensive and personalized family support programs, which include day care, health care, nutrition, housing, advocacy for the family, and vocational training for parents, are required, if children are to show or maintain improvement (Bronfenbrenner, 1974; Ryan, 1974). At long-term follow-up, success may be measured in maternal variables (employment, education, smaller family size) and such child measures as school attendance and reduced need for special education rather than IQ (Seitz et al, 1985).

Response to Physical Illness

Separation from parents by hospitalization is still difficult, even for a child who is comfortably able to separate in other circumstances. Castration and mutilation anxiety and the belief in immanent justice increase the child's fears. Preparation, when possible, by simple explanations and a visit to the hospital, may help. Regression, manifested by such behavior as whining, clinging, and loss of toilet training, is common. Interestingly, even adults may regress and demonstrate similar types of immature childlike behavior under the strain of illness and hospitalization or most any other major life stress.

MIDDLE CHILDHOOD (ELEMENTARY SCHOOL AGE): 6 TO 12 YEARS

This period of development is often called *latency,* or *middle childhood.* The age of 7 (plus or minus 1 year) represents a significant developmental milestone in virtually all present and past cultures (Shapiro and Perry, 1976). This is the age at which the child is considered to be ready for formal schooling, for apprenticeship, or for more active learning of adult skills and roles. For example, the Catholic Church has established the age of 7 as "the age of reason" and therefore time for First Communion. Other religions and cultures have similar rituals that mark this developmental stage. The child's increasing cognitive and motor capacities allow for gradual independence from the family.

Physical Development in Middle Childhood

Neurologic

Changes in the child's abilities, interests, and role in society coincide with significant maturation of the central nervous system (Shapiro and Perry, 1976). By age 7, the brain has attained about 90% of its adult weight. The cerebral cortex is completely myelinated, and the EEG is better synchronized, with a stable alpha wave pattern. Structural and functional changes at the microscopic level can be documented in the frontal lobe, perhaps facilitating verbal regulation of behavior. Children are able to perceive and understand more complex sensory stimuli. Their ability to integrate and coordinate various sensory and motor capacities improves dramatically.

They attain the ability to distinguish right from left, first in themselves, and then on others. Handedness is established around age 7, followed by dominance of one eye and one foot.

Gross Motor

Between the ages of 7 and 10, balance, equilibrium, control of large muscles, skill, and timing improve dramatically. Children are able to learn to play sports, most commonly skating, jumping rope, swimming, diving, and riding a two-wheel bicycle. Children who later excel in a sport often begin to learn it now.

Fine Motor–Adaptive

Small muscle control improves also, and average 8-year-olds can tie their shoes easily, wink, snap their fingers, and whistle. Games such as jacks are mastered. In drawings, the 8-year-old can use perspective and correct body proportions.

Sleep

At age 8, sleep averages 10 hours, decreasing to 8 to 9 hours by age 10.

Pubertal Changes

At age 10, girls and boys are approximately equal in size and sexual maturity. Girls are first to show subtle signs of puberty. The growth spurt begins at 9 or 10, with peak of growth at 12. Hip rounding, nipple projection, waist accentuation, and early pubic hair follow the growth spurt. Puberty begins on average 2 years later in boys. A slight increase in the size of the penis and testes, and the beginnings of pubic hair appear at age 10 or 11, with the growth spurt beginning at age 11 or 12. Appetite tends to increase around age 10, especially in boys.

Cognitive Development in Middle Childhood

Piaget's Stages

In the stage of *concrete operations* (age 7 to 11 years), the child acquires the ability to *decentrate,* that is, to consider more than one dimension at once (e.g., height and width). Ability to take the perspective of another person improves. Children become able to reverse operations mentally, a skill essential to addition and subtraction. They develop the ability to *conserve* quantity first (age 6 to 7 years), then weight (9 to 10 years), and finally volume (11 to 12 years). In other words, they come to understand that these properties of a substance are not changed by alterations in shape or size. Their explanations of conservation progress from negation or reversibility (you could just make it the way it was before), through identity (it's the same, none was added or taken away) to compensation or reciprocity (a short wide glass holds the same amount as a tall narrow one).

As moral development progresses, children are able to take into account what motivates behavior in judging right and wrong. Morality becomes *subjective,* as the child is increasingly able to understand the feelings of other people and the influence of their own actions on others.

Milestones

Perceptual–integrative abilities improve dramatically during this developmental period. School placement is crucial. If the work is too easy, it leads to boredom and poor study habits. If too hard, failure, loss of motivation, feelings of incompetence, and/or behavior problems result. Around 3% of school children are mentally retarded and need a special class or school. Approximately 10% to 25% are slow learners, with borderline or low normal IQ, 40% to 50% are average, 20% to 25% are bright or above average, and about 10% are gifted. Expectations vary among schools. A child with an average IQ may have difficulty getting good grades in a competitive suburban or private school. Girls tend to be better students than boys.

By 7 years old, correct understanding of time and calendar organization leads to a better understanding of the past and future and increased ability to delay gratification. Most 8-year-olds are able to read for pleasure, but their ideas still exceed their writing ability. Nine-year-olds are typically in the fourth grade and should have an improved ability to set and finish a task. Most children find school enjoyable but may fear failure. Some previously immature children show a rapid growth in learning at this time. Alternatively, increased demands for using reading and math skills may uncover a learning disability that was not previously noticed.

Most 10-year-olds memorize well but still have difficulty with abstraction. They can count indefinitely by ones, twos, fives, tens, and backward. They are also able to identify similarities and differences between objects, define concrete words, and add and subtract with ease.

By age 11, children should be able to interpret simple proverbs, multiply, and divide. They are, however, usually unable to understand irony or sarcasm.

A more realistic concept of death is developing in children age 10 to 11. Most understand that death is universal, especially those who have reached the Piagetian stage of concrete operations, but more than half of fourth graders do not yet clearly understand the irreversibility of death. Elementary school-age children tend to view death as a punishment for bad behavior (White et al, 1978).

Speech and Language in Middle Childhood

Five-year-olds literally think out loud, with a running description of their activities. By age 6 to 8, this becomes more covert, or private, and takes on a self-regulatory and then problem-solving function. Private speech also takes on a role in academic performance. By age 10 or 12, children have developed *metacognitive* abilities (i.e., they understand something about what they know and how they learn, and are able to consciously develop strategies for learning). Impulsive children with learning, conduct, or attentional problems either do not develop these skills or do not use them when appropriate. Specific interventions have been developed to teach them, with variable degrees of success.

Affective Development in Middle Childhood

Superego and Conscience

New cognitive abilities permit better inhibition and control of drives and postponement of action and gratification. Freudian developmental theory (described in

Chap. 3) proposes that the *superego,* which emerges as the oedipal crisis is resolved, is divided into the prohibiting and punitive *conscience,* and the *ego-ideal* or idealized model to which one aspires. The child identifies with the parents and gives these identifications authority, facilitating obedience to parental instructions without parental presence. Satisfying the ego-ideal leads to increased self-esteem, comfort, and well-being. Major discrepancy between the child's ego-ideal and the actual abilities of the child may lead to demoralization and low self-esteem, or a defiant refusal to try to achieve success. Early in this period the new superego may be alternatively overly punitive or ineffective. Guilt may be handled by projection or by provoking punishment. When children misbehave, or believe that they have, without parental awareness, they may then engage in further mischief until finally punished. A parent may say, "I don't understand it, Johnny was *asking* for it!" Under stress, children may be prone to regression, with loss of superego control. Emotions are often fluid, intense, and rapidly changing.

By age 8 to 10, the superego is more firmly established, and the ego is stronger and more firmly consolidated. Children should be able to distinguish right from wrong, and be honest and truthful. Behavior should be based on internalized values and consideration for others, rather than on seeking rewards or avoiding punishment. More mature obsessional defenses and sublimation can facilitate the discipline need for good school performance. Normal compulsive traits are seen in the strong interest in establishing and organizing collections typical of this phase. If pronounced, these defenses, along with increased repression, may lead to a decrease in creativity and spontaneity, and an increase in performance anxiety.

Sexuality

Although this period has been termed "latency" in psychoanalytic developmental theory, the only sexual drives and interests that are usually latent are sexual wishes toward, and fantasies directly concerning *parents.* Sexual exploration, comparing of genitals, and group or mutual masturbation are common among boys. Prepubertal boys show a renewed interest in anal or fecal humor and in using sexual or excretory terms as expletives. Sex education, which should have begun in early childhood, should be continued, although children this age may not be willing to confess ignorance by asking questions. As puberty approaches, school may no longer provide sufficient gratification and excitement or bind sufficient energy, and interest is transferred to sports, gangs, or teenage activities.

Fears

Some fears, such as those related to body integrity, may be dealt with by counterphobic defenses and risk-taking behavior. Many children worry about their own competence or appearance. Nightmares are usually related to daytime events, and children are easily calmed when awakened.

School-age children who are on their own after school and during the summer when their parents work ("latchkey children") are at risk for higher levels of fear and anxiety, as well as poorer social skills, juvenile delinquency, and accidents (Zigler and Hall, 1988).

Social Development in Middle Childhood

Eight-year-olds should have a firm grasp of basic rules and an ability to cooperate well when playing games. By age 9 or 10, they should be able to both cooperate and compete, although games may still be interrupted by disagreements about the rules. By age 11 or 12, a legalistic fascination with making, changing, and negotiating rules emerges. An entire afternoon may be spent setting up teams, leaders, rules, and punishments for breaking rules, addressing all possible contingencies, without ever getting to the game, but without disappointment. Children come to understand that rules have been invented by human beings and are maintained by mutual consent. Rules may be altered if the change is fair and all agree. Rules serve to promote social interaction, define socially unacceptable behavior, and strengthen the barrier against regression.

Both boys and girls generally prefer single-sex groupings for play, sports, and social events. There is extreme peer pressure, especially on boys, for culturally appropriate gender role behavior. Boys and girls often harbor rigid sexual stereotypes, even in families where parents have equivalent roles at home and at work.

Girls have more intense friendships than boys do, with one or two peers, and may develop "crushes" on older adolescents or young adult women, who concretely represent their ego-ideal. These feelings should not be regarded as signs of homosexuality.

Compared to earlier stages, the school-age child is far more exposed to and influenced by the environment outside of the home. Childhood has its own subculture, passed from child to child by word of mouth, without adult intervention. This includes rhymes, chants, superstitions, rituals, jokes, riddles, and secret codes. Both boys and girls engage in hero worship—of sports, rock, television or movie stars, coaches, or even teachers.

The ubiquitous sex and violence in the media exert a powerful influence. Viewing television violence has been demonstrated to increase aggression in children and adolescents (Pearl et al, 1982). Television also probably provides a significant amount of overstimulation regarding sexual matters and often presents poor role models of precocious sexuality in which sexuality is presented without regard to moral concerns, values, love, or commitment.

Groups and clubs are increasingly important, often with little purpose other than to include some children and exclude others. To be accepted by peers, children must learn to be loyal, to be able to compromise, to be good sports, and not to tattle. Social competence and peer acceptance result from specific skills and characteristics, such as the ability to size up a social situation and adapt to it, to respond positively to approach by peers, and to take a gradual, indirect, process-oriented approach to social goals (Asher, 1983). Children who are impatient or aggressive are rejected by peers.

Unfortunately, group behavior is not always positive. Teasing is often cruel and persistent at this age. Peer pressure may lead to dangerous or immoral behavior. Boys are especially vulnerable to dares or to suggestions of cowardice.

Even prior to adolescence, girls are acutely aware of cultural concepts of physical attractiveness. Many express unrealistic concern about obesity and try to diet, despite normal weight. In vulnerable girls, this may be accentuated at the beginning of puberty, with the normal increase in body fat, and may lead to the development of anorexia or bulimia nervosa.

Response to Physical Illness

School-age children usually tolerate acute illness and hospitalization relatively well, especially if they are prepared, parents visit daily for substantial periods, and preceding development was on course. Children this age may still have irrational explanations of illness. Oppositional or immature behavior is common. Unfortunately, nursing staff have limited tolerance for a child who whines, cries, clings, or refuses to cooperate with medical procedures. Loss of recently acquired skills due to illness or injury is a major blow to the child. Chronic illness interferes increasingly with normal developmental tasks, especially those related to school and to peer relationships.

ADOLESCENCE

The major tasks of adolescence are the development of a secure personal and sexual identity, occupational choice, and personal values. For many youth, prolonged education and the resulting economic dependence on the family extend the period of adolescence well into their middle and late twenties.

Physical Development in Adolescence

Neurologic

Dendritic connections attain their adult level, which is a reduction from earlier proliferation. By age 14, the EEG shows mature alpha rhythms.

Endocrine

Puberty is the attainment of reproductive capacity. There is wide diversity in timing among youth of each sex. Early maturation is generally an advantage for boys, but a disadvantage for girls. The average age of menarche in girls is now 12, as compared to 15 to 16 in the 1880s. The change is attributed to better nutrition and fewer serious childhood diseases. Combined with the prolongation of the adolescent period for economic and educational reasons, it results in a long period of sexual maturity before it is culturally appropriate to marry and start a new family. Boys attain sexual maturity 2 years later than girls, on the average.

Tanner has detailed the sequence of changes in primary (genitals) and secondary sexual characteristics for both males and females (see Hamburg and Wortman in Annotated Bibliography for more detail). Pubertal changes are normally complete by age 15 in girls and age 17 in boys.

Pubertal changes focus the adolescent's attention on his or her body. Many teens, especially girls, are extremely concerned about their physical appearance. Hormonal changes accompanying puberty, along with social and cultural factors, lead to an increased interest in sexuality and sexual experimentation. In addition, the pervasive sexuality in television, movies, music, and advertising may lead to over-stimulation and pressure to engage in sexual activity before the teenager is sufficiently cognitively and emotionally mature.

Cognitive Development in Adolescence

Piaget's Stages

A few children reach the stage of *formal operations* as early as 12 years old. It is attained by only 35% of 16 to 17-year-olds. Many adults never reach this stage, limiting their ability to deal in a flexible and rational manner with such abstract concepts as religion, ethics, morality, philosophy, and politics. At the level of formal operations, the youth is able to use abstract thought, to consider theoretic notions, and to devise hypotheses and ways of testing them. The adolescent becomes able to understand metaphor and complex, abstract subjects such as algebra and calculus. Even when the stage of formal operations is attained, emotional pressure may cause temporary regression to concrete operations.

Affective Development in Adolescence

Adolescent Turmoil

Adolescents in American society are beset by multiple stressors and pressures. The move from a smaller elementary school to a larger middle school or high school results in less supervision, more impersonal relationships with teachers, and a larger, more diverse peer group. Academic work is increasingly demanding, and there is a pressing need to make decisions regarding work or further education after high school.

Early psychoanalytic and Eriksonian theory propose that adolescent turmoil (i.e., psychologic upheaval leading to significant disruption in personality organization, disequilibrium, and disturbances in mood and behavior) is not only ubiquitous but necessary for successful separation from parents and formation of adult identity. Studies by Offer and colleagues (Offer et al, 1981) of normal adolescents and those with a variety of emotional and physical illnesses in the 1960s and 1970s found that serious emotional or behavioral problems are *not* normal in adolescents. Most teenagers were found to cope reasonably effectively, and without undue disruption of school or family life, with the tasks of adolescence. About 20% of youth experience tumult or diagnosable psychopathology in their teen years, most often those from less stable backgrounds and with more family conflict. About a quarter of adolescents, most often those who experience few stressors and have parents who encourage independence, demonstrate essentially continuous growth and good interpersonal relationships. The third group is characterized by developmental spurts alternating with periods of conflict. These youth are often "late bloomers," who report more disagreements with their parents and more feelings of depression and anxiety.

It is normal, particularly in early adolescence, to experience a transient disturbance of self-esteem, increased feelings of anxiety and depression, and oversensitivity to shame and humiliation, which do not reach a clinical level and are usually related to particular stressful situations. Interestingly, the 1970s' cohort of adolescents surveyed by Offer and associates (1981) reported feeling less self-confident, controlled, and trusting of others than the teenagers studied in the 1960s.

Prior to adolescence, behavioral and emotional disorders are more common in boys than girls. In adolescence, the girls catch up and even exceed boys in eating disorders and depression.

Critical Developmental Challenges and Issues of Adolescence

Shapiro and Hertzig (1988) identify eight issues that must be resolved in the course of adolescent development.

1. Dependence on versus independence from nuclear family.
2. Behavioral license versus intellectualized control.
3. Loyalty to family versus peer group.
4. Normalizing function of sharing thoughts and feelings with peers versus need for privacy.
5. Idealization versus devaluation of peers and adults.
6. Formation of identity, role, and character.
7. Consolidation of sexual role and sexual object choice.
8. Reshuffling of defenses and consolidation of style of functioning.

Mechanisms of Defense

Adolescents may show a temporary increase in less mature mechanisms such as *projection, externalization, denial, reaction formation,* and *repression,* as well as development of the more advanced *rationalization, identification,* and *sublimation.* On balance, adolescents have an improved ability to use mature defenses, to tolerate frustration, and to delay gratification.

Risk-Taking Behavior

Unfortunately, the entitlement and belief in their omnipotence and invulnerability common in adolescents may lead to dangerous experimentation and risk-taking behavior. The three leading causes of death in adolescents are accidents, homicide, and suicide. Although adolescents cognitively understand the meaning of death, they do not accept the reality of the possibility for themselves. Some teenagers have a heroic mental image of themselves "surviving in fantasy," imagining seeing how their parents and peers would react to their death, classically portrayed in Tom Sawyer's attendence at his own "funeral."

Adolescents commonly fluctuate between unrealistically positive and negative views of themselves. Compared to adults, they are more likely to attribute responsibility for their failures to others. They are generally able to take appropriate credit for success. In later adolescence, normal youth are able to give up their fantasies of omnipotence and recognize that some problems that need to be solved are inevitable in life.

Although overall rates of adolescent abuse of cocaine, heroin, sedatives, amphetamines, and hallucinogens have stabilized or declined, there is still cause for serious concern. In 1985, 54% of high school seniors reported having used marijuana at least once, with 5% admitting to daily use (Johnston et al, 1986). Five percent of teens drink alcohol daily. A third of all adolescents surveyed report that most or all of their friends get intoxicated at least once a week. Adolescence is the critical period for initiation of abuse. First onset of drug use is actually rare among adults. Interference with normal developmental tasks puts young adolescent drug users at greatest risk for serious substance abuse and its medical, cognitive, and emotional sequelae. Youth who are rebellious, place a low value on achievement, are alienated from their parents, are influenced by peers with behavior problems, and live in a chaotic environment without clear discipline are at especially high risk.

Cigarette smoking has declined over the last decade, after a period of increase, especially among girls (Petersen and Hamburg, 1986).

Sexuality

Masturbation is normal and, especially in early adolescence, serves a generalized function of reducing anxiety and discharging tension. Teens often experiment with a variety of masturbation fantasies, and transient homosexual fantasies and activities are not uncommon.

Previously steadily increasing rates of teenage sexual intercourse have now stabilized, at least among older youth (age 15 to 19). Adolescents who engage in unprotected and/or indiscriminate sexual activity run the risk not only of pregnancy, but of AIDS and other sexually transmitted diseases. The United States has the highest rate of teenage pregnancy of any industrialized nation. It has been estimated that one in every ten girls becomes pregnant during adolescence. The high physical and psychologic morbidity for both mother and child create a major public health problem.

Family Relationships

The adolescent should experience gradual independence and autonomy from the nuclear family. There is a normal increase in parent–child arguing around the time of puberty. The young adolescent is increasingly critical of his/her parents, oppositional, and deliberately provocative. This may represent evolutionarily determined preparation for leaving home. In American culture, however, young adolescents are not emotionally or financially prepared to leave home, although they may be biologically ready.

The *family romance* is sometimes revived in adolescence, with idealization of a peer's parents and scorn for one's own.

Social Development of Adolescents

Harry Stack Sullivan described early adolescent chumship characterized by an intense friendship with a youth of the same sex. Adolescents are acutely interested in their peers. The need for absolute peer conformity is more important to early adolescents than it is later. There is a new interest in establishing heterosexual relationships.

Renewed egocentrism leads to the belief that others are as obsessed as they are with their behavior and appearance, leading to a feeling of being under constant scrutiny. Painful self-consciousness peaks in early adolescence.

Response to Physical Illness

Adolescents are increasingly able to take pride in being responsible for their own body and medical care. When ill or injured, their fears are more realistic than those of younger children. Loss of autonomy and privacy is especially painful for teenagers.

In chronically ill or handicapped adolescents, concern with physical appearance often leads to a view of their bodies, and therefore themselves, as defective. Low self-esteem may decrease adolescents' belief in their own ability to control their fate, resulting in hopelessness, impaired ability to resist peer pressure, and noncompliance with medical regimens.

Both individual adolescents and the peer group are intolerant of differences in appearance or behavior. Adolescents with a handicap or chronic illness may be embarrassed about their disease. Compliance with medical treatment may be avoided, because it exposes the teen as different. Peers may even encourage violating treatment.

Chronically ill adolescents may use a variety of defense mechanisms, including denial, intellectualization, projection, displacement, regression, development of rituals, and identification with the aggressor (the physician). It is important to note that psychopathology is not inevitable in chronically ill adolescents.

Possible contributing factors to medical noncompliance include: denial or lack of acceptance of the disorder, frustration with the outcome or nature of treatment, lack of knowledge or skills, miscommunication or lack of relationship with medical caregivers, rebellion against parents, inability to resist peer pressure, and psychopathology in the adolescent.

THE ROLE OF THE FAMILY IN DEVELOPMENT

Cultural influences

While family systems theory and therapy are dealt with in Chapter 8, the role of family will be briefly introduced here within a developmental context. Societal expectations of families and their members vary widely in different cultures. Even in our own country, regional and ethnic differences can be identified. The changing role of women, the increasing prevalence of divorce, and the growing number of two-career families have significantly changed roles and functions in many American families. However, certain tasks and functions must be carried out in some way by every healthy family or family group.

Family Tasks

Fleck (1966) has identified seven essential tasks for families with children.

1. To form and maintain a *marital coalition* between the adults, which will meet their emotional needs.
2. To form and maintain a *parental coalition* between the adults who function as parents, to assure support and consistency when

dealing with the children. In joint custody arrangements following divorce, maintenance of the parental coalition, despite dissolution of the marital coalition, is essential for successful adaptation of the children.

3. To *nurture* the children, physically and emotionally.

4. To create and maintain appropriate *boundaries* between generations and persons within the family and between the family and the community. Families may have difficulties if the boundaries are too strong and rigid or too weak and permeable.

5. To *enculturate* the younger generation, instilling the values of the family and the culture.

6. To promote *independence* and then emancipation of the children.

7. To deal with *crises*.

Insufficient material or psychologic resources, parental psychopathology, and/or severe stressors can interfere with a family's accomplishment of these tasks, resulting in developmental difficulties or even psychopathology in the child.

Parenting Styles

Research in child development has identified patterns of parenting that correlate with, although by no means inevitably lead to, certain outcomes in children (Table 6-4). Discipline characteristics that have been associated with aggressive and delinquent children include inconsistency, parental response based on the parents' own mood rather than the child's behavior, expression of dislike for the child, and lack of

Table 6–4 **Parenting Styles**

STYLE	CHARACTERISTICS	POSSIBLE OUTCOMES
Authoritarian	Firm rules and edicts No bargaining or discussion with children	Weak conscience Low self-esteem Social withdrawal Unhappiness
Indulgent–permissive	Few controls or restrictions Accept children's demands	Low self-reliance Poor impulse control Aggression Unpredictable parental harshness
Authoritative–reciprocal	Firm rules Shared decision making Discuss children's demands	Social responsibility Self-reliance Self-esteem Low aggression
Indifferent–neglectful	Uninvolved	Aggression Low self-esteem Low self-control Poor parent–child relationship

(Data from Rutter M, Cox A: Other family influences. In Rutter M, Hersov L (eds): Child and Adolescent Psychiatry: Modern Approaches, 2nd ed. Oxford, Blackwell Scientific Publications, 1985)

positive direction (Patterson, 1982). Discipline and limit setting should not be confused or equated with corporal punishment. Corporal punishment attempts to control a child's behavior by fear and threat, is not particularly effective, and leads to anger and resentment. Behavioral strategies such as rewards, incentives, contingencies, and "time out" are far more effective (see Chap. 4).

Stages of Family Development

The New Baby

Parents and siblings of an infant must integrate a new, very demanding and totally dependent person into their lives, which requires major readjustments in their previous relationship. Parenting of infants is accompanied by fatigue and often anxiety. Fathers at times may jealously resent the attention given to the baby.

The Toddler

The child at this stage requires close supervision while making increasing demands for autonomy. Parents must be able to let the child go without pushing him/her away. Parents with a strong need to control their children's behavior and who interpret efforts at autonomy, self-assertion and independence as signs of defiance that should be punished may have great difficulty with the 2-year-old, believing their children to be "terrible."

The Child Age 3 to 6 Years

As children pass through the Oedipal stage, they may be quite overtly seductive to the parent of the opposite sex. Parents may be flattered and respond in an overstimulating way, particularly if the relationship with their spouse is not emotionally gratifying. The child's wish for an exclusive relationship with the parent may lead to jealousy and marital discord, if not understood and handled sensitively by the parents. Alternatively, parents may become guilty about their own fantasies that the child's attentions produce, and become overly punitive or withdraw from the child. The child may find a divorce particularly difficult at this time as it almost always is regardless of age.

The School-Age Child

With the beginning of mandatory schooling, the child is no longer the exclusive possession of the parents. School and peers become increasingly important. Parents may view a teacher's complaints about their child as a criticism of their parenting ability. On the more positive side, parents now have more time and energy for their own interests. Previously isolated parents may benefit from participation in their child's school, church, or recreational activities.

The Adolescent

The family of an adolescent needs to provide more privacy and to tolerate the teenager's increasing autonomy. Parents need to permit and encourage the degree of separation and independence that is appropriate for the youth's age and emotional development, and be able to understand and tolerate frequent shifts between apparent maturity and behavior typical of a much younger child. In many ways, it is reminiscent of parenting a toddler, but with a child who has much wider freedom of movement and is heavily influenced by peers. Parents must be flexible and titrate carefully between the dangers of holding too tight and precipitously letting go.

Parents who have difficulties with this stage of emancipation may find their loss of power and the adolescent's challenges to their authority intolerable. Other parents may compete with their teenager, in an effort to avoid recognition of their own aging. The most successful parents minimize power struggles and emphasize important rules and values, while ignoring many details of behavior, particularly in respect to clothing and hair styles. A style of collaborative negotiation and problem solving, begun prior to puberty, facilitates discipline and decision making.

Response to Physical Illness

Physical handicap or chronic or life-threatening illness places significant stress on both parents and siblings at any stage of life. Factors that may hamper a family's ability to function and to comply with medical regimens include an inability to encourage and foster independence as the child matures, unresolved parental guilt, denial, anger or fear, lack of an adequate support system, other stressors that strain family resources, and problems originating in other family relationships (e.g., marital discord) being acted out in conflict over the child.

CHILDREN AT RISK

Attempts to understand and prevent pathology in children and adolescents have led to an interest in children who may be vulnerable. The risk or liability of a particular outcome is determined by a complex interaction between *diathesis* (negative genetic factors), environmental stressors, and assets or protective factors.

Divorce

The number of children affected by divorce continues to climb (see Chap. 8). The effects of a divorce differ between boys and girls, and at different developmental stages. The likelihood of a negative outcome is increased by the degree of family conflict preceding and following the divorce, as well as by associated stressors (e.g., economic hardship; loss of extended family; need to move from familiar home, neighborhood, and school; or decreased emotional support from an angry or grieving parent). Children commonly blame themselves for the divorce or internalize the experience as a failure of theirs to keep the parents together. Most wish for their parents to be reunited, and many believe they have the responsibility and/or power to bring about a reconciliation.

Most children of divorced parents spend a period of time in a single parent home, but the frequency of remarriage is high. Marriage of a single parent with children creates what is known as a *reconstituted family.* An estimated one in every six American children under the age of 18 lives with a stepparent. The parents must simultaneously form a new marital and parental coalition, while dealing with the behavior and emotional adjustment of children of various ages, who have their own feelings about the divorce and remarriage. Teenagers may be particularly resistant to developing a positive relationship with the stepparent. If the natural parents are divorced, children may fear being disloyal to the other parent if they accept a stepparent.

Children of Alcoholic Parents

A significant minority of children of alcoholic parents have increased behavioral problems, especially conduct problems, restlessness, inattention, poor academic performance, dropping out of school, and alcohol abuse, as well as emotional symptoms such as anxiety and depression. Probable mediating factors include marital conflict, divorce, disrupted family routine, inadequate parental nurturance and supervision, economic hardship, and modeling of maladaptive coping styles (West and Prinz, 1987). Genetic contributions may add to risk, as well as the teratologic effects of a mother who drinks during pregnancy. Special self-help groups have evolved for both adolescent and adult children of alcoholics (ACOA).

Children of Mentally Ill Parents

Both genetic factors and the effect of mental illness on parenting skills and family environment increase risk. Children whose parents have a mood disorder have an increased (but by no means inevitable) incidence of both depressive symptoms and nonspecific behavioral and emotional disturbance (Beardslee et al, 1983). Children of schizophrenic parents are more likely to demonstrate abnormalities in attention and information processing, even before emergence of any overt symptoms (Masten and Garmezy, 1985).

Resilient Children

Graduated stressors or challenges that can be mastered may promote the development of flexible, diverse, and successful coping strategies and positive outcome. Children from high-risk groups who do not appear to suffer negative consequences have been called resilient or "invulnerable." There is great interest in elucidating how some children not only resist and cope with unusual stress but thrive and succeed despite adversity. Identified protective factors include a cohesive and emotionally supportive family environment; external support systems, such as caring extended family members or other adults, and/or institutional supports; and characteristics of the child, such as intelligence, hardiness, autonomy, positive social orientation, and self-esteem (Masten and Garmezy, 1985). Strong genetic endowments also probably play a major role in the resilience of such children to surviving and adapting to developmental stress and trauma.

SUMMARY

This chapter has been, by necessity, a dense, compressed, and abbreviated summary of the wealth of current theory and knowledge regarding human development from conception through adolescence. An understanding of the major concepts and principles of development will stand a physician in good stead, no matter what the ultimate specialty choice. In all spheres, normal development proceeds in certain predictable sequences, although rate varies considerably among healthy persons. There is a constant reciprocal interaction between children and adolescents and their environment, with each shaping the other. Developmental outcome is not simple to predict, but is the result of multiple factors within the child, the family, the school, and the larger culture. Developmental considerations beyond adolescence and into early adulthood will be discussed in Chapter 7.

ANNOTATED BIBLIOGRAPHY

Cohen DJ, Schowalter JE (eds): Child psychiatry. In Michels R (ed): Psychiatry, vol 2. Philadelphia, JB Lippincott, 1985

An easy-to-read, comprehensive, three-volume loose leaf text.

Chapter 2, Early child development, Provence S

Chapter 3, Primary school age development, Shapiro T

Chapter 4, Adolescent development and psychopathology, Hamburg BA, Wortman RN

Chapter 5, Family development, Gurwitt A, Muir RC

Chapter 71, In the best interests of the child: An overview, Solnit AJ, Schetky DH

Chapter 72, Pediatric consultation, Schowalter JE

Chapter 73, The chronically ill child and his family, Van Dongen-Melman JEWM, Sanders-Woudstra JAR

Chapter 74, The fatally ill child and his family, Van Dongen-Melman JEWM, Sanders-Woudstra JAR

Ginsburg H, Opper S: Piaget's Theory of Intellectual Development: An Introduction. Englewood Cliffs, NJ, Prentice-Hall, 1969

A brief, comprehensible summary of Piaget's work.

Heins M, Seiden AM: Child Care/Parent Care. Garden City, New York, Doubleday & Company, 1987

An exhaustively comprehensive medical and psychologic guide for parents and professionals working with children and their families, written by a pediatrician and a psychiatrist who are also mothers themselves. Excellent. Available in paperback.

Levine MD, Carey WB, Crocker AC et al (eds): Developmental-Behavioral Pediatrics. Philadelphia, WB Saunders, 1983

A comprehensive text directed toward pediatricians. Excellent reference.

Lewis M: Clinical Aspects of Child Development, 2nd ed. Philadelphia, Lea & Febiger, 1982

The best summary of normal development. Aimed at medical students, but useful for residents also.

Wolman B (ed): Handbook of Developmental Psychology. Englewood Cliffs, NJ, Prentice-Hall, 1982

A detailed compendium of current research in developmental psychology. Chapters integrate and present implications of research findings.

REFERENCES

Asher SR: Social competence and peer status: Recent advances and future directions. Child Dev 54:1427–1434, 1983

Beardslee WR, Bemporad J, Keller MB et al: Children of parents with major affective disorder: A review. Am J Psychiatry 140:825–832, 1983

Bowlby J: Developmental psychiatry comes of age. Am J Psychiatry 145:1–10, 1988

Bowlby J: Separation: Anxiety and anger. In Attachment and Loss, vol 2. New York, Basic Books, 1975

Bowlby J: Attachment. In Attachment and Loss, vol 1. New York, Basic Books, 1969

Brazelton TB: Crying in infancy. Pediatrics 29:579–588, 1962

Bronfenbrenner U: A Report on Longitudinal Evaluations of Preschool Programs, Volume II: Is Early Intervention Effective? Washington, DC, Office of Human Development, USDHEW, 1974

Crowell J, Keener M, Ginsburg N et al: Sleep habits in toddlers 18 to 36 months old. J Am Acad Child Adolesc Psychiatry 26:510–515, 1987

Fleck S: An approach to family pathology. Compr Psychiatry 7:307–320, 1966

Gesell A, Halverson HM, Thompson H: The First Five Years of Life: A Guide to the Study of the Preschool Child. New York, Harper & Row, 1940

Goldberg S: Parent–infant bonding: Another look. Child Dev 54:1355–1382, 1983

Green M, Solnit AJ: Reactions to the threatened loss of a child: A vulnerable child syndrome. Pediatrics 34:58–66, 1964

Hodapp RM, Mueller E: Early social development. In Wolman B (ed): Handbook of Developmental Psychology. Englewood Cliffs, NJ, Prentice-Hall, 1982

Johnston LD, O'Malley PM, Bachman JG: Drug Use Among American High School Students, College Students and Other Young Adults. Washington, DC, US Dept of Health and Human Services, 1986

Kagan J, Reznick JS, Snidman N: Biological bases of childhood shyness. Science 240:167–171, 1988

Kaplan, HI, Sadock BJ: Synopsis of Psychiatry, 5th ed, chap 33. Baltimore, Williams & Wilkins, 1988

Masten AS, Garmezy N: Risk, vulnerability, and protective factors in developmental psychopathology. In Lahey BB, Kazdin AE (eds): Advances in Clinical Child Psychology, vol 8. New York, Plenum Press, 1985

Money J: Sin, sickness, or status: Homosexual gender identity and psychoneuroendocrinology. Am Psychol 42:384–399, 1987

Offer D, Ostrov E, Howard KI: The Adolescent: A Psychological Self-Portrait. New York, Basic Books, 1981

Patterson, GR: Coercive Family Process. Eugene, OR, Castalia, 1982

Pearl D, Bouthilet L, Lazar J (eds): Television and Behavior: Ten Years of Scientific Progress and Implications for the Eighties. Washington, DC, US Government Printing Office, 1982

Petersen AC, Hamburg BA: Adolescence: A developmental approach to problems and psychopathology. Behav Ther 17:480–499, 1986

Piaget J, Inhelder B: The Psychology of the Child. New York, Basic Books, 1969

Rutter M, Cox A: Other family influences, In Rutter M, Hersov L (eds): Child and Adolescent Psychiatry: Modern Approaches, 2nd ed. Oxford, Blackwell Scientific Publications, 1985

Ryan S: A Report on Longitudinal Evaluations of Preschool Programs, Vol I: Longitudinal Evaluations. Washington, DC, Office of Human Development, USDHEW, 1974

Seitz V, Rosenbaum LK, Apfel NH: Effects of family support intervention: A ten-year follow-up. Child Dev 56:376–391, 1985

Shapiro T, Hertzig M: Normal child and adolescent development. In Talbott, JA, Hales RE, Yudofsky SC (eds): American Psychiatric Press Textbook of Psychiatry. Washington, DC, American Psychiatric Press, 1988

Shapiro T, Perry R: Latency revisited: The age 7 plus or minus 1. Psychoanal Study Child 31:79–105, 1976

Shepherd-Look DL: Sex differentiation and the development of sex roles. In Wolman B (ed): Handbook of Developmental Psychology. Englewood Cliffs, NJ, Prentice-Hall, 1982

Siegel LS: Infant tests as predictors of cognitive and language development at two years. Child Dev 53:545–557, 1981

Spitz, RA: Anaclitic depression. Psychoanal Study Child 2:313–342, 1946

Spitz RA: Hospitalism: An inquiry into the genesis of psychiatric conditions in early childhood. Psychoanal Study Child 1:53–74, 1945

Steinhausen H-C, Spohr H-L: Fetal alcohol syndrome. In Lahey BB, Kazdin AE (eds): Advances in Clinical Child Psychology, vol 9. New York, Plenum Press, 1986

Thomas A, Chess S: Temperament in Clinical Practice. New York, Guilford Press, 1986

US Bureau of the Census: Statistical Abstract of the United States: 1987. Washington, DC, US Government Printing Office, 1987

West MO, Prinz RJ: Parental alcoholism and childhood psychopathology. Psychol Bull 102:204–218, 1987

White E, Elsom B, Prawat R: Children's conceptions of death. Child Dev 49:307–310, 1978

Zigler E, Hall NW: Day care and its effect on children: An overview for pediatric health professionals. Dev Behav Pediatr 9:38–46, 1988

Zimmerman IL, Bernstein M: Parental work patterns in alternative families: Influence on child development. Am J Orthopsychiatry 53:418–425, 1983

7

Adult Development

Thomas Wolman and
Troy L. Thompson, II

There is a saying that it takes a lifetime to develop into a complete human being. The irony of this remark lies in our "having to give it up just when we have finished the job." But upon reflection, one might consider that life is, in large part, synonymous with growth and development. Someone who has ceased growing has, in a sense, stopped living. Therefore, one may define mental health in this way, as the capacity to adapt to the various developmental tasks that persons encounter over their entire lifespan. Human development, therefore, does not end in adolescence, although the relative lack of attention that has been devoted to adult development makes this perhaps one of the most understudied areas of human behavior.

Personal development is the unique path that each person takes through that sequence of milestones called the "lifecycle." The lifecycle is a universal framework or template whose features appear to remain generally constant for all persons, cultures, and eras. Stages of infancy, childhood, adolescence, courtship, adulthood, marriage, parenting, and old age are ubiquitous, and all require phase-specific developmental challenges.

Traditionally, knowledge about the lifecycle has resided in the folk wisdom of the culture. Great literature of all eras, from the Bible to Shakespeare, has reflected this knowledge. In modern times, people have looked to physicians for advice on problems encountered in lifecycle phases. Until recently, however, physicians were hampered by spotty and unsystematized research and knowledge of the specific biologic, psychologic, and social complexities of each developmental phase. At the turn of the century, even childhood was *terra incognita* as far as systematic and scientifically based knowledge of development was concerned. Freud (1958) and his followers began the exploration of childhood stages of psychologic development, and interest in this area has greatly expanded. In the 1960s, researchers, like Mahler (1975), produced the first detailed glimpse into the first 2 years of life. Adolescence also became the subject of much interest, thanks to the pioneering work of psychoanalytic workers like Anna Freud. Nevertheless, Erik Erikson (1963) in his "eight ages of man" (which are discussed more later in this chapter) was the first to view the *total* lifecycle as a continuum (Table 7-1).

As was mentioned earlier, our overview of the lifecycle has been seriously

Table 7–1 **Erikson's Psychologic Stages of the Lifecycle**

	USUAL AGE RANGE	FUNDAMENTAL ISSUES	ROUGH EQUIVALENT	STRENGTHS BASED ON FAVORABLE OUTCOME RATIOS
Stage 1	0–18 mo	Basic trust vs mistrust	Infancy	Drive and hope
Stage 2	18 mo–3½ yr	Autonomy vs shame and doubt	Toddler stage	Self-control and will power
Stage 3	3½ yr–5 yr	Initiative vs guilt	Oedipal stage	Direction and purpose
Stage 4	5 yr–12 yr	Industry vs inferiority	Latency	Method and competence
Stage 5	12 yr–20 yr	Identity vs role confusion	Adolescence	Devotion and fidelity
Stage 6	20 yr–35 yr	Intimacy vs isolation	Young adulthood	Affiliation and love
Stage 7	35 yr–65 yr	Generativity vs stagnation	Maturity	Production and care
Stage 8	65 yr and up	Ego integrity vs despair	Old age	Renunciation and despair

(Adapted from Erikson EH: Childhood and Society. New York, WW Norton, 1963)

skewed towards the early years, mostly encapsulated by infancy on one hand and adolescence on the other. In part, this is a legacy of Freud's hypothesis that the personality is largely "fixed" by the age of 5. Yet recent autobiographic studies of Freud himself (Anzieu, 1986) underscore the importance of his own "midlife crisis" in setting him on a course toward the discovery of psychoanalysis. This "distortion toward the young" has been partly overcome by recent work on aging and adult development (Colarusso and Nemiroff, 1981; Gould, 1972; Levinson et al, 1978; Vailliant, 1977). But it is still possible to find otherwise up-to-date texts of psychiatry with no or almost no mention of adult development (Nicholi, 1985).

The purpose of this chapter is to summarize recent discoveries about the adult lifecycle in a manner that is relevant to physicians in the practice of medicine. Events of the lifecycle will be related to health and illness, and the vulnerable points in the cycle, where pathologic change is more likely to occur, will be highlighted.

NEW DEVELOPMENTAL CONCEPTS

The Triad of Stage, Transition, and Normative Crisis

One of the important discoveries of recent years is that psychologic change and development are not uniform (see Table 7-2). Any lifecycle theory must account for periods of rapid change and periods of preparation for change, in addition to periods of slower consolidation. Life change may unfold through a typical sequence of preparation (a transitional period), rapid change (such as may occur with a normal developmental step, or "normative crisis"), consolidation (the achievement of a new life "stage"), and "plateauing." Such a formula helps to organize an approach to the lifecycle, provided it is not taken too literally. For example, adolescence (or any other period) may be viewed in part as a normative crisis, as a transition, and as a stage.

Stages

Most research on the human lifecycle, from Erikson onward, divides the developmental continuum into *discrete stages.* Each stage is characterized by its own specific tasks, conflicts, modes, and viewpoints. Some stages, such as those of childhood, maturity, and old age, are universal; others, such as those of the "age 30" transition, may be more culture-dependent. Stages indicate periods of developmental stability in which considerable time is spent on age-specific tasks; these are periods of *consolidation of skills* rather than of rapid change.

Transitions

A more specialized period of transition is needed to bridge the wide gulf between the demands of successive stages (Levinson et al, 1978). People require time to get used to new demands, challenges, and outlooks. At the same time, they need the time to consider what to relish and what to relinquish from earlier periods. Most people make a transition on a smaller scale every evening as they prepare themselves

Table 7–2 **New Developmental Concepts**

CONCEPT	BRIEF DEFINITION	EXAMPLES
Transition	Bridge or junction between successive stages	Late adolescence Midlife transition Courtship
"Limbo state"	A "stuck" point in development, usually at the transition between two stages	Pseudo-adulthood (prolonged adolescence) Courtship
Rite of passage	Social ritual that facilitates a transition	Graduation Marriage Funerals
Normative crisis	Period of rapid change and/or turmoil that strains person's adaptive capacity	Childbirth Midlife crisis Marital crisis
"Normal illness"	Hybrid state with features of both an illness and a normative crisis	Pregnancy Maternal preoccupation Bereavement
Stage	Period of consolidation of skills and capacities	Early adulthood Mature adulthood
Plateau	Period of developmental stability	Adulthood up to midlife
Developmental lines	Independent course of development of a particular skill or capacity	Love Work Play
Delay/precocity	Variations in the timing of developmental lines	Precocious adulthood "Late bloomer"
Regression	Temporary retrograde vector in development	Revival of adolescence or childhood in midlife
Repetition	Reworking and reliving all or part of previous stage(s)	The second separation—Individuation crisis of young adulthood/late adolescence

for sleep. Reverie and hypnagogic imagery are transitional states between conscious thinking and dreaming.

Transitional states are like vehicles that carry the person from one stage to another. Rites of passage perform the same function in a social context (Van Gennep, 1960). They help to concretize the change, giving it a sort of external "scaffolding," and making it more real to the participants. In addition, transitional states act to allay the anxiety of the person and the group, for whom change always represents a threat.

The Normative Crisis

This concept reflects the fact that the rate of change may vary considerably throughout life. Almost everyone is familiar with the experience of overwhelming changes that strain their capacity to adapt. One can define a normative crisis as any period in the lifecycle whose chief characteristic is turmoil. This turmoil can result from external factors, such as illness or misfortune, or it can result from internal conflicts between opposing alternatives: self versus others, freedom versus bondage, living versus dying. In many crises, childbirth for example, external and internal factors coexist.

The Normative Crisis in Health and Illness

In our culture, people have a marked tendency to define a normative crisis as a symptom of an illness. In the past, physicians have contributed to this trend, most notably in their attitudes toward pregnancy. An important task of today's physicians is in helping their patients reinterpret what is normative versus what is pathologic. At times, this may mean revising some of our attitudes toward developmental blocks, obstacles, plateaus, doldrums, and even reversals.

It may even be a good exercise to try to reinterpret the "obviously" pathologic as if it were a normative crisis. Doing this serves to place the illness inside the more manageable framework of the lifecycle, thus allowing greater adaptation and assimilation of what seems alien. For example, symptoms of anxiety in young adults may be interpreted in the context of some expected difficulties in leaving the parental home. Promiscuity in a middle-aged man may be a sign of the "midlife crisis." Even schizophrenia may be redefined in part in this way, and be viewed as an unfortunate outcome, precipitated by the stresses of a difficult adolescent transition.

On the other hand, the physician also needs to be knowledgeable about particularly vulnerable points in the lifecycle—those points that can more easily trigger actual illness. The transitional periods are particularly important in this regard: adolescence has been frequently associated with the onset of schizophrenia; the midlife crisis with severe depression. Transitions can sometimes become prolonged into "limbo states," where people languish indefinitely, postponing the process of further growth.

Lines

It has been known for some time that development is not a unilateral process. It is less like a single, uniform mass, and more like an army advancing along a broad front in a series of uneven "columns" or "lines." Each developmental line acts like an independent unit and proceeds at its own pace (Freud, 1963). Consequently, any two lines—such as those of love and work—may be considerably out of phase with each other. The same person can be advancing in some areas, retreating in others, and remaining stationary in still others.

Timing

This implies that development proceeds according to a person's own timetable. There is a certain fixed order to the stages and general age ranges for each, but these must not be interpreted too literally. There is an innate rhythm to each person's development which, unless extreme, should usually not be hurried or imposed upon by external factors. Each new stage is a challenge and a potential obstacle. It is best to reject fixed notions of the course of development as largely illusory. *Normal development is not synonymous with uniform forward progress; nor does it reach a peak at some predetermined point, followed by a rapid downhill course or shift toward another stage.*

There is considerable variation in rate of normal development. *Delay* and *precosity* are typical examples. Normative bias may prompt one to ask what is wrong in all cases of delay. But, in many cases, it is simply a function of the unique rhythm of that person's growth curve. Folk wisdom recognizes this in the expression "late bloomer." Similarly, there is a tendency to view precosity as superiority. Yet, cases are known in which precosity is followed by later failure.

Regression

During development, the person may appear to take two steps forward and then one step backwards (i.e., regress in some area). *Regression refers to the revival of earlier and more primitive coping strategies in response to stress.* It is an expected feature of most normative crises and transitions. For example, most people are familiar with the child who begins to act more like a baby after the arrival of a new brother or sister. Yet they sometimes forget that parents tend to regress under the same circumstances. The father, for example, may be secretly nursing a jealous grudge against the new baby for monopolizing his wife's attention, as he also may have done vis-a-vis his own mother when one of his younger siblings was born.

Repetition

People tend to underestimate the extent to which repetition is built into the lifecycle. Lulls and plateaus may be as intrinsic to the lifecycle as rapid spurts of development. But, to the person caught in one of these doldrums, the reality is that "he is not getting anywhere." Only careful assessment can determine whether the complaint indicates a normal degree of pause or if it represents a "stuck point" requiring intervention.

One adaptive aspect of repetition is the opportunity it affords to rework tasks and conflicts of earlier eras, particularly those of separation–individuation. In optimum cases, this amounts to a second chance at development through greater mastery of previously highly conflicted issues. Psychotherapy attempts to facilitate this "second chance." Because it is stressful to talk about conflicted issues, psychotherapy generally is also associated with some regression.

Transitional periods, in a sense, look backward as well as forward, in a kind of Janus-faced posture. *Transitions reflect the developmental need to reassess, rethink, reexperience, and rework the past.* Only in retrospect can one generally see the positive aspects of a lull or get a new perspective on a period of rapid life change that seemed to be a blur at the time. Perhaps this is why adult stages of development have been relatively neglected until recently. Most of those doing scholarly research are immersed in this "era," and it is generally much more difficult to look carefully and critically at one's self than at others.

Erikson's Eight Ages of Man

Erik Erikson's model of human development (Erikson, 1963) laid the foundation for later lifecycle studies. His intention was to fill in the total picture of the lifecycle in broad strokes. His eight ages of man (see Table 7-1) shows an underlying order in the lifecycle in a simple format, and its simplicity makes it a valuable tool for organizing life experience. Erikson divided the lifecycle into eight discrete, well-defined stages. Each stage is characterized by a specific task, usually a fundamental one that affects multiple life sectors. For example, *basic trust* applies to all human relationships, self confidence, and even religious faith. The pairing of each task fulfillment with its potential failure, or problems remaining within it, circumscribes a range of possible outcomes.

Each stage is a link in the chain of life. *Failure* is defined as a weak link or a break in the chain. This has been called the *epigenetic approach* (i.e., the initiation of and success with a new stage is partly dependent on the degree of successful negotiation of previous stages). The image of the chain emphasizes the continuity of life. Consequently, it implies that childhood is the foundation of adulthood. However, success with basic mastery of childhood stages carries proportionately more weight in determining the probability of later successful development. Failure or major problems early on tend to be less reversible and to cause broader ranging difficulties than problems later in life.

The merits of Erikson's approach also determine its limitations. It is a sketch of development, not a detailed blueprint. Some of his divisions are too broad to do justice to the subtleties of a person's life. They also may be too uniform to suggest the markedly different paths and rates of change that frequently occur during a life. The adult stages also seem meager in number and in substance. Occupation, for example, is not mentioned at all. Many of these "deficiencies" can be mitigated by viewing the adult stages as midpoints of multiple lines of development. By taking into account all related stages, each adult stage actually appears quite comprehensive. Each adult stage also takes on added significance when it is viewed in the light of the quest for an individual's personal identity.

Identity and the Lifecycle

Erikson (1959) saw the lifecycle as a lifelong quest to achieve a coherent personal identity. By identity, he meant an inner sense of "sameness" or continuity in the midst of change. Erikson was the first to affirm the importance of a sense of identity for success and happiness as a human being. A stable sense of identity is both a prerequisite for and an outcome of successful development. But even with a strong foundation in the early years, the sense of a stable personal identity can never be taken for granted. It is always a precarious achievement, liable to be upset or even overturned by the vicissitudes of change, such as a personal illness or external circumstances. Every normative crisis threatens to disrupt the ongoing sense of identity. The successful negotiation of adult stages requires extensive psychologic reworking, adaptation, and integration. Everyone is periodically challenged to rework, revise, and reorient his former ideas of whom he was, is, and wants to become.

The childhood stages contribute to each person's first sketch of his own identity and sense of self. *Basic trust* gives a child the conviction that he or she belongs in this world and has a right to exist in his or her own right. It forms the fundamental basis of how one responds to others and expects others to respond. The stage of *autonomy* works in the other direction by helping the child learn that it is acceptable at times to say "no" to others' demands, and that, in part, people may define themselves by what they oppose. The stage of *initiative* fixes the first blueprint of identity through the activities with which each person selects to be involved, and often relates to the parental ideals. *Industry* helps to consolidate and expand the new sense of self by learning that hard work tends to pay off and that identification with a peer group is important.

The transition to young adulthood (Erikson's stage of *identity consolidation versus role diffusion*) poses the first major challenge to identity for some persons. The range and intensity of life changes during young adulthood may strain the established psychologic structure to the breaking point. Often, the result is a state of flux. At this point, the person is vulnerable to more severe breakdowns in identity, including the extreme of psychosis; the latter is in part because the biologic vulnerability to schizophrenia appears to peak in late adolescence and the early twenties. But given some measure of success in the early stages, the person may be able to tolerate or postpone aspects of the chaos long enough for reintegrative psychologic forces to "catch up." Such a postponement of adult commitments, to allow more time to rethink or gradually address changes, Erikson calls a *moratorium.*

Early adulthood initiates the process of forging a new adult identity from the fragments of adolescent flux. Accomplishing this goal amounts to a major reorientation, a revolution, if you will, in the self-concept. The new structure will have to reconcile the competing claims of dependency, craving for autonomy, sexuality, and body image changes. Old attachments will have to be relinquished or preserved with modifications. New commitments will have to be entered into, at first tentatively, and later definitively in the stage of intimacy.

The stage of *generativity* ushers in a further modification and expansion of adult identity. The life space widens to include the next generation; there is an identification with the parental role in the broadest sense. Persons redefine their own contribution as a "passing of the torch" to their potential heirs. The need for bold self-assertion usually lessens. Occasionally, this new orientation is incorporated into a "mission" or life's work that concentrates on enhanced productivity, optimally a playful creativity, and a renewed partnership with others. In the full sense, generativity connotes a confluence of love, work, play, and identity.

The completion of one's identity is the task of late life, and Erikson labeled this the stage of *ego integrity versus despair.* Integrity implies a feeling of self-worth associated with a final self-reconciliation. Seeing life as a whole highlights a person's achievements, as well as failures. Integrity is based on an awareness of the limits of any human life. It may be hard to face these limits and to let go of one's omnipotence once and for all. But this final work of "delimitation" can also bring about a sense of underlying meaning, order, and uniqueness of the person's life.

THE STAGES OF ADULTHOOD

The Transition to Adulthood

After the initial period of adolescent flux, young people initiate their first tentative movement toward adulthood (see Table 7-3). The transitional identity of student or apprentice teaches them the background skills, without committing them to full responsibility (Levinson et al, 1978; Levinson and Gooden eh, 1985). In this guise, they can allow themselves the freedom to be experimental—to try out various roles. Such playful exploration is normative for a transitional stage and does not necessarily imply a lack of perseverance.

Table 7–3 **Some Postinfancy Aspects of Psychologic Stages in the Lifecycle**

STAGE	TRANSITIONAL ISSUES	RITES OF PASSAGE	SYMPTOMS OF CRISIS	PATHOLOGIC OUTCOME
Transitions before adulthood	Novice Student Apprentice	School matriculation	School Work phobia	Agoraphobia
Consolidation of adulthood	New title	Graduation	Repeated career changes	"Pseudo-adult"
Courtship	Experimentation	Dating, "trial marriage"	Premature or delayed commitment	Schizoid character Precocious adult
Transition to marriage	"Contract" with spouse	Marriage ceremony	Boredom or constant warfare	Separation or divorce
Pregnancy	Physical changes "New space"	Baby "shower" Childbirth education classes	Hypochondriasis Detachment	Denial or "pseudocyesis"
Childbirth	Pregnancy	Labor and delivery	Excessive anxiety: Prepartum and during labor	Postpartum depression
Parenting	Primary maternal preoccupation, "holding"	Naming ceremony	Marital unrest Developmental delay in child	Maternal deprivation or overstimulation of child
Midlife transition	Mourning	"40th birthday" or midlife crisis	Withdrawal, sudden life change	Depression, substance abuse
Transition to old age	Repository of cultural values	Retirement, illness, death of spouse and friends	Regression, "King Lear" complex	Depression

The tasks of the young adult are consistent with his transitional role of "novice" or learner. Several of these tasks merit consideration:

1. The relationship to the parents must undergo substantial modification. The old childhood dependence on the parents must be given up and replaced by a more mature partnership with them. Nobody is free to make strong future attachments while old ones are still totally in place. Moreover, one cannot feel truly independent while holding on to the expectation that a parental figure will always be there to help put things right. Such magic expectations undermine the motivation to accept personal responsibility and to develop adult initiative.

2. The identity of "student" or "novice" serves as a helpful transition to mature mutuality. The relationship of mentor to pupil includes some of the old parent–child dependent qualities. Medical students understandably often complain of their passive position in the

learning process: the long lectures, the hours of memorizing, the examinations—in short, their relative lack of control and initiative. On the other hand, the professor or mentor will hopefully help to model a more active and independent stance. Student may be progressively more encouraged to take their own positions, ask their own questions, and design their own projects.

3. Identification with the mentor both fuels and modifies young people's idealism. In this context, they elaborate this identification into dreams, and later into more articulated adult aspirations (Levinson et al, 1978). Idealism helps to bridge the gap between childhood fantasies and adult hopes and aspirations. Early childhood fantasies are modified and, in part, incorporated into the new adult identity. Continuity is thus maintained between past and future. Keeping this in mind will guard against the tendency to discourage idealism merely because it is unrealistic or rebellious in tone.

4. Studenthood is more specifically the transition to an occupation. It is a time of intense preparatory learning, during which students are protected from the full weight of responsibility for their performance. They can try out the work under supervision and in smaller doses. Normally, there is an atmosphere of toleration of student's needs to experiment with different styles, techniques, and roles, regardless of the inconsistencies these shifts may appear to entail. Possibly more disruptive, but still within the rubric of experimentation, is the tendency to go from one job to another, or one passionate interest to another.

5. The same bent for experimentation often rules the attempts to establish an intimate relationship. There may be a prolonged period of "playing the field," or a series of "trial relationships." It must be borne in mind that relationships require a period of learning as well. The peer group plus knowledge and fantasies about what the parent's early relationship was like may provide the equivalence of mentorship in this area. Notions about the ideal mate must be tested against reality. Views about sexuality and love must be explored in the "laboratory" of a real relationship.

"Sticking Points" and Failures in Early Adulthood

Problems in early adulthood are often associated with delay in initiating adult tasks, and by far the most frequent cause for these delays is the failure to relinquish the parents. Such failures are often brought to the attention of the physician in the form of anxiety or depressive symptoms. College students in their first year away from home are virtually all grappling to some degree with separation–individuation issues. The student's "school phobia" may screen a more profound pining and yearning for the parental home. The physician can often be helpful in bringing out the underlying depression and grief, and in helping the student adjust to their separation from home. Sometimes a period of regression is necessary, during which the student may move back home for a while, and frequent but brief trips back and forth from school can be recommended to permit emotional "refueling" to decrease the strain of abrupt separation and allow more time for the individuation process to mature.

The young person who fails entirely to leave home may present physicians with a somewhat more difficult problem. Such persons may have failed to initiate dating or job seeking. Their school phobia may have worsened into agoraphobia. Paradoxically, an escalation of their symptoms may also signal the alarm they increasingly feel in being isolated and removed from the mainstream of others their age. Often, it is the parents who bring these persons to medical attention out of concern that the symptom is exacerbating the young person's dependency, which, of course, it is designed to do. The literal fact of living at home is less important than the inner attachment to the parents. An occasional young person can be living in the parental home past the age of 30 and still possess a clear sense of personal independence. In contrast, there may be others who live thousands of miles away, yet are very tied to the parents or locked in unresolved conflicted relationships with them. In this case, geographic distance may be a substitute for the emotional distance that cannot be achieved by other means.

The "Pseudo-adult"

At times, the attachment to the parents, and to the world of childhood in general, leads to a kind of temporal dissociation, instead of to delay. Such persons feel that they can "have their cake and eat it too." They fabricate an adult "false self," while still maintaining their true identity as a child who never grows up. The condition has recently been dubbed the "Peter Pan" syndrome (Kiley, 1983), from the popular childhood story of a mythical boy who never had to grow up. In terms of the lifecycle, the pseudo-adult is stuck in a limbo—"never, neverland," if you will—between childhood and adulthood. This syndrome is well illustrated by certain men in their thirties.

A CASE STUDY

Mr. N, a charming and moderately successful artist in his mid-thirties, presented to a psychiatrist with symptoms of dissatisfaction with his marriage. Although talented, he had a formidable psychologic block against advancing his career. His "Peter Pan" identity allowed him to work well under conditions of play, but he rebelled when it came to keeping a regular work schedule. He loved to think up new ideas but hated the work necessary to implement them. The same basic problem plagued him in his marriage: he could not stand the idea of having to work and compromise with his spouse to resolve the inevitable conflicts associated with a long-term, intimate relationship. In effect, he was going through the motions of being an adult without putting his heart and soul into it. And yet, he found that he could easily fool others with his act. They marveled at his "togetherness." This reinforced his secret wish to have it both ways: success in the adult world without ever having to grow up.

Precocious Adulthood

For some, the problem is not one of attachment, but rather of precocious autonomy and independence. As children, these persons typically detached themselves from dependence on their parents at a very young age. In some instances, they may have resorted to "self-mothering" as a result of maternal deprivation. In other cases, they may have been allocated the role of "parental child" in a large family and been delegated the task of taking care of younger siblings or others. But regardless of etiology, their precosity would seem to obviate any need for a transition to adulthood—they are "already there." What is missing in them is their childhood "roots." Often they are perceived by others as highly competent and responsible, but at the same time as stilted, and as lifeless as robots. Their resemblance to automatons is based on an early identification with an ideal of total self-reliance.

Some of these persons exhibit a pressured and almost manic pursuit of this ideal, to the exclusion of any reflection or self-awareness. So immersed are they in life's externals, that their inner life dies stillborn. They often become the adult workaholic. Such flight into constant activity may carry them along for a surprising length of time, but they are at risk of having a traumatic midlife crisis.

Others with this type of precosity develop a schizoid indifference to interpersonal intimacy. The schizoid type preserves a rich inner life at the expense of an interpersonal life. One such patient presented at the age of 34 with the chief complaint of never having been intimate with a single person, man or woman. In a way, he was bothered more by what other people would think about this than by personal distress; yet, he retained a fleeting awareness that an important sector of life was passing him by.

The Consolidation of Adulthood

In favorable circumstances, the young adult reaches a point when he or she can say, "Now, I am a man (or woman)" (Blos, 1967). This stage of consolidation of adult identity usually occurs around the age of 30 (Vailliant, 1977). It may have gradually evolved out of a variety of components, or it may have "crystallized" with some degree of abruptness. In some cases, it does not come without some measure of inner struggle over the new "fixity" of adulthood and its associated commitments (Gould, 1972).

Recently, the term *consolidation* has become almost synonymous with the consolidation of occupational or professional identity. This is due in part to the expanded role that work plays in modern life (Simons, 1985). *Increasingly, some have come to see work not as something they do but as something they are.* It has become more of "a calling" than "a job." People whose work is "only a job" may feel a need to find their "real life's work." People who are failures at their work are sometimes considered failures in life. Accordingly, work has become a kind of microcosm of life. In addition to income, they look to work to provide them their sense of status, self-esteem, productivity, a creative outlet, as well as social life, friendly collaborations, and even their "subculture" (the corporate culture).

The rite of passage into true adulthood has evolved into a type of graduation ritual. Graduation confers upon students a new title or name, which formalizes their new identity as well as cancels their old student identity. While important in this regard, graduation has become more of a public recognition of a *fait accompli*. It is intended to give official, public recognition to what has already been accomplished, sometimes largely in private.

Medical students—the primary audience of this text—may offer an important example in this regard. If one asks medical students at the beginning of their third year how they prefer to be addressed, the majority will answer, "as a medical student, Mr., Ms., and so forth." If one asks them the same question again in the fourth year, many will say "Doctor." At some point in the fourth year, the student will start "living up" to that title. He or she will start thinking and acting much more like a doctor than like a freshman medical student. And the moment these students start making their own decisions, the less they will need others to tell them what to do; instead, they will begin to look on others more as consultants. Their newfound ability to give themselves to their calling may produce a sense of euphoria and power. That is due, in part, to the expansion of work to include play, relaxation, and a sense of mastery.

That "moment" is often marked by the change of title. Like any name, new doctors find that others address them in the same way that they address themselves. This coordination of internal and external recognition is important to the sense of identity. A discrepancy between the two signals may indicate trouble. Public recognition alone is not enough, as noted in the case of "pseudo-adults." On the other hand, a lack of public recognition often disguises a problem in private recognition. For example, students who always complain that the residents or professors are "keeping them down" probably do not fully yet believe in their own "coming of age." Such persons may not be able to reach full adulthood without undergoing somewhat of an "age 30 crisis" (Gould, 1972; Levinson et al, 1978; Levinson and Goodeneh, 1985).

A CASE STUDY

Dr. G, a young resident physician, presented to a psychiatrist with complaints of extreme anxiety over the performance of medical procedures. Lately, he had started to ask consultants to do this type of work for him. He felt so ashamed over this state of affairs that he actively considered abandoning his medical career. After a period of psychotherapeutic work, Dr. G related this fear to the image of a punishing father. He vividly recalled making rounds with his father, who was a veterinarian, and witnessing the castration of numerous farm animals. In effect, he had integrated the "maternal" aspects of being a doctor, but not the "paternal." He was a responsible physician who cared for his patients and worked hard on their behalf. But his inability to integrate the degree of "intrusiveness and aggressiveness" that is needed to complete some tasks into his image of himself was holding up his adult consolidation as a comprehensive physician. The resolution of his "age 30 crisis" involved some rapprochement between aspects of both parents.

The Triad of Courtship, Marriage, and Marital Crisis

Courtship

Courtship is part of the transition to marriage in the same sense that student status is part of the transition to an adult occupation. In the one, the focus is individual identity, while, in the other, it is "pair identity." Temporally, the stages of early adulthood and courtship usually parallel each other. The issue of intimacy occupies both stages. In courtship, its achievement is defined as the formation of a couple.

In American culture, dating functions as a rite of passage into the courtship stage. Its main function is to bring the young person into contact with the pool of possible marital partners. Young adults sometimes express the wish to bypass this process, complaining of the artificiality of the rituals involved. Nevertheless, some "artificiality" is a facet of all rituals and must be borne to some degree. The absence of dating in someone's life history is virtually always significant. It may signal a delay in the courtship phase, or it may indicate that those stages have been skipped, as in premature marriage.

"Trial marriage" or "living together" has also become an accepted part of courtship, at least in most Western industrial societies. Nowadays, it is more common for what was at least the stereotyped "honeymoon" to precede the marriage. Optimally, living together might function as a laboratory for the exploration of what the realities of marriage would be for the couple. In practice, however, this may be a relatively rare occurrence. When the "honeymoon" precedes the marriage, there is a strong temptation to postpone consideration of the more contractual aspects of couplehood until after marriage.

In the American society of today, courtship may easily degenerate into a kind of "limbo" that evades the transition to marriage rather than furthers it. For some couples, courtship may then become a prolonged honeymoon or even an indefinite extension of dating. Other couples may choose to live together like roommates, out of convenience or friendship, keeping their romantic liaisons outside the relationship. This tendency to split the romantic from the contractual aspects of the couple may sometimes continue into the marriage, which may result in stresses and possibly divorce, despite years of preparatory living together.

Marriage

Naturally, the psychologic formation of a "couple" will not always coincide with the marriage ceremony. In any case, some couples will have formed well in advance of their marriage; whereas, other couples do not crystallize until well after their marriage, and still others are effectively "divorced" before they get married. Nevertheless, it is probable that most couples go through some type of postcourtship transition to the married state.

Marriage takes for granted a certain degree of personal maturity in both partners. Ideally, each of them should be capable of seeing the other as a whole, separate person with his or her own life and viewpoints. Each must be able to tolerate the good as well as the bad in the other, as reflected in the words "for better or worse," which are frequently used in marital vows. And each must be able to empathize with (and not be overly threatened or annoyed by) the other's positions, even when they conflict with his or her own. In short, the partners will hopefully have acquired a sense of their own identity and self-worth as persons.

But some couples start married life before the partners have consolidated their own adult identities. They may decide early on to continue the mode of infantile dependence on each other. This kind of symbiosis can be mutually reinforcing in a way that prevents an evolution of the relationship along more mature lines. Other couples feel so threatened by the new level of intimacy of their married state that their precarious coalition is vulnerable to decompose into two warring persons.

Both the symbiotic couple and the "warring couple" lack clear boundaries between the partners. In the symbiotic couple, the partners function as "auxiliaries" for undeveloped aspects of each other. The warring couples are so threatened by defusion of boundaries that they must resort to opposition to reinforce and clarify those boundaries. The more exaggerated the differences in their positions, the easier it is to see and grasp their separate identities. The partners in the latter type of couple have too much privacy, just as in the first type the partners do not have enough. Neither type possesses the basis for a mature partnership between equals.

A clue to a solution of these problems may be contained in the marriage ceremony itself. This rite of passage aims to transform two separate persons into a new couple. The device that unites the pair is a simple contract. It is important to emphasize that marriage is a formal arrangement imposed on the couple by society. The contractual features are evident in several ways. First, there are legalistic trappings: the official representative of society (a priest, rabbi, judge, and so forth), the exchange of explicit vows, the presence of witnesses, and the finality of a signed document. Second, there is the almost arbitrary conventionality of the quid pro quo formula: one thing in return for another.

The marital contract offers the couple a framework for holding together and for keeping apart their status as individuals. We can look on it as a piece of scaffolding that can be discarded once the partnership is in place. In this sense, it is a transitional state between the individual and the couple—a connecting link between the individual agendas. Just as in the marital vows, each partner is expected to translate his private wishes into explicit, verbal statements. These statements are then put in the form of promises in the following formula: if you give me X, I will give you Y. With the contractual formula in hand, the partners can begin to negotiate agreements over the entire range of their shared life space. These include family finances, sexual etiquette, conflict resolution, allocation of privacy—even who sleeps on which side of the bed.

An especially thorny issue may be the question of the household division of labor. Traditionally, this matter was decided along the lines of stereotyped sexual roles. Nowadays, the couple must first decide where they stand on the sex role continuum before that of task allocation per se. Some successful marriages opt for a complete reversal of sex roles, while others stay with the more traditional arrangement; still others occupy a middle ground.

At some point in the process of working out these issues, the partners may recognize a renewed sense of mutuality based on working together as equals. They may see that working together validates their separateness at the same time as it draws them closer together. The partnership is now the property of the couple and no longer something imposed by society. The framework of the contract has helped them to discover a new mode of creative collaboration in which their different perspectives play off each other with novel results. Several of these may be an enriched sexual experience, a readiness for new ventures, and a vital miniculture of shared history and values.

Marital Crisis
We have seen how the transition to the married state can result in considerable turmoil for the couple. This is a time when the forces of individuation may threaten to tear apart a fragile alliance. A crisis may occur whenever new conditions place excessive strain on the old arrangements. According to this framework, a crisis will be

most likely during a transitional period. Childbirth, parenting, and the "empty nest syndrome" are typical examples. But a crisis may be delayed or postponed, especially if the development of the marriage is out of synchrony with that of the partners. Many marriages have existed for 7 to 10 years before one or both partners have reached maturity as adults. When individual partners "catch up," they are likely to feel disoriented and constrained within an outmoded arrangement. For example, a sudden spurt in occupational success can throw the previous "contract" out of kilter.

A crisis may be preceded by a prodromal period during which signs of trouble are ignored. The increasing turmoil may make itself felt as tension and fighting—or the reverse: excessive calm or boredom. Sometimes a fullblown crisis is necessary to get across the message that something is wrong. When this is recognized, the partners can spell out their dissatisfactions and so begin a process of reformulation of the marriage contract.

The reconciliation process is often complicated by the tendency toward regression that marks any crisis. In the context of the couple, this usually means a return to "nonpair" ways of relating. The prototypic example is a reversion to mutual blaming. In the first round of many marital squabbles, each partner will want to blame the other for the problem. Instead of viewing the problem in pair terms, he or she sees it solely as the other person's responsibility. Frequently, there follows an escalation of blaming during which the pair revives many of their past conflicts.

Couples who already have an established pattern of fighting may be especially vulnerable at this point. Such a couple is usually unable to resolve their crisis without help, because they cannot recover their "pair perspective." Spouse abuse is an ominous sign of such a deteriorating situation. If the couple can recover their perspective, they face the task of reassessing and then restructuring the marriage. They may have to renegotiate the old agreements from scratch. If so, they may want to bring back the old contractual framework as a temporary support. At best, they will have to substantially modify past agreements.

Although marital crises tend to occur at fairly specific points in the adult lifecycle, such as after childbirth, at midlife, or during the "empty nest" phase, it would be erroneous to view the time line of most marriages as a long period of stagnation or latent conflict, followed by an explosive climax. There is a unique evolution to every marriage, but some may indeed follow these patterns. But in a healthy marriage there is usually a dynamic sequence of growth, plateauing, stagnation, reassessment, and new growth. The time frame for this process may be years, months, or even weeks.

The Role of Counseling

Even a normative crisis may carry significant risks. For example, the high rate of divorce reflects the inherent instability associated with marital crises as much as it does the pathologic aspects of a marriage and the changing mores of society. It is thus quite natural and wise for a couple to look for outside professional help when they see no other way out of their difficulties. When the couple can no longer mediate between themselves, society can provide them with an outside mediator. The external mediator is, in a sense, a new version of the same official representative who married them in the first place. This role can be filled by any person in authority: a teacher, priest, physician (ultimately, often a psychiatrist), or even lawyers and a divorce court judge.

If the couple has never really learned how to negotiate, the psychiatrist or other psychotherapist may begin by teaching them this art. One entire style of marriage therapy—aptly called "contract therapy"—does just this (Sholevar, 1981). However, with most couples, it is more a question of restarting a stalled negotiation. The first step may be a search for a new area of compromise. Each partner may need help in articulating his or her position, or in refraining from attack and counterattack. Most of all, they need encouragement to keep talking. In acting as a mediator, the counselor or psychotherapist must be careful to remain in the middle. The partners will usually try to draw him or her to their side as an ally, or to do their talking for them. (This phenomenon is also known as "triangulation" and is discussed in Chap. 8). The counselor gently deflects all such invitations away from him or herself and back into the partners themselves. Similarly, the counselor discourages them from using other people, including children and in-laws, for the same purpose. The therapist thus stabilizes the coalition by decreasing access to the outside coalitions that undermine it.

It is quite common for physicians to encounter patients whose hidden or overt agenda is a failing marriage. The patient may want the physician's permission to exit a moribund marriage. Or he or she may want the spouse to be "treated"—in other words, "brought into line." Or it may be the spouse who wants the patient "treated." The clue to the underlying situation is often revealed when, inevitably, the spouse is drawn into the discussions. If physicians fail to see the hidden agenda, they may unwittingly encourage an unfruitful alliance with the patient that supports a bad marriage. (Family systems theory, family therapy techniques, and the physician's role in the referral process are also discussed in Chap. 8.)

Alternatives to Traditional Marriage and Parenting

The previous section has made it clear that collaborative partnerships are not an invariable outcome of marriage. Many marriages endure despite the absence of any true alliance. And many viable partnerships develop outside the confines of traditional marriages in stable, long-term relationships, or as a result of other social arrangements. The latter category includes working partnerships, the psychotherapeutic alliance between therapist and patient, and a community or religious network.

Hence, there is some justification for the reverse assumption, namely that the establishment of a collaborative partnership produces a "marriage." Increasingly, our society has come to recognize a relationship as "binding" when there is public evidence of the existence of a partnership. This broader definition might include common-law marriages and homosexual marriages. In this context, "marriage" is a metaphor for any dedicated, supraindividual relationship. The "other party" to this relationship is not limited to one special person. It may be a collection of persons, a group/organization, a life's work, a political cause, or even God, as exemplified in religious communities.

Parenting may supply the raison d'etre for such a "marriage," as the following sections will discuss. In examining the wide variations in parenting at all levels of society, family studies have stressed the importance of collaboration for successful family development. They have defined collaboration according to three invariant criteria: (1) A clear division of parental function between the role of mother and father, (2) some degree of recognition and representation of both parental roles, and (3) a barrier against crossgenerational alliances, and of incest in particular (Sholevar, 1981). (See also Chap. 8.)

According to these criteria, many apparent exceptions to the traditional model of parenting may prove quite capable of raising healthy families. Many successful families make effective use of surrogate parents. In single parent families, the role of surrogate may be played by a grandparent, uncle/aunt, or friend. Other families distribute the roles of mother and father among several people. This method was pioneered by the Israeli kibbutz and is typical of extended families and of postdivorce merged families. In homosexual parenting arrangements, the parental roles are divided between persons of the same sex. Such arrangements may be successful provided the couple can maintain sufficient differentiation between the two parent's roles. A third method leans on the new institutions of day care, professional babysitters, and neighborhood networks to provide "auxiliary parents." It is probably not uncommon for single parent families to call on all three methods at various times and settings. Even in so called "matriarchal" families, the place of the missing parent is often occupied by a symbolic figure, such as the local minister.

It is this latter view of marriage—and this point cannot be emphasized too strongly—that constitutes the true developmental task. Many persons find that some degree of partnership is achieved more easily through an alternate route. Indeed, there are some persons for whom traditional marriage is contraindicated for a variety of reasons. The prototypic unmarried professional person, for instance, by finding deep satisfaction in his/her dedication to their work arrives at a different path to "generativity" and validation of their self-worth.

The Triad of Pregnancy, Childbirth, and Parenting

Pregnancy

Nature usually offers expectant parents a 9-month grace period before the awesome travails of childbirth and parenting begin. Pregnancy gives the couple time to make room for a new person in their lives. Conception has the secondary meaning of a "new idea"—the idea of a child and new family member. Conception brings the idea of a child to life in the minds of the parents. The child becomes a subject of fantasy in both mother and father. The specific content of the fantasy is less important than its significance as the "potential space" in which the child will fit into the parent's lives.

The gradual physical changes in the mother-to-be give another support to the creation of this "space." At first, they are the only evidence of the "reality" of the child. Most mothers cannot ignore what is happening to their own body, but the father is, of course, more removed from the process. He can avoid a tendency toward denial by actively involving himself in what the mother is feeling, and by feeling the abdominal area for signs of movement (quickening).

Bodily changes also direct the mother's attention inward to a growing identification with the living child inside her (Bibring et al, 1961; Winnicott, 1965). It is normal for her to become relatively more preoccupied with herself during pregnancy, to the relative neglect of externals. Her early attachment to the new baby is dependent on her undergoing this "normal illness," known as primary maternal preoccupation. The father can help by arranging things so that mother need not be distracted from this state of mind. Nowadays, some have gone to the other extreme in expecting the mother to continue with her life as if nothing new is happening.

Mothers who cannot enter this state often have trouble forming an initial bond to their infant. In contrast, there are mothers who become excessively caught up in bodily sensations to the point of hypochondriasis. One can see that pregnancy creates some very real demands on the mother's sense of adult identity. The new space for the child may be experienced as a kind of incursion. Mothers with a poorly formed sense of themselves may be more vulnerable to postpartum depression and other psychiatric reactions.

For both parents, the baby in the womb is a metaphor for a new growing space in their lives. The first fantasies about the baby are elaborated into plans for the future. Usually an infant's room is decorated and furnished. Some account is taken of the parent's feelings about one sex or the other. Universal fears about the health of the child are aired, a process that helps to make the responsibility of parenting more concrete. The preparation reaches a climax with the choice of names for the baby. The name selection helps create a new place in the family network that hopefully will someday be filled by a living human being. Sometimes the naming is celebrated in a bris or other ceremony shortly after birth.

Childbirth

Even with 9 months of active preparation, childbirth is virtually always a normative crisis in the lives of the new parents. This is so because the rate of change in childbirth and the immediate postpartum period is tremendous. The experience may leave the couple in a state of emotional shock. It is not uncommon to experience some degree of feelings of depersonalization, derealization, and a distortion of time sense. At times, the shock can be masked by feelings of exhilaration after birth. Weeks or even months may go by before the reality of the event begins to sink in. During this phase of normal "let down," the new parents start to recognize the automaticity of their responses and the postponement of their affective reactions until well after the fact. Indeed, this pattern of automatic behavior and postponement of response often continues well into the first year.

The first challenge is posed by the tendency of labor pains to cause some degree of panic in the mother and father. Extreme pain of any kind signals the possibility of catastrophy for the organism (Simons, 1985). Somehow, a context must be found in which this pain is perceived as normative and indicative of work being done. In a sense, the new childbirth classes are trying to make labor and delivery a new rite of passage into parenthood. One of their main goals is to remove the alarm that accompanies extreme pain, by reinterpreting it in a new context. Toward this end, they teach basic physiology, as well as specific techniques for pain management. In addition, they place labor and delivery at the end point of the preparation process started in pregnancy. They stimulate the couple's anticipatory planning for the future in tandem with the working through of anxiety. They help lay the foundation for parenting by encouraging the couple to act as a team. Giving the father the role of "coach" helps to counter his sense of helplessness in the face of his wife's activities and possible suffering. The group context provides support as well as a circle of initiates on the threshold of parenthood.

However, it is important that the ideologic underpinnings of these classes do not foster magic expectations. Some pain is still a fact of life for most deliveries. Not all fathers can deal with the actual birth. Most couples know instinctively what goes beyond the limits of their endurance and that should be assessed and honored by the physician.

Parenting

The skills of parenting lean heavily on the established partnership of the couple. The demands of a new baby will probably challenge the couple to improve their team work even further. Usually, this will involve some modification and reallocation of roles and tasks. However, the new task orientation may present a danger to the intimacy of the couple. The partners may be tempted to communicate through the new "third party," instead of with each other directly. Parents must work to preserve and protect their private relationship in the service of teamwork. They thus ensure from the start that parenting will not undermine the marriage that supports it. Some couples use parenting as a way of hiding a bad marriage, and those couples are most vulnerable to "the empty nest syndrome" (when the children leave home).

The couple's teamwork forms the basis of a "holding environment" for the new baby (Winnicott, 1965). "Holding" refers in a general way to all their efforts to adapt to the baby's needs, both psychologic and physiologic. It takes into account the literal holding of the child, as well as the monitoring of the early physical environment, of which the establishment of a stable home life is an essential part. Also important is the protection from stimuli and outside impingements that are beyond the child's capacity to assimilate. The earliest holding environment builds on the mother's growing empathy with her infant, itself founded on primary maternal preoccupation. The father's role in the beginning is to "hold" the mother and child couple so they can devote themselves to each other. For this purpose, he may need to act as a substitute mother, thus allowing the mother some time to recover her "individual" identity.

Beyond the stage of intimacy, the father helps to facilitate the child's separation from the mother (Greenspan, 1982). In this new role, he can allow himself to be seen as someone different from the mother, who represents a limit or even an interference on the mother–child mutuality. Yet, in the same guise, he also supports the child's growing independence.

With the passage of time, these roles are freely distributed between the parents. Frequent role reversals help to solidify the partnership by defusing stress. For example, it permits the parents to alternate the role of "disciplinarian." Doing this supports the idea that discipline is a joint effort, rather than the work of one parent alone.

Raising children places a variety of stresses on the parental partnership. Even if both parents have achieved full adulthood, which is often not the case, they will be prone to some regression in the stage of the absolute dependency of a newborn. Such extreme dependency may evoke a range of reactions, from stoic counterdependency to childish resentment. But even if they can weather this phase, they must now adjust to strains, in quite the opposite direction, when the child begins to separate. At this point, a tendency toward overidentification may inhibit the child from gaining independence. Most of all, it is the rapidly oscillating and conflicting demands that create turmoil. With the onset of the rapprochement crisis (Mahler, 1972), at about 21 months of age, children alternate between intense clinging to and pushing away of the parents. This is often enough to drive the whole family into a "minicrisis."

The holding environment must be strong and flexible enough to assimilate later developments, such as sibling rivalry and adolescent rebellion. When children acquire a personality of their own, they learn to exploit conflict between the parents by playing one against the other. Or they may divide the parents into opposing sides in the sibling war. The parents must resist any action that threatens to drive a wedge between them. And this means being aware of their tendencies to aid and abet their children's divisive behaviors.

Nothing poses a greater challenge to parental teamwork than "acting out" by their children. Temper tantrums or an adolescent's breaking curfew both require the setting of limits. "Discipline" is really nothing more than limit setting in action. The idea is not so much to "punish" as it is to contain behavior that threatens the holding environment. Children usually react positively to limit setting, because they accurately interpret it as a willingness to address their problems.

As was briefly noted in Chapter 6, discipline should not be confused with "punishment." Physical or corporal punishment is ultimately ineffective in developing a true sense of right and wrong and is indicative of parental ignorance about effective methods of parenting. Physical punishment basically molds behavior around fear of retaliation and motivates children to avoid "being caught." The goal of development is ultimately to enable the child to internalize self-regulatory behavior, to appreciate the effects of their own actions on others, to develop empathy and consideration for the feelings of others, and to solidify the substrate of a moral, ethical, and social conscience. Corporal or physical punishment—even "mild" forms—should be condemned by physicians, and parents should be counseled as to other methods of limit setting such as brief periods of "time out" or withdrawal of rewards (see Chap. 4).

By challenging the parents to strengthen their internal cohesion as a couple, children act as a spur to adult development. The experience of being a parent teaches adults the meaning of reliability and consistency, which are essential to any position of responsibility, whether that be as a teacher, judge, or physician. It also affords a helpful distance from the self in its other-directedness, and in the opportunity it provides of reexperiencing and reworking some of their childhood stages as well. Thus, parents retain a vital connection with the world of childhood at the very time when they are detaching themselves further from it.

The Effects of Divorce

According to this argument, children react to the parental couple in two contradictory ways. On the one hand, they want to drive a wedge between the parents to try to dominate and control them. On the other hand, they have a deep need to get and keep the parents together in a productive relationship. These trends represent opposite attitudes toward the fact of dependency.

When parents divorce, the wish to split up the parental couple becomes a reality. Therefore, it should come as no surprise when children see themselves as the cause of the separation and react with guilt. This may be so painful to children that they may attempt to deny the reality of the divorce. Or if they accept the threat as real, they may engage in frantic reparative efforts to get the parents back together. If the parents themselves are vascillating on the issue of separation, children may discover that they alone are holding the parents together; such a sense of responsibility may only add to their burden of guilt, fear, and anger.

It goes without saying that divorce is almost always traumatic to some degree to children. Naturally, the child's capacity to cope is influenced by the family context. If the marriage has been a violent battleground, or a cold, barren desert, divorce may be anticipated with something approaching relief. In some cases, the parent's capacity for parental collaboration may improve when living apart. In any case, the outcome is likely to depend on the parent's being able to sustain some degree of collaboration. The use of a child as a pawn in the parent's games, sometimes played out in a courtroom, jeopardizes the holding environment. Some form of escape into premature independence by the child may be the only way out of such an intolerable situation. Some form of psychologic or psychiatric counseling for parents to minimize the deleterious effects of divorce on the children is almost always indicated.

The Midlife Transition

Sometime between the ages of 35 and 55, most adults realize that they have reached the "midpoint" of their life span. This realization has a special psychologic significance. Beyond the midpoint one can no longer say that most of one's life lies ahead. The end is now visible, as well as the beginning. It is like stepping outside of the stream of life and seeing its horizon for the first time. From this perspective, one may grasp life as a whole, along with its boundaries and limits. The confrontation with these limits forms the basis of the most thorough readjustment of the adult self.

Before the midpoint of life, adults are usually still basking in the mild euphoria of "consolidation." They are most probably continuing to make steady progress toward their professional and personal goals, have seen the possibilities life has to offer, and are so immersed in various "engagements" that little time is taken for introspection. Indeed, they may be quite prepared and even wish to postpone any such self-assessment indefinitely. It is much easier to be carried along unthinking, on the tide of youthful dreams.

It often takes some life crisis or trauma before this mild illusory state is interrupted. Midlife is the time when new realities make their appearance: the first signs of physical aging, including the onset of menopause in women and the first dimunition of sexual desire in some men, the "sandwiching" produced by the growing independence of adolescent children and the death or disability of aging parents, and plateauing of advancement at work. Not infrequently, a first major medical illness, such as a myocardial infarction, will begin to drive home the idea that death is inevitable, or the reality may dawn when a peer dies in the prime of life.

Some experience of disillusionment seems to be necessary in making the transition to mature adulthood. Coming face to face with these "narcissistic blows" may help people to give up their universal fantasy of unlimited possibilities (Jaques, 1965; Kernberg, 1980; Viorst, 1986). They may be motivated to undergo a comprehensive life review, in which the past and present are reassessed (Levinson et al, 1978). Each aspect of life will have to be measured against the new limits revealed in one's own mortality. The ultimate goal of this quest is a new integration of self, in which a number of conflicting polarities—love/hate, self/other, male/female—are partially reconciled (Levinson et al, 1978; Levinson and Goodeneh, 1985; Settlage et al, 1988). Although largely internal, such a radical readjustment is bound to influence future relationships with others. Some have formulated this change as one of new tragic awareness replacing an older romanticism (Schafer, 1970).

The term "midlife crisis" is sometimes used to describe a block or obstacle in the midlife transition. For example, Mr. C presented to a psychiatrist with apprehension about an extramarital affair. In many ways, Mr. C's feelings about the affair resembled his passionate attachment to flying an airplane, an experience he described as "better than sex." Flying represented his last stand against the limits of earthbound life. Up in the sky, nothing could stop him, nothing could pull him down, nothing could get in his way. The controls were in his hands. He was quite oblivious to the fact that he could "crash," or that his life was already heading for a "nose-dive."

Bereavement

Loss plays a necessary role in every life transition. Every step forward in development implies the letting go of an important piece of one's past life. Thus, every developmental gain requires the working through of reactions to loss, both real and imagined (Viorst, 1986). However, it may be helpful to distinguish between reaction to loss, which is a function of all transitions, and the more specific reaction to the loss of a real object, referred to in this chapter as bereavement. In overcoming any major loss—whether it be of a spouse, parent, child, relative, or even a body part—the person must commit all of his psychologic resources to the single task of reviewing and reliving his lost relationship (Freud, 1958). Such a task is necessarily painful and also painstaking, protracted, and time consuming. It is best viewed as a self-limited psychologic process that unfolds through a series of stages from initiation to resolution.

The initial reaction to sudden loss is often some form of denial. People are likely to react to any catastrophic event with exclamations like "No," "It can't be," or "You've got to be kidding." Some people react to loss with the almost total absence of emotion. They are the ones on whom others rely for support and the smooth execution of funeral arrangements. For many, the apparent absence of emotion is due to "shock" and psychic numbing. They continue to go about their business in a kind of altered state of consciousness, as if on "autopilot." In any case, the effect of such denial is that the actual grief experience is postponed.

Everyone recognizes the signs of true grieving, which is characterized by an intense emotionality that includes admixtures of sadness, tearfulness, and rage. Many of these feelings are worked through and reexperienced in private, because our society tends to discourage public displays of grief. Grieving people are usually preoccupied with their feelings and inner experiences. Quasihallucinatory phenomena, such as hearing the voice of the departed relative, may be considered within the normal range of bereavement.

An important task in grief is the coming to terms with ambivalence. Bereavement tends to exaggerate normal ambivalence toward family members by evoking fantasies of desertion in a context in which it is considered wrong "to speak ill of the dead." Hence, some degree of guilt feeling is a normal aftermath of grief. For example, bereaved persons may chastise themselves for tiny sins of omission, like not being present at the moment of death, or not trying some experimental treatment. For a brief period, the bereaved person may feel that any degree of ambivalence is unacceptable. He or she may tend to split their ambivalence by overidealizing the image of the lost object and by setting up scapegoats, whom they can blame for their loss. It is not uncommon for the physician to occupy this role, particularly if he has been guilty of some error in his management of the case. A certain number of malpractice suits take their origin from this emotionally charged situation. In the ordinary course of events, however, the bereaved are able to pull together their feelings of love and hate into a more integrated picture. If they can begin to see the lost person for what he was, they may find they can cherish his memory in a more meaningful way.

This task concluded, the stage is set for the final detachment from the lost object, and the resultant freeing up of emotional energy for new emotional investments. Such detachment is facilitated by the reality testing that takes place every time the bereaved person falls back into the illusion that the dead person is still alive, and then must remind himself that he or she is no longer to be found. Only with such gradual detachment can one truly "bury the dead" and go on with the business of living. For people whose grieving has been incomplete, the dead still "live" as ghosts, which haunt the survivor, refusing to let him go.

The whole grieving process is marked by appropriate rites of passage that include funerals, eulogies, vigils, fasts, condolence rituals, wakes, and burial rites (Van Gennep, 1960). Nowadays, the erosion and weakening of public mourning rituals has placed a greater burden on the person's private means and resources. Wherever possible, the reinforcement and encouragement of public mourning provide a valuable support for the person's solitary efforts. For example, seeing the body—the equivalent of "viewing"—may help some persons to accept this death as an undeniable reality (Simons, 1985). A funeral also helps the bereaved to remember the dead, and also to begin to relinquish their intense attachments. It emphasizes the continuity of life (the community of mourners, the link with the transcendent) as it dramatizes its transience.

To an extent, public mourning has been transferred from the religious setting to the medical setting. The physician now often takes the role formerly occupied by the clergy. Within this setting, the physician can be of great help in assisting the bereaved. The physician can use their position and skills to guide the bereaved person through the stages of grief. Simply by allowing patients to grieve, physicians lend support to the legitimacy of grief, a legitimacy that is sometimes undermined by society's phobic attitude toward bereavement in general. More specifically, the physician's presence works to counteract the patients' fear that something is wrong with them ("Doctor, am I depressed?") and the patients' guilt that they are overreacting emotionally. At the same time, the physician can respect patient's pain and distress, addressing these feelings with standard medical management.

Thus, bereavement is treated as a kind of normal "illness," analogous to pregnancy, menopause, puberty, and so forth. As a potential illness in the strict sense, it is up to the physician to diagnose and treat pathologic complications. In pathologic bereavement, one or more features of the grieving process become grossly exaggerated and/or fixated at one stage. Common examples include absent grief, chronic bereavement, excessive guilt, and the loss of reality (psychosis). These and associated conditions, such as depression, mania and psychosomatic illness, must be treated in their own right.

Psychotherapy for the bereaved can serve as a catalyst to the grieving process and as a means of unearthing blocks in its development. The extent to which all psychotherapy deals with issues of "stillborn" or inadequately resolved grief reactions has probably been underestimated. For example, a 33-year-old cabinetmaker consulted a psychiatrist for frequent outbreaks of panic and depression. In the course of therapy, he revealed that his father had died about 10 years ago, suddenly and unexpectedly. For several years preceding his death, the patient had noticed a certain reserve in his otherwise cordial relations with his father. Now, it seemed as if a cruel fate had made any considerations of feeling irrelevant. Instead of grieving in the manner of his distraught mother, he said to himself, "Now you are the man of the family, so you better act like one." Ever since then, he had resolved to suppress all evidence of emotion and to "face reality" in a cool, detached manner. His recent decision to start therapy was really his way of keeping the appointment with this postponed grief and of owning up to it for the first time.

The Transition to Late Life

Society's recent, more enlightened attitudes toward late life may tend to obscure its realities. Any older person with a sense of humor might say that "old age" is not exactly what he or she had in mind. The sacrifices of this life stage in terms of illness, physical decline, and the death of loved ones are very real. A misconception about old age is that these losses represent an end to life. Now they are recognized as the greatest challenge to keep on living. One sign of increasing recognition of this challenge, as well as the older person's capacity to meet it, is the resurgence of interest in psychotherapy and psychoanalysis for the elderly.

A major task of old age is to enhance and maintain a sense of inner integrity in the face of great external threats. Throughout the lifecycle, the sense of identity is often "propped up" by a variety of external supports, including a healthy body, a social network, some authority in the workplace, demonstrable productivity, and family. Even a healthy person in the prime of life may suffer from identity defusion when deprived of these supports, such as may occur in prisons or other prolonged separations from family and friends. Such stresses call on all of a person's inner resources in combating depersonalization and identity confusion.

Luckily, one does not usually have to endure such trials all at once in the transition to old age, but each potential threat to a person's emotional integrity must be met and conquered using a variety of techniques. Among these are a search for new externalized supports, experiments with new methods of self-validation, and psychotherapy. These lines of development lend themselves for discussion under the headings of retirement and the battle for integrity.

Retirement

The relinquishing of power and authority must stimulate a search for new sources of productivity and creativity (Levinson and Goodeneh, 1985). Retirement often marks this transition. Less tied to the demands of the workplace, the older person is free to explore new interests and to deepen old ones. Adult education presents a popular means to this end. Besides opening the way to new undertakings and often new friends, learning can serve as a basis for self-study or just be pursued as an end in itself.

The renewed student status reflects a basic change in older person's engagement with the world. Regardless of the specific activity, they reenter society from a different "angle." What they have to offer others, whether as a grandparent, teacher, employee, or advisor, is the sum of their experiences, their wisdom, in short. They are natural experts on the human lifecycle and a vital link with the traditions of the past. One social role for the elderly may be to embody those traditions and to serve as a kind of custodian of cultural values and history.

What the elderly may lose in actuality, they often can regain in symbolic forms. They must get used to the idea of being a "figurehead"—at least to some degree. Yet, even when they have to "delegate" almost everything, they still have worth as the embodiment of societal values. This is where society's attitude—veneration or vilification of their elderly members—makes a difference. Symbolism only works if society lends weight to it. Ironically, its effectiveness is most visible in the political arena where older persons have been able to parlay this role of "elder statesman" into increased power and influence.

This transition requires the construction of new social networks to replace the old ones that were centered in the nuclear family and the workplace. New peer relationships are made possible by the increasing numbers of people surviving into old age and the proliferation of institutions that cater to the needs of senior citizens. Grandparenting may offer a new connectedness to family members.

However, not everyone succeeds in this readjustment. Some are seduced into thinking that retirement means a return to childhood fantasy and, therefore, an end to work. These are the people who may go through a "honeymoon" phase after retirement, followed by "disenchantment." Others approach retirement with great reluctance, often refusing to give up the reins of power and authority. Or they may express their ambivalence by making a show of handing over the responsibility, while still holding on to the ultimate authority, as occurs in King Lear.

Some inner opposition to the "passing of the scepter" is probably inevitable. Sometimes the conflict is the occasion for a medical consultation.

A CASE STUDY

Mr. H, a 65-year-old hospital administrator, presented with the complaint of excessive anger at the prospect of being replaced by a younger man. He noted that his whole life had been a search for new "challenges," which would confirm his identity as an effective person. What made stepping down particularly distasteful was the fact that, in his eyes, the replacement lacked even the basic qualifications for the job. Yet despite this lack of respect, he felt guilty at begrudging a "son" figure the chance to make good. Verbalizing these feelings helped him overcome this obstacle to his retirement and to go on with his life in a fulfilling manner.

The Battle for Integrity

Isolation still remains the single most important threat to the sense of integrity of older persons. They are especially vulnerable to the stimulus deprivation that may result from decreasing sensory acuity. As inner resources decline, the importance of external supports increases. Surrounded by familiar people and objects, even a person with dementia may be able to maintain a sense of personal identity for a long time.

Physicians may be helpful in reversing the insidious combination of the effects of aging and the loss of external supports, such as lower income, illness or death of a spouse, and family relocation. They can support the family of an ill or demented older person by providing assistance in the management of the home environment. In addition to medical treatment, such measures will include frequent family visits; daily orientation to time, place, and person; a rigid daily schedule; family photographs on the wall; and the use of a night light.

In more optimal circumstances, older people are challenged to view sickness and death as a test of their personal integrity and inner resources. The near universality of some type of illness in the elderly may make illness a kind of "normative crisis" that the elderly recognize as a rite of passage into old age. By finding ways of overcoming the passivity and helplessness associated with a major illness, the elderly may learn to see illness and even death as experiences that underscore their basic humanity. The major "battle" between integrity and despair is often fought in that arena.

The approach of death may paradoxically open up new avenues for feelings of inner continuity. When the future is foreclosed, there may be a greater intensity to the present moment and a greater depth of self-awareness. At the end of the lifecycle, older persons may feel nearer to the beginning, nearer to the cycle of the generations of which they are a part. Having come full circle, they may approach their end with a heightened sense of mystery and an enriched interest in the transcendent, often expressed through an increased involvement with religious concerns.

ANNOTATED BIBLIOGRAPHY

Colarusso C, Nemiroff R: Adult Development. New York, Plenum Press, 1981

> This standard work presents a problem-oriented approach to the main stages of adult development

Erikson EH: Childhood and Society. New York, WW Norton, 1963

> This classic on adult development contains the "eight ages of man" schema, which has served as a foundation for much subsequent research in the field.

Gould RL: Transformations. New York, Simon & Schuster, 1978

> Gould's paradigm of adult development stresses transitional stages such as the "age 30 transition."

Levinson DJ, Darrow CM, Klein EB et al: The Seasons of a Man's Life. New York, Alfred A Knopf, 1978

> Based on more than a decade of rigorous research on the stages of adult development, Levinson's work achieved a fresh perspective on adulthood by viewing it as a series of transitions.

Mahler MS, Pine F, Bergman A: The Psychological Birth of the Human Infant. New York, International Universities Press, 1975

> The product of many years of observational study on mothers and their infants, this classic work offered a new developmental schema for the first 3 years of life, based on the notion of separation–individuation. It originated the idea of a normative crisis—the so-called rapprochement crisis—at the age of 21 months.

Vailliant G: Adaptation to Life. Boston, Little, Brown & Co, 1977

> This book discusses the results of a large prospective study of male college students in which psychologic traits were correlated with measures of physical and psychologic health over several decades.

Viorst J: Necessary Losses. New York, Ballantine Books, 1986

> Viorst elaborates the thesis that each advance to a new developmental stage is associated, to a greater or lesser extent, with the loss of an emotionally invested portion of the previous stage.

Winnicott DW: The Maturational Processes and the Facilitating Environment. New York, International Universities Press, 1965

> Winnicott's concepts of the "holding environment" "primary maternal preoccupation," and "the good enough mother" are essential for appreciating the task of parenting.

REFERENCES

Anzieu D: Freud's Self-Analysis. Madison, CT, International Universities Press, 1986

Bibring GL, Dwyer TF, Huntington DS et al: A study of the psychological processes in pregnancy and of the earliest mother–child relationship. Psychoanal Study Child 16:9–24, 1961

Blos P: The second individuation process of adolescence. Psychoanal Study Child 22:162–186, 1967

Colarusso C, Nemiroff R: Adult Development. New York, Plenum Press, 1981

Erikson EH: Identity and the Lifecycle. (Monograph) Psychological Issues, Vol. 1, No. 1. New York, International Universities Press, 1959

Erikson EH: Childhood and Society. New York, WW Norton, 1963

Freud A: The concept of developmental lines. Psychoanal Study Child 8:245–265, 1963

Freud S: Mourning and Melancholia. 1917. In Strachey J (ed): The Standard Edition of the Complete Psychological Works, vol 14. London, Hogarth Press, 1958

Freud S: Three Essays on the Theory of Sexuality. 1905. In Strachey J (ed): The Standard Edition of the Complete Psychological Works, vol 7. London, Hogarth Press, 1958

Gould RL: The phases of adult life: A study in developmental psychology. Am J Psychiatry 129:521–531, 1972

Greenspan S: "The Second Other": The Role of the Father in Early Personality Formation and the Dyadic–Phallic Phase of Development. In Cath S, Gurwitt A, Ross JM (eds): Father and Child. Boston, Little, Brown & Co, 1982

Jaques E: Death and the mid-life crisis. Int J Psychoanal 46:502–514, 1965

Kernberg O: Internal World and External Reality Object Relations Theory Applied. New York, Jason Aronson, 1980

Kiley D: The Peter Pan Syndrome. New York, Dodd, Mead, 1983

Levinson DJ, Darrow CM, Klein EB et al: The Seasons of a Man's Life. New York, Alfred A Knopf, 1978

Levinson DJ, Goodeneh WE: The Life Cycle. In Kaplan HI, Sadock BJ (eds): Comprehensive Textbook of Psychiatry, Baltimore, Williams & Wilkins, 1985

Mahler MS: The rapprochement subphase of the separation–individuation process. Psychoanal Q 41:487–506, 1972

Mahler MS, Pine F, Bergman A: The Psychological Birth of the Human Infant. New York, International Universities Press, 1975

Nicholi AM: The New Harvard Guide to Psychiatry. Cambridge MA, Belknap Press of Harvard University Press, 1985

Schafer R: The psychoanalytic vision of reality. Int J Psychoanal 51:279–297, 1970

Settlage CF, Curtis J, Lozoff M et al: Conceptualizing adult development. J Am Psychoanal Assn 36:347–369, 1988

Sholevar P (ed): The Handbook of Marriage and Marital Therapy. Jamaica, NY, SP Medical and Scientific Books, 1981

Simons RC (ed): Understanding Human Behavior in Health and Illness. Baltimore, Williams & Wilkins, 1985

Vailliant G: Adaptation to Life. Boston, Little, Brown & Co, 1977

Van Gennep A: The Rites of Passage. Chicago, University of Chicago Press, 1960

Viorst J: Necessary Losses. New York, Ballantine Books, 1986

Winnicott DW: The Maturational Processes and the Facilitating Environment. New York, International Universities Press, 1965

8

The Family in Human Development and Medical Practice

Nancy L. Kriseman, Joan Fiore, and Alan Stoudemire

Following along the lines of discussion in previous chapters in this section on sexuality, child and adult development, this chapter will more formally discuss the role of the family from a systems perspective. This chapter is intended to help future physicians gain a clearer understanding of how family relationships affect human development and how families are affected by medical illness. In addition, guidelines will be presented for identifying families in distress and referring them for evaluation and therapy.

DEFINITION OF FAMILY

How does one define "the family?" This has become a difficult task in the late 20th century. There are many different types of family systems in modern Western industrialized society. If one looks at a traditional definition of family, such as might be found in a Webster's dictionary, one would find something similar to the following: (1) A social unit consisting essentially of a man and woman and their offspring; (2) a group of people sharing common ancestry; (3) all the members of a household; (4) a group of like things. If one turns to the U.S. Census Bureau, the family would be defined as "two or more people who are related by blood, marriage or adoption and who live in the same dwelling." If one were to ask the general population to define a "family" of the 1990s, a variety of definitions might be elicited from a man and/or woman (married or single, or divorced with or without children), to a gay family, to several people of various sexes and ages "living together."

There are, nevertheless, basically two generic ways most family therapists would define the family, by its *structural* format and by its *functional* format. The *structural* format would include the biologic or adopted members who dwell together; also included would be extended family members. The *functional* format would include any other persons who have a close relationship or who help support the family. Social systems can be considered as a part of the functional component.

It is also helpful to keep in mind some statistics about the changing structure of the "typical" American family. Research has found that the basic family structure has changed in the last 10 to 20 years. While marriage continues to be a near universal experience, people are waiting longer to get married. The average age is about 23 years for women and 25 years for men. In addition, while people are still choosing to have children (90% of couples), they are waiting longer to have them and are having fewer children than their generational counterparts. While divorce rates have "leveled off" in recent years, they have leveled off at incredibly high rates—between 50% and 60% of first marriages currently end in divorce.

The "ideal" family of the 1950s (father and nonworking mother with children) accounts for slightly more than 8% of American families according to the Bureau of Labor Statistics, with two income, single parent, stepfamilies and childless couples making up the majority. Other changes in the American family over the past 40 years may be noted as well.

> Men and women marry later—in 1988 the median age for first marriages for women was 23.6 years and for men 25.9 years.
>
> Families are smaller with the typical family consisting of 3.17 persons, an all time "low." (Contributing to this phenomenon are high divorce rates, single parents with children, and a declining birth rate.)
>
> Families without children outnumber those with children (a phenomenon that was observed for the first time only in 1985).
>
> As noted above, marriages are decimated by high rates of divorce with 50% of all first marriages ending in divorce and 60% of all second marriages ending in divorce.
>
> Fewer households consist of "families" (two or more people related by birth, adoption, or marriage). Of 91.1 million households in the United States in early 1988, 71.5% were "families" compared to 90.3% 40 years ago.
>
> Single parent families are increasing. Twenty-seven percent of all families with children have only one parent present—90% of whom are women.
>
> Of *all births,* 22% are to unmarried women; 60% of black children are born to single mothers and about 15% of white children are born to single mothers.

Hence, there are more single parent families than ever before. Even when two parents are present, the dual career couple has become the norm rather than the husband as the only breadwinner.

People are also living longer, with an average age of about 78 years for women and 74 years for men. The 80 + age group is the fastest growing segment of the population, resulting in more pressure on middle-aged persons to care not only for their children but for their aging parents as well (the so-called sandwich generation).

Despite the diversity and changing demographic characteristics of the American family, several basic functions that the family serves in human development may be identified.

BASIC FUNCTIONS OF THE FAMILY

Satir et al (1975) conducted a 10-year study on healthy versus dysfunctional families. Four prominent distinguishing factors were found. Healthy families displayed the following functions:

Productivity

Healthy families, when faced with different crises or problems, were able to reach significantly greater number of decisions than maladaptive families.

Leadership patterns

Healthy families always seemed to have one person who became the leader and the others backed him/her up. There was an absence of any kind of leadership in dysfunctional families, which tended to be chaotic. Efforts at leadership were often undermined or sabotaged by other family members.

Conflict resolution

In healthy families, the members were able to express conflict openly and usually attain some sort of resolution. In the maladaptive families, however, there appeared to be either too much expression of conflict or not enough and generally little, if any, resolution.

Clarity of communication

Healthy families had clear communication channels. Dysfunctional families either had very minimal communication with each other or communicated in vague ways so that the members were unsure of as to whom the message was directed.

As was previously discussed in Chapter 6, Fleck (1985) also identified several essential family functions that are generally found in healthy families. A few of these functions are reiterated below and lised in Table 8–1.

Facilitation of Development of Autonomy, Identity, Self-esteem, and Competence in the Family Members

An important task of the family, primarily the mother and father, is to encourage and support its members (in particular its younger members) through the stages of the lifecycle. Adolescence is a lifecycle stage that appears to be the most difficult for parents who are not well differentiated as persons themselves. There is a tendency during this time for parents to "hold onto" or "overprotect" or alternately overcontrol their adolescents. Adolescents usually react by rebelling or developing some type of behavior in reaction to the parent's overprotectiveness or overcontrol. The most common problem, however, may be parental *inconsistency* in the setting of limits during this phase of development. Hence, parents who alternate between rigidity and permissiveness serve only to exacerbate the adolescent's personal turmoil.

Development of Appropriate Emotional and Role "Boundaries"

Parents need to be parents and children need to be children in an age-appropriate manner. A family becomes dysfunctional when emotional or sexual boundaries become blurred. Children look to their parents for guidance, protection, nurturance, and providing limits and parameters for their behavior and impulses. When parents fail to provide appropriate emotional and sexual boundaries, dysfunction in the family system may be inevitable. This is most dramatically demonstrated in families where there is sexual and physical abuse.

In some dysfunctional families, there may be intrusiveness and confusion over leadership and a lack of structure and stability. Clear boundaries in a family facilitate the proper development of other essential family functions, which include self-control, ethical standards, and setting of appropriate limits on behavior. Alternately, some families may be "too stable," that is, have rigid and uncompromising boundaries and rules that penalize differentiation and self-assertion.

Family Rituals

Family rituals are usually passed down from generation to generation, and they are unique to each family. Rituals provide a sense of belonging, a capacity for sharing, and help consolidate the family's identity and continuity. Religious ceremonies, holidays, family reunions, annual vacations, and birthday celebrations are all examples of family rituals. Rituals also help to structure families and provide for a sense of intergeneration support and cohesion. The lack of family rituals may lead to fragmentations of the family, a sense of isolation, and separateness.

Table 8–1 **Basic Functions of the Family**

Productivity
Leadership
Protection, support, nurturance—Physical and emotional
Appropriate boundaries—Identity, emotional, sexual
Clear communication of ideas, needs, and feelings
Conflict resolution
Development of individual autonomy and independence
Self-control
Respect for the needs and feelings of others; empathy
Education and values in regard to ethical standards of behavior
Formation of identity and self-esteem
Rituals—Consolidation of familial identity, intergenerational cohesion, and continuity over time

EVOLUTION OF FAMILY THEORY AND THERAPY

Historic Background

Many of the pioneers in family theory and therapy were psychiatrists who basically borrowed ideas from general systems theory. General systems approaches as applied to the functioning of the human body basically consist of seeing the organism as being a biologic system with mutually interdependent component subsystems. Most family therapists think of families within a similar systems model.

The family therapy movement began in the 20th century and was given impetus by the growth of psychoanalysis. Before Freud, mental illness was largely considered to be the result of pathologic organic dysfunction of the brain. Freud introduced the concept of mental illness as a function of the "mind" deriving from psychologic conflicts and problems in childhood development—although Freud never abandoned the possibility of certain psychiatric disorders resulting from primarily organic factors. Psychoanalytic and traditional psychodynamic treatment, however, originally focused primarily on the individual person. Therapists encouraged their patients to delve into their past, examining feelings about relevant people, and uncovering repressed traumatic developmental experiences that could be "worked through" and emotionally resolved. The focus on the person in treatment is in marked contrast to family-oriented approaches to therapy, which will be discussed below.

SCHOOLS OF FAMILY THERAPY/FAMILY THERAPY MOVEMENT

The family therapy movement started in the 1950s by clinicians who were concerned that psychoanalysis focused too much on the person and feeling that more consideration should be given to examining and treating dysfunctional aspects of family relationships that were contributing to the patient's condition. Haley, Minunchin, Bowen, Bateson, and Jackson were among those who began conducting family research, with much of the early work focusing on families with an affected member who had schizophrenia. Bowen set up a landmark project at National Institute for Mental Health in which *entire families* were hospitalized for observation and research (Guerin, 1976). Out of this seminal project came new ideas, which were developed to conceptualize dysfunctional family systems. This research stimulated further study of normal family systems in the late 1950s and 1960s.

DIFFERENT APPROACHES TO FAMILY THERAPY

There are many different approaches to conceptualizing family systems and strategies for family therapy. Describing each of them would be beyond the scope of this chapter. However, two major family therapy approaches (Bowen and Minunchin) will be described, and their main concepts will be presented. These are the most widely used by family therapists. These approaches will provide some insight about basic aspects of healthy and dysfunctional family interactions and the potential value of therapeutic interventions.

Family of Origin or Bowenian Family Therapy

Murray Bowen, M.D., conceptualized the family as an emotional unit in which the individual was a part. He believed that family dysfunction was more likely to occur when family members were less emotionally differentiated from each other, and hence the family was continually having to adapt to high levels of chronic anxiety. People with higher degrees of emotional differentiation were theorized to suffer from less chronic anxiety and could therefore tolerate greater amounts of acute stress before they became symptomatic. Bowen proposed that individuals who are less differentiated in relationship to their families have more anxiety about independence and assuming responsibility for themselves. As a result, some individuals never really "leave home" (emotionally, at least), while others pretend to separate but experience severe anxiety in the process and subsequently produce families with similar types of problems.

The major components of Bowen's theory are as follows:

1. *Scale of Differentiation*—Bowen conceptualized a scale of differentiation to capture his notion that people vary considerably (from 0 to 100, low to high) in how differentiated or separated they are from their family of origin. The more differentiated individuals are, the greater the "degree to which they are able to distinguish between the feeling process and the intellectual process," and the more their ability to *choose* between being guided by thoughts or feelings at any given moment (Kerr and Bowen, 1988, p. 97). This statement should not be construed to mean that an intellectual or obsessive individual is more differentiated than an emotionally aware and expressive person. Bowen is most concerned with "emotional reactivity," which is experienced with more frequency the lower one is on the scale of differentiation. An illustration of emotional reactivity would be the experience of going home for a family visit fully determined to behave in a mature way only to find oneself engaged in the "thousandth re-enactment" of a problematic interaction with one's mother that had been repeated since age twelve.

   Bowen and Kerr describe individuals at a low level of differentiation (0–25) as emotionally needy and highly reactive to others. Much of their energy is focused into "loving" or "being loved." They find it difficult to make statements such as "I believe, I am, I will do." People with moderate levels of differentiation (25–50) are much more adaptive and can tolerate more stress and life change than people at the lower end of the scale, but they are still excessively reactive to emotional disharmony and to the opinions of others. They tend to be very focused on creating a good impression and on seeking approval. Individuals with a moderately high level of differentiation (50–75) have more choice to flexibly move back and forth between intimate emotional closeness and goal-directed activity. Bowen and Kerr have described that rare individual who is highly differentiated (75–100) as sure of his beliefs and convictions; he is not dogmatic or fixed in his thinking. Capable of hearing and evaluating the viewpoints of others, he can discard old beliefs in favor of new. He can listen without reacting and can communicate without antagonizing others. He is secure within himself; his functioning is not affected by praise or criticism. He can respect the identity of another without becoming critical or emotionally involved in trying to modify the life course of another. Able to assume total responsibility for self and sure of his responsibility *to* others, he does not become overly responsible *for* others. He is realistically aware of his dependence on his fellow man and is free to enjoy relationships. He does not have a "need" for others that can impair functioning, and others do not feel "used." Tolerant and respectful of differences, he is not prone to engage in polarized debates. He is realistic in his assessment of self and others and not preoccupied with his place in the hierarchy. Expectations of self and others are also realistic. Intense feelings are well tolerated, and so he does not act automatically to alleviate them. His level of chronic anxiety is very low, and he can adapt to most stresses without developing symptoms. (Kerr and Bowen, 1988, p. 107).

2. *The Two Selves—Solid Self and Pseudo-Self.* Individuals low on the differentiation scale have little "solid" self. Solid self is contrasted with the "pseudo-self." Solid self is made up of firmly held convictions and beliefs, a sense of self that is not changed by coercion or persuasion by others. It is what allows people to maintain their individuality and their sense of themselves while in close emotional contact with another or with a group. These are not individuals who define themselves by group opposition or by trying to change other's beliefs, but rather, individuals who are self-confident about their identities. In contrast, pseudo-self is "negotiable" in relationships with others. Pseudo-self is particularly vulnerable to being molded in emotionally intense relationships such as marriage where each partner is trying to shape the other's beliefs and behavior. Often in marriages, one partner's views will gain in strength, and that individual will appear "stronger" and more differentiated, while the other will appear "weaker" and less differentiated, as if the latter gave the former his/her pseudo-self in trade for keeping the anxiety in the relationship down and the relationship intact. These individuals are actually equally differentiated (solid self), according to Bowen, and only *appear* to be different due to the lending and borrowing of pseudo-self. Typical examples

of these couples are those where one is symptomatic or much less likeable (e.g., the alcoholic and spouse, the competent overachiever and the incompetent underachiever, the sick patient and the helpful or neglectful well one). Who has not seen an individual who once looked weak in a marriage who then blossomed after a divorce?

3. *Triangles.* Another major concept of Bowen's family theory is the idea of *triangles.* Bowen described the triangle as the smallest stable relationship system. Within a given family system in periods of emotional stability, the "triangle" is made up of a comfortable twosome, and a less comfortable third "outsider." When anxiety in the system increases, the outsider third person becomes more involved, often decreasing the tension between the twosome and spreading the anxiety through three relationships. A typical sequence of triangulation might be that person A becomes an uncomfortable insider and pulls in the outsider C by complaining about the other insider B. If C responds by taking sides with A, C and A will feel close and B will be the new "outsider." For example, a wife starts to feel angry at her husband but wants to avoid conflict with him, so she complains about him to her eldest daughter who sympathizes. Mother and daughter feel close. Husband is now "outside," but the husband and wife, while distant, are at least not in overt conflict. Of course, husband and wife will never resolve anything either! Moreover, the confident daughter will likely be left with the angry feelings and will get into conflict with her father for her mother. *The more healthy a family, the more its members can deal with their tensions directly in dyads without triangulating third parties into the conflict.* The less differentiated a family, the more repeated and multiple interlocking triangles will occur. A physician can easily be the unsuspecting third in a triangle. If the physician sides with a member of a family, sees the problem as having "good guys and bad guys" rather than equally participating players, the physician will inadvertently maintain the dysfunction in the family.

    Bowen felt it was important if the third person were drawn into a triangle in this manner that that person remain objective or emotionally separate and avoid becoming involved in the conflict (detriangling). If the third person or outsider can maintain some emotional distance, this can help to diffuse the anxiety between the two conflicted individuals and restore their equilibrium. Friedman labeled this as taking a "nonanxious presence" (Friedman 1985). More often than not, however, introducing the third person into the triangle ensures that the anxiety-producing issues will not be resolved and that more distance will result between the original twosome than would have been possible without the triangle.

    Triangles within family systems tend to repeat themselves

and people tend to evolve into fixed roles and alliances in the family system. Thus, knowledge that families in conflict tend to form "triangles" as a way to manage their anxiety can be helpful in planning family intervention.

STRUCTURAL FAMILY THERAPY AND SALVADOR MINUNCHIN

Structural family therapy, developed by Minunchin, concerned itself with the way the family structured itself to maintain homeostasis or stability under chronic stress. Sometimes a family's "homeostasis" can be dysfunctional. The main therapeutic technique in this form of therapy was to change the communication pathways, which would facilitate structural changes. Four basic concepts make up the core of Minunchin's structural family therapy: transactional patterns, adaptation, subsystems, and boundaries.

Transactional Patterns

Transactional patterns in Minunchin's model are *repetitive* sequences of family interactions. The patterns or types of transactions point to the family rules and reveal who relates to whom about what within the family system. Transactional patterns generally determine the family's structure. Understanding the nature of transactional patterns within a family is helpful in identifying pathologic or dysfunctional relationships and formulating treatment interventions.

Adaptation

Simply stated, adaptation is the family's ability to modify their typical transactional patterns of behavior and interaction and adapt to a crisis or developmental stage of the family. Minunchin pointed out that dysfunctional families often were *rigid* and had poor "adaptability" as illustrated by the following example.

A CASE STUDY

Mr. Y is a 72-year-old man who has had a stroke. He is married to Mrs. Y, age 68. They have three children. Mr. Y's stroke has impaired him both physically and mentally. Although he is mobile, his coordination and reflexes are impaired. Mentally, his short-term memory is poor, and he often repeats himself. A neuropsychologic evaluation was done, which showed moderate to severe memory loss. Furthermore, Mr. Y has had an alcohol problem and has continued to drink. Although his wife is concerned about drinking, she refuses to recognize that he is not capable of performing the many tasks he used to do (i.e. driving, managing his affairs, and so forth. In addition, because of his dementia, he is incapable of recognizing or understanding his disabilities and impairments. Both he and his wife are having a difficult time adapting to these new

changes. They are unrealistically attempting to maintain their old pat-
terns of dependency before the stroke. For example, he had always as-
sumed the primary leadership role of handling the affairs of the family.
Mrs. Y, through her use of denial, is trying to hold onto the "old" Mr. Y.
Mr. Y, complicated by his dementia, is also using denial by trying to
maintain his leadership position in the family. What the family needs is
to try to come up with ways that Mr. Y can feel like he has some leader-
ship in the family that are appropriate to his physical and mental con-
dition. Mrs. Y needs to acknowledge her feelings of loss over the "old" Mr.
Y and begin to develop ways she can enjoy and relate to Mr. Y in spite
of the limitations imposed by his disability.

Subsystems

Subsystems in Minunchin's model are smaller units within a family (e.g., hus-band–wife, sibling–sibling, grandmother–grandfather). Groups of family members form subsystems within the overall family unit. Quite often, families come together to form different subsystems in order to obtain support or nurturance if chronic conflict exists within the family. Subsystems also serve normal and adaptive purposes. Healthy subsystems may exist within the family that have clear but semipermeable bound-aries. For example, the "marital couple" forms a subsystem in which the children should have access but in which certain issues (such as sex, finances, career) primarily remain the province of the parents' subsystem.

Boundaries

"Boundaries" within a family in Minunchin's theory refer to specific rules about who participates in individual subsystems. Boundaries serve to protect the unique-ness of each subsystem. For example, Minunchin found the most typical type of boundary problem involved parents and children where the parents were not func-tioning appropriately in their parental role. Thus, the goal of therapy is to rearrange the communication and roles within the family so that the "parental subsystem" becomes "in charge" again (Minunchin and Fishman, 1981). Boundary clarity is paramount to healthy family functioning; crossing of sexual boundaries is particularly disastrous.

Boundaries within a family are seen on a continuum from "disengaged" to "enmeshed." *Disengaged* generally refers to boundaries that are rigid, detached, and distant. *Enmeshment* generally refers to boundaries that are too close in which there exists emotional entanglement, excessive dependency, and poor differentiation be-tween family members. An enmeshed family will often experience profound and protracted distress and disorganization during an illness or death due to excessive emotional dependency and the incapacity of individual family members to function autonomously.

Minunchin worked extensively with "psychosomatic" families and with young family members who had anorexia nervosa, juvenile diabetes, and asthma in which exacerbations of the child's illness often appeared to be determined or related to abnormal relationships within the families—the so-called psychosomatic family system. Minunchin found that many of the transactional patterns of "psychosomatic" families were quite different from families with seriously ill but not "psychosomatic" children. He found *four core characteristics* in these dysfunctional "psychosomatic" families (Minunchin et al, 1978).

Rigidity

Defined as inflexible ways of relating to each other that tend to be fixed and not amenable to change or adaptation.

Overprotectiveness

Members are not permitted to make independent decisions; parents tend to "take over" for their children, shield, overprotect, and infantilize them.

Enmeshment

Members overreact to illness and other stresses and do not allow room for emotional growth that enhances individual autonomy.

Conflict avoidance

Members are not allowed, by covert or overt "messages," to openly disagree with each other (Minunchin et al, 1978). Conflicts within the family are hidden or avoided, often using the child's illness as an excuse to divert or distract the family from core emotional problems operative within the family system.

Being able to identify these dysfunctional characteristics in families help break dysfunctional patterns, not only of faulty communications but to decrease the "control" that the child's illness has on the family system. These same general concepts may be applied to families and patients of any age—including the elderly—if patterns such as those described above are observed in relation to illness.

GENOGRAMS

With these basic concepts of the function of the family and basic approaches to family therapy in mind, the next step is to examine how physicians might incorporate a "family systems way of thinking" into their clinical practices. An excellent and practical technique is to use a *genogram*, which will be described below.

What is a Genogram?

A genogram is a drawing of a family tree that records significant information about a family and generally dates back at least two or three generations. Genograms provide the clinician with the opportunity to obtain a great deal of information about a person and their family efficiently. Genograms are easy to read and provide the clinician with an immediate and expandable "picture" of the family. It can give clinicians information such as dates of birth, death, marriage, and other timely events in the family history. It may detail both medical and psychosocial information about life transactions, medical history, genetic patterns of illness, traumas, and lifecycle stages (i.e., retirement and dates and causes of death, and so forth). All this information can aid clinicians in understanding the patient's patterns of illness. The clinician may also elicit a sense for the types of family and interpersonal relationships that have existed for the patient.

The genogram can also be a helpful tool in assessing and tracking medical data. Critical medical information can be "flagged" on the genogram. In addition, current medical problems can be seen immediately in a larger familial and historic perspective (McGoldrick and Gerson, 1985).

Gerson and McGoldrick also point to the relevance of the genogram in management of medical treatment for the family and patient.

> Helps the physician "anticipate illness behavior" by recognizing recurrent behavior or patterns of illness in a family system.
> Aids in anticipating compliance and identifying resources for enhancing compliance.
> Documents life events and pinpoints stressors that affect treatment.
> Provides a better understanding of the psycho/social/biologic functioning of the patient and the family system.
> Helps with assessment of family functioning and determines whether a person needs to be referred for family therapy.
> Can sometimes uncover symptom patterns that can help with early detection of a problem or, in some cases, prevent or anticipate an illness by identifying patients at risk.

Genograms Role Between Patient and Doctor

It has been found that most patients after being given a 20-minute genogram interview feel that the interview and history taking could improve their medical care and their communication with their physician (McGoldrick and Gerson, 1985). Many patients also feel that knowing that their physician is concerned enough to take both the time to conduct a genogram and conduct a physical and social/psychologic history is reassuring and enhances trust in the doctor–patient relationship.

Data Physicians Need to Gather for a Genogram

I. Facts.
  A. Dates of birth, marriage, separation, divorce, illness and hospitalizations, retirement, death.
  B. Sibling position.
  C. Profession/education.
  D. Where the patient was born and where he or she lives now.
  E. Religious background.
II. Historic Information.
  A. Important family events.
  B. At least two to three generations of family history.
  C. Identify messages, rules, expectations that have been "passed down" from

generation to generation. (For example, in family "X" the expectation is that when parents become sick they move in with children.)

III. Relationships and Roles.

    A. Are there family members who do not speak to each other?

    B. How often are they in contact with one another?

    C. Are there any family members who are extremely close or distant (enmeshed–disengaged)?

    D. How differentiated are family members, in particular, spouses, adult children, and their parents?

    E. Are there marital difficulties?

    F. Who is most or least supportive to the patient?

    G. Who seems to have the most (or least) power and control? (This is a particularly important question in regards to compliance with diet and medication regimens.)

IV. Questions About Family Functioning.

    A. Are there any current serious family problems?

        (1) Medical or psychiatric.

        (2) Sexual abuse, incest.

        (3) Drugs/alcoholism.

        (4) Financial or legal.

    B. Work history.

        (1) Are there recent job changes such as unemployment, retirement, or relocation?

        (2) How much income is there? Are there financial stresses?

    C. How has person/family coped with stress in the past? Once physicians gather the above information they can identify specific aspects of the family history and structure that can impact on the patient. Particular attention should be paid to:

        (1) Repetitive patterns of behavior in the family system (suicide, alcoholism, divorce).

        (2) Coincidences of dates (i.e., death of a family member coinciding with a presenting symptom in another family member; anniversary reaction).

        (3) Impact of untimely life events (i.e., unexpected deaths, births, separations) (McGoldrick and Gerson, 1985).

A CASE STUDY

Mr. C, an 80-year-old man, (Fig. 8-1) was experiencing headaches and "dizzy spells." He called his physician and came for an appointment. The physician decided to gather some information for a genogram. In working from the genogram the doctor was able to place Mr. C's headaches and dizzy spells in a broader perspective. The following "red flags" became apparent: (1) There was considerable stress in the last two years in Mr. C's family. His wife had been diagnosed with Parkinson's disease and soon thereafter their daughter was diagnosed with breast cancer. (2) Mr. C had had most of the responsibility for caring for his wife. He only had one child, a daughter, an attorney, who lived lo-

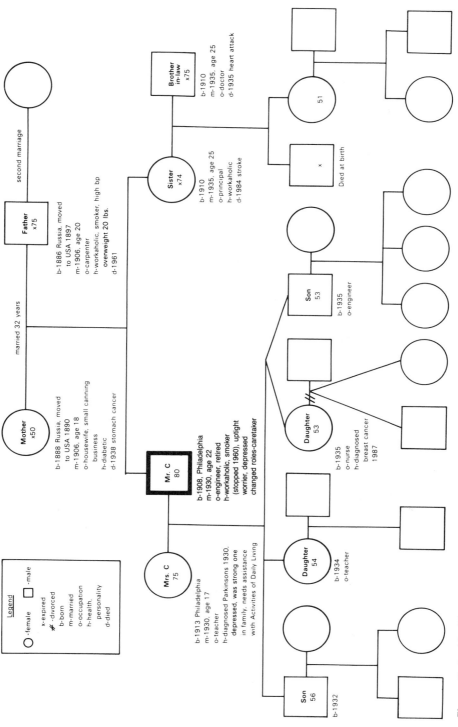

Figure 8–1. Mr. C's genogram.

*cally. (3) Based on the information gathered about his life patterns, it
was found that Mr. C has always been "high strung" and always has
had difficulty relaxing. He has never been the "patient" type and gets
easily upset. Furthermore, his wife has always been the one who organized their social life and made the decisions in the family. (4) "Workaholic" or obsessional personality types tended to run in his family (i.e.,
his father, sister and self). (5) Heart disease runs in his family; his father and sister both died of strokes. (6) Mr. C classified himself as a
"worrier" and was very concerned about his wife and daughter. He has
also worried excessively about finances even though he did well as an
engineer. (7) Mr. C mentioned that he doesn't know how to cope with his
wife's depression and feels overwhelmed by the responsibility of caring
for her.*

    *Based on the above information, the physician felt that it was most
probable that Mr. C's dizzy spells and headaches were stress-related
symptoms for his feelings of helplessness and anxiety about his situation. After a medical evaluation ruled out other causes of his symptoms,
the physician then suggested that Mr. C see a psychiatrist who could
help him and his family.*

Developing the genogram was a structured and organized technique to elicit
critical information about Mr. C and his family so that a thorough assessment of the
presenting physical problem could be made. Without this information, the physician
may have overlooked or missed the significance of his physical symptoms and their
relationship to his stressful life situation.

    The second example highlights how important it is to gather data by using a
genogram to "catch" hidden problems.

A CASE STUDY

*Mrs. Y (Fig. 8-2) went to her internist because she was feeling depressed,
anxious, and fearful. Furthermore, she was not sleeping at night and
had lost her appetite. She was 72 years old and had a history of various
illnesses and relatively minor surgeries. She had never presented with
these particular symptoms before. At first glance, it seemed apparent
that she was suffering from anxiety and depression, so the physician
placed her on a minor tranquilizer for depression/anxiety, reassured
her she would be okay, and sent her home. Two weeks later she was back
in his office with even more pronounced symptoms. This time her
daughter also came with her. Her daughter was worried and concerned.
She stated her mother had been calling her three and four times a day
and that her mother could not sleep or eat. Mrs. Y has lost weight and
has been tearful and refuses to drive, stating she's afraid. The physician
decides to increase her medication and suggests that Mrs. Y move in
with her daughter for a while until the medication takes effect. If that is
not possible, the physician suggests she hire someone to stay with her to*

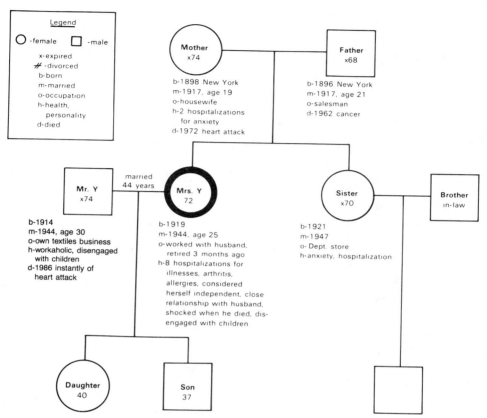

Legend

○ -female □ -male

x-expired
♯ -divorced
b-born
m-married
o-occupation
h-health,
    personality
d-died

Mother
x74

b-1898 New York
m-1917, age 19
o-housewife
h-2 hospitalizations
    for anxiety
d-1972 heart attack

Father
x68

b-1896 New York
m-1917, age 21
o-salesman
d-1962 cancer

Mr. Y
x74

b-1914
m-1944, age 30
o-own textiles business
h-workaholic, disengaged
    with children
d-1986 instantly of
    heart attack

married
44 years

Mrs. Y
72

b-1919
m-1944, age 25
o-worked with husband,
    retired 3 months ago
h-8 hospitalizations for
    illnesses, arthritis,
    allergies, considered
    herself independent, close
    relationship with husband,
    shocked when he died, dis-
    engaged with children

Sister
x70

b-1921
m-1947
o- Dept. store
h-anxiety, hospitalization

Brother
in-law

Daughter
40

Son
37

Figure 8–2. *Mrs. Y's genogram.*

cook her meals and drive to where she needs to go. Again she was sent home. In 2 days' time, the daughter called the physician and stated her mother was doing much worse. At this point, the doctor reinterviewed the patient, focusing on her psychosocial history and drew up a geno-gram, which revealed the following: (1) Mrs. Y has been widowed for 2 years. However, in the last 3 months, she has retired from the business she and her husband owned. (2) Her sister, with whom she had been very close, died last month. She is now the only living sibling. (3) Her daughter married a year ago and just recently moved away. (4) She has a history of depression in her family; both her mother and sister were hospitalized for depression. (5). When asked about her husband's death and the impact it had on her, it was evident that she never really grieved for him. She had been "too busy" having to take over the busi-ness and so forth. The same was true with her sister's death. The physi-cian recognized that Mrs. Y needed some help in working through her grief. Medicine alone would not help. Furthermore, there were unre-solved family issues that needed to be addressed.

After referral to a psychiatrist for grief oriented psychotherapy and changing her to an antidepressant medication, Mrs. Y was able to reconstitute herself, recover from her acute depression, and complete the grieving process.

While it might appear that a genogram would be too time-consuming to perform on every new patient, one can nevertheless usually be taken easily in 15 to 20 minutes. When one thinks about the amount of time that is often misdirected because of missing psychosocial information driving a patient's symptoms, genograms have significant value in respect to cost and time efficacy. If the physician is too pressed for time, nurses or other office personnel can take the information, and the results can be reviewed by the physician with the patient.

Once the essential information from the family history and genogram has been gathered, the specific medical or psychiatric intervention that is indicated can be more precisely determined. There are general clinical symptoms or "red flags" that patients present with, which should alert the physician that there is a good possibility of family dysfunction and other types of stresses that are precipitating the patient's physical symptoms.

CLINICAL "RED FLAGS"

Each case must be evaluated on an individual basis, however, the following are medical symptoms often seen in medical patients as a sign of psychosocial distress that, more often than not, point to family dysfunction, interpersonal stress, or a major psychiatric disorder (Doherty and Baird, 1983).

1. Atypical headaches of longstanding duration and other unexplained pain complaints.
2. Chronic fatigue or anxiety.
3. Unexplained chronic gastrointestinal complaints: nausea, diarrhea, pain, constipation.
4. Insomnia.
5. Multiple physical complaints of a nonspecific nature.
6. Nonspecific allergies (itching/rashes).
7. In children:
   a. Enuresis.
   b. Poor appetite (even though child looks healthy).
   c. Poor sleep patterns.
   d. Hyperactivity.
   e. Poor school performance/behavior problems.

The presence of *stress* in the patient's life is another "red flag." It is important to find out from the patient what stresses they might be experiencing in their family, occupational, and social life. The following are a few to be alert for:

1. Major lifecycle changes and transitions (divorce, separation, illness, deaths in family, relocation, children leaving or returning home, job changes, retirement, and so forth).
2. Untimely events (early death, illness).
3. External stressors (financial or legal problems).

The last category of "red flags" involves the serious chronic psychosocial problems some families experience. Leading candidates are as follows:

1. Chemical dependency (alcohol and drugs).
2. Chronic depression and anxiety.
3. Child abuse, spouse abuse, incest, eating disorders.
4. Chronic dysfunctional family patterns (marital problems, weight problems, and so forth).

WHEN TO REFER OR NOT REFER

An understanding of the referral process for psychiatric evaluation and psychotherapy is important. In medical practices, physicians are confronted with a number of patients and families who will require more than just a "sympathetic ear" from a physician or "office counseling." Physicians are in the best position to refer patients for psychiatric assessment and psychotherapy, because they are trusted and generally experienced by the patient or the family as "the expert." This is especially true of longstanding patients and families or of older patients. Thus, a physician who learns the skills needed to refer patients appropriately for psychiatric evaluation or family therapy in a timely and effective manner can provide an important service for their patients. Furthermore, the physician and psychiatrist or other mental health professional can form a very effective team. Each can support and help the patient and the family by providing encouragement and reinforcement for therapy.

To ensure the best possible chance that the patient will follow through on a referral for psychotherapy, the physician should try to consider the following:

1. The confidence and enthusiasm that the physician places in the value of psychiatric treatment and psychotherapy is critical. Patients will readily pick up ambivalence and skepticism about psychiatry and psychotherapeutic treatment. Physicians should often recommend the therapist as someone *they* know personally and in whom they have trust and confidence and who has been helpful to other patients. Patients should be reassured that these types of problems are relatively common, understandable, and nothing to be ashamed of or embarrassed. The suggestion for a psychiatry consultation or therapy should always be placed in the context of the patient's ongoing medical care (i.e., the physician should reassure the patient that they will continue to be followed by the physician carefully for their physical symptoms, underlying medical problem and general health care). Some patients may feel the doctor is

"trying to get rid of them" by a psychiatric referral and need to be reassured about the physician's ongoing interest.

2. Have the names and telephone number of therapist(s) readily available to give to the patient.

3. Call the therapist personally to explain the reason for the referral and ask the therapist to keep you informed about the patient's progress.

4. Ask the patient to make an appointment while they are still in the physician's office.

5. Ask the patient to call you once they have gone to see the person.

6. Check with the patient if they have not called you within 3 weeks.

7. Check to see how the therapy is going (Doherty and Baird 1983).

Being aware of family dynamics is essential to medical practice. Patients do not exist in a vacuum, and any significant chronic or acute illness will affect the family system. Incorporating a systems approach to medical care is a principle that is repeated throughout this text. Construction of a genogram as part of the office or hospital record is a practical way to elicit the family history and will often prove invaluable to both the medical and psychologic care of the patient.

ANNOTATED BIBLIOGRAPHY

Doherty W, Baird M: Family Therapy and Family Medicine. New York, Guildford Press, 1983
> This is the most comprehensive book available for physicians and other health-care professionals who work in medical settings and are interested in learning about how family system concepts can be applied in a medical setting. The authors thoroughly cover all aspects of how to treat patients within a family medical model, describe a few family therapy approaches that can be applied to medical settings, discuss a variety of treatment issues such as noncompliance and various clinical "red flag" cases. This book is well documented, easy to read, and serves as an excellent reference for physicians.

Doherty W, Campbell T: Families and Health. Newberry Park, CA, Sage, 1988
> This book focuses on examining acute and chronic illness from a family systems perspective. The authors thoroughly cover how acute and chronic illness impacts on the person, family, and lifecycle. There are many case examples, which illustrate how the physician can intervene by including the person and family and why it is important to include the family when treating the person.

Gerson R, McGoldrich M: Genograms in Family Assessment. New York, WW Norton & Co, 1985
> This book describes what a genogram is, how it is used, and why it could be a very effective diagnostic/treatment tool for physicians and other health professionals. It is easy to read and easy to follow. A must for physicians who are truly interested in working with the "total" patient.

REFERENCES

Bowen M: Family Therapy in Clinical Practice. New York, Jason Aronson Press, 1978
Doherty W, Baird M: Family Therapy & Family Medicine. New York, Guildford Press, 1983
Fleck S: The family and psychiatry. In Kaplan HI, Sadock BJ (eds): Comprehensive Textbook of Psychiatry, vol 1, 4th ed, pp 273–294. Baltimore, Williams & Wilkins, 1985

Friedman E: Generation to Generation: Family Process in Church & Synagogue. New York, Guildford Press, 1985

Guerin P: Family Therapy Theory & Practice. New York, Gardner Press, 1976

Kerr ME and Bowen M: Family evaluation. New York, W. W. Norton & Co, 1988

McGoldrick M, Gerson R: Genograms in Family Assessment. New York, WW Norton & Co, 1985

Minunchin S, Fishman H: Family Therapy Techniques. Cambridge, MA, Harvard University Press, 1981

Minunchin S, Rosman B, Baker L et al: Psychosomatic Families: Anorexia Nervosa in Context. Cambridge, MA, Harvard University Press, 1978

Satir V, Stachowiak J, Taschman H: Helping Families to Change. New York, Jason Aronson Press, 1975

9

The Behavioral and Psychobiologic Effects of Developmental Trauma

Bessel A. van der Kolk

Section 2 and the preceding chapters in this section on human development have laid the groundwork for considering the possible consequences of developmental stresses for human behavior and vulnerability to psychiatric illness. A growing body of psychiatric research has confirmed that stress within the family system may cause abnormalities in psychologic development with lifelong effects on the individual's personality, susceptibility to stressful events in later life, and vulnerability to certain types of mental illness. Moreover, the long-term *neurobiologic* effects of developmental stress have also begun to be elucidated. These findings, some of which will be summarized here, provide an excellent model to integrate biologic, psychologic, and social theories of human behavior and mental illness. This chapter will provide an overview of some of this evidence from a psychobiologic perspective. This chapter will also provide an entrée and transition to Section 4, which considers in some detail neurobiologic aspects of behavior.

It has been an unfortunate tradition in medicine and psychiatry to separate mental illness into "organic" or "functional" problems. This dichotomy implies that the origins and cure of mental problems are *either* biologically *or* psychologically determined. These assumptions are based on the existence of a body–mind dichotomy: that nature and nurture act on different parts of the mind, and that biologic and psychologic processes can somehow be segregated into two disconnected determinants of behavior. Human beings, however, are biologic organisms that develop within an interpersonal and social context; much of the maturation of the central nervous system (CNS) occurs after birth.

In the past few decades, research has clarified the interaction between social environment and ongoing neurobiologic development (Edelman, 1987; Kandel and Schwartz, 1985). Contemporary science has started to elucidate how *the most ordi-*

nary everyday events—sensory stimulation, deprivation, and learning—have biologic consequences, causing disruptions of synaptic connections under some circumstances and activation of neural connections under others. While genetic and embryonal processes determine the basic structure of the brain, *the pattern of interconnections between neurons depends largely on experience,* particularly during the first decade of life. The degree of impact of environmental events on the CNS and, therefore, on behavior varies with age.

It is thus no longer scientifically justifiable to make clear distinctions between psychologic and biologic processes; rather we need to define our understanding of the degree to which genetic, developmental, toxic, and social factors converge to result in certain clinical syndromes. Both psychopharmacologic and psychotherapeutic interventions must work by acting on the CNS and, thus, on the connections between nerve cells. This general approach is consistent with a biopsychosocial model of understanding human behavior both in normal development and psychopathological states. The following discussion presents evidence that provides scientific confirmation of this integrated model.

THE PSYCHOBIOLOGY OF ATTACHMENT AND SEPARATION

Nobody grows up and lives in isolation. We all have been shaped by and continually are affected by our social surroundings. This process starts with the mother–infant bond and continues with ever-wider interpersonal and cultural forces. Human attachment starts as a vital biologic function, without which survival is not possible (Bowlby, 1969, 1973). Human beings by nature seem to be *monotropic* i.e., they tend to form specific relationships and preferences for particular people. By being attached to familiar caregivers as children, and a predictable environment and moral values as adults, people are assured of a "safe base" from which they can explore their inner and outer world. Secure caregiving experiences in infancy set the stage for the development of a capacity for safe, meaningful interpersonal relationships and for trust.

Mammals have developed highly complex ways of maintaining attachment bonds between caregivers and their offspring. The separation cry of infants induces adults to respond to provide safety, nurturance, and social (i.e., pleasurable) stimulation. Nonhuman primates express attachment bonds mainly with physical contact such as clinging. Humans have evolved to be able to supplement such behavior with language to maintain relationships. MacLean (1985) considers human verbal communication to be an evolutionary development from the infantile attachment cry of infants. He sees the human capacity to maintain attachment bonds over space and time by means of verbal communication as one of the principal reasons for the human ascendancy in the animal kingdom. This capacity also has a dark side: "when mammalians opted for a family way of life, they set the stage for the most distressful forms of suffering, a condition that, for us, makes being a mammal so painful, and that is having to endure separation and isolation from loved ones, and, in the end, the utter desolation of death" (Maclean, 1985).

Anxiety and Social Deprivation

When primate infants cannot find their caregivers, they emit a separation cry; these protest signals are aimed at bringing the primary attachment figure back, and they cease upon the adult's return. Failure of the caregiver to return results in withdrawal, grief, and mourning. If, after prolonged protest or mourning, no reunion or resolution follows, primates develop a detached stance, in which they turn away from mutually gratifying social interactions. Starting with Harlow's work (Harlow and Harlow, 1971), a long series of studies have demonstrated the remarkable similarities between the response of *nonhuman primates* to separation from mothers and peers and those of *human infants* and children. Harlow's isolated monkeys always sought the presence of mother surrogates in preference over food. In monkeys, social isolation for various periods during the first year of life produced grossly abnormal social and sexual behavior. Young monkeys who are separated from their mothers respond with self-stimulation such as huddling, self-clasping, self-sucking, and biting. This is accompanied by social withdrawal and unpredictable aggression. These primates do not learn to discriminate such social stimuli as facial expressions, because they lack the early experience of the synchrony between mother and child and its associated expressions.

Spitz (1945), as mentioned in Chapter 6, first described how essential interpersonal stimulation is for normal growth and development in infants. He compared children raised in a foundling home for abandoned children with those raised in a nursing home attached to a women's prison. In both places the children were clean and well cared for. However, the prisoners showered the children with physical affection for brief periods each day, while in the foundling home the children were hardly touched by anybody, except for the most perfunctory contact around feeding and changing. They even were unable to observe each other from their cribs. They led lives of severe sensory deprivation. After 1 year, the foundling home children who suffered from a deficiency of nurturing maternal contact developed a socially acquired immunodeficiency syndrome, in addition to severe depressions that made them unresponsive to human interaction.

The Relevance of Critical Periods and the Persistence of Latent Effects

The effects of social deprivation in primates can be partially reversed by reunion with peers and adult caregivers, and by integration in a social structure (Kraemer, 1986; Reite and Field, 1985). Both the age at which the separation trauma occurs and individual genetic vulnerability affect the extent of long-term damage. After an initial period of marked aggression against their newly acquired peers, previously isolated monkeys slowly develop appropriate behavior when they are put back in a social setting. Kraemer and his colleagues have shown that by 3 to 4 years they are nearly indistinguishable from their socially reared counterparts. *However, this normal adaptation can be lost under stress, or after being given psychostimulants or alcohol.* These stimuli cause these formerly deprived monkeys to respond either with social withdrawal or with indiscriminate aggression. Even monkeys that recover in other respects may have persistent deficits in sexual behavior and continue to misperceive social cues, for example, failing to withdraw after a threat by a dominant animal. The increased alcohol consumption seen in the previously isolated monkeys, compared with normal controls, indicates that, in addition to the genetic vulnerability to substance abuse, there is a neurobiologic linkage between early social attachment mechanisms, social stressors, and vulnerability to alcohol abuse and addiction.

Early Experience Contributes to Physiologic Reactivity

Field (1987) has shown that normal play and exploratory activity in children requires the presence of a familiar attachment figure who modulates their physiologic arousal by providing a balance between soothing and stimulation. In the absence of the mother, infants experience extremes of under- and overarousal that are physiologically disorganizing. Unresponsive or abusive caregivers may cause chronic hyperarousal states, which have a long-term effect on the child's ability to modulate strong emotions. These changes persist over time, even though under ordinary conditions there are no readily observable behavioral concomitants of this biologic alteration. Field (1987) notes: "On a continuum from low to high physiologic arousal there is an optimal level for every organism. The shape of an individual's optimal stimulation curve depends, in part, on their early life experiences."

The response to social isolation or stress also depends on age. Children under the age of 12 months admitted for elective surgery generally have little trouble with either separation from, or reunion with their parents. They hardly differentiate between their mothers and strangers; the only sign that something is wrong is that they may be unusually quiet. Hospitalized children over 2 years of age usually respond anxiously or angrily to strangers, and they often are demanding and clinging with their mothers. Upon return home, they tend to cling tenaciously to their mothers and are very distressed when left alone.

Increased Attachment in the Face of Danger

Both children and adults seek increased attachment in the face of external danger. This occurs even when the threat emanates from the attachment object itself; thus, attachment increases even when a caregiver no longer provides effective protection and nurturance (Rajecki et al, 1978). Children are most vulnerable to such pathologic attachments, because they have much fewer choices than do adults about whom to turn to for protection. Thus, while only conditions of captivity will make adults turn to tormentors for attachment, abused children, as a rule, display anxious attachment and exceptional loyalty to their abusing parents.

Freud already noted that one of the earliest indications that a child will later become neurotic can be seen in an insatiable demand for his or her parent's affections. This is, of course, another way of describing a child who shows excessive anxiety about separation and loss of love (See Chapter 3).

What makes children vulnerable to such excessive separation anxiety? At least five factors now have been identified:

1. Kagan and associates (1987) have demonstrated the large *temperamental differences* between children, which show up behaviorally as shyness, neophobia, and clinging, and neuroendocrinologically as increased catecholamine and blunted cortisol responses to environmental stimuli.

2. Safety of the attachment bond. Children who are abused and neglected are afraid of new stimuli, unable to change sets, and physiologically hyperreactive. They tend to vacillate between being anxious and withdrawn socially, and being hyperaggressive and insensitive to other children's needs. This syndrome has been noted in children with prior experiences with sudden parental separations and loss, abuse, and confusion about boundaries and roles within the family, such as occurs in parental drug and alcohol abuse, suicidal threats, and incest (Cicchetti, 1984; van der Kolk, 1987).

3. Intactness of the central nervous system (CNS). Mentally retarded or intoxicated children and adults and those with other organic brain syndromes are much more likely to react to separation and change with anxiety or aggression.

4. "Spoiling." An excess of gratification interferes with the development of mastery and trust in one's inner capacities to solve problems. Not learning the pleasures of mastering difficult problems leads to excessive worry, fear of not being able to face new challenges, and clinging to parents and other authority figures.

5. Excessive threats of separation and abandonment by parents. One study showed that 27% of parents used threats of abandonment as a method of discipline. Many studies have shown that offspring from such parents are prone to chronic anger and anxiety.

Separation Anxiety and Hostility

Separation anxiety, abandonment, and abuse activate hostility. Separation from mother, parental rejection of children, and lack of acknowledgment of legitimate grievances by loved ones and authority figures in adults all give rise to anger. Studies of neglected and abused children have demonstrated a vulnerability to grow up angry and disturbed (Burgess et al, 1987; Lewis et al, 1979). Separated children play violent games with dolls representing parental figures. Hostility tends to subside after reunion or acknowledgment. Bowlby has called this a situation in which a person's need for security competes with anger at abandonment. He points out that anger initially serves as an attempt to reestablish a broken connection. When this fails, many people do to others what has been done to them. This "identification with the aggressor" allows feelings of helplessness to be replaced with invulnerability and omnipotence. Reenactment of victimization is a major cause of violence in society. Abuse and victimization of children have been linked with the development of drug abuse, juvenile delinquency, and adult criminal behavior.

Identification with the aggressor may also lead to self-destructive behavior. Many abused children engage in headbanging, biting, burning, and cutting. There are, very frequently, childhood sexual abuse histories in adults who engage in various forms of self-harm later in life, particularly cutting and self-starving. Their self-destructive acts clearly are a repetition, both on a behavioral, and possibly on a biologic level, of encounters with hostile caretakers during the first years of life.

When abused and neglected children grow up, and the possibility of intimacy arises, the expectation of a recurrence of loss and betrayal is likely to be accompanied by inappropriate hostility and anxiety. Thus, hostility and anxiety go hand in hand; they may be turned against the self, against others, or they may be expressed indirectly and manifest themselves in psychosomatic symptoms, where hostility and helplessness are reexperienced both by the patient and his caregivers.

Numerous studies have documented the relationship between early loss of safe attachment and later psychiatric illness. However, studies of refugees and other traumatized children regularly uncover a multiplicity of creative solutions and the development of particular gifts that allow many people to transcend horrendous early life experiences, at least to survive, though often in a world of impoverished interpersonal attachments.

Information Processing and Memory Storage

Memories of past experiences determine a person's interpretation of contemporary life events. These memories are not necessarily conscious (i.e., encoded as verbal memory traces). Developmental psychologists have identified three modes of information processing: *enactive, iconic,* and *symbolic/liguistic* (Kihlstrom, 1984). These three modes of representation closely parallel Piaget's notions of sensorimotor, preoperational, and operational thinking, which reflect stages of development of the CNS (Piaget, 1973). Over the course of development there is a shift from sensorimotor (motoric action), to perceptual representations (iconic), to symbolic and linguistic modes of organization of mental experience. During periods of stress, people often return to processing events mainly on a visceral or motoric level (i.e., with somatic sensations or with action). Severe stress leaves people in a state of "unspeakable terror." Words do not allow for meaningful constructs. The terror overwhelms and cannot be integrated. In those cases, the experience is organized on a sensorimotor or iconic level—as anxiety attacks, nightmares, visceral sensations, or as fight/flight/freeze reactions (van der Kolk, 1987).

Children are particularly vulnerable to physiologic disorganization in the face of stress, and they rely principally on their caregivers for modulation of arousal. The development of cognitive schemes that help to give meaning to current life experiences is crucial for learning how to interpret and thus modulate physiologic arousal in the face of threat: cognitive schemata serve as a buffer against being overwhelmed. Thus, the cognitive preparedness (development) of a person interacts with the degree of physiologic arousal to determine the capacity to organize potentially disturbing experiences. Frightening experiences can be stored in memory in a somatosensory mode without linguistic representation (i.e., conscious awareness). These experiences then are "remembered" as anxiety attacks and panic disorders, which result in increased clinging and neophobia.

Recent research on state-dependent learning sheds some light on why children are more likely to process stress on a somatosensory level rather than in conscious, verbal, memory (Jacobs and Nadel, 1985). The hippocampus, which serves a mapping function for locating memories for experiences in space and time, does not fully mature until the third or fourth year of life. However, the maturation of the *taxon system,* which subserves memories related to the quality (feel and sound) of things, occurs much earlier. Thus, in the first few years of life only the quality of events, but not their context, can be remembered. During subsequent development, the locale system remains vulnerable to disruption. Stress interferes with the functioning of the hippocampally based locale system and potentiates the taxon system (i.e., it leads to context-free fearful associations that are hard to locate in space and time). The hippocampus is rich in corticosteroid receptors, which are selectively activated during stress. *Severe or prolonged stress, with its accompanying increase in corticosteroid levels can result in a suppression of hippocampal functioning and thus amnesia for traumatic experiences.* Lacking localization in space and time, they are encoded in sensorimotor form and, therefore, cannot be easily translated into the symbolic language necessary for linguistic retrieval (Squire, 1987).

Forgotten Memories Return under Stress

Learning is state-dependent. Information can only be retrieved in a state similar to the one in which the memory was encoded. State dependency can be roughly related to arousal levels and, thus, is affected by a large variety of stimuli that affect a person's mental state (e.g., both psychostimulants and depressants, meditative states, and situations of terror). Reactivation of past learning is relatively automatic. *Contextual stimuli* directly evoke stored memories without conscious awareness of the transition (Squire, 1987). The more similar the contextual stimuli are to conditions prevailing at the time of the original storage of memories, the more likely the probability of retrieval. *In practice, this means that feeling states are reactivated when a person is exposed to situations similar to the ones that occurred at the time that the original memory was stored.* This is true for both positive and negative experiences. Strains of music or smells may cause one to return to a happy frame of mind associated with past experience, but, similarly, when people who grew up in violent homes, and who as adults behave competently, are exposed to a threatening situation, they reexperience themselves as terrified children and may behave accordingly (van der Kolk, 1988).

These observations have implications for psychotherapy, because an essential feature of explorative psychotherapies is the necessity of "reliving" in memory and feeling traumatic experiences as part of the healing process. It is through the reactivation of emotionally traumatic affective (feeling) states and the memories associated with them that the person is freed up from these disabling influences on personality and interpersonal relationships. Distortions and problems in interpersonal relationships that have their roots in difficult developmental experiences are addressed in this reconstitutive process. The emotional "working through" occurs within a new intellectual and maturational framework, which the person now is able to utilize to reinterpret past experience.

Stress causes a return to earlier behavior patterns throughout the animal kingdom. In a state of low arousal, animals tend to be curious and seek novelty. When hyperaroused, they will seek the familiar, regardless of the rewards that follow. Because novel stimuli themselves cause arousal, an animal in a state of high arousal will avoid mildly novel stimuli even if it would reduce exposure to pain. Thus, highly stressed animals will return to a familiar, electrified box, in preference to an unfamiliar, but physically safe environment. The similarity between this behavior and that of people who seem unable to extricate themselves from painful relationships is obvious (Mitchell et al, 1985).

THE SOCIAL ENVIRONMENT AND CNS DEVELOPMENT: THE THEORY OF NEURONAL GROUP SELECTION

The work of Kandel, Edelman, and others has begun to shed some light on the way in which the CNS uses experience to form the unique structures that characterizes each person in his or her complexity. Edelman (1987) has pointed out that the task of the CNS is to "carry on adaptive perceptual categorization in an unlabeled world...that cannot be prefigured for an organism." After birth, a person's neural structure is basically in place, and the focus of development "now turns to modifications in the strengths of the synapses between neuronal groups, so the connections that are modified are between these groups, rather than between specific cells." The initial arrangement into groups is known as the primary repertoire; further experience is responsible for the creation of a secondary repertoire, which is involved in the subsequent behavior of the organism. The connections between the neuronal groups that are created in the secondary repertoire enable a person to "get around in the world." From Edelman's point of view, "the brain is a selective system more akin in its working to evolution than to computation or information processing." Both sensors and effectors are involved in this process of group selection. Action is fundamental to perception. Both sensory sheets and motor ensembles must operate together to produce perceptual categorization. Edelman believes that categorization (i.e., the way in which the mind imposes structures on a world which has no inherent labels) is the most fundamental of mental activities. Thus, he views memory as "the enhanced capacity to categorize and generalize associatively, not the storage of features, not objects as a list." In this model, learning consists of altering "the linkage of global mappings to hedonic centers through synaptic changes in classification couples. Such changes yield a categorization of complexes of adaptive value under conditions of expectancy."

Affiliation and the Brain

The leap from Edelman's theory of group selection to mental states is considerable. However, there now is considerable speculation that what is remembered best are not facts, things, or even faces, but what is known as the *taxon system*, the feelings and quality of experience. As Minsky (1980) puts it, "So we shall view memories as entities that predispose the mind to deal with new situations in old, remembered ways—specifically, as entities that reset the states of parts of the nervous system. Then they can cause that nervous system to be 'disposed' to behave as though it remembers. This is why I put 'dispositions' ahead of 'propositions.' "

Harlow and his successors have conclusively demonstrated that secure attachment is not merely a psychologic event; it is essential for the development of core neurobiologic functions in the primate brain. Early attachment patterns determine, to a large degree, how a child categorizes his interpersonal world. *Early disruption of the social attachment bond causes long-lasting psychobiologic changes that reduce the capacity to cope with stress, interfere with learning and motivation, and disturb parenting processes, causing a similar vulnerability in the next generation* (van der Kolk, 1987).

Research in the past few decades has established that the limbic system guides the emotions that stimulate the behavior necessary for self-preservation and survival of the species. The limbic system is largely responsible for such complex behaviors as feeding, fighting, fleeing, and reproduction. Studies of people with temporal lobe epilepsy show that the limbic system is also responsible for free-floating feelings of what is real, true, and meaningful (Kling and Steklis, 1976). While neocortical activity is not necessarily involved in attachment behaviors, destruction of various parts of the limbic system in nonhuman primates abolishes social behavior, including care of the young. In young animals it also abolishes play, which is necessary to learn to experiment with peer attachments and social collaboration.

Neuroanatomical Correlates of Affiliative Behavior

The relationship of affiliative behaviors and specific anatomical areas in the brain is still speculative. However, brain lesion studies in nonhuman primates provide some indications that bonding, nurturance, and social cohesion are severely affected by ablations of the limbic system. Lesions of the amygdala, the cingulate cortex, the anterior temporal pole, and the prefrontal cortex all cause dramatic deficits in social behavior, such as nest building, nursing, and retrieval of the young. Cingulectomized animals treat others as if they were inanimate—walking over them and sitting on them. This does not lead to fights because they avoid even aggressive contact with others (Kling and Steklis, 1976). In human beings, cingulotomy has been used to treat obsessive–compulsive disorder and other emotional disturbances related to conflicts about social relationships.

Kling's electrical recording studies from the amygdala suggest that the amygdala responds to an external stimulus with an intensity proportional to its "emotional" significance. Kling believes that the intensity of the discharge may determine the extent of the projection field from the amygdala to the hypothalamus, brain stem, and possibly, cortical structures. Thus, temporal lobe lesions decrease facilitatory inputs and diminish amygdaloid activity. This reduces the capacity to make differential responses to specific stimuli and thus impairs affiliative behavior.

There are critical periods of development after which the CNS loses its plasticity and damage becomes irreversible. In the first year of life, there appears to be considerable *plasticity* of the nervous system. One study found that neonate rhesus macaques who sustained bilateral ablations of the amygdala and were returned to their mothers 6 to 12 hours later grew up no different from normal controls. In nonhuman primates, social affiliative bonds remain relatively intact after prefrontal and temporal cortical ablation during the first two years of life, provided that there is adequate mothering. However, monkeys with either prefrontal or amygdaloid lesions are even more responsive to the effects of maternal deprivation than are intact monkeys.

Psychophysiologic and Biochemical Responses to Separation

In most young mammals, dependency on adult caregivers is so strong that mere separation from the mother, even without external danger, causes distress in infants. Pups of many species show a physiologic response to removal from the mother, which includes a drop in temperature, cardiac and respiratory depression, and behavioral arousal. Even brief separations in squirrel monkeys cause highly elevated plasma cortisol levels; repeated maternal separations lead to chronic elevations of plasma cortisol (Reite and Field, 1985). Increased cortisol leads to elevated tryptophan hydroxylase, which, in turn, results in a decrease in serotonin, the neurotransmitter most implicated in the modulation of affect and aggression. Kraemer and McKinney (1986) have demonstrated that monkeys with early separation experiences have low resting cerebrospinal fluid (CSF) catecholamine levels, but extreme norepinephrine responses to social stressors and to amphetamines. These changes in serotonin, adrenal gland catecholamine synthesizing enzymes, plasma cortisol, and immuno-resistance are not minor, and they persist over time. The opiate system seems to play an important role in mediating affiliative behavior. Minute amounts of morphine abolish the separation call in infants, as well as maternal protection of their pups. The areas of the brain with the highest binding for Mu-like opiate receptors are precisely those that have been found to be involved in the maintenance of social bonding. There is some evidence that social isolation directly affects the number or sensitivity of brain opiate receptors, at least during critical stages of development (Panksepp, 1982).

The precise behavioral results of these neurochemical changes are difficult to determine. Because any given behavior is undoubtedly influenced by a large variety of interacting neurochemical systems, any attempt to establish connections between a particular neurotransmitter and a specific type of behavior is bound to result in an oversimplification.

The Social Environment as Mediator of Brain Development

In contemporary psychiatry, much research has been done to elucidate the relationship between subtle, implicitly genetic, brain abnormalities and human psychopathology. However, studies on nonhuman primates indicate that the CNS of neonates are plastic enough to permit compensation for some gross brain abnormalities in early life, provided that parental care is adequate. On the other hand, animal studies show that mothers of damaged and unresponsive offspring tend to show an aversion to close physical contact with their infants and show little emotional expressiveness.

Nonhuman primate data, however, indicate that early social deprivation itself can be the cause of lasting changes in neuronal functioning. David Hubel (1978) was the first to suggest that "it seems conceivable that early starvation of social interaction, such as contact with mother, may lead to mental disturbances that have their counterpart in actual structural abnormalities of the brain." There are intriguing similarities between the behavioral effects of maternal neglect on monkeys and those of ablations of the amygdala and the cingulate cortex. Both monkeys who have been amygdalectomized and those who were socially isolated or abused as infants develop an attentional deficit, with distractability and difficulty in performing complex tasks and both tend to neglect or abuse their own offspring.

There are no morphologic studies yet to indicate that the behavioral sequelae of amygdalectomy and early social deprivation are, in fact, based on the same structural abnormalities. However, it is striking that the effects of social deprivation are most pronounced during critical periods in a monkey's life. These critical periods may coincide with the myelinization of those parts of the nervous system that are related to bonding and affiliative behavior. *Thus, it is conceivable that early social deprivation causes lasting damage to brain structures concerned with affiliation and bonding.* This would be analogous to the irreversible damage from sensory deprivation during critical periods that has been observed in the visual system.

TRAUMA AND PSYCHIATRIC ILLNESS

In recent years, there have been consistent reports that at least 50% of psychiatric inpatients have a childhood history of severe chronic physical and/or sexual abuse (Carmen et al, 1984). While the variety of current psychologic symptoms and maladaptive behaviors obscure the etiologic role of the childhood traumatic stressors, most of these patients continue to show such symptoms as physiologic hyperreactivity, a subjective sense of loss of control, chronic passivity alternating with uncontrolled violence against the self or others, and sleep disturbances. Data from these studies indicate that the hallmark of psychiatric patients with chronic childhood trauma is the multiplicity of clinical presentations that they exhibit over time, the variety of diagnoses that are given, and the number of different medications received.

In order to gain a greater understanding of the spectrum of trauma-related psychiatric disorders, much work remains to been done to map out the differential effects of environmental trauma on people with different temperaments at varying stages of development. The biphasic protest/despair response to abandonment and fear in childhood could be related to hyperactivity or underactivity of neurotransmitter systems.

Norepinephrine, dopamine, serotonin, and the endogenous opioid and endocrine systems are all involved in the protest/despair response. This illustrates how complex the interactions between biologic abnormalities and behavior are; depending on the age at which the trauma occurred, the nature of social support, predisposing biologic factors, and the nature and severity of the trauma, childhood trauma can manifest itself in many ways: as somatic sensations in the form of anxiety and panic, as behavioral reenactments of aspects of the trauma, or integrated into the totality of a persons' personality organization, in which violence against self or others has become a way of life. As people mature they become less vulnerable to gross disruptions in their environment.

SUMMARY: ENVIRONMENT, GENETICS, AND HUMAN DEVELOPMENT

Contemporary psychiatry has justifiably paid much attention to both the neurologic and genetic concomitants of mental disorders. While numerous studies have found intriguing leads toward a greater understanding of the biology of such psychiatric disorders as schizophrenia, mood (affective) disorders, phobias, and attention deficit disorder, there often has been an implicit assumption that abnormal biologic conditions must be genetically transmitted and encoded in DNA. However, the social environment can have profound effects on neurobiologic maturation. The precise relationship between early experiences and subsequent psychopathology remains as elusive as that between DNA and mental illness. However, given the fact that secure social attachment bonds during infancy are essential for normal development in humans, and loss, abuse, and neglect are often devastating, it is obvious that understanding the psychobiologic effects of early disruptions in attachment bonds and the subsequent development of psychopathology is one of the great challenges of contemporary psychiatry. The following section will discuss in some detail derivatives of this psychobiologic approach to understanding human behavior from ethologic, in neurobiologic and genetic perspectives.

ANNOTATED BIBLIOGRAPHY

Bowlby J: Attachment and Loss. Vol 1: Attachment. New York, Basic Books, 1969

Bowlby J. Attachment and Loss. Vol 2: Separation. New York, Basic Books, 1973

> Bowlby's monumental but very readable work integrates current knowledge about the development of attachment and affectional bonds and the consequences of their disruption at various stages throughout the life cycle.

Edelman GM: Neural Darwinism: The Theory of Neuronal Group Selection. New York, Basic Books, 1987

> This challenging work makes a major contribution toward explaining the evolution of neuronal solutions to information processing tasks. Its wide-ranging theory integrates knowledge from a range of neurosciences, from molecular genetics to evolutionary and developmental biology and the newly emerging field of cognitive science.

Kandel ER, Schwartz JH: Principles of Neural Science. New York, Elsevier, 1985

> This work addresses in depth and with a grand vision the questions of how life events are translated into neuronal changes and interconnections, and how mind and body are embedded in the same basic matrix.

Rajecki DW, Lamb ME, Obmascher P: Toward a general theory of infantile attachment: A comparative review of aspects of the social bond. Behav Brain Sci 3:417–464, 1978

> This lengthy article reviews and integrates current knowledge about the ethology of attachment throughout the animal kingdom and the role of external events on imprinting, bonding, and individuation.

Reite M, Field T (eds): The Psychobiology of Attachment and Separation. Orlando, Academic Press, 1985

> A comprehensive and detailed review of the scientific data of the neurobiologic and behavioral ramifications of early separation and attachment. This challenging book reviews the current status of our knowledge about the psychobiology of attachment and separation primarily in nonhuman primates. Its data about the specificity of the attachment bond, the long term psychobiological effects of early trauma, and the development of the limbic system in the context of environmental stimuli are particularly noteworthy.

van der Kolk B: Psychological Trauma. Washington, DC, American Psychiatric Press, 1987

> This book attempts to integrate current knowledge about the developmental, psychodynamic, cognitive, and biological aspects of human traumatization and discusses the need for a treatment approach that integrates all these dimensions when treating children and adults who have been traumatized.

REFERENCES

Bowlby J: Attachment and Loss. Vol 1: Attachment. New York, Basic Books, 1969

Bowlby J. Attachment and Loss. Vol 2: Separation. New York, Basic Books, 1973

Burgess AW, Hartmann CR, McCormack A: Abused to abuser: Antecedents of socially deviant behavior. Am J Psychiatry 144:1431–1436, 1987

Carmen EH, Reiker PP, Mills T: Victims of violence and psychiatric illness. Am J Psychiatry 141:378–379, 1984

Cicchetti D: The emergence of developmental psychopathology. Child Dev 55:1–7, 1984

Edelman GM: Neural Darwinism: The Theory of Neuronal Group Selection. New York, Basic Books, 1987

Field T: Interaction and attachment in normal and atypical infants. J Consult Clin Psychol 55:1–7, 1987

Harlow HF, Harlow MK: Psychopathology in monkeys. In Kimmel HD (ed): Experimental Psychopathology. New York, Academic Press, 1971

Hubel D: Effects of deprivation on the visual cortex of cat and monkey. Harvey Lect 72:1–51, 1978

Jacobs WJ, Nadel L: Stress-induced recovery of fears and phobias. Psychol Rev 92:512–531, 1985

Kagan J, Reznick S, Snidman N: The physiology and psychology of behavioral inhibition in children. Child Dev 58:1459–1473, 1987

Kandel ER, Schwartz JH: Principles of Neural Science. New York, Elsevier, 1985

Kihlstrom JF: Conscious, subconscious, unconscious: A cognitive perspective. In Bowers KS, Meichenbaum D (eds): The Unconscious Reconsidered. New York, John Wiley, 1984

Kling A, Steklis HD: A neural substrate for affiliative behavior in non-human primates. Brain Behav Evol 13:216–238, 1976

Kraemer GW: Causes of changes in brain noradrenaline systems and later effects on responses to social stressors in rhesus monkeys: The cascade hypothesis. In Antidepressants and Receptor Function (Ciba Foundation Symposium 123). Chichester, Wiley, 1986

Lewis D, Shanok SS, Pincus JH et al: Violent juvenile delinquents: Psychiatric, neurological, psychological and abuse factors. J Child Psychiatry 18:307–319, 1979

MacLean PD: Brain evolution relating to family, play, and the separation call. Arch Gen Psychiatry 42:505–417, 1985

Minsky M: K-lines. A theory of memory. Cognitive Science 4:117–133, 1980

Mitchell D, Osborne EW, O'Boyle MW: Habituation under stress: Shocked mice show non-associative learning in a T-maze. Behav Neural Biol 43:212–217, 1985

Panksepp J: Toward a general psychobiological theory of emotions. Behav Brain Sci 5:407–468, 1982

Piaget J: Structuralism. New York, Basic Books, 1973

Rajecki DW, Lamb ME, Obmascher P: Toward a general theory of infantile attachment: A comparative review of aspects of the social bond. Behav Brain Sci 3:417–464, 1978

Reite M, Field T (eds): The Psychobiology of Attachment and Separation. Orlando, Academic Press, 1985

Spitz R: Hospitalism: An inquiry into the genesis of psychiatric conditions in early childhood. Psychoanal Study Child 1:53–74, 1945

Squire LR: Memory and the Brain. New York, Oxford University Press, 1987

van der Kolk B: Psychological Trauma. Washington, DC, American Psychiatric Press, 1987

van der Kolk BA: The trauma spectrum: The interaction of biological and social events in the genesis of the trauma response. J Traumatic Stress 1:273–290, 1988

Biological Basis of Behavior

10

Ethology and Human Behavior

Doris Zumpe and Richard P. Michael

ETHOLOGY, BEHAVIOR, AND MEDICINE: INTRODUCTION

Today, more than ever before, medicine is aware of the impact of behavior on human health and disease. This impact is felt almost from the moment of conception to the grave. There is now little doubt that if a mother uses heroin or abuses alcohol and cigarettes during pregnancy, the physiology and psychology of her offspring may be adversely affected. This is also true when the fetus is exposed to other drugs, to hormones, and to stress. If a child is reared in an impoverished emotional environment or, worse still, is abused physically or emotionally, this can have devastating, lifelong effects on health. It is recognized that behavior patterns that are laid down early can result in the excessive consumption of sugar, salt, and fat, particularly in urban societies, which leads to much pathology and increased mortality rates. We are now confronted by the rapid appearance in many communities of lethal, sexually trans-mitted diseases whose spread depends on certain behavioral patterns and life-styles that have always been looked at askance by the more conservative establishment. Modern medicine accepts that one must tackle the emotional and motivational under-pinnings of some forms of aberrant behavior (although not all) in order to effect lasting changes. This was one of Freud's most important contributions. Emotional and motivational conflicts themselves may translate into a wide variety of psychosomatic disorders, and the interaction between the body and the emotions is understood to be a two-way process.

Comparative morphology has taught us well, and we thoroughly understand that our anatomical form has its roots in the distant, phylogenetic past. But it is less obvious that many of our motivational and behavioral tendencies also have distant origins and that behavior as well as anatomy has been molded by evolutionary selection pressures. Behavior that might have been highly adaptive and successful in, for example, a hunter-gatherer society may be quite maladaptive in a modern industrialized setting

241

today, yet can still be inexorably, although inappropriately, expressed. Could it be that the insatiable craving for fatty foods and excessive calories, which can be fatal to some people now there is unlimited access to them, stems from an era when such nutrients were extremely scarce (indeed, they still are in many parts of the world)? Perhaps the irrepressible drive toward sexual consummation, barely curbed by threats from lethal disease, is an adaptation to the fact that infant mortality was very high and survival to reproductive age only about fifty percent throughout most of human history? Such questions are probably unanswerable, but they certainly make one think.

Ethology describes behavior in terms of its form and function and traces its development during both ontogeny (the lifespan of the individual) and phylogeny (the evolutionary history of the species). This approach is very similar to that taken by comparative anatomists and physiologists in their efforts to understand how the body functions. Behavior is, of course, more susceptible to environmental and cultural influences than is morphology, but behavior and bodily form cannot exist or function without the other; that they must have co-evolved during phylogeny is a truism. To help provide the educated physician with a broader biological perspective on human behavior, this chapter gives a brief overview of the more important concepts of ethology in an admittedly capsular form and illustrates the concepts with examples from animal and human behavior.

HISTORY, DEFINITION, AND AIMS OF ETHOLOGY

The attempt to understand and classify the behavior of animals and humans goes back at least to Aristotle and Plato. What we know today as psychology actually developed in Europe during the 19th century from philosophy. Ethology, on the other hand, developed from zoology, from the study by naturalists of animals in their natural environments. The term *ethology* derives from the Greek word *ethos*, meaning habit or manner, and was once applied to what today we know as ecology. But from the turn of this century it gradually came to be used to describe the study of the naturalistic behavior of animals, and since 1951 it has been the generally accepted term for this branch of natural science. The founding father of modern ethology was Konrad Lorenz. Lorenz, the Dutch ethologist Nikolaas Tinbergen, and Karl von Frisch (who described the communicatory "dance" of the honey bee) together shared the Nobel Prize for Physiology or Medicine in 1973 for the tremendous insights into the workings of animal behavior that they provided (Fig. 10-1).

The basic tenet of ethology is that animals evolve not only morphologically but also behaviorally to interact successfully, if not optimally, with their environment so as to survive and reproduce. Ethology is therefore concerned with understanding how animals interact with each other and cope with their environment (i.e., how they feed, avoid predation, seek and court a mate, raise their young, and so forth). A major thrust of many ethologic studies is to determine (1) the factors that influence an animal's motivational or emotional state, (2) how the latter creates predisposition to behave in certain ways, and (3) how these predispositions are communicated to others of the same or different species. *Because of the great impact of Darwin on biology, ethologic research was originally directed almost exclusively toward innate (or inborn) behavior, especially that of fishes and birds, giving rise to the common misconception that ethologists consider all behavior to be innate and little affected by learning or experience.* This is certainly true in some cases. For example, a chick hatched by a duck immediately scratches the ground and pecks at seeds, just like all chicks do, whereas a duckling hatched by a hen runs to water, swims, dives, and oils its feathers. This happens straight from the egg, and learning cannot be responsible for these widely different species-specific behavior patterns. *The modern view,*

Figure 10–1. *The three Nobel laureates for Physiology or Medicine in 1973.* **A:** *Konrad Lorenz, considered the founding father of ethology (photo: H. Kacher).* **B:** *Niko Tinbergen (photo: B. Tschanz).* **C:** *Karl von Frisch (photo: M. von Frisch). (Reproduced with permission from Slater PJB: An Introduction to Ethology. New York, Cambridge University Press, 1985)*

and the view emphasized by this text, is that both "nature" and "nurture" are generally involved in determining behavior. There is a genetic predisposition to perform certain behavior patterns and to learn certain things, and experiential factors are involved to a greater or lesser degree in shaping the form of the behavior itself and the context in which it occurs.

The aims of ethology are given in capsular form in Table 10-1. For ethology as for anatomy, the distinction between homology and analogy is important for understanding functional and evolutionary relationships. Homologous structures and behaviors are those that were derived during evolution from a common source. The whale's flipper, the bat's wing, and the human arm differ greatly in form and function, but they can all be traced to the primitive tetrapod forelimb. Analogous structures and behaviors, on the other hand, have a close external resemblance because they serve similar functions, for example, the wings of birds and insects, but they possess no common structural or evolutionary features. In view of the similarities between the aims of morphology and those of ethology, it is not surprising that some of the methods adopted by ethologists (Table 10-2) resemble those used by anatomists.

Table 10–1 **Aims of Ethology**

To establish for each species a comprehensive list of all functional units of behavior (an *ethogram*), and then determine for each unit of behavior:
    Its adaptive function
    Its ontogeny
    Its phylogeny
The environmental and physiologic factors regulating it

Table 10–2 **Methods Used by Ethology to Achieve Its Aims**

1. *Construction of ethogram:* Observe many members of the species in their natural habitat, record all behavioral sequences (postures, movements, facial expressions, vocalizations, and so forth), and break them down into their smallest functional units.
2. *Determination of adaptive function:* Analyze chains of "who does what to whom" to classify the relation between the behavior-eliciting situation, the behavior itself, and the effects of the behavior.
3. *Determination of ontogeny:* Discover when the behavior pattern first appears in the life of the individual, and record any subsequent changes in form and function.
4. *Determination of phylogeny:* Examine if the behavior pattern
   a. Occurs in closely-related species.
   b. Occurs in geographically isolated populations.
   c. Develops in individuals isolated from conspecifics since birth.
   d. Has specific morphologic and/or physiologic correlates.
5. *Physiologic and environmental regulation:* Conduct experiments to determine the effects of changing one variable while holding constant all others.

ETHOLOGIC CONCEPTS AND PHENOMENA

Imprinting

The process of *imprinting* appears to have been independently discovered at different times by different people, including an English monk, St. Cuthbert, living between 635 and 687 AD, Sir Thomas More in the 16th century, Sigmund Freud (1905), and Konrad Lorenz, who formulated the modern concept in the 1930s from his observations on jackdaws, a species closely related to ravens and crows. Imprinting, considered to be a specialized form of early learning, is an example of what Lorenz called the "instinct-learning intercalation," namely, an innate predisposition to acquire some very specific pieces of information that are important, either immediately or much later on, in the life of the individual. Imprinting is characterized by a number of features (Table 10-3), some of which are shared with other learning processes.

It takes place during a circumscribed sensitive or critical period early in life. The young of many ground-nesting birds are very well-developed when they hatch and must follow their mother away from the nest almost immediately, for example, to water in the case of ducks and geese. To recognize and respond reliably to their mother by normal learning processes would take too long and would expose the young to predation. The imprinting process occurs very rapidly and has, in this context, enormous adaptive advantage. It has been shown (Hess, 1959) that ducklings become imprinted on whatever object they are exposed to (normally the mother) during a critical period between 13 and 16 hours after hatching. If they are exposed to a moving object such as a striped box during this period, they will follow it in preference to another object such as a cone.

The imprinted information may not, however, be used until later in life. When male ducklings are imprinted on their mother, they also receive visual and auditory information about the species to which they belong and about the sex with which to mate when adult (females do not readily imprint sexually). Species and sexual imprinting, therefore, takes place within the first day of life, although sexual imprinting is not expressed until many months later. Male wood ducks raised together but

---

Table 10-3 **Major Ethologic Concepts. I. Imprinting**

Imprinting is regarded as a specialized form of early learning involving:
1. A sensitive or critical period when the information is acquired.
2. Information that can be acquired before being put to use.
3. Information that concerns supraindividual, species-specific characteristics.
4. Retention of the acquired information for life.
5. Specificity of the behavioral response.

---

otherwise socially isolated become sexually imprinted on male wood duck. This becomes evident only after sexual maturation when they begin to court male rather than female wood ducks. One might be tempted to analogize to human fixations! Only the supraindividual characteristics of a species are imprinted. A gander imprinted on humans may follow and court any human being, not just the person on whom it was imprinted, and a cockerel imprinted on mallard drakes will try to follow and court all mallard drakes. Information acquired by normal learning processes is susceptible to forgetting, but imprinted information is retained for life. If a male wood duck imprinted on other male wood ducks is maintained in the absence of males but in the presence of females, it may eventually mate with the females. However, if another male is introduced, even many years later, the imprinted drake immediately abandons the females and resumes courting the male. Finally, only specific responses are imprinted. A jackdaw raised by Lorenz directed filial and sexual activities toward the imprinted species, namely humans, but flew with hooded crows as flight companions and directed parental behavior towards young jackdaws.

We do not know whether imprinting-like processes are important in the human, and ethical considerations preclude experimentation. Primates, and especially humans, have a uniquely long period of infant dependency, giving ample opportunity for the acquisition of important environmental and social information by associative learning processes as discussed in previous chapters. This, together with the massive neocortical development of primates, might make the rapid, irreversible acquisition of information early in life less useful; mammals provide fewer clear-cut examples of imprinting than do birds. Nevertheless, language acquisition appears to have a sensitive period during the early years, when both native and foreign tongues are readily understood and acquired without accent; these skills are lost before puberty. There is much to suggest that the foundations of many adult attitudes, beliefs, and actions are laid down irrevocably during early life, long before such attitudes and beliefs become functional. For example, dietary habits and taboos (about meats and alcohol) acquired during childhood, sometimes by religious proscription, are extremely difficult to break in adulthood.

Socialization in many mammals including primates (see below) also has an early critical period. Domesticated species like cats and dogs, when raised by their mothers in isolation from humans (e.g., on large farms), remain totally "wild" for the rest of their lives, while feral species such as the wolf or dingo, when raised by humans, can become domesticated and treat humans as pack members. However, there are marked individual differences in the strength of effects in these species, and it is likely that differences would be even greater in humans. It is conceivable, but a speculation, that early events at a critical time with negligible impact on one child may have far-reaching, imprinting-like effects on another, and we do not at present have an understanding of the possible role of these mechanisms in the etiology of adult mental disorder.

Bonding

One process of importance that occurs quite rapidly and early on, and which may involve imprinting because the consequences pervade the lifespan, is the formation of the *mother–infant bond in primates.* Using orphaned rhesus monkeys, Harlow and colleagues analyzed the features of the surrogate mother that contribute to bonding (Harlow and Zimmermann, 1959) and demonstrated how breaking the bond by enforced separation results in deprivations whose behavioral symptoms (Fig. 10-2) have many similarities to those described for anaclitic depression in hospitalized infants and children (Bowlby, 1969; Robertson, 1958; Spitz, 1946). Separation studies with infant macaques have shown that, as in the child, there are three phases of distress: agitation–protest, withdrawal–despair, and, finally, total detachment. Some authorities feel this provides a model both for mourning and for certain types of human depression, and that the experimental results confirm the views of clinicians, such as Melanie Klein (1932), that object loss (the depressive position) in childhood contributes significantly to vulnerability to depression in later life. These theories are bringing about an interesting convergence and potential integration between ethology, psychoanalytic theory, and other biologic perspectives.

In monkeys, the mother–infant relationship, the effects of separation, and the infant's responsiveness to its environment all depend on characteristics of the mother or mother-surrogate (Mason and Capitanio, 1988), on complex feedback interactions

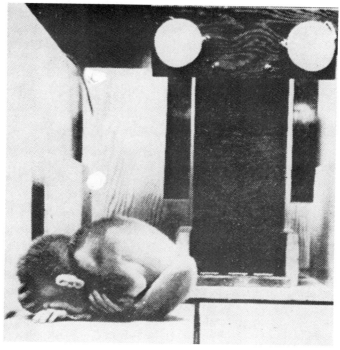

Figure 10–2. *Behavioral response of an orphaned rhesus monkey, raised on a mother surrogate, when separated from the latter and placed in a fear-evoking environment. (Harlow HF, Zimmerman RR: Affectional responses in the infant monkey. Science 130:421, 1959. With kind permission of the American Association for the Advancement of Science)*

between mother and infant, as well as on the social setting and on food availability (Hinde, 1983; Rosenblum and Paully, 1984). If early deprivations are very severe, both monkey and human infants show much self-directed behavior, notably self-hugging, sucking, and biting. They perform stereotyped movements such as rocking and react to others with inappropriate fear and aggression. There is a failure to thrive, and immune responses are compromised. In infant rhesus monkeys that have been in total isolation for 12 months, resocialization is practically impossible. The animals maintain abnormal, catatonic postures and cannot reproduce after puberty. Again, analogies have been made between the experimental situation in monkeys and Kanner's syndrome of early infantile autism, and we have yet another possibility of a model for the major psychoses. On the basis of comparisons with normal children, ethologists (Tinbergen and Tinbergen, 1972) have interpreted the behavior of autistic children to be an expression of the motivational conflict between avoidance and approach in a social context. In autism, for unknown reasons, the avoidance component is abnormally intense and overrides the affiliative component, leading eventually to increasing withdrawal and social isolation. Although socially isolated female monkeys generally cannot respond to males appropriately enough to be mated, some have become pregnant. These females fail to show normal mothering behavior toward their infants and are, in effect, neglecting and, because of their indifference, abusing mothers. Perhaps in the human, as in rhesus monkeys, failure to form adequate parent–offspring bonds may lead to a generalized failure to bond with individuals in later life, be they friend, mate, or offspring. We are only just beginning to understand something of the vast implications of these processes for the welfare of the individual and, indeed, of our social institutions.

Fixed Action Patterns

Fixed action patterns are units of behavior characterized by their unvarying form and independence of environmental stimuli; they are innate, and totally unaffected by experience or learning. However, environmental stimuli may be necessary to elicit them. Fixed action patterns can occur in well-coordinated sequences, which are also unvarying in form and independent of environmental stimuli. They are not, as commonly believed, simply chains of conditioned or spinal segmental reflexes. The best examples come from locomotor behavior in forms as diverse as the eel, the chicken, and the human. In eels, the undulating swimming pattern is independent of proprioception and depends on the endogenous production of excitation within the central nervous system. In birds, flight develops according to an ontogenetic maturational program independent of the chick's posthatching experiences and of afferent inputs from its wings and wing muscles (Provine, 1981). Locomotion in human infants also depends on coordinated sequences of fixed action patterns, which are fully functional long before the maturation of the musculoskeletal system necessary for their full expression. Premature babies, whose body weight is small enough to be supported by the limbs, can show fully coordinated walking, hanging, and climbing movements. Normal babies at 6 weeks show spontaneous kicking movements that mirror the temporal parameters of the adult walking cycle (Thelen et al, 1981).

As in the case of anatomical features, fixed action patterns may be characteristic of the species, the genus, or of an even larger taxon, and they can be as useful as an anatomical feature for evaluating taxonomic relationships and tracing evolutionary pathways. A classic example of this is the comparative study by Lorenz on the fixed action patterns of ducks and geese. The piping of a lost duckling, for example, is common to all species of duck and goose, whereas the courtship behavior of "displacement shaking" is common to all ducks but absent in all geese, and so forth. Sometimes genetic studies can reveal the potential presence of a fixed action pattern that is absent from the ordinary behavioral repertoire. For example, the "down-up" courtship behavior of many ducks is absent in pintail and yellow-billed ducks but reappears in their hybrids.

These studies exemplify the techniques used to identify innate components of behavior, and some of them can be used in human ethology. A common phylogenetic basis is likely if a behavioral pattern or sequence has an identical form and function in different but related species, as in the stereotyped sequence of movements of the head, face, and mouth with which babies and all primate neonates search for the nipple. A behavior pattern is also likely to be a fixed action pattern, or a sequence of fixed action patterns, if it occurs in identical form in different, geographically isolated populations, and this is the case for components of human greeting, courtship, and aggression. A fixed action pattern is also assumed if a behavior occurs in the absence of any opportunity for learning, for example, in deaf- and blind-born children who show many facial expressions of emotion such as smiling, laughing and crying (Fig. 10-3) although there has been no opportunity for imitation or learning (Eibl-Eibesfeldt, 1970).

Conflict Behaviors

In their normal environments, animals are exposed to many conflicting stimuli simultaneously, and such conflicts must be resolved rapidly and efficiently for survival. It may seem an extravagant statement, but all initial approaches between conspecifics are thought to be associated with conflicting behavioral tendencies and emotions. Many of the greeting ceremonies of social vertebrates, including humans, are derived from competing tendencies to approach and withdraw, namely, from the activation of two or more incompatible tendencies. As noted earlier, ethologic studies suggest that the behavior of autistic children in social situations is an expression of such motivational conflicts. We can consider some of the ways in which motivational conflicts are resolved (Table 10-4).

An *intention movement* is seen when a behavior occurs in an abbreviated form and not in its entirety. It results when the tendency to perform a behavior is too low to elicit the complete behavioral sequence or when the behavior is partially blocked by a conflicting tendency. Thus, a student leans forward and places both hands on the arms of his chair during an unpleasant interview with his professor. The sequence of getting up from the chair is blocked by his respect for, or fear of, the higher-ranking person; the movements can be both made and perceived unconsciously.

Redirection, or *redirected behavior,* occurs when a stimulus simultaneously arouses two conflicting tendencies, such as attack and sexual activity. The individual

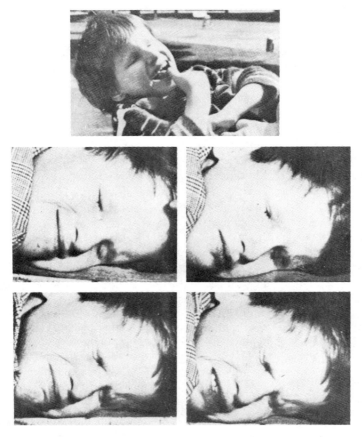

Figure 10–3. *Facial expressions of emotion in a congenitally deaf and blind girl deprived of all opportunities for imitation or learning.* **Top:** *laughing at age 7;* **middle and bottom:** *transition from smiling to weeping and finally crying at age 9 (photos: I. Eibl-Eibesfeldt). (Reproduced with permission from Eibl–Eibesfeldt I: Ethology: The Biology of Behavior. New York, Holt, Rinehart & Winston, 1970)*

responds by performing a behavior appropriate to one drive, for example an attack, but instead of directing this attack toward the eliciting stimulus, such as a potential mate, it redirects the attack away from the latter onto another conspecific or even an inanimate object in the environment (e.g., kicking the furniture). Aggression directed by a parent at a child after an unsuccessful verbal conflict with the spouse would be another example of redirection; in psychoanalytic terminology, this would be displacement. Law officers must be especially careful when intervening in domestic violence because they are liable to be attacked by both parties; the highest death rate among police occurs in answering these calls. *Physicians are often the target of redirected frustration and anger toward illness and disease that patients and their families experience.*

Table 10–4 **Major Ethologic Concepts.**
II. Conflict Behaviors

Conflict behaviors are postures, movements, facial expressions, and vocalizations that result from the simultaneous activation of two or more incompatible behavioral tendencies:
1. Intention movement.
2. Redirected behavior.
3. Displacement activity.
4. Vacuum activity.
5. Alternation.
6. Compromise.
7. Ambivalence.

Redirected aggression is seen during the early phases of courtship in many different species including primates (Zumpe and Michael, 1979). If the aggression aroused by the prospective mate cannot be effectively redirected, courtship activity can break down, actual fighting occurs, and bonding cannot proceed. However, if courtship progresses, each partner may join in with the other's redirected threats, so that both are "threatening-away" together in the same direction, and this appears to have a very strong bonding effect. As noted above, rather unfortunately, redirection is known as "displacement" in the psychoanalytic literature, and the latter term is used in ethology for a quite different form of conflict behavior (see below). The use of the same terms for different mechanisms in different disciplines causes much confusion.

As just mentioned, another type of conflict behavior is *displacement activity.* This is typically a low-priority maintenance activity such as scratching, preening, or self-grooming that seems entirely irrelevant to the behavioral context in which it occurs. Fights between laboratory rats, for example, are commonly punctuated by bouts of self-grooming and self-licking, which are irrelevant to the behavioral context. In humans, displacement activities often take the form of repetitively adjusting one's hair or clothing at times of conflict and tension. Yawning and stretching repeatedly at times of stress (waiting for a fateful interview) can be another displacement behavior that humans share with many other vertebrates. Current thought holds that these low-priority maintenance behaviors become disinhibited as a consequence of the mutual but total inhibition of two conflicting high-priority tendencies, such as attack and flight in our rat example.

A *vacuum activity* is a behavior that occurs quite spontaneously in the absence of its normal eliciting stimulus, as though the individual were responding to a hallucination of the latter. This occurs when the tendency to perform the behavior is very strong, either after a prolonged period when the behavior has been inhibited by conflicting tendencies or after a prolonged period without an eliciting stimulus. Lorenz first coined the term when he saw his tame starling, fed since hatching from a bowl containing boiled eggs and other delicacies, fly up to the ceiling of his room, snap at a nonexistent fly and swallow it in an unmistakable and typical behavioral sequence (Lorenz, 1982). A dog that has been penned up in the house for an unusually long time will rush into the yard when freed and bark at nonexistent cats and intruders.

Three other types of conflict behavior might be mentioned here: alternation, compromise formation, and ambivalence. *Alternation* occurs when first one, and then another, of the competing behavioral tendencies briefly overrides the other, so that the animal alternates between the two appropriate responses, for example, between approach and withdrawal. The classic example in ethology is the zig-zag "dance" of the male stickleback (a freshwater fish) when courting the female and leading her to the nest he has built. *Compromise formation* occurs when an individual performs a behavior that is appropriate to both conflicting tendencies. Finally, *ambivalence* is expressed when intention movements appropriate to each of the two conflicting tendencies are combined into a single pattern. Many facial expressions and body postures in both animals and humans result from ambivalence between sexually motivated or aggressively motivated approach on the one hand and flight-motivated retreat on the other. Fig. 10-4 illustrates how the facial expressions and body postures of the cat change with changing combinations of conflicting tendencies to attack and flee. As mentioned earlier, many greeting ceremonies in social vertebrates are derived from such conflicting tendencies, and the human is no exception. Frame-by-frame analyses of moving films of greetings between the host and guests at social functions have demonstrated predictable and well-ordered sequences of interactive behavior (Kendon and Ferber, 1973). At a distance, initial eye contact is associated with a brief raising of the eyebrows ("eyebrow flash"—see below) and a smile. This is followed by a dip of the head with closed eyes and subsequent gaze aversion during the approach. As the guest comes closer to the host, eye contact is reestablished, the head is tilted to one side, and the guest brings his or her arm across the front of the chest in a protective gesture and then reorients from a position directly facing the host to one at a right-angle that readily permits departure. These kinds of studies have shown that agonistic (aggressive and submissive) tendencies play a part even in the relatively informal greeting interactions of friends and acquaintances. Many vertebrate courtship displays can be traced to the conflict between sexual and aggressive tendencies, and in rhesus monkeys there is considerable evidence that some degree of agonistic tension between partners is necessary for the optimal expression of sexual activity. This is also true for the human. Certainly, many of us are aware of the agonistic component in human courtship, particularly during adolescence, when actual aggression between partners can easily occur and the balance between affectionate and aggressive behavior is precarious.

A few words more about aggression. The term "aggressive behavior" covers a wide variety of often quite dissimilar things, and definitions differ between disciplines. The aggression of a stallion in preserving his harem of mares is clearly different from that of a highland cow separated from her calf. Some authors include predation among aggressive behavior, but others do not because predation is often associated with a quite different type of affect. Not surprisingly, the determinants of human aggression, particularly of violence and warfare, remain obscure despite the many theories invoked, from original sin to those involving precise and localized neuropathology. To an ethologist, it is of great interest that most nonhuman primates show intense xenophobia (fear of strangers) and initially react agonistically (aggressively and fearfully) to individuals not belonging to their own social group. Bands of rhesus monkeys generally avoid each other (transfer of an individual to another group cannot

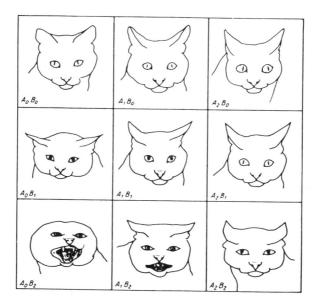

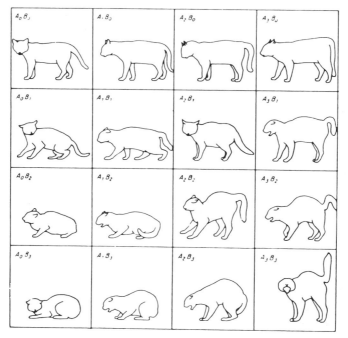

Figure 10–4. *Varying mixtures and intensities of aggression and fear expressed in the facial expressions and body postures of the cat. In each section, aggressiveness increases from left to right and fear increases from top to bottom. (Reproduced with permission from Leyhausen P: Katzen—Eine Verhaltenskunde. Berlin and Hamburg, Paul Parey, 1982)*

be dealt with), but intertroop fights may occur if they meet, and larger bands generally dominate smaller ones. This suggests a biologic basis for tribal conflicts (within the species) and for the ubiquitous human predisposition to distinguish "them" from "us." This can apply to different branches within the same family, to neighbors, sexes, races, religions, socioeconomic groups, political parties, nations, and so on. It had been thought that humans possess a unique propensity for killing their own kind despite signals of distress and submission, but similar behavior has recently been reported among chimpanzees in the wild, where the males of one social band systematically stalked and killed all members of another over a period of months in an act reminiscent of genocide. Whether this can be regarded as similar to the human phenomenon remains an open question.

Ritualization

In the interests of rapid and unambiguous communication, many conflict behaviors have become specialized during the course of evolution in both form and frequency, and are said to have become ritualized into displays. *Ritualization,* as used here, applies to an evolutionary process, and the behavior resulting from it in the present is called the *display.* We are all familiar with examples of ritualized fighting between males as displayed, for example, by stags during the rut. They lock their horns and push, but serious damage is infrequent and almost accidental. Ritualization may involve a number of specializations (Table 10-5). The movements often show remarkable stereotypy and inflexibility. In woodpeckers, for example, the rhythmic drumming on a hollow branch, which attracts females and signals other males that the territory is occupied, is a stereotyped version of the hammering movements used to drill the nest hole. When a behavioral sequence shows this constancy of form over a wide range of drive intensities it is said to have a typical intensity. More usually, the intensity with which a behavior is performed parallels the intensity of the underlying motivation. At the expense of some loss of informational content, the standardization brought about by a typical intensity enhances the signal value of a display and minimizes its chances of being misunderstood by conspecifics; this is very useful and highly adaptive. A first component of greeting between two people who catch sight of each other is a rapid raising and lowering of the eyebrows, the "eyebrow flash," accompanied by a smile.

Table 10–5 **Major Ethological Concepts.**
III. Ritualization

Ritualization is a specialization, in the interests of unambiguous communication, in the form, frequency, and intensity of a behavior. It may involve:
1. Stereotypy.
2. Typical intensity.
3. Associated morphologic specialization.
4. Threshold changes.
5. Motivational changes.

This occurs across all cultures that have been studied (Fig. 10-5) and is a ritualized display having a typical intensity. Frame-by-frame analyses of film records of people all over the world have shown that the entire behavioral sequence has a uniform duration of about 0.3 seconds, and that the eyebrows are maximally raised for about 0.16 seconds (Eibl-Eibesfeldt, 1970).

Ritualization may involve other specializations, one of which is that the exaggerated behavior patterns may be associated with conspicuous morphologic structures, such as antlers in stags. The behavior and the morphology serve to enhance the signal value of each. A courtship display by cocks in all species of game birds (domestic fowl, pheasants, turkeys, and peacocks) is derived from pecking the ground for food, which attracts the female. This behavior exposes the tail of the cock to the hen, and most of us are familiar with the picturesque tail feathers that emphasize this courtship display and reach great elaboration in peacocks. In the eyebrow flash in humans, the presence of distinctive eyebrows greatly enhances the signal value of the

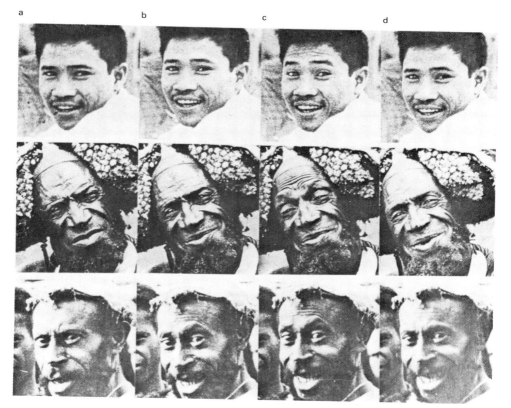

Figure 10–5. *Selected film frames of eyebrow-flashes in a Balinese* **(top)***, Papuan of the Huri tribe* **(middle)***, and Papuan of the Woitapmin tribe* **(bottom)***. Taken at 48 frames/second with a camera whose objective was mounted on a prism so that it filmed at a right angle and not to the front; this permitted filming without the subjects being aware (photos: I. Eibl-Eibesfeldt) (Reproduced with permission from Eibl-Eibesfeldt I: Ethology: The Biology of Behavior. New York, Holt, Rinehart & Winston, 1970)*

behavior. A similar behavior pattern occurs in some nonhuman primates where its visibility is enhanced, in the absence of eyebrows, by conspicuously colored eyelids. Eyebrow position conveys much information about the emotional state (anger or sadness). It is used by actors and has become culturally ritualized (see below) in the Kabuki theater. The face and eye region have special importance in nonverbal communication, and primates preferentially scan the faces of conspecifics, especially around the eyes. There are neurons deeply placed in the superior temporal sulcus in primates that respond selectively to the sight of faces (Perret and Rolls, 1983); damage to this area in the human may be responsible for prosopagnosia (inability to recognize familiar faces—sometimes including one's own).

Ritualization can involve changes in the threshold of a display in closely related species and can require more intense stimulation for its expression in some species than in others. This can be so extreme that the display is entirely absent from the normal behavioral repertoire but reappears in hybrids, as described earlier. Ritualization may also involve a complete change in the underlying motivation; thus, a display originally based (in evolutionary terms) on redirected aggression may now depend entirely on sexual motivation for its expression, as in the courtship displays of many species of fishes, birds, and mammals. Certain movements made during redirected threats by courting rhesus monkeys have become ritualized into more stereotyped movements and now serve as sexual invitations by which the female initiates mounts by her male partner; the original aggressive motivation has been replaced by a sexual one (Zumpe and Michael, 1970).

Dominance fights among wolves, which have a complex social hierarchy, are abruptly terminated when the loser suddenly adopts a submissive posture by offering its throat to the opponent; this inhibits the winner from continuing its attack for as long as the posture is held. Are there any human analogies? In considering this, mention should be made of what is termed cultural ritualization, which demonstrates several features of the evolutionary process (Lorenz, 1977). The analogy between the submissive postures of social canids and bowing, kneeling, and general kowtowing in the human is, of course, quite compelling. The greeting ceremony in which a man briefly lifts his hat, as well as the military salute of touching the forehead (cross-cultural), are thought to be ritualized gestures derived from those times when warriors signaled their nonaggressive intentions by displaying vulnerability (uncovering their heads). Handshakes and kissing rituals between men are still regular matutinal forms of the greeting ceremony in European countries, for example between office workers.

Innate Releasing Mechanisms

We have described innate predispositions to perform behavior patterns, but there are also innate predispositions to respond to certain stimuli. In other words, there can be a genetic basis for receiving as well as for sending signals that have adaptive importance. Environmental stimuli that evoke special, highly appropriate responses on very first exposure are said to be "releasers" or "key stimuli," and the response that is triggered depends on an "innate releasing mechanism." This concept was developed by Lorenz and Tinbergen. Some releasers can be inanimate aspects of the environment. For example, naive chicks and kittens hesitate at a precipice even when it is covered by a glass plate, and the same effect can be demonstrated by a visual illusion employing a checkerboard drawn in perspective to mimic a precipice. The response to the optical stimulus is immediate and not learned and initially overrides the tactile information. In other cases, conspecifics or other species (notably predators) serve as very specific releasers of behavior. Studies with models have shown that it is often a very simple characteristic of the natural releaser that triggers the behavioral response. Tinbergen (1951) demonstrated this in his studies on the three-spined stickleback. During the spring mating season, male sticklebacks develop a red belly and begin fighting one another for suitable breeding territories, whereas the bellies of females become swollen with ripening eggs. Tinbergen showed that it was the simple characteristic of "red belly underneath" that elicited territorial attacks by males. Lifelike models lacking a red belly, or models provided with a red back rather than red belly, were less effective in eliciting aggression than were shapeless objects characterized merely by a red patch along the bottom. Tinbergen also demonstrated that the swollen belly of the fertile female is the characteristic that elicits male courtship. Humans, too, appear to make quite complex judgments about others on the basis of very simple cues. Eyebrow position and movement communicate not only emotional state, as noted earlier, but also seem to be perceived as indicators of social dominance. Adults and children of different nationalities judged models with lowered eyebrows as more dominant than models posing with slightly raised eyebrows. Indeed, there is evidence that judgments about an individual's personality and leadership qualities, made on the basis of simple facial characteristics such as eyebrow thickness and jaw angle, may influence that individual's career throughout life (Mazur et al, 1984).

Oddly enough, an exaggeration of the feature that normally triggers a response, in other words, a supranormal stimulus, is often more effective than the naturally occurring feature. For example, many ground-nesting birds retrieve eggs that roll off their nest by means of a characteristic sequence of movements of the bill, head, and neck. This behavior can be elicited by models of natural eggs, but when models up to ten times larger than natural ones are offered, attempts are made to retrieve them in preference to real eggs, although the bird is physically incapable of succeeding in the task. Perhaps the fine-tuning of the perception of a releaser that would be needed to exclude supranormal stimuli never took place because, until inquisitive ethologists provided them, they were simply not encountered. Humans also respond to supranormal releasers. The best-known example is the so-called infant schema. Compared with adults, young animals, babies, and small children have much more rounded heads and bodies, and shorter faces, especially between the eyes and the lower jaw. These individuals are perceived as "cuter" and "more lovable" and elicit more caregiving behavior than do individuals showing the adult form (Fig. 10-6). Studies with models have shown that men, women, girls, and, to a lesser extent, boys, all perceive exaggerations of the infant schema in humans and in other species as more appealing than the corresponding natural infant. This is exploited widely in marketing and advertising and is apparent in the form taken by popular dolls and by Disney cartoon characters.

The juvenile characteristics of women, in addition to their secondary sexual characteristics, are frequently exaggerated in drawings for fashion magazines, in dolls, and in poses by models for product marketing.

In summary, ethologic concepts and methods have been extremely helpful in understanding and interpreting the genetic bases of behavior and especially the relationships between the individual and its environment during phylogeny and ontogeny. Ethology has helped us gently put to rest the sterile controversies of earlier years between the vitalistic and mechanistic schools, which looked on behavior as a result either of inexplicable instincts or of chains of reflexes. By using a comparative approach to behavior, ethology has provided fresh insights into some human motiva-

Figure 10–6. *The "infant schema" that releases human parental care responses. Head proportions typical of the infant* **(left)** *are perceived as cuter and more lovable than head proportions in the same or closely related species that are typical of the adult* **(right)**. *(Reproduced with permission from Lorenz K: Die angeborenen Formen möglicher Erfahrung. Z Tierpsychol 5:235–409, 1943)*

tional systems and has given us a useful framework for observing and understanding much nonverbal communication, notably that of the infant and child. An appreciation of the major ethologic concepts, together with the recognition that the evolution of biologic systems proceeds more slowly than cultural and technologic evolution, may help remind physicians that some of our morphology and behavior is probably more appropriate to the environments and lifestyles of the past than to those of today. Nevertheless, we must bear the weight of this evolutionary past on our shoulders.

ANNOTATED BIBLIOGRAPHY

Harlow HF, Zimmermann RR: Affectional responses in the infant monkey. Science 130:421–432, 1959

> This classic article describes the series of experiments that first demonstrated that infant rhesus monkeys require bodily contact for the development of affectional bonds with the "mother," and enumerates other variables subsequently proven also to be important. There are also detailed and touching descriptions of the infants' responses to separation from the surrogate mother.

Hinde RA: Human non-verbal communication. In Biological Bases of Human Social Behavior, pp 117–146. New York, McGraw-Hill, 1974

> This chapter concisely reviews certain human communicatory gestures and facial expressions, some ethologic hypotheses about their phylogenetic and cultural origins, and a classificatory scheme for nonverbal communication. It ends with a section comparing nonverbal with verbal communication. This will be a useful starting point for the physician who considers it important to acquire the "clinical eye" referred to by Lorenz in the reading suggested below.

Lorenz KZ: Introductory history. In The Foundations of Ethology. The Principal Ideas and Discoveries in Animal Behavior, pp 1–12. New York, Simon & Schuster, 1982

> This highly readable, personal account of the nature/nurture controversy provides a good synopsis of the ethologic view of animal and human behavior. Chapter II, "The Methodology of Biology and Particularly of Ethology," pp 36–65, is also recommended for its account, richly illustrated with anecdotes, of basic "dos and don'ts," some of which may have almost as much relevance for the practicing physician as for the ethologist.

Tinbergen EA, Tinbergen N: Early childhood autism—An ethological approach. Z Tierpsychol Suppl 10:1–53, 1972

> While laying no claim to an understanding of the biologic causation of autism, the authors advance a strong argument for the use of ethologic techniques of observation and motivational analysis to identify behavioral feedback mechanisms that may have therapeutic implications. The photographs alone are very compelling.

REFERENCES

Bowlby J: Attachment and Loss. New York, Basic Books, 1969

Eibl-Eibesfeldt I: Ethology: The Biology of Behavior. New York, Holt, Rinehart & Winston, 1970

Freud S: Three Essays on the Theory of Sexuality. In Complete Psychological Works of Freud, Vol VII. London, Hogarth Press, 1905

Harlow HF, Zimmermann RR: Affectional responses in the infant monkey. Science 130:421–432, 1959

Hess EH: Imprinting. Science 130:133–141, 1959

Hinde RA: Feedback in the mother–infant relationship. In Hinde RA (ed): Primate Social Relationships, Section 6.2. Sunderland, MA, Sinauer Associates, 1983

Kendon A, Ferber A: A description of some human greetings. In Michael RP, Crook JH (eds): Comparative Ecology and Behavior of Primates, pp 591–668. New York, Academic Press, 1973

Klein M: Psycho-Analysis of Children. London, Hogarth Press, 1932

Lorenz KZ: The Foundations of Ethology. The Principal Ideas and Discoveries in Animal Behavior. New York, Simon & Schuster, 1982

Lorenz KZ: Behind the Mirror. A Search for a Natural History of Human Knowledge. London, Methuen & Co, Ltd, 1977

Mason WA, Capitanio JP: Formation and expression of filial attachment in rhesus monkeys raised with living and inanimate mother substitutes. Dev Psychobiol 21:401–430, 1988

Mazur A, Mazur J, Keating CF: Military rank attainment of a West Point class: Effects of cadets' physical features. Am J Sociol 90:125–150, 1984

Perret DI, Rolls ET: Neural mechanisms underlying the visual analysis of faces. In Ewert J-P, Capranica RR, Ingle DJ (eds): Advances in Vertebrate Neuroethology, pp 543–566. New York, Plenum Press, 1983

Provine RR: Development of wing-flapping and flight in normal and flap-deprived domestic chicks. Dev Psychobiol 14:279–291, 1981

Robertson J: Young Children in Hospital. London, Travistock Publications, 1958

Rosenblum LA, Paully GS: The effects of varying environmental demands on maternal and infant behavior. Child Dev 55:305–314, 1984

Spitz RA: Anaclitic depression. An inquiry into the genesis of psychiatric conditions in early childhood. Psychoanal Study Child 2:313–342, 1946

Thelen E, Bradshaw G, Ward JA: Spontaneous kicking in month-old infants: Manifestation of a human central locomotor program. Behav Neural Biol 32:45–53, 1981

Tinbergen EA, Tinbergen N: Early childhood autism—An ethological approach. Z Tierpsychol Suppl 10:1–53, 1972

Tinbergen N: The Study of Instinct. Oxford, Clarendon Press, 1951

Zumpe D, Michael RP: Relation between the hormonal status of the female and direct and redirected aggression by male rhesus monkeys (*Macaca mulatta*). Horm Behav 12:269–279, 1979

Zumpe D, Michael RP: Ovarian hormones and female sexual invitations in captive rhesus monkeys (*Macaca mulatta*). Anim Behav 18:293–301, 1970

11

Neurobiologic Aspects of Behavior

Cort A. Pedersen, Robert N. Golden,
Dwight L. Evans, and
John J. Haggerty, Jr.

Chapter 10 elucidated some of the apparently genetically programmed, innate patterns of behavior that may be seen in both animals and humans that have an inherently neurobiologic basis. Following on these same lines, the neurobiologic basis for behavior will be discussed in some detail. It should again be reiterated that human behavior is multifactorially determined, and the concepts discussed here briefly review the core evidence that biologic factors are inextricably involved in determining the ultimate effects of social, psychologic, and environmental factors that will determine behavior and vulnerability to mental illness. Enormous *advances* in neuroscientific research in recent years have provided the basis for exciting insights into the biologic basis of behavior and invigorated the search for the biochemical and genetic basis for the major psychiatric disorders. This chapter will present an overview of the major neural networks and primary neurochemical systems that underlie complex behavior. The basic neurochemical systems will be reviewed (norepinephrine, serotoninin, acetylcholine, dopamine, and so forth) as well as the major neuroendocrine systems. The neurobiology of learning and memory will be reviewed as well as basic neurobiologic aspects of behaviors such as reproductive behavior, consumptive behavior, aggression, and stress responses. Finally, a brief overview of sleep architecture and physiology will be presented.

MAJOR COMPONENTS OF BEHAVIOR AND THEIR NEURAL SUBSTRATES

Behavior may be understood as the product of integrated activity of a number of interacting brain systems. *Among these systems are mechanisms that monitor internal and external sensory input, focus and maintain attention to significant stimuli, and arouse other brain regions involved in behavioral response pat-*

terns. For example, if an external stimulus (e.g., food) harmonizes with an internal drive state (e.g., hunger), a specific motivational system (e.g., feeding) activates goal-directed motor sequences. If the "reward" (i.e., food) is achieved, the internal drive state temporarily abates and the motivated behavior (i.e., food seeking and eating) ceases. Conversely, an aversive stimulus (e.g., predator, unfamiliar object) activates an avoidant or aggressive motivational system, which initiates motor sequences appropriate to the situation, such as "fight or flight," freezing, or a generally cautious approach. If the resulting behavior response decreases proximity to the threatening stimulus or increases familiarity with a novel anxiety-provoking stimulus, avoidant or aggressive motivation subsides.

Activation of the brain's motivational system is accompanied by arousal of endocrine and autonomic responses. Affective or mood-related systems also influence the intensity and quality of behavioral responses and, in higher animals and humans, generate a range of subjective experiences known as emotions.

The basic characteristics of rewarding or aversive stimuli determine the degree of affective arousal in the organism. Frustration in achieving the goals of motivated or avoidant behavior also mobilizes affective responses. Learning modifies behavior by allowing stimuli that might be otherwise neutral (conditioned stimuli) to become associated with rewarding or aversive stimuli (unconditioned stimuli). Through the learning process, conditioned stimuli become capable of activating arousal and attention mechanisms as well as motivational and affective systems. Thus, behavior is shaped by the following basic processes: arousal and attention, motivation, affect, motor performance, and learning. (Those basic concepts of behavioral and learning theory have also been discussed in depth in Chap. 4.) Brain systems subserving these fundamental components of behavior are summarized below.

Arousal and Attention

A diffuse network of neurons with widespread connections runs along the entire length of the midline brainstem. This system, referred to as the *reticular formation,* has long been known to influence level of consciousness (Kandel and Schwartz, 1985). We describe below (in the section entiled "'Classic' Neurotransmitters") ascending *monoamine-containing pathways,* which originate in the midbrain and ascend to forebrain structures. Neuronal cell bodies giving rise to these noradrenergic, dopaminergic, and serotonergic projections are located within the reticular formation. Reticular monoaminergic pathways influence the processing of sensory information at higher brain centers as well as at the level of the dorsal horn of the spinal cord where primary sensory neurons connect with the central nervous system (CNS). They also regulate behavioral arousal and control levels of awareness. In particular, *noradrenergic* pathways ascending from the *locus ceruleus,* a pontine nucleus, play a key role in establishing and maintaining focused attention on significant stimuli. Monoaminergic pathways ascending from the reticular formation project to many other regions of the CNS including areas involved in initiation of motivated behaviors, affect, organization of motor output, and learning. Thus, arousal and attention systems, originating in the midline brainstem, activate the neural substrates of other components of behavior.

Motivation

Drive states originate within motivational systems located in the preoptic–hypothalamic area of the brain (Kandel and Schwartz, 1985). Some drive states (e.g., thirst, hunger, desire for warmth) result from changes in homeostasis of the internal physiologic milieu. Indeed, specialized cells that monitor certain parameters of the internal state (plasma osmolarity, blood glucose concentrations, body temperature) are located within the preoptic–hypothalmic area and may be directly involved in activating drive states. Sex-specific motivated behaviors (e.g., mating, parenting, social aggression) depend on reproductive hormone conditions and the availability of appropriate external stimuli (e.g., receptive females, newborns). Threatening or painful conditions elicit avoidant, defensive, or submissive behaviors depending on the nature of the aversive situation. Output from motivational systems descends along the midline or through the medial forebrain bundle to the rostral brainstem where connections are made with pathways that control specific motor sequences. Beginning with the work of Olds and Milner in 1954, numerous investigators have found that *electrical stimulation at some locations within the hypothalamus and associated structures (the limbic system and the medial forebrain bundle) acts as a potent reward.* Animals with electrodes in these regions stimulate themselves at very high rates for long periods of time even if they are in no drive state (i.e., are not hungry, thirsty, sexually aroused, and so forth). *Stimulation at other hypothalamic sites elicits escape, aggressive, or submissive behavior.* Dopaminergic pathways are particularly important in maintaining electrical self-stimulation and may have a more general role in the mediation of reward.

Motor Performance

The essence of behavior is purposeful movement. Motor neurons arising in the anterior horn of the spinal cord or cranial nuclei are controlled directly or indirectly by cerebrospinal or cerebrobulbar neurons that originate in the motor cortex. The motor output of this system is regulated by associated structures (Kandel and Schwartz, 1985). Voluntary movement requires a plan of action (motor plan), which is formulated in the premotor and prefrontal cortices. The basal ganglia, which receive input from all cortical regions as well as the substantia nigra, communicate with the prefrontal and premotor cortices by thalamic nuclei. The cerebellum compares descending motor control signals with sensory signals resulting from motor action and then adjusts the motor signals at the level of the motor cortex and brainstem motor nuclei.

It is not clear at this time how motivational and affective systems influence motor planning and execution. Many motivated behaviors are mediated by descending projections to the midbrain. Ascending monoaminergic pathways that originate in the midbrain and terminate in the basal ganglia and frontal cortex may shape motor planning to conform to motivational states. The nucleus accumbens, which receives input from ascending monoamine pathways as well as structures of the limbic system (see below), projects to frontal cortex and may also convey motivational as well as affective influences on motor planning.

Affect, Mood, and Emotions

The hypothalamus appears to be the center of coordination of autonomic, endocrine, and behavioral aspects of affect and emotion (Kandel and Schwartz, 1985). Ablation of the hypothalamus almost totally eliminates affective responses to stimuli. Papez hypothesized some 50 years ago that connections between the cortex and hypothalamus may modulate affective responses originating from the hypothalamus and may also account for the effects of affect on cognition and other cortical functions. He proposed that a circuit including the cingulate gyrus, hippocampal formation, mamillary bodies, anterior thalamic nuclei, and their interconnecting pathways may be the anatomical substrate of affect. Later, McLean speculated that other structures are also involved in affect, including the septum, nucleus accumbens, amygdala, neocortical areas such as the orbitofrontal cortex, and some of their connecting pathways. Collectively, these structures are referred to as the limbic system. Rostral structures within the limbic system have various modulating effects on the behavioral, autonomic, and endocrine output of the hypothalamus. For instance, in some species, lesions of the amygdala produce a placid state with muted affective responses. On the other hand, lesions of the septum produce increased irritability and exaggerated rage responses to aversive stimuli. In primates, lesions of the orbitofrontal cortex, which connects with underlying limbic structures, eliminate normal levels of aggression and affective responsiveness, while electrical stimulation in this region has opposite effects.

NEUROCHEMICAL DETERMINANTS OF BEHAVIOR

"Classic" Neurotransmitters

The Discovery of Neurotransmission

Although scientific interest and curiosity about the nervous system date back to antiquity, the concept of biochemical compounds acting as the mediators of neural transmission is less than 100 years old. In the late 19th century, a number of investigators demonstrated that adrenal extracts could produce physiologic effects that were strikingly similar to those seen following stimulation of sympathetic nerves; adrenaline (epinephrine) was subsequently identified as the active compound in these extracts. In 1904, Langely demonstrated that pilocarpine could mimic the effects of parasympathetic nerve stimulation. The next year, Elliot pulled together these observations in formulating a hypothesis of chemical neurotransmission. Elliott proposed that nerve endings might release small amounts of a chemical substance, such as adrenaline, which might then act on effector sites (Elliot et al, 1977).

The initial proof of the hypothesis of neurochemical transmission focused on acetylcholine (ACH). Dixon, in 1907, reexamined the physiologic effects of muscarine and argued that parasympathetic nerves release a muscarinelike compound. Over the next decade, Dale and colleagues performed a series of studies that led them to conclude that ACH was involved in parasympathetic neurotransmission. Dale proposed that the parasympathetic nerve fibers should be described as "cholinergic," and that ACH and similar compounds should be called "parasympathomimetic". Then, in 1921, Loewi performed a series of elegant experiments on isolated frog hearts connected by perfusion media; he found that vagus nerve stimulation of innervated heart produced a compound, which he called "vagusstoff," which slowed the second, denervated heart. Vagusstoff was found to be acetylcholine (Elliot et al, 1977).

During the same year of Loewi's classic experiments, Cannon and Uridil isolated "sympathin," a compound that was released following stimulation of sympathetic nerves. Later studies showed that sympathin was released by all sympathetic nerves. In 1946, Von Euler identified norepinephrine as the "sympathin" neurotransmitter of the sympathetic nervous system (Elliot et al, 1977).

As interest in neurotransmission grew, a number of criteria were established for determining whether a particular substance is, in fact, a neurotransmitter (Table 11-1). It is quite difficult to demonstrate for a given substance that all of these criteria have been met. Thus, we often refer to "putative" neurotransmitters, because most, but not all, of these criteria have been met for a number of substances.

Below, we briefly review the physiology of some of the "classic" neurotransmitters. We have selected those that seem to be most relevant and most extensively studied in reference to normal and pathologic human behavior. How does one, however, establish a link between a neurotransmitter and behavior? This is an exceedingly complex challenge, because the study of both neurotransmission and of behavior is difficult. Nonetheless, Reis (1974) has provided useful guidelines for establishing a connection between these complex phenomena (Table 11-2).

Table 11–1 **Criteria for a Neurotransmitter**

1. Neurons contain the substance.
2. Neurons synthesize the substance.
3. Neurons release the substance upon depolarization.
4. The substance is physiologically active on neurons.
5. The postsynaptic physiologic response to the substance is identical to that of the neurotransmitter released by neurons.

(Adapted from Coyle JT: Neuroscience and psychiatry. In Talbott JA, Hales RE, Yudofsky SC (eds): Textbook of Psychiatry. Washington, DC, American Psychiatric Press, 1988)

Table 11–2 **Criteria for Linking a Neurotransmitter to a Behavior**

1. The neurotransmitter must be present in the central nervous system.
2. Precursors and enzymatic machinery for synthesis and degradation must be present in association with the transmitter.
3. A characteristic pattern of transmitter release should occur in relation to the behavior.
4. Elicitation of the characteristic transmitter release pattern should evoke the behavior.
5. Destruction of the involved neuronal system should both deplete the transmitter and abolish normal control of that behavior.
6. Increases or decreases in transmitter activity should have opposing behavioral effects.

(Reis DJ: Considerations of some specific behaviors or disease. J Psychiatr Res 11:145–148, 1974)

Representative "Classic" Neurotransmitters

Norepinephrine. Historically, the catecholamine norepinephrine (NE) has been viewed as a stress-related hormone. Hans Selye described the critical role it plays in orchestrating the physiologic response to stress. Cannon identified NE and epinephrine (EPI) as key components in the mobilization of the organism for a "fight–flight" response to stimuli that are perceived as threatening.

The metabolic pathways involved in the synthesis of NE, as well as the other catecholamines dopamine (DA) and EPI, are shown in Figure 11-1. The amino acid tyrosine is taken up into the neuronal cell body where it becomes the basic "building block" for catecholamine synthesis. The rate-limiting step involves hydroxylation by the enzyme tyrosine hydroxylase. Catabolism of the catecholamines is accomplished by several enzymes acting in an extensive pathway. Monoamine oxidase (MAO) is the enzyme that is principally involved in the intraneuronal degradation of catecholamines, where it catalyzes the oxidative deamination of NE. Catechol-O-methyltransferase (COMT) plays a similar role in the extraneuronal catabolism of NE and

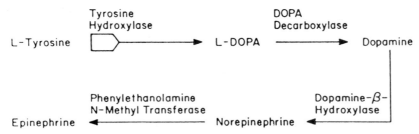

Figure 11–1. *The biosynthetic pathway for catecholamines. Tyrosine hydroxylase is activated by phosphorylation by protein kinases and the synthesis of phenylethanolamine-N-methyl transferase depends on glucocorticoids. (Reproduced with permission from Coyle JT: Neuroscience and psychiatry. In Talbott JA, Hales RE, Yudofsky SC (eds): Textbook of Psychiatry. Washington, DC, American Psychiatric Press, 1988)*

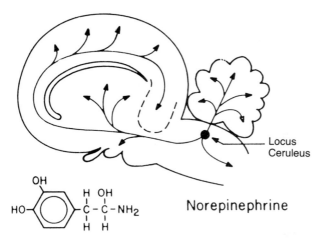

Figure 11–2. *The primary projections of the noradrenergic locus ceruleus. (Reproduced with permission from Coyle JT: Neuroscience and psychiatry. In Talbott JA, Hales RE, Yudofsky SC (eds): Textbook of Psychiatry. Washington, DC, American Psychiatric Press, 1988)*

the other catecholamines. The O-methylated products of COMT catabolism also become substrates for further degradation by MAO. MHPG (3-methoxy-4-hydroxy-phenylglycol) is a major metabolite of NE (Cooper et al, 1986).

In humans, noradrenergic neurons are organized into anatomically and functionally discrete nuclei in the upper brainstem. Two of the most important are the locus ceruleus, which projects extensively within the CNS (Fig. 11-2 and 11-3), and the nucleus of the tractus solitarius, which projects to the brainstem and the peripheral autonomic nervous system. Noradrenergic neurons are also organized into ganglia in the peripheral sympathetic nervous system.

Neurotransmission in noradrenergic systems is representative of synaptic transmission for the biogenic amines (NE, EPI, DA serotonin). When NE, which is stored in presynaptic vesicles, is released, it diffuses across the synaptic cleft and interacts with postsynaptic receptors (Fig. 11-4 and 11-5). This leads to a cascade of events, by a "second messenger" system involving activation of adenylate cyclase and cyclic AMP formation (Fig. 11-6), which ultimately produce excitation (or inhibition) of the postsynaptic neuron (Hyman, 1988).

Noradrenergic receptors are classified, and subclassified, based on their characteristic responsivity to different agonists (Table 11-3). Thus for *alpha₁-adrenergic* receptors, the pharmacologic potency (i.e., amount of drug required to produce a particular effect) of agonists can be "rank ordered" as EPI > NE > isoproterenol (ISO); for *alpha₂-receptors,* the rank order of agonist potency is NE = EPI > ISO; the

(*Text continues on page 270*)

Table 11-3 Drug and Neurotransmitter Receptors Relevant to Psychopharmacology

RECEPTOR TYPE	CHARACTERISTICS
Adrenergic	
Alpha₁	Located postsynaptically in both sympathetic nervous system and brain (where it is found on both neurons and blood vessels). Produces vasoconstriction. Agonist potency: EPI>NE>ISO.
Alpha₂	Mostly presynaptic autoreceptor (in sympathetic terminals, locus ceruleus) but also postsynaptic (e.g., in pituitary: mediates growth hormone release.) Agonist potency: NE=EPI>ISO. Clonidine is selective agonist; yohimbine is selective antagonist.
Beta₁	Localized in heart>lung; found regionally in brain. Stimulates heart. Agonist potency: ISO>EPI=NE. Practolol is selective antagonist.
Beta₂	Localized in lung>heart; found in brain, glia>neurons. Produces bronchodilation, vasodilation. Agonist potency: ISO!EPI>NE. Salbutamol, terbutaline are selective agonists. Classification still controversial.
Serotonin (5-HT)	Three subtypes:
5-HT₁	Found in gut and dorsal raphe nucleus in various species. Appears
5-HT₁ₐ	to mediate contraction in gut, neuronal inhibition in brain. Spiperone is antagonist; the anxiolytic, buspirone, is partial antagonist.
5-HT₁ᵦ	Found in cortex and sympathetic nervous system. Mediates contraction of smooth muscle and neuronal inhibition.
5-HT₁c	Found in stomach; mediates contraction.

(continued)

Table 11–3 *(continued)*

RECEPTOR TYPE	CHARACTERISTICS
5-HT$_2$	Found in brain, platelets, gut, uterus. Down-regulated by antidepressant treatment. Mediates "serotonin syndrome." Methysergide, cyproheptadine, and ketanserine are antagonists.
5-HT$_3$	At least three subtypes exist, all found peripherally. Stimulation causes neuronal depolarization (transmitter release, nociception).
Dopamine	Two types; evidence for others poor.
D$_1$	Located in parathyroid, not pituitary. Present on intrinsic neurons of corpus striatum and in retina. Physiologic role poorly understood.
D$_2$	Located in anterior pituitary (inhibits prolactin release) and on neurons receiving nigrostriatal and mesolimbic dopamine projections. Probably responsible for therapeutic effects of antipsychotics and extrapyramidal effects. Bromocriptine selective agonist. Butyrophenones (e.g., haloperidol) selective antagonists.
Muscarinic Cholinergic	Antagonized by atropinelike drugs, but also by tricyclic antidepressants, many antihistamines, and low-potency neuroleptics, resulting in side effects. Loss of muscarinic cholinergic transmission in Alzheimer's disease may be partly responsible for cognitive decline. Two types generally recognized pharmacologically, but four types predicted by cloning.
M$_1$	Located in sympathetic ganglia, frontal cortex, corpus striatum, hippocampus.
M$_2$	Located in brainstem, cerebellum, heart. Recently shown to open a K$^+$ channel by a G protein-linked mechanism causing hyperpolarization and, therefore, bradycardia.
GABA	Two types:
GABA$_A$	Mediates classic inhibitory transmission in higher brain centers. (Glycine serves this purpose in the brainstem and spinal cord.) Thus, receptors found on majority of neurons in forebrain. The receptor also contains binding sites for benzodiazepines and barbiturates. Binding of these drugs increases the affinity of the receptor for GABA. Muscimol is a selective agonist; bicuculline (proconvulsant) is an antagonist.
GABA$_B$	Works through G proteins, not Cl$^-$ channel (nonclassic effect). Baclofen is selective agonist.
Opiate	At least three types; naloxone is an antagonist at all types with affinity: $m{\rightarrow}d{\rightarrow}k$.
mu (*m*)	Localized in periaqueductal gray, thalamus, substantia gelatinosa of spinal cord, and other regions. Mediates analgesia and indifference to pain, miosis, and respiratory depression. Morphine and related opiate alkaloids are exogenous agonists; beta-endorphin and the enkephalins are endogenous agonists.
delta (*d*)	Highest density in limbic system. Mediates analgesia, hypotension, and miosis. Enkephalins are endogenous agonists. No selective agonists in clinical use because only peptide agonists known.
kappa (*k*)	Located in deep cortical layers. Mediates sedating analgesia, miosis. Benzomorphan drugs (e.g., ketamine, pentazocine) selective agonists. Dynorphins are the endogenous agonists.

Note: Where possible, clinically relevant agonists and antagonists are listed. The most selective agonists and antagonists are often not clinically important.
Abbreviations: Epi = epinephrine, NE = norepinephrine, ISO = isoproterenol.
(Hyman SE: Recent developments in neurobiology. Psychosomatics 29:157, 1988)

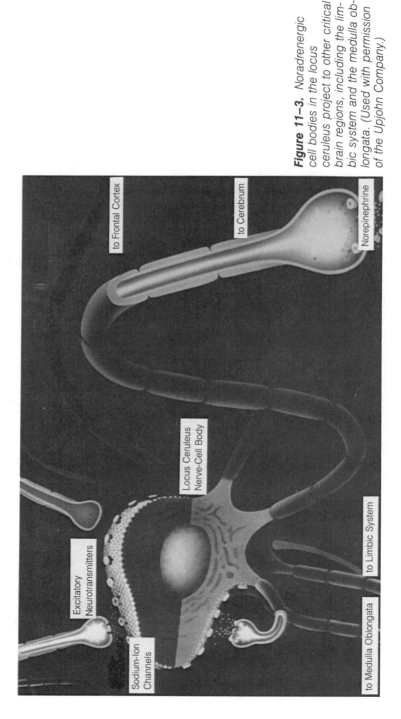

Figure 11–3. *Noradrenergic cell bodies in the locus ceruleus project to other critical brain regions, including the limbic system and the medulla oblongata. (Used with permission of the Upjohn Company.)*

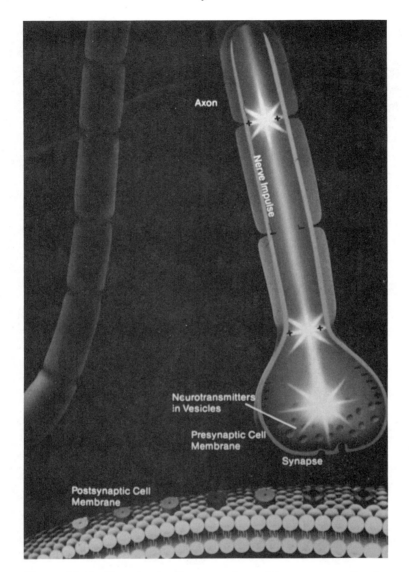

Figure 11—4. *Neurotransmitters are released from presynaptic storage vesicles and diffuse across the synaptic cleft, where they interact with the postsynaptic cell membrane. (Used with permission of the Upjohn Company.)*

rank order of agonist potencies for *beta$_1$-* and *beta$_2$-adrenergic* receptors is ISO > EPI = NE and ISO > EPI > NE, respectively.

Alpha$_1$ receptors are found postsynaptically in both the sympathetic nervous system and the brain. Alpha$_2$ receptors are often located presynaptically, in the locus ceruleus and in sympathetic terminals, where they are thought to function as autoreceptors that modulate output by serving as homeostatic regulators; they are also found postsynaptically in certain sites, such as the pituitary gland, where they play a

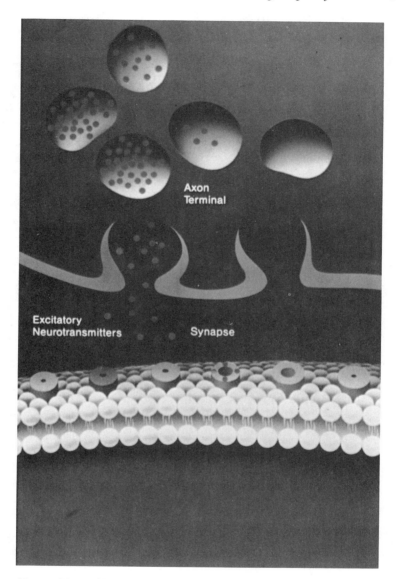

Figure 11–5. *Neurotransmitters, when released from storage vesicles in the presynaptic axon terminal, bind to those postsynaptic receptors that offer the best "fit." (Used with permission of the Upjohn Company.)*

role in regulating growth hormone release. Beta$_1$ receptors are found regionally in the brain, and beta$_2$ receptors are located on glial and neural tissues in the brain.

Electrophysiologists have advanced the concept that NE serves as an "orchestrator" or modulator of other signals in the CNS. In the cerebellum, for example, NE released following locus ceruleus stimulation decreases the spontaneous firing of Purkinje cells, thereby increasing the relative signal generated by exogenous stimuli. Thus, NE increases the "signal-to-noise" ratio in that area of the brain, thereby

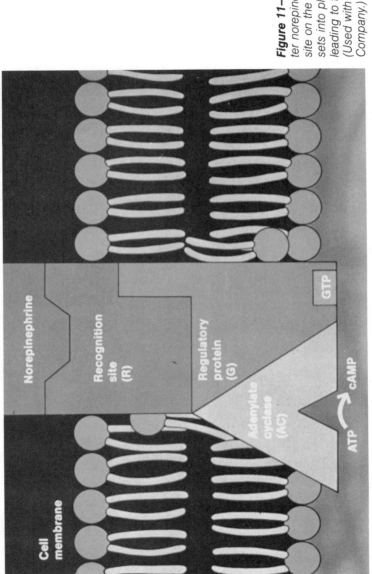

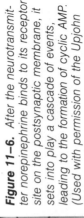

Figure 11–6. *After the neurotransmitter norepinephrine binds to its receptor site on the postsynaptic membrane, it sets into play a cascade of events, leading to the formation of cyclic AMP. (Used with permission of the Upjohn Company.)*

increasing reactivity to stimuli. In a similar way, projections from the locus ceruleus to other areas in the brain, such as the hypothalamus and cortex, may enhance responsiveness to exogenous stimuli (Golden and Potter, 1986).

Historically, NE has played a pivotal role in the development of biologic theories relating to the pathogenesis of mood disorders such as depression. Two decades ago, the original formulations of the "catecholamine hypothesis of depression" identified decreased functional activity of central NE systems as an etiologic mechanism in the development of depressive illness (Bunney and Davis, 1965; Schildkraut, 1965). More recently, with our growing appreciation for the complex dynamic regulatory mechanisms of neurotransmitter control, researchers have emphasized relatively subtle forms of NE systems dysregulation rather than absolute deficiencies (Golden and Potter, 1986).

More recently, the role of the locus ceruleus and the norepinephrine system has received attention as being involved in the pathogenesis of panic disorder, a severe anxiety disorder often accompanied by agoraphobia. Although the exact mechanisms are not clear, it is believed that some sort of disruption or dysregulation in the locus ceruleus/norepinephrine system results in a flooding of the CNS with anxiety and a plethora of secondary physiologic and psychologic symptoms.

Serotonin. Serotonin, or 5-hydroxytryptamine (5-HT), plays a critical role in the regulation of such diverse functions as sleep, temperature homeostasis, pain sensitivity, appetite, neuroendocrine secretions, and mood regulation. Many of these functions are felt to be regulated, in part, by 5-HT input to the hypothalamus. Cell bodies of 5-HT containing neurons are localized in a series of nuclei in the upper pons and lower midbrain, called the raphe nuclei. Axons ascending from the raphe project to almost all brain regions (Fig. 11-7).

Serotonin within these cell bodies is formed from the amino acid tryptophan, which is an "essential" amino acid in that dietary intake regulates its availability. Tryptophan is taken up into 5-HT neurons by active transport across the blood–brain barrier. The enzyme tryptophan hydroxylase catalyzes the rate-limiting step of hydroxylating tryptophan into 5-hydroxytryptophan, which is then decarboxylated to form 5-HT.

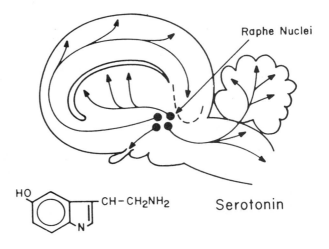

Figure 11–7. *The pathways of the raphe serotonergic neurons. (Reproduced with permission from Coyle JT: Neuroscience and psychiatry. In Talbott JA, Hales RE, Yudofsky SC (eds): Textbook of Psychiatry. Washington, DC, American Psychiatric Press, 1988)*

As with NE (see above), 5-HT is inactivated by reuptake into the presynaptic nerve terminal following its release and interaction with postsynaptic receptors. There it is oxidized by MAO to form 5-hydroxy-indoleacetic acid (5-HIAA), which is released into the cerebrospinal fluid (CSF) and eventually excreted in urine.

5-HT receptors are also classified based on agonist affinity; the classification is currently an area of extensive investigation and is somewhat controversial (see Table 11-3). 5-HT$_{1A}$ receptors are found in the gut and in the dorsal raphe nucleus in some species. These receptors appear to mediate contraction in the gut and neuronal inhibition in the brain. The anxiolytic medication buspirone is a partial 5-HT$_{1A}$ agonist. 5-HT$_{1B}$ receptors are found in cortex and in the sympathetic nervous system; they mediate smooth muscle contraction and neuronal inhibition. 5-HT$_{1C}$ receptors mediate contraction in the stomach. 5-HT$_2$ receptors are localized in the brain, platelets, gut, and uterus. Several antidepressant medications have been found to down-regulate (i.e., decrease the density and responsivity of) these receptors. 5-HT$_3$ receptors have recently been described and appear to be located peripherally (Hyman, 1988).

At about the same time that American researchers were developing the catecholamine hypothesis of depression (see above), British scientists began to emphasize the role that 5-HT might play in depressive illness (Coppen et al, 1965). Prange and associates (1974) synthesized these two bodies of data in formulating the "permissive hypothesis" of affective illness: a decrease in the functional activity of central 5-HT systems could permit the development of depressive illness when coupled with a deficiency in central NE, while the coexistence of decreased 5-HT and increased NE could lead to the emergence of mania. Recently, a number of investigators, using various pharmacologic "challenge tests" have identified 5-HT dysregulation in depressed patients as measured by altered neurohormonal response to 5-HT agonists. 5-HT has also been implicated in the pathogenesis of many other major psychiatric syndromes, including schizophrenia, personality disorders, obsessive–compulsive disorder, anxiety disorders, alcoholism, and chronic pain syndromes (Coccaro and Murphy, in press).

Dopamine. Dopamine (DA), like NE, is a catecholamine neurotransmitter synthesized from the amino acid tyrosine (see Fig. 11-1) and metabolized by MAO and COMT. There appear to be two major classes of DA receptors: D$_1$ receptors are linked to an adenylate cyclase "second messenger" system, and D$_2$ receptors appear to be independent of adenylate cyclase activity and are involved in the neuroendocrine control of growth hormone and prolactin release, drug-induced parkinsonism, and the antipsychotic activity of neuroleptic medications (see Table 11-3).

There are three major DA systems in the brain: the meso-cortico-limbic midbrain-forebrain system, the nigrostriatal system, and the tuberoinfundibular system (Fig. 11-8). The meso-cortico-limbic system is felt to play an important role in regulating mood and behavior. The nigrostriatal system is involved in the control of fine movement, and disruption of DA neurotransmission in this area by neuroleptic medication can lead to the emergence of "extrapyramidal" side effects (i.e., acute dystonia, parkinsonian symptoms, and akathisia). The tuberoinfundibular system primarily contains D$_2$ receptors; dopamine released into the hypothalmic–pituitary portal venous system regulates prolactin and growth hormone secretion (Hyman, 1988).

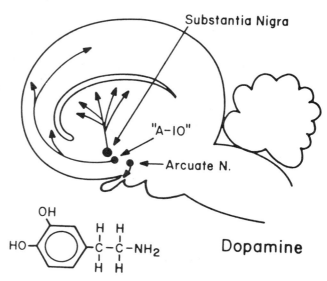

Figure 11–8. *The three major dopaminergic pathways. These include the nigrostriatal, the mesocorticolimbic (A-10), and the tuberoinfundibular pathway from the arcuate nucleus to the infundibulum. (Reproduced with permission from Coyle JT: Neuroscience and psychiatry. In Talbott JA, Hales RE, Yudofsky SC (eds): Textbook of Psychiatry. Washington, DC, American Psychiatric Press, 1988)*

Most research exploring the relationship between DA and human psychopathology has focused on psychoses. The "dopamine hypothesis" of schizophrenia was derived, in part, from two observations: (1) clinically effective antipsychotic medications (e.g., phenothiazines, butyrophenones, reserpine, and so forth) share a common property of diminishing central DA neurotransmission; (2) amphetamine and other psychostimulants that enhance central dopaminergic activity have been associated with the emergence of psychotic syndromes that in some ways resemble schizophrenia. In addition, hypotheses have been developed that link alterations in central dopaminergic systems with mania and depression (Janowsky et al, 1988).

Acetylcholine. Although acetylcholine (ACH) was the first neurotransmitter to be discovered, until recently limitations in technology have slowed the pace of investigations of its role in CNS function (Janowsky et al, 1988). ACH is synthesized by choline acetyltransferase, using acetyl-coenzyme A and choline as substrates. Brain ACH formation is relatively dependent on bloodborne choline derived from dietary intake, because choline cannot be synthesized in the brain in adequate amounts.

In the brain, there are nicotinic and muscarinic, pre- and postsynaptic receptors, as well as other cholinergic receptors that do not appear to belong to either of these classic types. Muscarinic receptors (see Table 11-3) are more plentiful in the brain than nicotinic receptors and play a more vital role in behavioral regulation. Unlike the catecholamine neurotransmitters, ACH inactivation following synaptic release does not depend on reuptake, but instead takes place by hydrolysis by either neuronal acetylcholinesterase or nonneuronal (glial) pseudocholinesterases.

The limbic system and the cerebral cortex, two brain systems that are felt to play major roles in the regulation of emotion in humans, receive considerable cholinergic innervation (Fig. 11-9). Thus, there is a theoretical basis for anticipating that ACH may play a role in the regulation of mood and in the pathogenesis of mood disorders. In 1972, Janowsky et al. proposed a cholinergic–adrenergic balance hypothesis of affec-

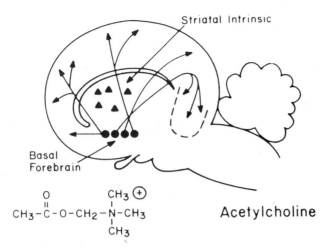

Figure 11-9. *The forebrain cholinergic neurons. Cholinergic neurons in the basal forebrain (including the nucleus basalis of Meynert, the diagonal band of Broca, and the medial septal nucleus) innervate the cerebral cortex, hippocampus, and limbic structures. The striatum contains local circuit cholinergic interneurons. (Reproduced with permission from Coyle JT: Neuroscience and psychiatry. In Talbott JA, Hales RE, Yudofsky SC (eds): Textbook of Psychiatry. Washington, DC, American Psychiatric Press, 1988)*

tive illness, which postulated that affect (mood) may represent a balance between cholinergic and adrenergic neurotransmitter activity in the areas of the brain that regulate mood. Depressive illness could represent a disease state of relative cholinergic predominance, while mania could result from relative adrenergic predominance. Numerous animal studies, clinical observations, and human studies lend support to this theory, although contradictory data also exist (Janowsky et al, 1988).

Cholinergic projections to the cortex and hippocampus also play a critical role in cognition and its disorders (see section entitled "Learning and Memory").

Gamma-aminobutyric acid. Gamma-aminobutyric acid (GABA) is synthesized from the amino acid glutamic acid through a decarboxylation reaction. Approximately 99% of all GABA in human is found within the CNS, where it functions as an inhibitory neurotransmitter (Fig. 11-10).

There are at least two types of GABA receptors, $GABA_A$ and $GABA_B$ (see Table 11-3). The former is linked to the benzodiazepine receptor and chloride ion channel and thus has been linked to the development of and treatment of anxiety disorders. The benzodiazepine receptor is believed to act synergistically with the GABA receptor to increase the affinity for the neurotransmitter. In addition to its association with anxiety disorders, GABA has been implicated in the pathogenesis of affective illness, such as depression, although the data related to GABAergic theories of affective disease are quite preliminary (Janowsky et al, 1988).

Neuropeptides

Neuropeptides are small proteins containing two to several dozen amino acids. They are, therefore, much larger than the "classic" small molecule neurotransmitters described above. The diversity of structure of neuropeptides is great. At least 50 are known and certainly many more will be found (Table 11-4). They occur in the CNS at

Figure 11–10. Major GABA-ergic pathways. The inhibitory neurotransmitter GABA (gamma-aminobutyric acid) is synthesized by local circuit stellate cells within the cerebral cortex, by the cerebellar Purkinje cells, and by striatonigral neurons. (Reproduced with permission from Coyle JT: Neuroscience and psychiatry. In Talbott JA, Hales RE, Yudofsky SC (eds): Textbook of Psychiatry. Washington, DC, American Psychiatric Press, 1988)

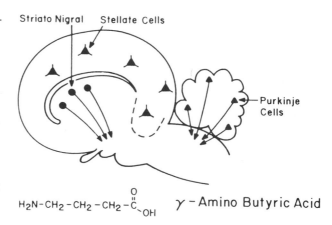

Table 11–4 **Some Putative Neuropeptide Neurotransmitters**

ACTH	Interleukin-1
Angiotensin II	Leu-enkephalin
Atriopeptin	Luteinizing-hormone-releasing factor
Beta-endorphin	Met-enkephalin
Bombesin	N-acetyl aspartyl glutamate (NAAG)
Bradykinin	Neurotensin
Calcitonin gene-related peptide (CGRP)	Neuropeptide Y
Carnosine	Oxytocin
Cholecystokinin	Pancreostatin
Corticotropin-releasing factor (CRF)	Somatostatin
Dynorphin	Substance P
Galinin	Thyrotropin-releasing hormone (TRH)
Gastrin	Vasoactive intestinal peptide (VIP)
Glucagon	Vasopressin
Insulin	

concentrations far lower than classic small molecule neurotransmitters. Neuropeptides have a broad range of physiologic and behavioral effects, which are exerted at concentrations three or more orders of magnitude lower than small molecule neurotransmitters. Neuropeptides also tend to have durations of effect considerably longer than classic neurotransmitters. These effects often persist well after proteolytic degradation of the neuropeptide.

Synthesis of neuropeptides is similar to that of other proteins (i.e., it involves translation of messenger RNA sequences on ribosomes; Coyle, 1988). This process occurs exclusively within the cell bodies and possibly dendrites of neurons. Translation usually produces a relatively large preproprotein or precursor of the neuropeptide. Initial proteolytic cleavage of the precursor protein occurs in the endoplasmic reticulum and the Golgi apparatus. The final stages of posttranslational processing occur after the precursor and proteolytic enzymes are packaged into neurosecretory granules, which are then transported to neuron terminals for storage or release. Processing may include further proteolytic cleavage to produce shorter peptides as well as C-terminal amidation, N-terminal acetylation, cyclization of glutamate to form pyroglutamate, disulphide bond formation, glycosylation, phosphorylation, or sulfation. Precursor molecules in some neuropeptide-synthesizing neurons contain several amino acid sequences of the same neuropeptide. This allows the neurons to produce multiple copies of a particular neuropeptide and thereby multiply the signal produced by translation of the precursor molecule. Precursor molecules in neuropeptide-synthesizing neurons may also contain amino acid sequences of several different neuropeptides. Changes in the cleavage pattern in the precursor can produce different clusters of neuropeptides, each of which may have quite different effects.

Release of neuropeptides from presynaptic sites depends on Ca^{++} influx. Neuropeptides act at specific postsynaptic receptors either by stimulating changes in membrane conductance or by releasing second messengers. Thus, mechanisms of release and receptor activation within synapses are very similar in neuropeptides and small molecule neurotransmitters. Inactivation of neuropeptides appears to depend entirely on extracellular proteolysis. Unlike many small molecule neurotransmitters, presynaptic reuptake and recycling of neuropeptide molecules does not occur. Extracellular proteolysis may produce fragments that have physiologic effects similar or quite different from the parent neuropeptide.

There has been much speculation about whether neuropeptides are true neurotransmitters or play a less specific neuromodulatory role. While no neuropeptide to date has been demonstrated to meet all of the exacting criteria required for neurotransmitter status (see Table 11-1), very likely many neuropeptides function as neurotransmitters. Neuromodulators are substances that are also released presynaptically but which act both locally and at more distant postsynaptic sites to diminish or amplify the effects of neurotransmitters. Neuromodulators may also influence the rate of release of neurotransmitters from presynaptic sites. Many neuropeptides have been localized within neurons containing small molecule neurotransmitters or other neuropeptides (Cooper et al, 1986). These observations suggest that neuropeptides may be coreleased with and serve as neuromodulators of small molecule or neuropeptide neurotransmitters. Neuropeptides very likely exert their effects well beyond the synapses into which they are released. Neuropeptide receptors are often located some distance from the terminal fields of neurons synthesizing those neuropeptides.

Endogenous opioids have received more investigative attention than any other family of neuropeptides. Approximately 18 separate opioid molecules have been described so far, among which beta-endorphin, leu-enkephalin, met-enkephalin, and dynorphin are of primary interest. All opioids arise from three major precursor molecules, pro-opiomelanocortin, pre-proenkephalin, and pre-prodynorphin, each of which is synthesized in a different population of neurons. The proteolytic cleavage products of pro-opiomelanocortin are summarized in Figure 11-11. Processing of opioid precursors varies with brain region. Enkephalin and dynorphin-containing neurons form discrete pathways in many regions of the CNS. Enkephalins are found in high concentration in the basal ganglia and are often colocalized in neurons with monoamines or other neuropeptides such as substance P. Beta-endorphin is synthesized primarily in neuron cell bodies in the arcuate nucleus from which project long ascending and descending pathways. A number of separate opiate receptor types

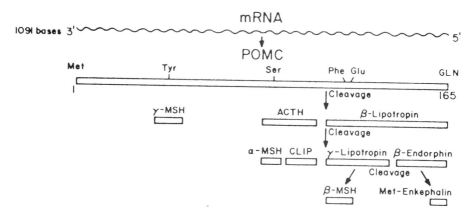

Figure 11–11. *Processing of proopiomelanocortin (POMC). The precursor protein, POMC, which contains 165 amino acids, is enzymatically cleaved to yield the physiologically active peptides indicated. Depending on the cellular localization (anterior pituitary, hypothalamus, midbrain nerve terminals), certain of these neuropeptides are expressed and others are not. (Reproduced with permission from Coyle JT: Neuroscience and psychiatry. In Talbott JA, Hales RE, Yudofsky SC (eds): Textbook of Psychiatry. Washington, DC, American Psychiatric Press, 1988)*

have been described (see Table 11-3), and several classification schemes have been suggested. Individual opioid molecules have different affinities for each of these receptor types.

Many other families of neuropeptides are found within the CNS. Neuronal processes containing the posterior pituitary hormones, vasopressin and oxytocin, project from the paraventricular nucleus of the hypothalamus to many sites in the limbic system, brainstem, and spinal cord. In addition, nests of vasopressinergic neurons are located at a number of sites outside the hypothalamus. Many hypothalamic neuropeptides that regulate release of anterior pituitary hormones are also synthesized and released in other regions of the brain. Among these are corticotropin-releasing factor, thyrotropin-releasing hormone, luteinizing hormone-releasing hormone, and somatostatin. Some peptides that were first localized in the gastrointestinal tract, such as cholecystokinin and vasoactive intestinal peptide, have also been identified in the brain. Neurotensin, first isolated from brain tissue, was subsequently found to be widely distributed in the gut. Summaries of physiologic effects and brain localization of these and other neuropeptides can be found in Nemeroff and Dunn (1984).

Steroid Hormones

Although steroid hormones have profound effects on behavior and other brain functions, they are all synthesized in peripheral tissues. Gonadal steroids are synthesized primarily in the ovaries (estrogens and progestins) or the testes (androgens), although the adrenal cortex synthesizes significant amounts of sex steroids. The adrenal cortex is the primary site of glucocorticoid and mineralcorticoid synthesis. After secretion into the blood, steroid molecules are either tightly bound to specific steroid-binding globulins or less tightly bound to albumin. Steroids bound to albumin, much more so than steroids bound to specific binding globulins, readily dissociate, diffuse across the blood–brain barrier, and gain access to all regions of the CNS. Steroids also diffuse readily into the neuronal cytoplasm where they may undergo a variety of metabolic transformations (see below).

Mechanisms of Effect

Mechanisms of possible steroid effects on neurons are summarized in Figure 11-12. Steroids appear to have their most profound and prolonged effects by altering genomic regulation of protein synthesis (Luttge, 1983). After diffusion into neuronal cytoplasm, steroids form noncovalent high-affinity attachments to macromolecules called cytoplasmic steroid receptors. Binding of cytoplasmic steroid receptors is quite

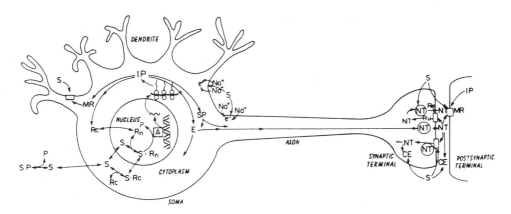

Figure 11–12. *Diagrammatic representation of various possible molecular and electrophysiologic actions of steroid hormones in mammalian brain neurons. In the extracellular space, cerebrospinal fluid, and blood, the steroid may exist in either the free (S) or carrier-protein bound (S·P) state. The free steroid enters the neuron either by diffusion or carrier-mediated transport, after which it may be metabolized or bind to a cytosolic receptor macromolecule (Rc) and diffuse as a steroid–receptor complex (S·Rc) to the nucleoplasm, or it may directly enter the nucleoplasm and then bind to the nuclear receptor (Rn). The intranuclear steroid–receptor complex (S·Rn) may then undergo a poorly understood "activation" process that facilitates its interaction with acceptor proteins (A) and DNA. This S·Rn·A interaction in the chromatin may, in turn, precipitate the production of specific mRNAs that code for the production of specific "induced proteins" (IP) and enzymes (E). Examples of IPs include structural proteins (SP) (e.g., tubulin), membrane receptor proteins (MR) (e.g., MRs for biogenic amines, acetylcholine, GABA, neuropeptides), cytoplasmic receptor proteins for steroids (Rc) (e.g., E_2 and P_4 receptors), and various anabolic and catabolic enzymes (CE) (e.g., ChAcT). Release (Re) and reuptake (Ru) of neurotransmitters (NT) may also be modulated by the direct actions of steroids. Last, steroids may interact directly with the neuronal soma or axonal plasma membrane to modulate the transmembrane diffusion or distribution of ions (e.g., Na^+) and thereby produce an electrophysiologic response (e^-) or alter the conduction velocity of a response. (Reproduced with permission from Luttge WG: Molecular mechanisms of steroid hormone actions in the brain. In Svare BB (ed): Hormones and Aggressive Behavior. New York, Plenum Press, 1983)*

specific in individual neurons, allowing genomic regulation of a target cell only by a particular type of steroid molecule even though other types of steroid molecules may enter that cell. Hormone–receptor complexes diffuse through pores in the nuclear membrane into the nucleoplasm where the complex interacts with nuclear "acceptors" and DNA, resulting in changes in synthesis of messenger RNA sequences coding for specific proteins. The steroid–receptor complex may then be processed so that the receptor is either recycled to the cytoplasm for reutilization or is catabolized and destroyed.

While genomic mechanisms of action have been most thoroughly studied, steroids may influence neurons in other ways. Steroids have short latency effects on postsynaptic electrical activity resulting from presynaptic neurotransmitter release. While steroids do not appear to have membrane-bound receptors like those of small molecule or peptide neurotransmitters, their affinity for the lipid-rich membrane environment may allow steroids to affect directly the physicochemical properties of neuronal cell membranes.

Location of Steroid Binding in the Brain

Neuronal cell bodies that bind specific steroids are located in discrete regions of the brain (Luine and McEwen, 1985; Luttge, 1983). Estrogen and androgen binding is located in the anterior and medial portions of the hypothalamus, the preoptic and septal areas, the amygdala, as well as midbrain sites such as the mesencephalic central gray. Implantation of gonadal steroids into these sites, but not into other brain sites, elicits hormonal and behavioral effects that are dependent on these steroids. Brain areas that bind gonadal steroids have been implicated in the regulation of reproductive behaviors (see section entitled "Reproductive Behaviors: Sex and Mothering"), other sexually differentiated behaviors, and gonadotropin release.

Progesterone-binding is localized in the same areas as estrogen binding with the exception of the amygdala. Synthesis of progesterone receptors requires estrogen stimulation. Progesterone receptor concentration peaks between 24 and 48 hours after estrogen treatment. If progesterone levels rise simultaneously with estrogen levels, progesterone receptor proliferation does not occur.

The pattern of glucocorticoid binding within the brain is markedly different from the pattern of gonadal steroid binding. Glucocorticoid binding is most prominent in the hippocampus (in the pyramidal cells in the CA_1 and CA_2 fields of the horn of Ammon and the granule neurons of the dentate gyrus) and, to a lesser degree, in the septal area, the amygdala, and some areas of the cerebral cortex. Behavioral effects of glucocorticoids are exerted in these limbic brain areas.

Estrogen, androgen, and glucocorticoid-concentrating cells have also been found in the lower brainstem and in the spinal cord. Androgen or glucocorticoid-labeled cells predominate in some somatomotor cranial nerves and spinal cord regions, while estrogen-labeled cells predominate in some sensory cranial nerves and spinal cord regions.

Metabolism of Steroid Hormones

In the brain, regional differences in metabolism influence local availability of specific steroid molecules (Luttge, 1983). Estradiol (E_2) is the major estrogen secreted by the ovary as well as the most potent estrogen in neural and nonneural tissues. However, other estrogen species, estrone (E_1), estriol (E_3), as well as catechol estrogens (2-OH-E_2, 2-OH-E_1, 4-OH-E_2, 4-OH-E_1), are synthesized in peripheral and brain tissues. Many brain regions are capable of interconverting E_1, E_2, and E_3. The relative amount of each estrogen species resulting from interconversion differs with brain region. For instance, E_1 is relatively increased by metabolism of estrogen molecules in the posterior hypothalamus, while E_2 is the primary metabolic product in the anterior hypothalamus and the preoptic area. Estrogen metabolism in the hypothalamus, preoptic area, septum, and amgydala produces relatively more E_2, less E_3, and about the same amount of E_1 as does estrogen metabolism in the hippocampus and cortical regions. Catechol estrogens, which are synthesized primarily from E_2, are found in greater abundance in the hypothalmus than in cerebral cortex and increase markedly during proestrus in rats. Catechol estrogens, especially 4-OH-E_2, compete with E_2 for high-affinity binding to cytoplasmic estrogen receptors in brain tissue and are as potent as E_2 in inducing female sexual behavior and LH secretion. Catechol estrogens also have high affinity for some enzymes involved in small molecule neurotransmitter synthesis and catabolism (e.g., tyrosine hydroxylase, catecholamine-O-methyl-transferase, and others).

Progesterone (P_4) is the major progestin synthesized in peripheral tissues of mammals. However, other progestins, such as 20 alpha-OH-P_4, are also synthesized and penetrate the blood–brain barrier. The principal metabolic conversion of progestins in the brain is 5 alpha-reduction which is irreversible. P_4 is converted by 5 alpha-reductase to 5 alpha-DHP. Both P_4 and 20 alpha-OH-P_4 are preferred substrates over testosterone for 5 alpha-reductase, suggesting that progestins may inhibit 5 alpha-reduction of testosterone to DHT, a conversion that is important for some behavioral effects of testosterone.

Testosterone (T) is the primary androgen in mammals, although a number of other androgen molecules are also found in the circulation. Interconversion of T and androstenedione (AE) by 17 beta-oxidoreductase occurs in many brain regions. The 5 alpha-reduction of T to DHT, which is irreversible, occurs primarily in the hypothalmus. Some androgens are converted to estrogen by the enzyme aromatase (e.g., T or AE conversion to E_2 or E_1), while other androgens cannot be aromatized (e.g., DHT). Aromatase activity in the male rat brain is highest in the medial preoptic area, periventricular nucleus of the preoptic area, and the medial amygdala, while lower levels are found in the lateral preoptic area, mediobasal hypothalamus, and the lateral hypothalamus. Nonlimbic brain areas contain little if any aromatase activity.

Corticosterone is the primary circulating glucocorticoid in some mammals (e.g., rats), while cortisol predominates in other mammalian species (e.g., lower primates and humans). Other glucocorticoids, such as cortisone, are also found in blood. Reversible and irreversible metabolic conversion of glucocorticoids may occur in the brain. Interconversion of cortisol and cortisone and cortisol conversion to corticosterone have been reported. However, little, if any, conversion of corticosterone has been demonstrated. This may explain why, in some primates where the major circulating glucocorticoid is cortisol, corticosterone appears to be concentrated preferentially by nuclear receptors in a number of brain areas.

Regulatory Effects of Steroids

Steroid hormones affect synthesis, release, turnover, reuptake, catabolism, and receptor concentration of small molecule neurotransmitters. These effects differ with type of steroid and vary with brain region. While less studied, evidence to date suggests that synthesis, release, and receptor concentrations of several neuropeptides are also regulated by steroids. Steroids exert most of these effects by altering expression of genes coding for specific proteins. However, some neurons that respond to steroids with changes in neurotransmitter synthesis, release, or receptor concentration do not contain steroid receptors. Mechanisms that can account for steroid effects on neurons that do not bind steroids have yet to be delineated.

Thyroid Hormone

The thyroid gland and its hormones constitute but one part of a larger regulatory system, the hypothalamic–pituitary–thyroid (HPT) axis. Key hormonal components of this system include the thyroid hormones thyroxine (T_4) and triiodothyronine (T_3), thyroid-stimulating hormone (TSH), and thyrotropin-releasing hormone (TRH). The thyroid hormones T_4 and T_3 are iodinated bi-mers of the amino acid, tyrosine. TSH, a glycoprotein synthesized in the pituitary gland, regulates the production of T_3 and T_4. TSH, in turn, is regulated by TRH, a tripeptide (pro-his-pro), which is synthesized by neurons in the hypothalamus, released in the median eminence, and delivered to the pituitary by the hypophyseal portal venous system. The activity of this system is also partially regulated by other extrathyroidal factors, such as thyroid-binding globulin, which serves as the main serum reservoir for thyroid hormone, and peripheral enzymes that convert T_4 either to T_3 or to its metabolically inactive form, reverse T_3.

Some hormonal components of the thyroidal system are found in virtually all animal species suggesting that it developed early in evolution and serves fairly basic biologic ends. By interacting with membrane as well as nuclear receptors, thyroid hormone affects a variety of cellular functions including energy utilization, enzymatic rates, and cell growth and division. While evolution appears to have adapted the HPT axis for multiple functions, its main job may be to modulate and coordinate overall metabolic activity. The ability to adjust cellular energy utilization to different circumstances such as growth, procreation, and seasonal change would provide obvious adaptational advantage.

Since the turn of the century it has been know that deficiency or excess of thyroid hormone is associated with psychopathology. Severely hypothyroid adults are often depressed, demented, or psychotic. Hyperthyroid persons are typically anxious or appear to have agitated depressions. The components of the HPT axis are probably partially involved in a variety of behavior responses. Based on available data, we can identify three key areas in which HPT axis activity influences behavioral adaptation: regulation of nervous system development, augmentation of catecholaminergic stress response, and modulation of biologic rhythms.

Nervous System Development

Thyroid hormone has a nerve growth factor-like effect on neurons in the CNS. Dendritic and axonal growth is enhanced by thyroid hormone and is impaired in thyroid deficiency states. There appears to be a developmental window, occurring perinatally in most species, during which thyroid hormone availability is absolutely essential for brain maturation (Sokoloff, 1967). In humans, deprivation of thyroid hormone prenatally or in early infancy leads to the severe and irreversible form of retardation known as cretinism. The HPT axis probably also facilitates neuronal maintenance and repair in the mature organism. Administration of TRH appears to stimulate cell growth and enhance recovery of function following brain and spinal cord trauma. Although the adult CNS is more tolerant of thyroid deficiency than that of the infant, prolonged thyroid deficiency states may cause irreversible cognitive decline in adult humans.

Stress Responses

Thyroid hormone augments the firing of beta-adrenergic neurons. This is mediated by a facilitating interaction at postsynaptic beta-adrenergic receptors (Whybrow and Prange, 1981). Thus, the HPT axis may help mediate the increase in catecholaminergic neurotransmission that is an essential component of the general stress response (see section entitled "Stress and Behavior") perhaps by way of a centrally induced neurohormone cascade involving TRH, TSH, and thyroid hormone. The HPT axis, in turn, can be directly tuned up or down by the sympathetic nervous system, which innervates the HPT axis at several levels. The ability of the HPT axis to enhance beta-adrenergic neurotransmission may be an important factor in recovery from the mood disorder depression, which appears to be associated with deficient or inefficient catecholaminergic neurotransmission. A slight increase in the tone of the thyroid axis may be able to compensate, at least partially, for such a deficiency (Whybrow and Prange, 1981). This concept is strongly supported by the observation that T_3 administration augments response to antidepressant medication. Conversely, one of the earliest and most consistent neuroendocrine findings is that 20% to 30% of depressed patients exhibit a diminished TSH response to exogenously administered TRH. Prange has postulated these findings to be the consequence of prolonged reliance in depressed persons on the ability of the HPT axis to compensate for deficient catecholaminergic neurotransmission; tachyphylaxis develops at the pituitary level to chronic TRH overdrive.

Modulation of Biologic Rhythms

As with other hormonal systems, HPT axis activity fluctuates diurnally and possibly seasonally. However, there is also evidence that HPT axis activity itself regulates the length of biologic rhythms (Schull et al, 1988). TRH mediates the change from hibernation to the active state in some species. In mice, the thyroid changes the length of motor activity cycles. The extent to which the HPT axis affects normal biologic rhythms in humans is unknown. However, there is evidence for HPT axis abnormalities in bipolar affective disorder, a disease state in which mood and activity cycle at an abnormal rate and to an excessive degree. In particular, an association has been observed between hypothyroidism and rapid cycling bipolar disorder. Administration of thyroid hormone will stabilize cycling in a portion of these patients.

It can be seen from the above overview that there has been a dramatic and rapid expansion in our understanding of the neurobiology of behavior and an emerging body of data in elucidating the biochemical basis for not only normal behavior but several of the major mental disorders as well. In the next section, the neurochemical basis of certain specific behaviors such as learning, memory, reproductive activity, feeding, and aggression will be discussed.

THE NEUROBIOLOGY
OF SPECIFIC BEHAVIORS

Learning and Memory

An impressive array of cognitive abilities enables humans to analyze situations, review past experiences, consider options, anticipate developments, and rehearse future actions. Therefore, human behavior depends on and is the result of a great deal of cognitive activity within the brain before overt, observable behavior occurs. Despite the critical nature of cognitive function in the shaping of human behavior, exploration of the biologic basis of most cognitive functions is in its infancy. Many cognitive abilities do not appear to be localized. In brain-damaged persons, impairment of cognitive functions such as attention, concentration, calculation, inductive and deductive logic has been related to the total amount of cortical damage but has not been associated with damage in specific areas. Some brain regions, however, have been implicated in particular cognitive tasks. The frontal lobes, for instance, play a key role in abstract thinking and planning. The neurobiologic basis of most cognitive functions is unknown. However, progress has been achieved in our understanding of the mechanism of learning and memory.

The Components and Dimensions
of Learning and Memory

Learning is the capacity to change behavior in response to experience. Memory is the retained record of experience and is composed of a short-term and a long-term phase. Short-term memory, lasting seconds to minutes, is probably based on a sustained pattern of activity of the primary sensory neural substrate stimulated by the new experience. Distraction by other stimuli, which disrupts the pattern of activity of the primary sensory neural substrate, results in loss of the new information stored in short-term memory. Acquisition of long-term memory requires persistent physical change either in the primary sensory neural substrate activated by the new information or physical change in cerebral cortex where information is stored after processing in the hippocampus (see below). Changes in neural structures underlying acquisition of long-term memory depend on protein synthesis. After initial acquisition, long-term memories require a period of *consolidation* before they can no longer be abolished by pharmacologic or electroconvulsive means. Consolidation of long-term memory requires a few hours to a few days in animals. Electroconvulsive therapy in psychiatric patients produces loss of some memories acquired as much as 3 years prior to treatment (Squire, 1987). This observation suggests that complete consolidation of memory in humans can require long periods of time. *Retrieval* of memories from long-term storage operates by mechanisms that differ from those mediating acquisition of memory. Retrieval does not involve information processing in the hippocampus nor does it depend on protein synthesis.

Recent investigations of the amnestic syndrome in humans, which results from a variety of neurologic insults, have provided new insights into the complexities of long-term memory. The amnestic syndrome is characterized by impaired acquisition of memories without accompanying sensory, motor, or other neurologic deficits. Amnesics have intact short-term memory and have no problem retrieving information stored in long-term memory prior to the neurologic insult. Moreover, cognitive functions other than acquisition of memories (e.g., concentration, calculation, logic, and so forth) remain intact.

Detailed investigation of which types of information can and cannot be learned by amnesics suggests the existence of different types of long-term memory mechanisms (Squire, 1987). *Procedural memory* involves acquiring knowledge of motor or cognitive sequences (e.g., tying knots, solving puzzles, and so forth). *Semantic memory* is the retention of abstract knowledge or events in time (e.g., the chemical composition of water or the assassination of President Kennedy). *Episodic memory* is the recollection of personal experiences (e.g., one's last visit to the doctor). *Semantic and episodic memory together are termed declarative memory.* It is generally agreed that amnesics can acquire procedural memory but are impaired in acquiring declarative memory. This produces the interesting situation in which amnesics can increase their retention of procedural information with training but have no memory of having learned and, in fact, have no awareness of their increased knowledge. There is debate about the extent of the deficit in acquiring declarative memory in amnesics. Some argue that episodic memory is specifically eliminated in the amnestic syndrome while semantic memory capability persists. Others argue that acquisition of both episodic and semantic memory is impaired. Careful neuropsychologic studies should resolve this controversy. Because amnesics have discrete impairment of declarative but not procedural memory these separate types of memory are probably acquired by different mechanisms.

Studies of the effects of priming on memory retrieval in amnesics also suggest that different mechanisms underlie procedural and declarative memory (Squire, 1987). Amnesics are very poor at free recall of lists of words. However, when given the first three letters of words they have previously seen, amnesics are able to complete accurately the spelling of many words. If normal subjects are given a list of words and instructed to focus on features of the words other than their meaning (such as counting vowels), subsequent recall is also poor. However, when given the first three letters of those words, recall is much improved, demonstrating a learning effect very similar to that seen in amnesics. These results suggest that amnesics can learn but cannot store information based on meaning or category. Declarative memory, which is impaired in amnesics, may, therefore, involve processing and storage of information based on meaning and category, while procedural memory, which is intact in amnesics, involves processing and storage based on the more concrete and literal aspects of information.

Localization of Learning and Memory

Where does acquisition of memory occur? Where is memory stored? The answers to these questions depend on the complexity of learning that occurs.

Habituation, the decline and extinction of a response with repeated presentations of a particular stimulus, is the simplest type of learning. *Sensitization* is another simple learning process involving the enhancement of responses following a strong noxious stimulus. *Classical conditioning* is a more complex learning task involving the association of a conditioned and unconditioned stimulus. Classical conditioning always requires that the conditioned stimulus precedes the unconditioned stimulus in time, and that only a brief period of time elapses between the conditioned and unconditioned stimulus. The neurobiologic basis of simple learning has been investigated in a number of animal models.

The marine snail *Aplysia californica* has a respiratory organ, the gill, and a spoutlike organ, the siphon, which is used to discharge sea water and body waste. Light tactile stimulation of the siphon causes a reflexive withdrawal of the gill and siphon. With repeated moderate tactile stimulation of the siphon, the withdrawal reflex habituates. On the other hand, strong noxious stimulation, such as electroshock of the tail of *Aplysia,* produces a subsequent increase, or sensitization, of the gill and siphon withdrawal reflex. This reflex can also be classically conditioned.

The mechanisms underlying habituation, sensitization, and classic conditioning of the gill and siphon withdrawal reflex in *Aplysia* have been studied in great detail (Kandel and Schwartz, 1985). The nervous system of *Aplysia* is relatively uncomplicated. The neural circuit mediating the gill and siphon withdrawal reflex consists of sensory neurons directly synapsing on motor neurons that effect the response. Although action potentials are generated in sensory neurons by each stimulation, release of neurotransmitter from the presynaptic processes of sensory neurons decreases with repeated tactile stimulation. As a result, synaptic transmission declines until the motor neuron is no longer activated. Electroshock of the tail of *Aplysia* activates pathways that converge on and stimulate the presynaptic processes of sensory neurons involved in the gill and siphon withdrawal reflex. Subsequently, more neurotransmitter is released from the sensory neuron in response to tactile stimulation of the gill, resulting in increased activation of motor neurons. Intracellular mechanisms underlying habituation and sensitization of the gill and siphon withdrawal reflex are summarized in Figure 11-13. If light tactile stimulation is consistently given just prior to tail shock, *Aplysia* become conditioned to withdraw the gill and siphon vigorously in response to tactile stimulation alone. Pairing of the conditioned and unconditioned stimulus in this manner selectively increases neurotransmitter release from the presynaptic processes of sensory neurons by a mechanism similar to that which mediates sensitization.

Brain mechanisms underlying classic conditioning have also been studied in other animal models. In the rabbit, a brief puff of air directed at the cornea reliably produces an eyeblink response. This reflex can be conditioned by pairing a brief tone just before the puff of air. In pigeons, foot shock reliably produces an increase in heart rate. When bright illumination of the visual field is repeatedly presented prior to foot shock, heart rate acceleration becomes conditioned to the light stimulus. Classic conditioning in both of these cases does not depend at all on the cerebral cortex or other forebrain structures but rather occurs within discrete areas of the lower brain where neurons conveying sensory information converge on neurons activating motor or autonomic outputs (Squire, 1987). The studies described above collectively suggest that acquisition and storage of simple learning tasks are located entirely within the direct or nearly direct connections between sensory neurons and neurons mediating relevant responses.

Complex learning occurs by mechanisms that differ from those subserving simple learning. Midtemporal brain structures, especially the hippocampus, are essential for acquisition of complex memory (Squire, 1987). Lesions in this area eliminate

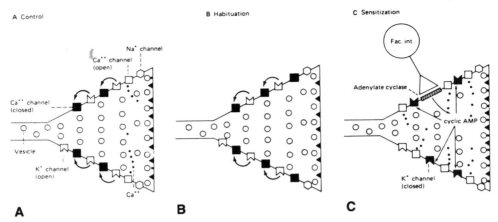

Figure 11–13. *These schematic models of presynaptic terminals show the mechanisms of short-term habituation and sensitization.* **A:** *In the control state an action potential in the sensory neuron opens up a number of Ca^{++} channels in parallel with the Na^+ channels of the membrane. As a result, some Ca^{++} flows into the terminals and allows a certain number of transmitter-containing synaptic vesicles to bind to release sites and be released. The opening of the K^+ channel repolarizes the terminal and prevents other Ca^{++} channels from opening (indicated by arrows).* **B:** *Repeated action potentials in the terminals, leading to habituation, decrease the number of open Ca^{++} channels in the sensory terminal and, at the limit, may shut them down altogether. The resulting depression in Ca^{++} influx functionally inactivates the synapse by decreasing mobilization to active zone release sites and by preventing synaptic vesicles from binding the external membrane, a necessary step for release by exocytosis.* **C:** *Sensitization is produced by interneurons, some of which are thought to be serotonergic. Serotonin and other facilitating transmitters act on an adenylate cyclase in the terminals, which converts ATP to cyclic AMP. Cyclic AMP, in turn, acts to decrease the repolarizing K^+ current and leads to a broadening of the action potential. The increase in the duration of the action potential prolongs the time during which Ca^{++} channels can open, leading to a greater influx of Ca^{++}, and therefore, to increased transmitter release. (Reproduced with permission from Kandel ER, Schwartz JH (eds): Principles of Neural Science. New York, Elsevier, 1985)*

the ability of animals to learn complex conditioning and operant tasks successfully. Examination of the brain of decreased amnesics invariably reveals damage to the midline temporal lobe area. Connections between the hippocampus and the cerebral cortex may be essential for processing and storing complex information. For instance, in the human and lower primate brain, the frontal association cortex (which connects with the hippocampus), the sulcus principalis, and the inferior prefrontal convexity play a critical role in sorting information in time. After processing, complex information is probably stored within the cortical areas that were involved in the processing. The importance of the cerebral cortex in the storage of complex memories is suggested by two lines of evidence. First, lesions that are restricted to the cortex interfere with the acquisition of complex learning. The size of the lesion, more so than the location, appears to be related to the degree of impairment. Second, repeated learning trials have been observed to produce hypertrophy within cortical regions that are known to process the types of sensory and motor information involved in the execution of the learned response (Squire, 1987).

In a manner analogous to simple and complex learning in animals, procedural and declarative memory in humans may depend on different neural substrates. Procedural memory may be acquired and stored within subcortical connections between neurons conveying sensory information and neurons activating responses. However, acquisition of declarative memory may require initial sorting, categorizing, organizing, and so forth that can only be accomplished with an intact mid-thalamic–hippocampal apparatus interacting with the cerebral cortex. When this apparatus is damaged, as in the amnestic syndrome, impairment or complete loss of the ability to acquire declarative memory occurs.

The Neurochemical Basis of Learning and Memory

Cholinergic pathways in the brain play a role in the acquisition and retrieval of memories (Bartus et al, 1987). Muscarinic neurotransmission facilitates initial acquisition of learning tasks but inhibits retrieval of memories from about 5 to 14 days after training. However, around 28 days after training, muscarinic neurotransmission facilitates memory retrieval. These observations suggest that memory consolidation is composed of a number of successive phases, each mediated by differing cholinergic mechanisms. Brain regions involved in learning, such as the hippocampus and the frontal cortex, are heavily innervated by cholinergic pathways. Dementia of the Alzheimer's type has been associated with loss of cholinergic neurons in the nucleus basalis of Meynert, the major source of cholinergic projections to the cortex. Noradrenergic neurotransmission enhances learning primarily by increasing attention. Several neuropeptides affect learning and memory. ACTH or vasopressin administration after a learning trial facilitates retention of learned avoidance behavior. Oxytocin, on the other hand, inhibits retention of learned avoidance behavior. Learning and memory effects of vasopressin and oxytocin are mediated within the dentate gyrus of the hippocampus, the dorsal septum, and the midbrain dorsal raphe nucleus. ACTH effects are exerted primarily in the caudal thalamus (Squire, 1987).

Reproductive Behaviors: Sex and Mothering

Sexual interest is obviously a major influence on behavior in animals and humans. Perhaps less appreciated as a behavioral motivator is the drive of parents, especially mothers, to nurture and protect their offspring. Maternal behavior, along with female and male sexual behavior, are classified as reproductive behaviors because they result in propagation of species and they are under the control of reproductive hormones.

Components and Dimensions
of Reproductive Behaviors

Female sexual behavior includes proceptive behavior, which elicits sexual advances from males, and receptive behavior, which facilitates attempts by males to copulate. In the presence of sexually active males, female rats signal their receptivity to mating by hopping, darting, wiggling their ears, and proffering their backsides.

During copulation, tactile stimuli from the male elicit adjustment in the female's body position that enhances penetration by the male. For example, a receptive female rat arches its back into an exaggerated lordosis posture and moves its tail to one side. Brain pathways mediating sensory signals that trigger lordosis are summarized in Figure 11-14.

Female sexual behavior is exhibited in most species only during a brief period of the ovarian cycle near the time of ovulation when fertilization is possible. Cyclic changes in estrogen and progesterone levels that stimulate ovulation also initiate female sexual behavior. In the absence of ovarian steroids, for instance after ovariectomy, sexual behavior ceases in animals and some, but not all, women.

Male sexual behavior includes penile erections, repeated intromissions, and ejaculation. In addition to proceptive behaviors, rodent males are attracted to receptive females by the odor of vaginal secretions. Primate males are attracted by the swelling and changes in pigmentation of the females' external genitalia that occur near ovulation. The initiation of male sexual activity depends on testosterone. Sexually experienced males of subprimate species undergo a gradual decline in sexual behavior after castration. However, men and primates sometimes experience no loss of sexual interest or potency after castration.

Maternal behavior is composed of a number of integrated activities that result in the cleaning, feeding, and protection of offspring. The specific behaviors vary widely

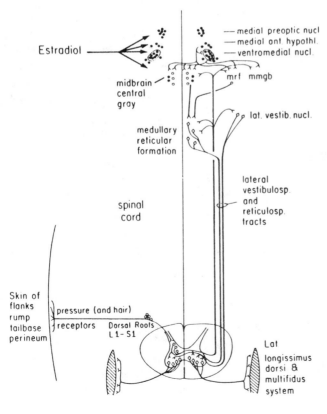

Figure 11–14. *Schematic representation of the minimal neural circuit for lordosis behavior in the female rat. Estradiol effects are mediated at estrogen-binding neurons in the hypothalamus and the central gray. Ascending spinal fibers conveying sensory information necessary for induction of lordosis travel in the anterolateral columns of the spinal cord. mmgb = medial division of the medial geniculate body; mrf = dorsal mesencephalic reticular formation. (Reproduced with permission from Pfaff D, Modianos D: Neural Mechanisms of Female Reproductive Behavior in Adler N, Pfaff D, Goy RW (eds): Handbook of Behavioral Neurobiology, Vol 7: Reproduction. pp 423–493. New York, Plenum Press, 1985)*

between species. Nursing is also associated in a number of species with increased food intake, enhanced aggressiveness, and diminished fearful and avoidant responses to aversive stimuli. The initiation of maternal behavior after parturition depends, in most subprimate mammals, on the rise in estrogen and fall in progesterone occurring in late pregnancy. In primates and humans, early social experience is critical in preparing females to provide effective mothering behavior.

Brain Sites Implicated in the Regulation of Reproductive Behaviors

Brain mechanisms have been more thoroughly investigated for female sexual receptivity than for other reproductive behaviors (Adler et al, 1985). Pathways initiating receptive posturing in rats project from the anterior and ventromedial hypothalamus to midbrain structures such as the mesencephalic central gray. This apparatus regulates descending multisynaptic pathways that control motor neurons innervating muscle groups involved in lordosis (see Fig. 11-14). The medial preoptic area and the septum exert a tonic inhibitory effect on receptive behavior that is probably mediated by pathways that descend to the midbrain. Estrogen facilitates receptive posturing by suppressing the inhibitory influence of the medial preoptic area and increasing the facilitating influence of the ventromedial and anterior hypothalamus. Estrogen also enhances female sexual behavior by stimulating synthesis of progesterone receptors. Tactile stimulation essential to the activation of the lordosis reflex ascends through the anterolateral columns of the spinal cord. If permissive ovarian steroid conditions are present, this sensory information activates the hypothalmic–midbrain apparatus that initiates the lordosis posture. Other than dependence on ovarian steroids, very little is known about the mechanisms of proceptive behavior.

Male sexual behavior is initiated within pathways that originate in the medial preoptic area (Adler et al, 1985). Testosterone acts throughout the preoptic-anterior hypothalmic area to stimulate male copulatory behavior. Depending on the species, male reproductive behavior depends on conversion of testosterone to one or several metabolites: androstenedione, dihydrotestosterone, other androgens, or estrogen. Inputs from limbic brain structures influence male motivation to copulate. For instance, lesions of the temporal lobe that include the basolateral nucleus of the amygdala produce hypersexuality in monkeys and cats. On the other hand, lesions of the corticomedial nucleus of the amygdala in rodents depress male sexual behavior probably by interrupting olfactory inputs indicating female reproductive state.

Maternal behavior is mediated by pathways that originate in the medial preoptic area, project laterally, and then descend through the medial forebrain bundle to rostral midbrain structures such as the substantia nigra (Adler et al, 1985). Estrogen acts in the medial preoptic area to initiate mothering. Limbic structures such as the hippocampus and septum play a more prominent role in the regulation of maternal behavior than in other reproductive behaviors.

The Neurochemical Basis of Reproductive Behaviors.

A large number of drugs that affect classic neurotransmitter systems have been tested for their effects on reproductive behaviors, especially sexual behaviors (Adler et al, 1985; Pedersen and Prange, 1987). Serotonergic neurotransmission inhibits both female and male sexual behavior. Selective destruction of serotonergic neurons in the hypothalamus increases receptive behavior. Peripheral drug treatments that enhance dopaminergic neurotransmission increase proceptive behaviors (the mobile component of female sexual behavior), decrease receptive posturing (the immobile component of female sexual behavior), and increase male mounting behavior. However, in the medial preoptic area and the ventromedial nucleus, dopamine agonists increase while dopamine antagonists decrease receptive posturing, suggesting that dopamine may have different effects in separate brain regions involved in female sexual behavior. Destruction of noradrenergic pathways that descend to the spinal cord suppresses proceptive and receptive behavior as well as components of male sexual behavior. The ascending ventral noradrenergic bundle is critical to receptive but not proceptive female sexual behavior. Peripheral treatment with different adrenergic drugs has a variety of effects on sexual behavior that do not fit into a coherent mechanistic scheme, probably because adrenergic pathways play different roles in different brain regions. Muscarinic cholinergic neurotransmission in the hypothalamus facilitates receptive behavior.

The neuropeptide, luteinizing hormone-releasing hormone (LH-RH), stimulates female receptivity and male copulatory behavior. In females, LH-RH acts in the medial preoptic area, ventromedial nucleus of the hypothalamus, and the central gray area of the midbrain. In males, LH-RH exerts its effects in the medial preoptic area. Administration of LH-RH in humans has been reported to increase sexual interest in some persons but not others. Endogenous opioids (beta-endorphin, enkephalins) inhibit female and male sexual behavior, observations that are consistent with the effects of narcotics in humans. Central administration of other peptides derived from pro-opiomelanocortin (ACTH, MSH) induce repeated erections, ejaculations, and copulatory movements and may enhance receptive behavior. Oxytocin also acts in the brain to increase receptivity and penile erections and may prolong the postejaculatory refractory period (Pedersen and Prange, 1987).

Maternal behavior has been subjected to much less neuropharmacologic investigation than sexual behavior. Peripheral administration of dopamine antagonists block maternal behavior. Adrenergic as well as muscarinic neurotransmission may be critical for the initiation but not the maintenance of maternal behavior. Increased aggression and food intake as well as decreased avoidance behavior during lactation could reflect increased central GABAergic neurotransmission. Morphine potently blocks both the initiation and maintenance of maternal behavior. Central release of oxytocin contributes to the initiation of maternal behavior (Pedersen and Prange, 1987).

Consumptive Behavior

Feeding behavior can be broken down into several discrete functions: initiation of feeding, food selection and maintenance of eating, and satiety. The first two are coordinated by neural structures located within the hypothalamus, especially the paraventricular nucleus. Satiety is mediated by a combination of central and peripheral mechanisms. The manner in which specific neurotransmitter systems interact varies with function, as indicated in Table 11-5. Other subcortical structures such as brainstem motor nuclei, the nigrostriatal tract, and sympathetic pathways play a role

Table 11–5 **Neurohormonal Regulation of Eating Behavior**

	NE	5HT	DA	END	CCK	NPY	INS	SAT	CRF
Initiation of feeding	I	–	–	D (P,I)	D	I	I	D	D
Food choice									
CHO	I	D	–	–	–	I	–	–	–
Fat	I	–	–	I	–	–	–	–	–
Pleasure	–	–	I	–	–	–	–	–	–
Satiety	–	I	–	–	I	–	–	I	–

Abbreviations: End = Endorphin, Ins = Insulin, Sat = Satietin, D = Decrease, I = Increase, – = No difference, P = Peripheral administration.

in carrying out the eating impulse by mediating stereotyped ingestive behaviors such as chewing and swallowing. In humans, it is clear that cortical structures can exert considerable influence over appetitive behavior, to the point of completely overriding hunger. The mechanisms by which this occurs are not yet well understood (Halmi et al, 1987).

The initiation of feeding is evoked in part by decreases in serum glucose concentration. Noradrenergic neurons have a strong facilitating influence on the initiation of feeding, perhaps mediated through inhibition of corticotropin-releasing factor, which has a powerful anorexic effect. Neuropeptide Y and opioids also initiate eating. Glucocorticoids facilitate eating and may regulate feeding (Morley, 1987).

Maintenance of homeostasis requires that an organism be able to select those nutrients that best fit current metabolic needs. The mechanisms involved in food choice are closely linked with reward centers in the hypothalamus. Dopaminergic neurons play a prominent role in the pleasurable reinforcement of food choice and in the maintenance of eating. Endorphins also influence food choice and, in particular, increase the consumption of fat. Noradrenergic stimulation increases fat and carbohydrate intake, while serotonergic stimulation decreases carbohydrate choice (Morley, 1987).

Satiety is initiated in the gut in part by food-triggered secretion of the gastrointestinal peptides cholecystokinin (CCK), satietin, and bombesin. Gut peptides exert their effects on feeding through afferent neuronal connections between the gastrointestinal tract and the CNS. For example, CCK satiety signals are transmitted to the brain through the vagus nerve. However, injection of CCK into the paraventicular nucleus also induces satiety, suggesting that direct peptide regulation of central ingestive systems may also occur (Morley, 1987).

Aggression

Aggression occurs in a number of distinct behavioral contexts. In animals and humans, aggression is one component of a larger repertoire of social behaviors, the goals of which are reproductive success as well as acquisition and protection of resources, territory, and status. Aggression is also one of a number of behavioral responses to aversive situations other than social conflict. Unfortunately, excessive, maladaptive violence directed toward others or self occurs in the form of assault, murder, or suicide. This section will focus primarily on the neurobiology of social aggression but will also review our limited understanding of pathologic violence. The neurobiology of behavioral responses to stress is reviewed in the next section of this chapter. Rodent studies have provided insight into brain mechanisms that regulate social aggression while primate studies have elucidated situational and hormonal determinants that may be of particular relevance to humans.

Social Aggression in Rodents

Adult rodents do not, as a rule, live in groups but rather establish individual territories. Aggressive behaviors are a part of a larger set of social behaviors including offensive attack, defensive attack, submission, and behaviors that establish territory such as patrolling and scent-marking with urine or other specialized secretions. Adult rodents, particularly males, attack same sex intruders into their territory. Aggression is most likely when there is competition for desirable goals (e.g., copulation). When attacked in another's territory, rodents respond either with defensive behavior if the animals have not previously encountered each other or submissive behavior if prior confrontations have established territorial rights. Encounters between adult conspecifics of opposite sex stimulate increased marking behavior in both sexes and, in nonpregnant, nonlactating females, submissive behavior. Reproductive and other motivated behaviors are strongly influenced by social situation and territorial considerations. For instance, males copulate more frequently in areas that they have previously marked.

Offense, defense, and submission in rodents each involves distinct postures and motor sequences, and is mediated by different neural circuitry (Svare, 1983). Offensive attack includes repeated series of bites and kicks directed at the flanks of the opponent launched from a stereotypical aggressive posture. Defense involves lunging and biting directed at the face of the attacker. Submissive behavior is characterized by ultrasonic vocalizations and stereotyped posturing. Offense is mediated by the preoptic area and the lateral hypothalamus; defense and submission are under the control of the midbrain central gray and tegmentum. Projections to the midbrain from the ventromedial nucleus of the hypothalamus suppress defense and enhance submission. Limbic brain regions (e.g., septum, amygdala), which analyze olfactory and other sensory cues, are essential for the interpretation of social situations. Projections from the limbic brain to the preoptic area, hypothalamus, and midbrain regulate both the initiation and direction of aggressive and submissive behavior. Note the similarity in neural circuitry mediating aggression and sexual behaviors (see section entitled "Reproductive Behaviors: Sex and Mothering").

Gonadal steroids regulate aggression and other dimensions of social behavior by acting on the neural apparatus outlined above (Coe and Levine, 1983; Sheard, 1987; Svare, 1983). Sexual differentiation of the nervous system determines the pattern of aggressive and social behavior during development and adulthood. Male juveniles engage in more rough and tumble play with age-mates than female juveniles. Adult males display higher rates of aggression, especially offensive behavior, in virtually all mammalian species. Testosterone and its metabolites facilitate offense toward other males but, in the presence of estrogen-treated females or their odors, suppress offense and increase patrolling and marking. In females, estrogen decreases offense toward all types of opponents but increases patrolling and marking behavior in the presence of testosterone-treated males or their odors. Progesterone enhances estrogen effects. During pregnancy and lactation, rodent females display much more offensive and defensive behavior and will readily attack males that approach their nests. Aggression in rat mothers appears to be under the same ovarian steroid control as other components of maternal behavior (see section entitled "Reproductive Behaviors: Sex and Mothering").

Neurotransmitter regulation of social aggression has been extensively studied in rodents (Eichelman, 1987; Svare, 1983). Noradrenergic and dopaminergic neurotransmission are essential for offensive behavior but play a less critical role in defense. Serotonin also facilitates offensive attack, while serotonergic antagonists increase submissive, defensive, and escape behaviors. Social aggression is inhibited by muscarinic antagonists and nicotinic agonists. Opioids also diminish aggression. Defeat in social confrontations produces analgesia, which is also opioid-mediated.

Social Aggression in Primates

Primates tend to live in groups in which each individual establishes a position in a dominance hierarchy. Outright physical assault is rare. Rather, individuals, especially males, establish and maintain their social rank by means of behavioral displays that vary with species. Aggression between males is much greater when sexually receptive or estrogen-treated females are introduced into the group. Display behavior increases dramatically at puberty in male primates, concomitant with the rise in testosterone levels. Adult aggression in male primates depends both on prenatal testosterone exposure during sexual differentiation and on increased testosterone secretion during sexual maturation. However, once established, the adult pattern of aggression is not necessarily dependent on testosterone. Testosterone levels in men do not correlate well with measures of aggression. Castration of adult primates often has no effect on dominance rank. Similarly, castration of sex offenders or excessively violent men frequently has no ameliorating behavioral effect (Coe and Levine, 1983).

While hormones play a limited role in initiating aggression in adult primates, success or failure in achieving dominance within a group has a powerful effect on the hypothalamic–pituitary–gonadal (HPG) and hypothalamic–pituitary–adrenal (HPA) axes (Coe and Levine, 1983; Sheard, 1987; Svare, 1983). A dominance hierarchy is rapidly established after formation of a new group. Individual testosterone and cortisol levels prior to new group formation fail to correlate with subsequent dominance rank. However, testosterone levels rise considerably in dominant males but fall in subordinate males shortly after formation of new groups. Cortisol levels increase both in dominant and subordinate males after group formation. The influence of dominance rank on HPG and HPA activity of males is more pronounced when females are included in new groups. Testosterone and, to some extent, cortisol levels rise earlier and to higher levels during the mating season in dominant than in subordinate males. Elevated testosterone may be related to the much greater reproductive success of dominant male primates. Competition influences activity of the HPG axis in humans as well. Triumph during tennis matches and other competitive situations increases testosterone levels while defeat lowers levels.

Human Violence

Investigation of the neurobiology of human violence is in its infancy (Eichelman, 1987). A history of repeated violent aggression has been associated with high CSF levels of the norepinephrine metabolite MHPG and low levels of the serotonin metabolite 5-HIAA. Low blood levels of serotonin have been measured in hyperaggressive men. Brain concentrations of 5-HIAA were also low in persons that had committed violent suicide. Thus, elevated norepinephrine and decreased serotonin activity in the CNS have been associated with violent assaultive and suicidal behavior in humans.

Stress and Behavior

The environment often subjects animals and humans to aversive stimuli and situations (stressors). Stress is the internal response to aversive conditions, which includes situationally specific patterns of hormone release, central neuroendocrine change, and autonomic activation. Stressors also elicit behavioral responses, which vary widely with the type and magnitude of aversive stimulus. Hormonal and neuroendocrine components of the stress response act within the brain to stimulate appropriate behavioral responses to specific stressors.

Behavioral Responses to Stressors

Stressful conditions can be grouped under three general categories, which will be discussed below (Field et al, 1985). Specific behavioral responses as well as endocrine and autonomic responses differ with type of stressful condition. The first category is composed of *stressors for which the organism has readily available effective coping responses*, which may include escape, offensive or defensive attack, or other proactive behaviors that allow the organism to diminish or master the aversive situation. Under these conditions, cardiac output, heart rate, blood pressure, and vasodilation in skeletal muscle all increase. The second category is composed of *stressors for which the organism has no active coping option*. Under these conditions, organisms become hypervigilant but immobile, adopting either a frozen or submissive posture. Peripheral resistance and blood pressure rise while heart rate and blood flow through skeletal muscle decrease. The third category of stressors includes *unfamiliar, novel, or uncertain stimuli or situations*. Reactions to such conditions include initial hypervigilance and immobility followed by cautious exploration interspersed with behaviors that are thought to be manifestations of anxiety (e.g., self-grooming in animals; tapping, clearing the throat, pacing, and so forth in humans). Cardiovascular responses to novelty are initially (during the immobile hypervigilant phase) similar to those occurring when active coping strategies are not available, but, as the organism begins to explore and emote, the cardiovascular response shifts to that associated with active coping. The sudden onset of high-intensity aversive stimulation often elicits an initial immobile, hypervigilant response with attendant cardiovascular changes even if active coping strategies are readily available. *Repeated exposure to aversive conditions that cannot be controlled produces a state of "learned helplessness" in which the organism will passively endure stressors even when coping options become available.* Aversive stimuli also inhibit reproductive, eating, drinking, and other motivated behaviors.

Exposure to stressors early in development profoundly affects behavior and stress responses in adulthood. Male offspring of rodent mothers that were stressed during pregnancy are both demasculinized and feminized; female offspring are little affected. For instance, as adults, these males display much reduced mounting and increased lordosis behavior (Adler et al, 1985). Prenatal stress alters catecholamine levels in a number of brain sites. In humans, prenatal stress has been associated with behavioral, psychiatric, and sexual identity problems. Separation of infants from their mothers also has lifelong effects on behavioral, endocrine, and autonomic responses to stressors (Field et al, 1985; Reite and Field, 1985). Repeated brief periods of separation and handling of rat pups result in improved modulation of stress responses in adulthood. However, prolonged isolation of infant rhesus monkeys produces exaggerated stress responses in adulthood that resemble clinical depression in humans. Thus, stability in the face of stressors in adulthood may be enhanced by short periods of early maternal separation but impaired by excessive parental deprivation. Approximately 15% of human infants display exaggerated fear of unfamiliar objects and situations. Fearful infants had higher levels of cortisol and norepinephrine as well as elevated heart rates compared with other infants (Kagan et al, 1987). Early differences in individual temperament may also influence adult patterns of stress response.

Neuroendocrine Components of the Stress Response and Their Behavioral Effects

The hypothalamic–pituitary–adrenal (HPA) axis is particularly responsive to stressors. As established by the pioneering work of Selye, vigorous release of adrenal glucocorticoids and pituitary ACTH is a prominent feature of the stress response. Levels of beta-endorphin, which is coreleased with ACTH from the anterior pituitary, also rise in response to stressors. Norepinephrine and epinephrine release from the adrenal medulla is the other component of the classic stress response (Goldstein and Halbreich, 1987).

Early stress researchers conceptualized HPA axis activation and catecholamine release as a general, nonspecific response to all types of stressors. However, more recent studies demonstrate that the pattern of release of peripheral neuroendocrine components of the stress response varies under differing stressful conditions (Field et al, 1985). Release of ACTH and adrenal glucocorticoids are most dramatic when organisms are confronted with aversive stimuli that are unfamiliar or for which they have no readily apparent coping mechanism. Epinephrine release is also relatively greater than norepinephrine release under these more psychologically stressful conditions.

Hypothalamic neuropeptides that are secreted into the hypophyseal portal system regulate the activity of the HPA axis by modulating the release of ACTH from the anterior pituitary. The most potent of these is corticotropin-releasing factor (CRF). However, vasopressin and oxytocin amplify CRF stimulation of ACTH release. The degree to which vasopressin and oxytocin are released into portal blood varies under different stressful conditions. Neural pathways containing CRF, vasopressin, oxytocin as well as beta-endorphin, enkephalins, and ACTH fragments are widely distributed within the brain. Stressors very likely stimulate central release of these neuropeptides. Indeed, various kinds of stressors decrease concentrations of opioids and CRF and increase opioid binding in some brain regions. Turnover and synthesis of norepinephrine, epinephrine, and serotonin all increase in a number of brain regions in response to acute stressors. Exposure to prolonged uncontrollable stress has been associated with depletion of total brain norepinephrine (Field et al, 1985).

Neuroendocrine components of the HPA axis influence behavioral responses to stressors. Glucocorticoids increase immobility and submissive behavior. ACTH, on the other hand, increases attack, as will exploratory behavior (Svare, 1983). Self-grooming behavior is activated by ACTH, vasopressin, oxytocin, beta-endorphin, and CRF. ACTH, vasopressin, and oxytocin all influence acquisition of avoidance behavior (see section entitled "Learning and Memory") suggesting that they may be crucial in gaining familiarity with novel stimuli, remembering aversive aspects of situations, and learning coping strategies. Stress inhibition of some behaviors may also be mediated by central neuroendocrine components of the HPA axis. Glucocorticoids, CRF, vasopressin, and beta-endorphin all inhibit sexual behavior, while CRF and beta-endorphin also antagonize food consumption. Central noradrenergic pathways play a key role in focusing attention and arousing appropriate behavioral responses to acute stressors. Depletion of brain norepinephrine resulting from exposure to repeated uncontrollable stress may contribute to the behavioral suppression associated with learned helplessness (Field et al, 1985).

Psychoneuroimmunology

Accumulating evidence for reciprocal interactions among neuroendocrine, affective and behavioral components of the stress response, and the immune system has spawned a new field of research called psychoneuroimmunology (Ader, 1981; Jankovic et al, 1987). Early investigators noted that thymic and lymphoid tissue involution are integral parts of the general stress response. Stressful psychologic states, such as bereavement and clinical depression, are associated with decreased numbers and function of lymphocytes as well as decreased natural killer cell activity (Evans and Nemeroff, 1988). Uncontrollable stress produces similar immune deficits in animals. Some endocrine components of the stress response, such as increased levels of adrenal glucocorticoids, may suppress the immune system. However, studies in adrenalectomized animals demonstrate that some immune deficits produced by uncontrollable stress occur independently of glucocorticoid levels. Ader and Cohen were the first to make the fascinating observation that immunomodulation can be learned (i.e., increases and decreases in the activity of various components of the immune system can be conditioned). Lesions in the hypothalamus alter immune function. Neuropeptides have various effects on cells of the immune system. These observations demonstrate that the brain directly controls immune function. In turn, the immune system may regulate neuroendocrine axes and behavioral substrates in the brain. Interleukin-1, a monokine released by macrophages and monocytes, potently stimulates the release of ACTH. Also, lymphocytes synthesize a number of peptides (e.g., ACTH, endorphins) that have neuroendocrine and behavior effects.

Sleep

Sleep is a fundamental, complex, and essential behavior. Sleep was regarded as a homogeneous, passive experience until 1935, when Loomis and colleagues described distinct states of sleep that could be identified by specific electroencephalogram (EEG) patterns. By the mid-1950s, scientists had observed that bursts of conjugate rapid eye movements (REM) appear periodically during sleep; these REM sleep periods were subsequently linked to dreaming. In the last 3 decades, increasingly sophisticated technology has allowed us to decipher more of the mysteries of the experience we call "sleep." Yet even today, many medical school physiology courses virtually ignore the biology of sleep, when in fact, the cardiovascular, respiratory, and neurochemical physiology of sleeping humans differs in many ways from the waking physiology that is usually taught.

Sleep Architecture

As Hauri (1982) has pointed out, sleep is an active, complex state, similar to a building with various components; thus, the expression "sleep architecture" is used to describe the stages and cycles of sleep and their interrelationships. The different stages of sleep are defined by distinct patterns of brain electrical activity and by distinct behavioral and physiologic states.

Sleep Stages. Sleep can be divided into two broad categories: rapid-eye-movement (REM) and non-rapid-eye-movement (NREM) sleep. NREM sleep can be further subcategorized into four stages. Stages 1, 2, 3, and 4 can be conceptualized as representing a progression from very light to very deep sleep, with concurrent EEG changes from fast (high-frequency) low-amplitude waves to slow (low-frequency) high-amplitude patterns (Fig. 11-15).

Stage 1 consists of the transition from wakefulness to sleep. In normal sleepers, it lasts from 30 seconds to 7 minutes. During this stage, reactivity to external stimuli is blunted, thinking becomes less "reality oriented," and short dreams may develop as thoughts begin to drift. Many people will report that they felt that they were awake during this stage.

Stage 2 sleep is heralded by the onset of "sleep spindles" on the EEG (i.e., bursts of 12- to 14-Hz activity lasting 0.5 to 2 seconds) and "K-complexes," (i.e., sudden, high-amplitude bipolar spikes; see Fig. 11-15). By convention, sleep researchers define the onset of sleep by the appearance of the first sleep spindle or K-complex. Mentation during stage 2 consists of short, fragmented, mundane thoughts, and most people who are awakened during stage 2 will acknowledge that they were asleep and will not remember any dreams, although they may recall fragments of thoughts.

Stage 3 and stage 4 sleep, collectively referred to as delta sleep, is characterized by slow, 0.5- to 2-Hz, high-amplitude waves on the EEG (see Fig. 11-15). Delta sleep can be thought of as "deep," or "heavy" sleep.

REM sleep derives its label from the periodic vertical and horizontal darting eye movements that are observed in this stage. The EEG during REM sleep presents a picture of low-voltage, mixed-frequency waves that resemble the pattern of stage 1 sleep except for the additional presence of sawtooth waves (see Fig. 11-15). When people are awakened during REM sleep, they will recall dreams about 80% of the time, while only 5% of NREM awakenings are associated with complete dream recollection.

Sleep Cycles. During normal sleep, sleep stages do not occur at random; a pattern of progression can be described for a normal *sleep cycle* (Fig. 11-16). A healthy young adult typically moves from an awake state into a period of NREM sleep.

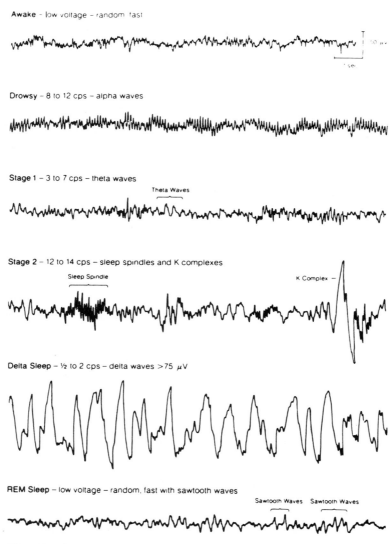

Awake – low voltage – random fast

Drowsy – 8 to 12 cps – alpha waves

Stage 1 – 3 to 7 cps – theta waves

Theta Waves

Stage 2 – 12 to 14 cps – sleep spindles and K complexes

Sleep Spindle

K Complex –

Delta Sleep – ½ to 2 cps – delta waves >75 μV

REM Sleep – low voltage – random, fast with sawtooth waves

Sawtooth Waves   Sawtooth Waves

Figure 11–15. *Stages of human sleep. (Reproduced with permission from Hauri P: The Sleep Disorders. Kalamazoo, The Upjohn Co., 1982)*

After a brief period (e.g., 5 to 10 minutes) of relaxed, drowsy wakefulness, the sleeper passes through a brief 1- to 5-minute period of stage 1 sleep, then descends into deeper stage 2 sleep. Thirty minutes into the sleep process, the sleeper enters delta (stage 3 to stage 4) sleep, which then lasts about 30 to 60 minutes. Typically, the sleeper then "ascends" back to stage 2, during which a brief, first REM period is experienced. Following this initial REM period, the sleeper returns to stage 2, and the

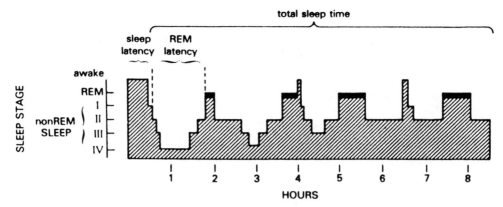

Figure 11–16. *Sequence of sleep stages in a healthy young adult. (Reproduced with permission from Mendelson WB: Human Sleep: Research and Clinical Care. New York, Plenum Press, 1987)*

second "sleep cycle" is begun. Thus, the first sleep cycle lasts about 90 minutes, with a brief REM period occurring 70 to 90 minutes after the initiation of sleep.

The typical healthy young adult sleeper will pass through four to six sleep cycles over the course of the night, and as Figure 11-16 shows, these cycles are not identical. Following the first cycle described above, subsequent cycles show progressively less delta sleep. REM periods become progressively longer over the course of the night.

Sleep and the Lifecycle

The normal process of aging is accompanied by changes in the sleep cycle. In fact, age is the single most powerful determinant of a person's sleep physiology. Total sleep time and the total nightly amount of time spent in each of the sleep stages are age-dependent. In general, total sleep time is greatest in infancy, decreases during childhood, and remains relatively stable during the adult years until a late life decline is seen. Sleep becomes more "fragmented" over the course of a lifetime; the amount of waking time and the number of awakenings after sleep onset increase (Hauri, 1982).

In addition to these general parameters, the proportion of the various sleep stages also changes with aging. The percentage of REM sleep is highest in infancy and childhood, decreases and levels off in adulthood, and then declines in the geriatric years. Stage 4 sleep is also highest in infancy, then progressively declines with age.

The incidence and types of sleep disturbances change over the lifecycle. In childhood, sleep problems tend to include principally night terrors, enuresis, and bedtime fears and anxiety. Adolescents often are chronically sleep deprived and have difficulty getting up in the morning. In the elderly, there is a marked increase in the occurrence of insomnia, as well as in the specific sleep disorders of sleep apnea and nocturnal myoclonus. The quality of insomnia itself seems to vary with age; the elderly are inclined to experience more frequent and longer nighttime awakenings or early awakenings, while young insomniacs more often complain of difficulty falling asleep. In general, these changes occur earlier in women than in men (Lacks, 1987).

Circadian Rhythms

The sleep–wake cycle requires about 24 hours to complete in most humans. Thus, it is an example of a *circadian* rhythm. Other important biologic functions also follow a circadian rhythm in humans, including body temperature (which reaches a nadir during nighttime sleep and peaks during the day), certain endocrine systems, and some metabolic processes. There is considerable variation among people regarding the exact shape of some of these 24-hour oscillations. Scientists have suggested that people who seem to be "early birds" in terms of their preferred time of day for maximal performance may have different points of maximal efficiency for some of their circadian biologic systems compared to "night owls."

When humans are placed in environments where there are no external time cues (e.g., a constantly lit, soundproof room with plenty of food but no clock), they still maintain a circadian rhythm. However, under these constant conditions, their sleep–wake cycles usually do not last exactly 24 hours. Most people settle into rhythms lasting between 24 and 28 hours, although sleep–wake cycles lasting as long as 50 hours have been observed under these conditions.

Neurobiology of Sleep

Nearly 100 years ago, Mauthner suggested that sleep induction was regulated by the area of the brain surrounding the third cranial nerve nuclei. A half century later, Bremer concluded that the junction between the diencephalon and the brainstem was crucial to sleep and wakefulness, based on his encephale isole and cerveau isole experiments (Hauri, 1982). Both Mauthner and Bremer viewed sleep as a "passive" process in which decreased cortical activation leads to a loss of wakefulness. It was later proposed that the reticular activating system plays a key role in maintaining arousal.

Other sleep researchers began to argue that sleep is a function of an active sleep-inducing center. Both stimulation and lesion experiments in animals, performed in the 1940s and 1950s, lent support to this view. Today, most sleep scientists have reconciled the "active" versus "passive" debate into an integrated theory.

Following transection at the midbrain, the forebrain above and the midbrain below both show wake–NREM sleep cycling, suggesting that there is no single center for NREM sleep. However, there are regions that do facilitate waking, including the ascending reticular activating system and the posterior hypothalamus, and regions that facilitate sleep (i.e., the basal forebrain, the area surrounding the solitary tract of the medulla, and possibly the dorsal raphe). Also, the superchiasmatic nucleus seems to serve as the major biologic "clock" for most circadian rhythms and, thus, is also involved in the sleep–wake cycle.

Thus, it appears that there are two systems that regulate the sleep–wake cycle: a sleep-promoting system and a wakefulness-promoting system. For sleep onset to occur, activity in the more powerful arousal system must first passively decrease; following this, the less powerful sleep-promoting system can actively begin to play a role. Earlier, it had been suggested that serotonin controls NREM sleep, but currently it is recognized that the neurochemical control is much more complex. It appears that serotonin, acetylcholine, norepinephrine, as well as other neurotransmitters modulate the sleep–wake cycle in a complex, interactive manner.

In addition to the sleep–wake cycle, the REM–NREM cycle has been the subject of considerable study and debate. In the early 1960s, Jouvet (1965) reported the discovery of a REM-inducing system in the higher pons. More recently, Hobson and associates (Hobson et al, 1975) have developed a model in which two classes of neural systems control the REM–NREM cycle. An aminergic system, which includes serotonergic neurons in the dorsal raphe and noradrenergic neurons in the locus ceruleus and nucleus peribrachialis lateralis, discharges at its highest rate during wakefulness, progressively decreases its discharge rate during NREM sleep, and produces very low discharge rates during REM sleep. A cholinergic reticular system, located primarily in the mesencephalic, medullary, and pontine gigantocellular tegmental fields, demonstrate the opposite pattern of activity. Thus, according to the Hobson McCarley model, these two opposing systems continuously interact to produce the cycling between REM and NREM sleep. This model is not universally accepted, and this area remains an important focus of ongoing research.

SUMMARY

After 2 decades of breathtaking discovery, it is clear that we are now in the golden age of neuroscience. Much progress has been made in our understanding of the brain mechanisms involved in behavior. Most of this knowledge has been obtained through investigation of animal behavior. The challenge for the future is to achieve as much insight into the biologic basis of human behavior. Fortunately, we are on the brink of a new era in which technical advances are opening the way for safe, noninvasive study of human brain function. For instance, the availability of an increasing number of radio-emitting substances allows quantification and precise localization of blood flow, glucose utilization, and binding of specific molecules in the living brain. These methods will permit identification of brain regions and neurochemical systems involved in human behavior, cognition, and emotion. New capabilities of this sort may revolutionize our ability to diagnose and treat behavioral and psychologic disorders in humans.

ANNOTATED BIBLIOGRAPHY

Ader R (ed): Psychoneuroimmunology. New York, Academic Press, 1981

> This is an excellent and comprehensive review of an emerging area in psychiatry. The field of psychoneuroimmunology is supplanting older theoretical approaches of psychosomatic illness with a solid scientific basis, and this text provides the most comprehensive treatment of the subject to date.

Cooper JR, Bloom FE, Roth RH (eds): The Biochemical Basis of Neuropharmacology. New York, Oxford University Press, 1986

> A concise but superb review of neuropharmacology; a classic small text that is "must" reading for all medical students.

Coyle JT: Neuroscience and psychiatry. In Talbott JA, Hales RE, Yudofsky SC (eds): Textbook of Psychiatry. Washington, DC, American Psychiatric Press, 1988

> Basic concepts in neuroscience as they relate to clinical psychiatric disorders are reviewed in this well-written chapter.

Kandel ER, Schwartz JH (eds): Principles of Neural Science. New York, Elsevier, 1985

> This is a masterful text that is remarkable for its clarity and depth; an extremely valuable resource for students interested in recent advances in the neurosciences.

Meltzer HY (ed): Psychopharmacology: The Third Generation of Progress. New York, Raven Press, 1987

> A compendium of the field of psychopharmacology and biochemical treatments for mental illness; excellent reference for research and in-depth reading.

REFERENCES

Ader R (ed): Psychoneuroimmunology. New York, Academic Press, 1981

Adler N, Pfaff D, Goy RW (eds): Handbook of Behavioral Neurobiology, Vol 7: Reproduction. New York, Plenum Press, 1985

Bartus RT, Dean RL, Flicker C: Cholinergic psychopharmacology: An integration of human and animal research on memory. In Meltzer HY (ed): Psychopharmacology: The Third Generation of Progress. New York, Raven Press, 1987

Bunney, WE Jr, Davis JM: Norepinephrine in depressive reactions: A review. Arch Gen Psychiatry 13:483–494, 1965

Coccaro EF, Murphy DL: Serotonin in Psychiatric Disorders. Washington, DC, American Psychiatric Association, in press

Coe CL, Levine S: Biology of aggression. Bull Am Acad Psychiatry Law 11:131–148, 1983

Cooper JR, Bloom FE, Roth RH (eds): The Biochemical Basis of Neuropharmacology. New York, Oxford University Press, 1986

Coppen A, Shaw D, Malleson A, et al: Changes in 5-hydroxytryptophan metabolism in depression. Br J Psychiatry 3:993–998, 1965

Coyle JT: Neuroscience and psychiatry. In Talbott JA, Hales RE, Yudofsky SC (eds): Textbook of Psychiatry. Washington, DC, American Psychiatric Press, 1988

Eichelman B: Neurochemical and psychopharmacologic aspects of aggressive behavior. In Meltzer HY (ed): Psychopharmacology: The Third Generation of Progress. New York, Raven Press, 1987

Elliot GR, Holman RB, Barchas JD: Neuroregulators and behavior. In Barchas JD, Berger PA, Ciaranello RD et al (eds): Psychopharmacology: From Theory to Practice. New York, Oxford University Press, 1977

Evans DL, Nemeroff CB: Depression and aging: Psychoneuroendocrinology and psychoneuroimmunology. Progress in Neuroendocrinimmunology, 1:21–27, 1988

Field TM, McCabe PM, Schneiderman N (eds): Stress and Coping. Hillsdale, NJ, Lawrence Erlbaum Associates, 1985

Golden RN, Potter WZ: Neurochemical and neuroendocrine dysregulation in affective disorders. Psychiatr Clin North Am 9:313–327, 1986

Goldstein S, Halbreich U: Hormones and stress. In Nemeroff CB, Loosen PT (eds): Handbook of Clinical Psychoneuroendocrinology. New York, Guilford Press, 1987

Halmi KA, Ackerman S, Gibbs J, et al: Basic biological overview of the eating disorders. In Meltzer HY (ed): Psychopharmacology: The Third Generation of Progress. New York, Raven Press, 1987

Hauri P: The Sleep Disorders. Kalamazoo, The Upjohn Co, 1982

Hobson JA, McCarley RW, Wyzinski PW: Sleep cycle oscillations: Reciprocal discharge by two brainstem neuronal groups. Science 18:55–58, 1975

Hyman SE: Recent developments in neurobiology. Psychosomatics 29:157–165, 254–263, 373–378, 1988

Janković BD, Marković BM, Spector NH (eds): Neuroimmune Interactions: Proceedings of the Second International Workshop on Neuroimmunomodulation. Ann NY Acad Sci 496:1987

Janowsky DS, El-Yousef MF, Davis JM et al.: A cholinergic-adrenergic hypothesis of mania and depression. Lancet 2:6732–6735, 1972

Janowsky DS, Golden RN, Rapaport M et al: Neurochemistry of depression and mania. In Georgotas A, Cancro R (eds): Depression and Mania. New York, Elsevier, 1988

Jouvet M: Paradoxical sleep: A study of its nature and mechanisms. In Himwich WA, Schade JP (eds): Sleep Mechanisms: Progress in Brain Research. Amsterdam, Elsevier, 1965

Kagan J, Reznick JS, Snidman N: Temperamental variation in response to the unfamiliar. In Krasnegor NA, Blass EM, Hofer MA et al (eds): Perinatal Development: A Psychobiological Perspective. Orlando, Academic Press, 1987

Kandel ER, Schwartz JH (eds): Principles of Neural Science. New York, Elsevier, 1985

Lacks P: Behavioral Treatment for Persistent Insomnia. New York, Pergamon Press, 1987

Luine VN, McEwen BS: Steroid hormone receptors in brain and pituitary: Topography and possible functions. In Adler N, Pfaff D, Goy RW (eds): Handbook of Behavioral Neurobiology, Vol 7: Reproduction. New York, Plenum Press, 1985

Luttge WG: Molecular mechanisms of steroid hormone actions in the brain. In Svare BB (ed): Hormones and Aggressive Behavior. New York, Plenum Press, 1983

Mendelson WB: Human Sleep: Research and Clinical Care. New York, Plenum Press, 1987

Morley JE: Behavioral pharmacology for eating and drinking. In Meltzer HY (ed): Psychopharmacology: The Third Generation of Progress. New York, Raven Press, 1987

Nemeroff CB, Dunn AJ (eds): Peptides, Hormones, and Behavior. New York, SP Medical & Scientific Books, 1984

Pedersen CA, Prange AJ Jr: Effects of drugs and neuropeptides on sexual and maternal behavior in mammals. In Meltzer HY (ed): Psychopharmacology: The Third Generation of Progress. New York, Raven Press, 1987

Pfaff D. Modianos D: Neural Mechanisms of Female Reproductive Behavior. In Adler N, Pfaff D, Goy RW (Eds.): Handbook of Behavioral Neurobiology, Vol 7: Reproduction, pp. 423–493. New York, Plenum Press, 1985

Prange AJ Jr, Wilson IC, Lynn CW et al: L-tryptophan in mania: contribution to a permissive hypothesis of affective disorders. Arch Gen Psychiatry 30:56–62, 1974

Reis DJ: Considerations of some specific behaviors or disease. J Psychiatr Res 11:145–148, 1974

Reite M, Field T (eds): The Psychobiology of Attachment and Separation. Orlando, Academic Press, 1985

Schildkraut J: The catecholamine hypothesis of affective disorders: A review of the supporting evidence. Am J Psychiatry 122:509–522, 1965

Schull J, McEachron L, Adler NT et al: Effects of thyroidectomy, parathyroidectomy and lithium on circadian wheelrunning in rats. Physiol Behav 42:33–39, 1988

Sheard MH: Aggressive and antisocial behavior. In Nemeroff CB, Loosen PT (eds): Handbook of Clinical Psychoneuroendocrinology. New York, Guilford Press, 1987

Sokoloff L: Action of thyroid hormones and cerebral development. Am J Dis Child 114:498, 1967

Squire LR: Memory and Brain. New York, Oxford University Press, 1987

Svare BB (ed): Hormones and Aggressive Behavior. New York, Plenum Press, 1983

Whybrow PC, Prange AJ Jr: A hypothesis of thyroid–catecholamine–receptor interaction. Arch Gen Psychiatry 38:106–113, 1981

12

*Behavioral Genetics**

Miron Baron

Major advances in population genetics, cytogenetics, biochemistry, and molecular biology have heightened the awareness that much of the variation in human behavior may be attributed to complex interactions among hereditary, social, developmental, and environmental factors. Attempts to quantify the relative contributions of genetic and environmental factors in behavior have led, by necessity, to an interdisciplinary framework of scientific thought, which has replaced previously held artificial dichotomies between biologic and psychologic or "nature *versus* nurture." In actuality, both interact to determine behavior and vulnerability to mental illness.

This interdisciplinary framework is consistent with the thesis that has been repeated throughout this text—that human behavior should be understood from multiple perspectives: psychologic, biologic, and sociologic. This chapter will review methods of genetic investigation as they bear on studies of human behavior and mental illness. Areas to be discussed will include the classic methods of family, twin, and adoption studies; pedigree analysis; the study of biologic susceptibility traits and chromosomal markers; and the basic techniques of molecular biology. The implications of recent research for current trends in behavioral and psychiatric genetics will also be discussed.

METHODS OF GENETIC INVESTIGATION

Family, Twin, and Adoption Studies

These strategies constitute the most traditional approach to behavioral genetics. *Family risk studies* attempt to determine the rate of a disorder or trait among the relatives of identified index cases who are themselves affected with the condition. For the most part, family risk studies focus on first-degree relatives, but more distant relatives can be considered as well. Because many behavioral disorders have variable age at onset, the observed familial rates must be adjusted by age. The *age correction*

* Supported by a Research Scientist Development Award MH00176 from the National Institute of Mental Health.

procedure yields expectancy rates or morbidity risks. The risk figures for the various groups of relatives can be compared with the expectancy rates for normal controls or the general population to determine the degree to which the condition being studied has a familial component.

Prediction studies are a variant of the family risk study. Prediction studies are concerned with the identification of behavioral or biologic precursors of the disorder in subjects who are at high risk for the disorder in question by virtue of their being related to specific family constellations, for example, the children of one or two affected parents. These studies are prospective by nature and require a longitudinal approach.

Family risk studies can provide empirical risks for given conditions but are inconclusive with respect to the genetic versus environmental contribution to the observed familial patterns. By contrast, twin and adoption studies offer a way of separating genetic and environmental influences. The use of twins in genetic research is commonly based on comparing the *concordance rate* (when both twins of a pair are affected they are said to be concordant) in monozygotic (or identical) and dizygotic (fraternal) twins. Because monozygotic twins share all their genes whereas dizygotic genes share only 50% of their genetic endowment, a higher concordance rate in the former is taken as evidence that genetic factors are important in etiology. From the concordance rates it is possible to derive the *heritability,* which is a measure of the proportion of the genetic component in the overall familial resemblance. The concordance rate is somewhat dependent on the method of computation. Higher concordances result from the use of the proband method whereby pairs are counted twice if each twin has an ill proband ascertained independently. In contrast, the pair method considers every pair only once. The probandwise concordance (using the proband method) is more widely used, because it can be compared with the population risk.

Adoption studies are based on three principal designs: (1) The *adoptees family method* determines the risk for a given condition to the biologic and adoptive parents of index cases versus controls. A higher risk among the biologic relatives of the index cases compared with the control group points to the importance of genetic factors in the development of the disorder. A higher risk to the adoptive relatives of index cases indicates that rearing influences contribute to etiology. (2) The *adoptees study method* is concerned with the adopted-away children of affected parents. A higher risk for the disorder in this group of adoptees compared with a matched control group indicates that heredity plays an important role in the development of the disorder. (3) The *crossfostering method* compares adoptees who have an affected biologic parent (but whose adoptive parents are normal) with adoptees whose biologic parents are normal but who are reared by an adoptive parent who is affected with the condition under study. Knowledge of the risk for the disorder in the two groups of adoptees is useful in evaluating the relative contributions of heredity and rearing influences. These three designs are summarized in Table 12-1.

Questions of ascertainment (case selection), adequate controls, phenotypic classification (e.g., diagnosis), and zygosity (twin studies) require careful consideration in these research strategies. These and related issues are discussed in greater detail by Rosenthal (1970) and Emery (1976).

Table 12–1 **Adoption Studies**

TYPE	DESIGN	INTERPRETATION
Adoptees family method	Compares the risk for a given condition among the biologic and adoptive parents of index cases (group I and II, respectively) and matched controls.	A higher risk to group I compared with the control group indicates that heredity contributes significantly to the condition studied. An increased risk to group II points to the importance of rearing influences.
Adoptees study method	Determines the risk for a given condition in the adopted-away children of affected parents (group III) versus matched controls.	An increased risk to group III points to the importance of genetic factors.
Crossfostering method	Compares adoptees whose adoptive parents are normal, but who have an affected biologic parent (group IV) with adoptees whose adoptive parents are affected, but whose biologic parents are normal (group V).	A higher risk to group IV compared with group V supports the role of heredity and minimizes the role of environment. An increased risk to group V indicates that the environment plays an important role in the disorder studied.

Pedigree Analysis

The studies described in the preceding section can point to the presence of genetic factors in etiology. However, they do not address the question of the underlying genetic mechanisms. Specifically, the mode of genetic transmission remains unknown. Discerning the mode of inheritance can strengthen the genetic evidence and can be useful both in the design and interpretation of genetic investigations (e.g., genetic linkage studies, see below) and in genetic counseling.

The search for mode of inheritance can be conducted through the use of statistical models that test the fit of specific genetic hypotheses to observed familial patterns. The method most commonly used for hypothesis testing is based on maximum likelihood, with "likelihood" referring to the probability of observing a given data set under a specific hypothesis (Thompson, 1986).

Most behavioral disorders do not have a clear single gene inheritance that conforms to mendelian laws. The deviation from classic mendelian inheritance has led to the introduction of concepts such as *reduced or incomplete penetrance, phenocopies or sporadic cases, and multifactorial-polygenic* effects. *Reduced penetrance* refers to the incomplete manifestation of the trait in persons who have the genotype, usually ascribed to an interaction with other genes or to nongenetic factors. *Phenocopies* are persons who do not carry the genotype but who nevertheless manifest the trait, a phenomenon commonly attributed to other genetic or nongenetic causes. *Multifactorial-polygenic* effects result from a large number of underlying genes and other factors that contribute to the person's liability to a given trait.

The most commonly employed genetic formulations are the single major locus (or gene) (SML) and multifactorial-polygenic (MFP) models. The SML model stipulates that the transmission of a trait or disorder can be explained entirely by a single gene with two alleles resulting in three genotypes, two homozygous states and a heterozygous condition. Several subhypotheses can be tested under the SML model, such as dominant (where one dose of the abnormal allele may bring about the disorder) and recessive (where a double dose of the allele is required) modes of inheritance, as well as contributions from the environment. The parameters of the model are the frequency of the allele, the genotypic means of the three genotypes, the threshold (a point on a liability scale beyond which the penetrance is 100%), and a measure of environmental variance.

The MFP model invokes multiple genes and random environmental factors (each of small and additive effects) that contribute to phenotypic expression. The model incorporates such features as the liability of the general population and that of affected persons, and a threshold (a point on a liability scale above which all persons are affected and below which all are normal); the threshold corresponds to the genetic-environmental load that is sufficient to bring about the phenotype. Nongenetic factors such as cultural influences that are transmitted between generations, and environmental factors that are not transmissible can also be incorporated in the models.

Other models that are thought to address more fully the complex transmission pattern of some behavioral disorders have been devised. These include the (1) "mixed" model that combines single gene transmission, a polygenic background, and environmental effects; (2) the two-locus model that postulates two separate genes with varying degrees of interaction; (3) SML models with more than two alleles; and (4) a polygenic model with graduated effects across the different loci.

One should note that the results of pedigree analysis must always be interpreted with due attention to methodologic issues such as etiologic heterogeneity, epistasis (the interaction between genes), reduced fertility, and assortative mating (the tendency of persons with like behavioral dispositions to marry and reproduce).

Susceptibility Traits and Gene Markers

Pedigree analysis aims to examine the fit of a given data set to a particular genetic model; however, in the absence of additional information on inherited biologic traits or chromosomal markers, statistical formulations cannot uncover the underlying genetic abnormality.

Biologic susceptibility traits derive from etiologic or pathophysiologic hypotheses. They span diverse fields such as biochemistry, neurophysiology, and neuroanatomy, and are thought to be part of the pathway from the genotype to phenotype.

Potential susceptibility traits include neurotransmitter enzymes, receptor proteins, and metabolites; attentional and electroencephalographic measures; and indices on brain scanning such as with positron emission tomography (PET). To qualify as a genetic susceptibility trait, the biologic characteristic must be *heritable and state independent* (stable over time, regardless of clinical state); in addition, it should *segregate* with the disorder in families of affected probands (Reider and Gershon, 1978). Although the specific mode of inheritance need not be known, traits of interest can be incorporated in genetic models that examine the underlying genetics of both the behavioral disorder and the biologic trait.

Gene markers refer to chromosomal loci with known genomic position. They can be assigned to two general categories: (1) classic or conventional markers, such as leukocyte antigens (HLA system); red blood cells antigens (i.e., blood groups); serum proteins; and observable traits, such as color blindness, and (2) the new generation of DNA markers, namely, inherited variations that are detectable by molecular genetic techniques (see below).

The relation of gene markers to a trait or disorder can be determined by linkage analysis (Ott, 1985). Genetic linkage refers to the tendency of chromosomal loci to be coinherited. The distance between loci can be inferred from the recombination frequency (recombination is an exchange of material between homologous chromosomes during meiosis leading to a rearrangement of alleles in the offspring generation). The closer the loci are to each other, the less likely is recombination to occur between them. The odds ratio (the ratio between the probability of there being linkage at a given recombination frequency and that of there being no linkage), more commonly known as the lod score (the logarithm of odds), serves as the principal statistical measure of linkage.

By definition, gene markers have a mendelian mode of inheritance. Unlike susceptibility traits, they need not stem from etiologic or pathophysiologic hypotheses of the disorder being studied. By virtue of their coinheritance with the gene for the disorder they point to its presence and approximate chromosomal location. The most efficient approach to the study of linkage markers requires extended pedigrees with large sibships and high density of illness. An alternative approach, known as the *sibpair method*, is concerned with pairs of affected siblings and does not require multigeneration family pedigrees. Gene markers can also be studied for association with a given trait in the general population; such an association can imply a causal link between the marker locus and the trait.

The demonstration of linkage with gene markers is interpreted as proof of single gene inheritance in the informative pedigrees and can also provide external validation for behavioral assessments. In addition, the study of inherited biologic traits and chromosomal markers can offer a means of addressing the important question of etiologic heterogeneity. For example, linkage or association of a trait with different gene markers in different family pedigrees or populations would suggest the presence of several independent genetic forms.

Molecular Biology

Perhaps the single most important development in human genetics in recent years involves the application of molecular biology techniques. The insights gleaned by these methods can be briefly summarized as follows. First, the new technology can reveal numerous DNA variations that span the entire human genone. In conjunction with linkage analysis, these DNA markers can lead to the chromosomal localization of the genes responsible for many inherited conditions. DNA markers have already been used to map the abnormal genes in several human disorders, such as Huntington's disease, Duchenne muscular dystrophy, X-linked mental retardation, and familial Alzheimer's disease. Second, the structure and function of the abnormal genes can be determined. This, in turn, can shed light on the underlying molecular mechanisms. A case in point is Duchenne muscular dystrophy where the gene has been characterized and its protein product identified. Third, the molecular biology approach can increase the precision of genetic diagnosis and might lead to improved preventive and treatment measures. The chromosomal mapping and the gene defects for some neurobehavioral disorders are summarized in Table 12-2.

DNA markers, also known as restriction-fragment-length polymorphisms (RFLPs), are detected by a method known as Southern hybridization whereby a DNA molecule digested by restriction enzymes (endonucleases) is hybridized to a genetic probe specific for the DNA segment suspected to be variant. The resultant pattern of DNA fragments that contain complementary genetic information can then be displayed by autoradiography and tested for linkage with presumed genes for a given disorder. Localization of the gene to a specific chromosomal region can be inferred from prior evidence that the marker is on a particular chromosome, or by physical methods such as somatic cell hybridization.

As noted earlier, a linked marker merely points to the approximate chromosomal location of the gene of interest but is not likely to contain it. Several molecular genetic methods have been developed to bridge the distance between RFLPs and the putative disease gene. These include chromosome "walking" and "jumping" and pulsed-field gradient electrophoresis. Once the DNA segment containing the gene has been identified and its structure (nucleotide sequence) has been determined, both the messenger RNA and the associated protein product can be characterized according to the principles of transcription and translation. Conversely, knowledge of the gene product can lead to the identification of the gene itself. Namely, the DNA sequence corresponding to the nucleotide code of the protein can be synthesized, cloned, and used as a probe to screen for the DNA segment that include the relevant gene. This method has been used successfully to identify the genes for the hormones insulin and erythropoietin, coagulation factor VIII, and the globin chains, among other protein-

Table 12-2 **Genetic Mapping of Neurobehavioral Disorders**

DISORDER	CHROMOSOMAL LOCATION	GENE DEFECT	REFERENCE
Tay-Sachs	15q22-25	Hexosaminidase (α chain)	Gilbert et al, 1975
Duchenne	Xp21	Deletions Dystrophin	Murray et al, 1982 Hoffman et al, 1987
Huntington's	4p16	Unknown	Gusella et al, 1983
Lesch-Nyhan	Xq27	HPRT	Nussbaum et al, 1983
Wilson's	13q14	Unknown	Frydman et al, 1985
Neurofibromatosis	17cen	Unknown	Barker et al, 1987
Manic depression (Bipolar disorder)	Xq27-28	Unknown	Baron et al, 1987 Mendlewicz et al, 1987
	11p15	Unknown	Egeland et al, 1987
Alzheimer's	21q21	Unknown	St. George-Hyslop et al, 1987

Note: q,p: the long and the short arms of the chromosome, respectively; cen: the centromere; preceding these notations are the chromosome numbers; following the q,p notations are the numbers of the chromosomal bands.

encoding genes. In behavioral disorders, such genes, also known as candidate genes, include genomic regions that code for neurotransmitter receptors and enzymes.

The availability of tightly linked DNA markers or gene-specific probes can provide powerful and accurate tools for genetic diagnosis of a given trait or disorder. These tools can also be used for risk prediction (and thereby genetic counseling) by the detection of carriers of abnormal alleles. Inherited disorders where these methods are being applied include sickle-cell disease, thalassemia, phenylketonuria, and Lesch-Nyhan syndrome. The characterization of genes and their products can lead to specific drugs of a therapeutic or preventive nature; in some instances (e.g., insulin, erythropoietin, and the antihemophilic factor VIII), the product itself can be used for treatment purposes. Eventually, the replacement of defective genes with normal clones could be contemplated. The clinical applications of molecular biology techniques to some medical disorders are listed in Table 12-3.

The principles that underlie the new DNA technology and its implications for psychiatry are reviewed in detail elsewhere (Gurling, 1985; Martin, 1987; Baron and Rainer, 1988).

Phenotypic Classification

An accurate definition of the phenotype is crucial in behavioral genetics. The current emphasis on structured, criterion-based approaches to the assessment of behavior has improved reliability and consensus between investigators and practitioners. "Ill" versus "well" dichotomies largely depend on descriptive diagnostic practices in the absence of external validating measures. The question of external validity pertains to the likely heterogeneity both within and among diagnostic categories. Additional information, such as biochemical measures, can aid in refining behavioral and psychiatric nosology and lead to the demarcation of homogeneous subgroups, which, in turn, may enhance the prospects of genetic studies. Conversely, data on biologic vulnerability traits, linked genetic markers, and differential familial loading can aid in the classification of behavioral conditions by circumventing the uncertainties inherent in descriptive diagnostic phenomenology, which is largely based on behavioral signs and symptoms.

Table 12-3 **Clinical Applications of Molecular Biology Techniques**

	APPLICATION	
DISORDER	**Risk prediction**	**Treatment***
Sickle cell anemia	+	
Thalassemia	+	
Phenylketonuria	+	
Lesch-Nyhan	+	
Cystic fibrosis	+	
Diabetes mellitus		+ (Insulin)
Hemophilia	+	+ (Coagulation factor VIII)

*Therapeutic products produced by molecular biology techniques.

Genes and Environment

Although the main emphasis in this review is on the genotypic determination of inherited conditions, *the environment can play an important role in the pathway from genotype to phenotype.* The environment shapes and modifies the transmission and expression of the genetic makeup, at all levels, from the cellular to the behavioral. This regulation may be in the form of activation or suppression of the underlying genetic mechanisms.

The contribution of the environment to phenotypic expression in most behavioral disorders can be readily evidenced by the incomplete concordance in identical monozygotic twins. To some extent, this contribution can be quantified by statistical measures, such as heritability, and the incorporation of reduced penetrance, sporadic cases or phenocopies, multifactorial influences, and other types of environmental variance in the genetic analysis of pedigrees. The study of biologic inherited traits may provide a more definitive approach to the elucidation of gene–environment interaction. For example, if a specific environmental factor operates in conjunction with the underlying genotypic makeup, this factor will more likely be present in the affected than in the unaffected relatives when the illness in both groups of subjects is linked to a particular genetic marker. A complementary approach, which falls under the rubric of high-risk paradigms, would be to study prospectively putative environmental factors in persons who carry the genetic marker and are therefore at risk for developing the disorder.

PSYCHIATRIC GENETICS

The Major Psychoses

Family, Twin, and Adoption Studies

The major mental disorders, schizophrenia and bipolar disorder, (manic–depressive illness), occupy center stage in psychiatric genetics because both conditions run in families. In the recent well-designed studies, the morbidity risk for schizophrenia in first-degree relatives of schizophrenic patients is 3% to 6% as compared with 0.2% to 0.6% in the general population. The corresponding rates for bipolar disorder are 4% to 9% and 0.2% to 0.5%, respectively. (When major depression, also known as unipolar major depressive disorder and thought to be a milder manifestation of the bipolar genotype in families of bipolar patients, is included in the bipolar "spectrum," the risk to first-degree relatives of bipolar probands is 13% to 35% versus 5% to 8% in the general population.) The variable rates among studies are attributable in part to different diagnostic practices and other methodologic issues, such as sampling scheme. For example, the rate at which schizophrenia is diagnosed can vary several fold depending on how narrow or how broad the criteria are (Baron, Gruen, Kane et al, 1985). Similarly, the familial rate of major depressive disorder can be reduced considerably by requiring "impairment incapacitation" as an essential inclusion criterion (Gershon et al, 1982). It is of interest, however, that, despite the varied methodology, the relative risk (the ratio of the risk to patients' relatives to the risk to relatives of normal controls) is high (approximately 10 to 20 for schizophrenia;

17 to 20 for bipolar disorder), indicating significant familial aggregation. When major depression is considered independently of bipolar disorder, the risk to first-degree relatives of patients with major depression is 11% to 18% compared with 5% to 6% in controls; the relative risk is 2 to 3. Thus, the evidence for familial clustering is not as impressive as that for schizophrenia and bipolar disorder but is nevertheless significant. The results overall support earlier family studies dating to the beginning of the century. Morbidity risk data on schizophrenia and mood disorders are presented in Table 12-4.

Twin studies have consistently shown higher concordance in both mood disorders and schizophrenia rates in monozygotic than in dizygotic twins, consistent with a genetic hypothesis. The ratio of monozygotic versus dizygotic concordance rates is approximately 4:1 for schizophrenia and bipolar disorder, although the absolute rates vary among studies. The heritability estimates based on these data are 30% to 50% and 60% to 80% for schizophrenia and bipolar disorder, respectively. As with the family risk data, the evidence for a genetic component in major depression is not as strong; the monozygotic:dizygotic ratio in concordance rates is only 2:1. It is noteworthy that an appreciable proportion of the monozygotic twin pairs are discordant for schizophrenia and bipolar disorder (approximately 50% and 20%, respectively), pointing to the important role of environmental factors in the pathogenesis of these disorders.

Using both the adoptees family method and the adoptees study method, adoption studies have reinforced the notion that genetic factors play an important role in schizophrenia and major mood disorders. In addition, a crossfostering study has shown that the adopted-away offspring of schizophrenic parents are at increased risk for the illness compared with the adopted-away offspring of nonschizophrenic par-

Table 12-4 **Morbidity Risk for Schizophrenia and Mood Disorders**

DISORDER	MORBIDITY RISK IN FIRST-DEGREE RELATIVES (%)	MORBIDITY RISK IN RELATIVES OF CONTROLS (%)	RELATIVE RISK	REFERENCE*
Schizophrenia	5.8	0.6	9.7	Baron, et al, 1985
	3.7	0.2	18.5	Kendler et al, 1985
Bipolar disorder†	3.9	0.2	19.5	Tsuang et al, 1980
	4.5(8.6)	0.0(0.5)	(17.2)	Gershon et al, 1982
	3.9(8.1)	No data		Andreasen et al, 1987
Major depression	11.0	4.8	2.3	Tsuang et al, 1980
	17.5	5.9	3.0	Weissman et al, 1984
	22.8	No data		Andreasen et al, 1987

*The studies cited fulfill modern criteria for genetic-family investigations. They represent four large scale research efforts: the Iowa 500 (Tsuang et al, 1980; Kendler et al, 1985); the New York-Columbia University Study (Baron, et al, 1985); the NIMH Study (Gershon et al, 1982); the New Haven-Yale University Study (Weissman et al, 1984); and the NIMH Collaborative Study (Andreasen et al, 1987).
†Bipolar disorder has two variants: bipolar I, the more severe illness form (depressive and manic episodes), and bipolar II (depression and hypomania). The figures in parenthesis are the combined morbid risks for bipolar I and bipolar II disorders; the other risk figures are for bipolar I disorder.

ents. The adopted-away offspring of normal biologic parents reared by schizophrenic parents showed no increase in the risk for schizophrenia. This study has been interpreted as evidence against a strong environmental component in the etiology of schizophrenia.

Taken together, family, twin, and adoption studies support the role of heredity in the major psychoses. A spectrum of conditions thought to be related to the "core" disorders have also been considered in the genetic framework. For example, some forms of schizoaffective illness (a mixed pattern of schizophrenic and affective symptoms), schizotypal, and paranoid personality disorders are believed to belong in the schizophrenia spectrum, whereas other subtypes of schizoaffective disorder and some forms of alcoholism, sociopathy, anxiety, eating disorders, and minor disorders with affective coloring such as cyclothymia may be related to the affective spectrum. These studies are reviewed in detail elsewhere (Andreasen et al, 1987; Baron et al, 1985; Gershon et al, 1982; Gottesman and Shields, 1982; Kendler et al, 1985; Weissman et al, 1984).

Pedigree Analysis

Numerous applications of genetic models to family data have been reported, including the SML and MFP models and variations thereof. Despite the advances in statistical genetics, the analysis of clinical genetic data has not led to consistent results. Based on these studies, the mode of inheritance of either schizophrenia or major mood disorders remains elusive. The inconsistency among studies has been attributed to variations in the methods for data collection (sampling scheme, diagnosis) and analysis (mathematical formulations) and to the likely heterogeneous nature of these disorders. The prevailing wisdom is that the analysis of familial patterns using statistical genetic techniques in not likely to unravel the underlying genetic mechanism without the added benefit of biologic susceptibility traits and chromosomal markers. Detailed reviews of this topic are provided by Baron (1986) and by Goldin and Gershon (1983).

Biologic Susceptibility Traits and Gene Markers

A large array of biologic variables, including biogenic amine enzymes and metabolites, neuroreceptor sensitivity, neuromuscular function, immune response, attentional and electrophysiologic measures, and brain morphology have been examined as potential vulnerability traits for schizophrenia and mood disorders. As has been noted in recent reviews of this area (Baron, 1986), some of these traits, such as attentional (Continuous Performance Test and eye tracking), neurophysiologic (auditory evoked response), and brain morphology measures (brain ventricular size) appear promising, but the data are as yet not adequate to arrive at firm conclusions. In bipolar affective disorder (manic-depression), alterations of the GABA (CSF GABA and GABA-transaminase) and cholinergic (muscarinic receptor sensitivity) systems show promise as elaborate potential susceptibility traits. For example, induction of REM sleep by the muscarinic agonist arecoline has been claimed to distinguish euthymic bipolar patients from controls, and is concordant in monozygotic twins, suggesting genetic control of this trait. The information available to support this theory fully is incomplete (Goldin and Gershon, 1983). Based on the available evidence, none of the proposed biologic traits qualifies as a major factor in the genetic susceptibility to the major psychoses.

Potential breakthroughs in this area have come about by means of linkage studies with chromosomal markers. Baron and associates (1987) reported close linkage of bipolar affective illness to the X chromosome markers color blindness and glucose-6-phosphate dehydrogenase (G6PD) activity, thus supporting earlier suggestions that a gene on the distal long arm of the X chromosome plays a role in a subset of bipolar disorder (see Baron et al, 1981; Risch and Baron, 1982). Subsequently, Mendlewicz and associates (1987) provided further supportive evidence for the X-linkage hypothesis by demonstrating linkage between bipolar illness and a DNA marker associated with the factor IX (F9) locus on the long arm of the X chromosome. Another group of investigators (Egeland et al, 1987) reported linkage between two DNA markers on the short arm of chromosome 11, the Harvey-ras (HRAS1) and insulin loci, and bipolar illness in an Old Order Amish pedigree. Consistent with the notion that bipolar disorder is a heterogeneous group of disorders, it appears that there are at least two genetic forms of the illness tied to different chromosomes. Because other pedigrees do not show linkage to either set of markers (Risch and Baron, 1982; Baron and Rainer, 1988), the generality of these findings remains to be determined; they nevertheless can be construed as major steps toward unraveling the molecular mechanisms of some illness forms. A similar strategy was applied to schizophrenia where linkage was reported between the illness and DNA markers on chromosome 5 (Sherrington et al, 1988); this linkage study used as an indicator an earlier report on a cytogenetic abnormality, a balanced translocation between chromosomes 5 and 1 in a family segregating schizophrenia (Bassett et al, 1988). Ongoing studies using a large array of gene markers and other molecular biology techniques seek to expand and replicate these findings and to identify other genetic mechanisms that underlie the major psychoses.

Other Mental Conditions

Other psychiatric disorders with possible genetic components include organic mental disorders, alcoholism, behavioral conditions associated with chromosome anomalies, and nonpsychotic states such as panic, eating disorders (bulimia nervosa and anorexia nervosa), agoraphobia, somatization disorder (Briquet's syndrome) and some of the personality disorders, and several neuropsychiatric disorders.

Linkage studies with DNA markers have shown the chromosomal sites for three organic mental conditions with neurologic and behavioral features: Huntington's disease (chromosome 4), Lesch-Nyhan disorder (the X chromosome), and a familial form of Alzheimer's disease (chromosome 21). Huntington's and familial Alzheimer's disease follow a dominant mode of inheritance whereas Lesch-Nyhan syndrome is inherited as an X-linked recessive trait.

Alcoholism appears to have a genetic component as evidenced by family, twin, and adoption studies, but the mode of inheritance has not been established. The role of genetic factors seems clearer in males than in females. Environmental factors have also been invoked. In some instances, alcoholism is thought to be related to affective disorder and antisocial personality, but the precise relation is unclear. It is of interest that familial alcoholics are distinguishable from the nonfamilial cases with respect to the severity of alcohol-related problems (more severe), onset of physical dependence (earlier), and treatment outcome (poorer). The two groups of alcoholics also differ on some physiologic and endocrine measures. These findings point to the heterogeneous nature of this condition.

Chromosome anomalies marked by behavioral features chiefly involve the sex chromosomes. These are Klinefelter's syndrome (XXY karyotype) and the XYY aberration. The behavioral manifestations in Klinefelter's syndrome can range from mild personality changes to delinquency to psychosis-like behavior. The XYY anomaly seems to occur more often than expected among delinquent and criminally inclined persons who show episodic violence and other forms of aggression and impulsive behavior. The interaction between the extra sex chromosome and other factors in the development of these behavioral conditions is not well understood.

Genetic contributions to panic disorder, eating disorders, agoraphobia, somatization disorder, and schizotypal, borderline, and antisocial personality disorders have been surmised from family, twin, and adoption studies, although these studies are not as comprehensive as those carried out on the major psychoses. In some studies, the familial pattern of panic disorder is consistent with single gene inheritance. Panic disorder, eating disorders, agoraphobia, borderline personality disorder, and antisocial personality disorder appear to share a comorbidity with mood disorders, whereas schizotypal personality disorder is thought to be part of the schizophrenia spectrum. The biologic and genetic basis of these conditions and their possible relation to the major psychiatric disorders require further elucidation.

The genetics of the disorders reviewed in this section are discussed further by Rainer (1985). Morbidity risk data on some of these disorders are presented in Table 12-5.

The Genetics of Personality

Although the focus of interest in behavior genetics, especially within the framework of psychiatry, has been on psychopathology, personality is an increasingly important area of inquiry. Most of the evidence on the role of heredity in shaping

Table 12–5 **Morbidity Risk for Some Psychiatric Disorders**

DISORDER	MORBIDITY RISK IN FIRST-DEGREE RELATIVES (%)	MORBIDITY RISK IN RELATIVES OF CONTROLS (%)	RELATIVE RISK	REFERENCE
Alcoholism	16.1	1.6	10.1	Pitts and Winokur, 1966
Panic disorder	17.3	1.8	9.6	Crowe, 1985
Anorexia nervosa	2.3	0.5	4.6	Strober et al, 1985
Agoraphobia	11.6	4.2	2.8	Crowe, 1985
Briquet's syndrome (somatization disorder)	7.7	2.5	3.1	Cloninger et al, 1986

personality stems from twin studies. In Loehlin and Nichols' (1976) pioneering study, a wide array of personality traits measured in identical versus fraternal twins were shown to have substantial heritabilities of about 50%. No effect of shared environment was detected. In a study of identical twins reared apart, Bouchard and McGue (1981) confirmed the high heritability rates for personality traits and showed that the correlations for identical twins reared apart and those reared together were very much alike, indicating that the contribution of common environment to the similarity between twins reared together is fairly small compared with genetic influences. Of interest are the findings that genes also seem to influence social attitudes and that some environmental influences are genetically mediated.

Taken together, these studies suggest that genes play a major role in determining personality traits. Compared with the person's genetic endowment, the common environment appears to exert a negligible influence on personality. The results are somewhat reminiscent of the substantial heritability shown for various cognitive abilities as measured in IQ tests. The similarity carries over to the controversy that such findings evoke, partly owing to potential social and political implications. In the absence of a clear biologic substrate, questions of the nature and interpretation of personality measurement scales, prenatal and perinatal factors, and gene–environment interaction will continue to arouse debate and stimulate further investigation in this complex area. This subject matter is discussed in greater detail by Loehlin and Nichols (1976) and by Plomin and Daniels (1987).

IMPLICATIONS

The burgeoning field of human genetics has yielded important insights into several conditions affecting behavior. Applications of the classic genetic methodologies, involving family, twin, and adoption studies, underscore the role of heredity in various behavioral manifestations ranging from personality traits to severe psychopathology. Studies with biologic susceptibility traits and genetic linkage markers, in conjunction with molecular biology techniques, have advanced our knowledge as to the specific genetic mechanisms that underlie some mental conditions. Of particular note is the identification of two putative genes for bipolar affective illness (manic depression) located in two different genomic regions, the X chromosome and chromosome 11. These findings, coupled with the rapid advance in genetic methodologies, hold great promise for the elucidation of etiology and pathophysiology, the identification and characterization of abnormal genes, refinement of phenotypic classification, disentangling gene–environment interaction, risk prediction, and, eventually, improved prevention and treatment measures.

ANNOTATED BIBLIOGRAPHY

Baron M, Rainer JD: Molecular genetics and human disease: Implications for modern psychiatric research and practice. Br J Psychiatry 152:741–753, 1988

Reviews the principles and potential applications of molecular biology techniques in medicine and psychiatry.

Emery EH: Methodology in Medical Genetics, New York, Churchill Livingstone, 1976
  Reviews statistical methods and research designs in medical genetics.

Goldin LR, Gershon ES: Association and linkage studies of genetic marker loci in major psychiatric disorders. Psychiatr Dev 4:387–418, 1983
  Reviews strategies and findings in studies of schizophrenia and affective disorders using genetic linkage markers and biologic susceptibility traits.

Rainer JD: Genetics and Psychiatry. In Kaplan HI, Sadock BJ (eds): Comprehensive Textbook of Psychiatry, 4th ed. Baltimore, Williams & Wilkins, 1985
  Overall review of genetic theories and findings in psychiatry.

Rosenthal D: Genetic Theory and Abnormal Behavior. New York, McGraw-Hill, 1970
  Reviews classic research designs and methodologies in psychiatric genetics.

REFERENCES

Andreasen NC, Rice J, Endicott J et al: Familial rates of affective disorder: A report from the National Institute of Mental Health Collaborative Study. Arch Gen Psychiatry 44:461–469, 1987

Barker D, Wright, E, Nguyen L et al: Gene for von Recklinghausen neurofibromatosis is in the pericentromeric region of chromosome 17. Science 236:1100–1102, 1987

Baron M: Genetics of schizophrenia. I. Familial patterns and mode of inheritance. Biol Psychiatry 21:1051–1066, 1986

Baron M: Genetics of schizophrenia. II. Vulnerability traits and gene markers. Biol Psychiatry 21:1189–1121, 1986

Baron M, Gruen R, Kane J et al: Modern genetic criteria and the genetics of schizophrenia. Am J Psychiatry 142:697–701, 1985b

Baron M, Gruen R, Rainer JD et al: A family study of schizophrenia and normal control probands: Implications for the spectrum concept of schizophrenia. Am J Psychiatry 142:447–454, 1985

Baron M, Rainer JD: Molecular genetics and human disease: Implications for modern psychiatric research and practice. Br J Psychiatry 152:741–753, 1988

Baron M, Rainer JD, Risch N: X-linkage in bipolar affective illness: Perspectives on genetic heterogeneity, pedigree analysis and the X-chromosome map. J Affective Disord 3:141–157, 1981

Baron M, Risch N, Hamburger R et al: Genetic linkage between X-chromosome markers and bipolar affective illness. Nature 326:289–292, 1987

Bassett AS, McGillivray BC, Jones BD et al: Partial trisomy chromosome 5 cosegregating with schizophrenia. Lancet 8589:799–801, 1988

Bouchard TJ Jr, McGue M: Familial studies of intelligence: A review. Science 212:1055–1059, 1981

Cloninger CR, Martin RL, Guze SB et al: A prospective follow-up and family study of somatization in men and women. Am J Psychiatry 143:873–878, 1986

Crowe RR: The genetics of panic disorder and agoraphobia. Psychiatr Dev 2:171–186, 1985

Egeland JA, Gerhard DS, Pauls DL et al: Bipolar affective disorder linked to DNA markers on chromosome 11. Nature 325:783–787, 1987

Emery EH: Methodology in Medical Genetics. New York, Churchill Livingstone, 1976

Frydman M, Bonne-Tamir B, Farrer L et al: Assignment of the gene for Wilson's disease to chromosome 13: Linkage to the esterase D locus. Proc Natl Acad Sci USA 82:1819–1821, 1985

Gershon ES, Hamovit J, Guroff JJ et al: A family study of schizoaffective, bipolar I, bipolar II, unipolar, and normal control probands. Arch Gen Psychiatry 39:1157–1167, 1982

Gilbert F, Kucherlapati R, Creagan RP et al: Tay-Sachs and Sandhoff's diseases: The assignment of genes for hexosaminidases A and B to individual human chromosomes. Proc Natl Acad Sci USA 72:263–267, 1975

Goldin LR, Gershon ES: Association and linkage studies of genetics marker loci in major psychiatric disorders. Psychiatric Dev 4:387–418, 1983

Gottesman II, Shields J: Schizophrenia: The Epigenetic Puzzle. Cambridge, Cambridge University Press, 1982

Gurling HMD: Application of molecular biology to mental illness. Analysis of genonic DNA and brain mRNA. Psychiatric Dev 3:257–273, 1985

Gusella JF, Wexler NS, Conneally PM et al: A polymorphic DNA marker genetically linked to Huntington's disease. Nature 306:234–238, 1983

Hoffman EP, Brown RH, Kunkel LM: Dystrophin: The protein product of the Duchenne muscular dystrophy lucus. Cell 51:919–928, 1987

Kendler KS, Gruenberg AM, Tsuang MT: Psychiatric illness in first-degree relatives of schizophrenic and surgical control patients. Arch Gen Psychiatry 42:770–779, 1985

Loehlin JC, Nichols RC: Heredity, Environment and Personality. Austin, University of Texas Press, 1976

Martin JB: Molecular genetics: Applications to the clinical neurosciences. Science 238:765–772, 1987

Mendlewicz J, Simon P, Sevy S et al: Polymorphic DNA marker on X-chromosome and manic depression. Lancet 8544:1230–1232, 1987

Murray JM, Davies KE, Harper PS et al: Linkage relationship of a cloned DNA sequence on the short arm of the X chromosome to Duchenne muscular dystrophy. Nature 300:69–71, 1982

Nussbaum R, Brennand J, Chinault C et al: Molecular analysis of the hypoxanthine phosphoribosyltransferase locus. In Caskey CT, White RL (eds): Recombinant DNA Application to Human Disease, pp 81–90. New York, Cold Spring Harbor Laboratory, 1983

Ott J: Analysis of Human Genetic Linkage. Baltimore, The Johns Hopkins University Press, 1985

Pitts FN, Winokur G: Affective disorder. VII. Alcoholism and affective disorder. J Psychiatr Res 4:37–50, 1966

Plomin R, Daniels D: Why are children in the same family so different from one another? Behav Brain Sci 10:1–60, 1987

Rainer JD: Genetics and psychiatry. In Kaplan HI, Sadock BJ (eds): Comprehensive Textbook of Psychiatry, 4th ed. Baltimore, Williams & Wilkins, 1985

Rieder RO, Gershon ES: Genetic strategies in biological psychiatry. Arch Gen Psychiatry 35:866–873, 1978

Risch N, Baron M: X-linkage and genetic heterogeneity in bipolar-related major affective illness: Reanalysis of linkage data. Ann Hum Genet 46:153–166, 1982

Rosenthal D: Genetic Theory and Abnormal Behavior. New York, McGraw-Hill, 1970

St. George-Hyslop PH, Tanzi RE, Polinsky RJ et al: The genetic defect causing familial Alzheimer's disease maps on chromosome 4. Science 235:885–889, 1987

Sherrington R, Brynjolfsson J, Petursson H, et al: Localization of a susceptibility locus for schizophrenia on chromosome 5. Nature 336:164–167, 1988

Strober M, Morell W, Burroughs J et al: A controlled family study of anorexia nervosa. J Psychiatr Res 19:239–246, 1985

Thompson EA: Pedigree Analysis in Human Genetics. Baltimore, The John Hopkins University Press, 1986

Tsuang MT, Winokur G, Crowe R: Morbidity risks of schizophrenia and affective disorders among first degree relatives of patients with schizophrenia, mania, depression and surgical conditions. Br J Psychiatry 137:497–504, 1980

Weissman MM, Gershon ES, Kidd KK et al: Psychiatric disorders in the relatives of probands with affective disorders: The Yale University-National Institute of Mental Health Collaborative Study. Arch Gen Psychiatry 41:13–21, 1984

Clinical Applications

5

13

Supportive Psychologic Care of the Medically Ill: A Synthesis of the Biopsychosocial Approach in Medical Care

Stephen A. Green

This entire text has led up to this concluding chapter, which will address how a knowledge of human behavior contributes to the compassionate psychologic and emotional care of patients, focusing on the critical importance of the doctor–patient relationship. In addition, the basic themes of the biopsychosocial model introduced by Cohen-Cole will again be discussed in light of the multiple perspectives that have been presented in previous chapters as well as its practical application in patient care.

THE DOCTOR–PATIENT RELATIONSHIP AND THE BIOPSYCHOSOCIAL MODEL

The interaction between physician and patient is too often an impersonal, mechanistic encounter due to their shared cause-and-effect mindset concerning the diagnosis and treatment of specific symptoms. Medical practice has long been considered an exercise of determining etiology, prescribing the indicated therapeutic regimen, and monitoring the patient's response, a perspective that highlights intellectual problem solving while neglecting central emotional factors that influence the course of an illness. This approach is based on the biomedical model, discussed in Chapter 1, which is a parochial viewpoint rooted in the Renaissance notion of a mind–body duality.

A strictly biomedical model compromises patient care by supporting the inaccurate belief in a mind–body dichotomy and perpetuating the simplistic notion that complex pathophysiologic phenomena are ultimately explained by a single principle (Engel, 1977). For example, it defines peptic ulcer disease as the anatomical end product of gastric hypersecretion, implying that definitive treatment consists solely of appropriate medication and dietary restrictions. Undoubtedly, these are necessary measures; however, they may be no more than palliative if medical interventions fail to address specific psychosocial issues affecting and affected by the patient's ulcer. The biomedical model promotes "the physician's preoccupation with the body and disease and the corresponding neglect of the patient as a person," and it fails to consider "how the patient behaves and what he reports about himself and his life [because] it does not include the patient and his attributes as a person, a human being" (Engel, 1980). In sum, the biomedical model suggests that treating one's specific organic pathology is synonymous with treating the patient, which ignores the fundamental truth that all illness simultaneously affects the mind and body.

Every patient must be seen as a singular human being if medical care is to be appropriate and effective. This requires application of the biopsychosocial model, a theoretic construct that assesses a person within the distinctive context of supports and stressors affecting his/her daily functioning. As discussed in Chapters 1 and 2, an understanding of the interplay among one's organic pathology, intrapsychic life, and the positive and negative impact of his/her external environment is important for several reasons.

First, the genesis and exacerbation of an illness (Rahe, 1973), even mechanisms of sudden death (Engel, 1968; Reich et al, 1981), are affected by numerous psychosocial factors. Second, extensive scientific research has demonstrated mind–body interactions in specific physiologic, endocrinologic, and immunologic processes, and in generalized stress reactions, work that has spawned related clinical investigations. Third, one's willingness and ability to cooperate in prescribed care is often affected by a myriad of nonphysical factors, including intrapsychic issues (Lipowski, 1975) and sociocultural norms (Zola, 1963). Finally, physical illness itself can precipitate a variety of abnormal psychologic states that adversely influence the disease process, or reach a degree of severity so intense that they become more threatening to the patients than their original organic pathology (Green, 1985).

The preceding discussion demonstrates that optimal medical treatment requires the biopsychosocial treatment approach, which Engel (1980) conceptualizes by interposing the patient between two hierarchies that combine to form an overall hierarchy of natural systems (Fig. 13-1). The person is at the same time at the highest level of an organismic hierarchy, which ranges from subatomic particles through the nervous system, and the lowest stratum of a social hierarchy, which ranges from a two-person system to the biosphere. These two hierarchies are in a dynamic equilibrium, because every system (e.g., cells or two-person) within each hierarchy is a distinctive whole that is simultaneously interrelated with every other system. Consequently, disturbances at any system level can alter any other system level; through feedback controls, they may modify or aggravate the system originally affected. Engel presents a clinical case to illustrate the workings of this medical model, which, as discussed

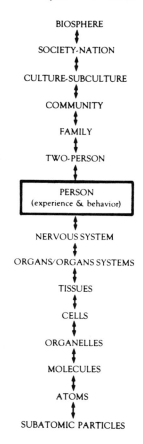

Figure 13–1. *Hierarchy of natural systems. (Reprinted with permission from Engel G: The clinical application of the bio-psychosocial model. Am J Psychiatr 137:535–544, 1980)*

below, is ultimately based on the clinician's appreciation of the meaning of illness to an individual patient.

ILLNESS DYNAMICS

The biopsychosocial model demonstrates that nonphysical issues are part and parcel of the disease process and can transform the same organic pathology into vastly different illnesses in different patients. Consider that premise in terms of the following two men who suffered similar myocardial damage from a heart attack. Their histories highlight the many psychosocial factors that influenced when and to what degree they became ill, as well as their response to treatment and ultimate prognosis.

TWO CASE STUDIES

Mr. A, a 40-year-old widower, is a midlevel manager diligently working his way up the corporate ladder while supporting three young children. In addition to family responsibilities and professional obligations, he devotes considerable time to a flourishing relationship with a coworker he hopes to marry. His past history is significant for the unexpected death of his mother from a cerebrovascular accident when he was 13 years old.

In contrast, Mr. B is a 63-year-old executive vice-president on the threshold of retirement, a husband of 40 years eagerly anticipating more leisure time with his wife and grown family. He has consistently enjoyed good health; his only major medical event, a cholecystectomy, was a scheduled procedure that caused minimal disruption to his life. Although Mr. B's father died at the age of 70 of metastatic carcinoma, his mother, siblings, wife, and children are all in good health.

After surviving the immediate threat of death from myocardial infarctions, each man exhibited a unique reaction to his damaged myocardium. Mr. A's initial anxiety was progressively supplanted by a growing sense of helplessness. The death of his mother at an early age generally sensitized him to loss, and specifically affected his psychologic development by enhancing dependent yearnings. Moreover, because she died of a cardiovascular illness, he more closely associated his heart disease with her sudden demise. He also identified with his childrens' concerns, as he had experienced the same anxiety that comes from recognizing that one's future is largely dependent on the welfare of a single parent. Significant feelings of anger and depression arose when he considered the impact of his illness on the course of his career and the developing relationship with his girlfriend. All these factors contributed to a heightened affective response to his heart attack, making it more difficult to resolve those intense feelings and fostering an increasing helplessness and dependency on those around him.

Mr. B, on the other hand, was also angered and depressed by his bad luck, but basically because it occurred at a stage of life primarily reserved for relaxation. However, the intensity of his feelings was tempered by the knowledge that his family was grown, that his loving spouse had consistently provided reassurance and support when needed, that he had already realized his professional ambitions, and that he was financially secure. For these reasons, Mr. B. more easily worked through the emotions stirred by his physical impairment and quickly returned to his premorbid level of functioning.

Although these patients suffered the exact same anatomical and physiologic pathology, each reacted to the period of ill health in a highly distinctive fashion due to the impact of idiosyncratic psychologic and social issues. Mr. A's heart attack precipitated a considerable emotional upheaval, marked by anxiety, depression, and helplessness, because it reawakened traumatic memories and painful feelings related to his mother's death, and he experienced it as a significant threat to many important aspects of his current life. Although some concerns were more imagined than real, they interfered with his ability to accurately assess and, consequently, accept the effect of an uncomplicated heart attack on his daily existence.

The relationship among one's biologic status (e.g., genetic constitution and physical pathology), emotional makeup, and the supports and stresses of a social matrix constitutes that person's *illness dynamics* (Green, 1985). This idiosyncratic standard, which represents the patient's understanding of a specific disease during a particular period of life, is portrayed schematically in Figure 13-2. The shaded area defines the distinctive interrelationship between the conscious and unconscious psychosocial factors affecting and affected by a patient's biologic status (Table 13-1), which predisposes to certain diseases and protects against others. Illness dynamics incline one to assess all illness-related information in light of singular values, wishes, needs, and fears, *ultimately causing the patient to perceive, assess, and defend against the loss of health in a highly subjective manner.* As demonstrated by the preceding case histories, this may significantly affect the patient's ability to cope with disease.

Both Mr. A and Mr. B shared the common organic pathology of an uncomplicated myocardial infarction; however, the most significant biologic component of Mr. A's illness dynamics was his mother's genetic endowment. The affected organ system also bore special meaning, raising doubts that he would have sufficient strength and stamina to devote to a rising career or to meet the emotional—and sexual—demands of a second marriage. Mr. A's excessive dependency was an important psychologic component of his illness response, a probable legacy of the early loss of his mother that was intensified by the death of his wife. And his stage in the lifecycle contributed to his significant depression, because the heart attack occurred at a time when persons are more focused on the challenges and joys of life than the fear of death. The predominant social determinants of Mr. A's illness dynamics concerned family relationships. His heart disease had considerable effect on his young children whose welfare depended on his wage-earning ability, a lack of flexibility in the family system that placed greater stress on him to recuperate rapidly and completely. All of these issues were in contrast to the impact of a heart attack on Mr. B's life. His physical resilience,

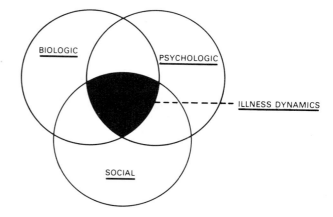

Figure 13–2. *Illness dynamics. (Reprinted with permission from Green S: Mind and Body: The Psychology of Physical Illness. Washington, DC, American Psychiatric Press, 1985)*

Table 13-1 **Major Components of Illness Dynamics**

Biologic

Nature, severity, and time course of disease
Affected organ system, body part, or body function
Baseline physiologic functioning and physical resilience
Genetic endowment

Psychologic

Maturity of ego functioning and object relationships
Personality type
Stage in the lifecycle
Interpersonal aspects of the therapeutic relationship (e.g., counter-
    transference of healthcare providers)
Previous psychiatric history
Effect of past history on attitudes toward treatment (e.g., postoperative
    complications)

Social

Dynamics of family relationships
Family attitudes toward illness
Level of interpersonal functioning (e.g., educational and occupational
    achievements; ability to form and maintain friendships)
Cultural attitudes

psychologic strength, and the supports of his social network combined to help him readily negotiate this period of ill health.

These patients' distinctive illness dynamics, illustrated in Figure 13-3, greatly influenced their ability to cope with heart disease *by affecting a grief process that normally accompanies loss of health.* Emotionally processing an episode of illness, reaching an accommodation with the diverse and powerful feelings that accompany it, is a prerequisite for return to healthy functioning. As discussed below, the working through of these emotions, in order to prevent them from intruding on one's daily responsibilities and interpersonal relationships, is analogous to grieving for a loved one.

THE GRIEF PROCESS AND ILLNESS

Illness is universally experienced as a loss, namely the loss of health, because it decreases one's degree of autonomy. Illness imposes restrictions on people, which may be transient and mild (e.g., immobilization of a sprained joint) or chronic and severe (e.g., hemiparesis following a cerebrovascular accident). Although feelings of loss are most intense when a serious health problem permanently and profoundly alters one's physical status, they also occur with minor ailments. The bedridden patient suffering a febrile viral syndrome often feels anxious, frustrated, and depressed about the inability to pursue his or her daily activities and responsibilities. Illness also precipitates a sense of loss due to its various symbolic meanings. The concrete demonstration of

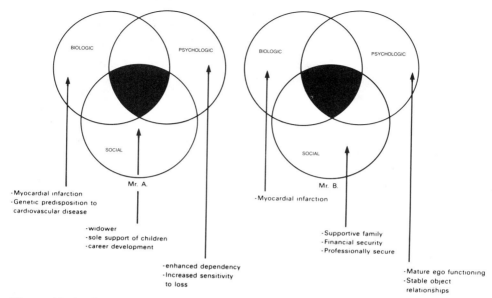

Figure 13–3. *Comparative illness dynamics. (Reprinted with permission from Green S: Mind and Body: The Psychology of Physical Illness. Washington, DC, American Psychiatric Press, 1985)*

physical vulnerability deprives one of infantile omnipotence, while idiosyncratic reactions to disease cause patients to experience more specific losses, such as Mr. A's conviction (founded on his mother's medical history) that his heart attack inevitably signaled an early death.

Whether illness has a predominantly symbolic or concrete effect, it precipitates a predictable psychologic reaction—namely, a grief reaction during which patients mourn the loss of their previous healthier functioning. The process is identical to bereavement, causing an outpouring of varied and shifting emotions as the patient acknowledges his/her current state of health and contrasts it with a premorbid level. Grieving entails recognition of the good and bad associated with a particular loss, which prompts a series of feeling states—*denial, anxiety, anger,* and *depression*—that a person must progress through before resolving those emotions and coming to terms with a temporary or permanent health impairment. The emotional response to a myocardial infarction illustrates this process.

Although well aware that severe precordial pain may signal an evolving heart attack, patients often attempt to deny that reality by minimizing the symptom or explaining it away as indigestion, myalgia, or bronchitis. That denial recedes as persisting angina underscores the medical reality and precipitates a host of intense feelings. There is immediate anxiety about the prospect of dying, the discomfort of acute treatment, and the need to abdicate considerable responsibility and autonomy to anonymous caretakers.

Anxiety persists into the recuperative period due to concern about long-range effects of the illness (e.g., dietary and physical limitations), although anger becomes the predominant feeling once patients feel secure that they will survive the medical emergency. During this phase of illness, patients direct their resentments globally, as well as towards specific targets. They curse the gods for their bad luck, while blaming specific family members, friends, and medical personnel for real and imagined transgressions and omissions that promoted ill health. As the anger abates, patients may experience a growing depression, characterized by emotional, behavioral, and cognitive changes that reflect their extreme preoccupation with real and potential losses brought on by the heart attack. In the short term, all aspects of their lives (e.g., family, professional, and social committments) must assume secondary importance to health concerns. Patients also mourn longer term losses caused by their diseased myocardium, such as restricted physical activities because of persistent angina.

The grief process proceeds toward closure as patients begin to achieve a realistic perspective concerning the consequences of illness. This entails acknowledgment of all limitations imposed by the disease, and of one's physical vulnerabilities and ultimate mortality. "Working through," or attempting to resolve those issues, is a dynamic process that allows reestablishment of the emotional equilibrium that characterized premorbid functioning, illustrated by Mr. B. Patients unable to resolve feelings precipitated by loss may develop one of several syndromes that characterize pathologic grief reactions (Brown and Stoudemire, 1983). These may take the form of a mood disturbance (e.g., the heightened anxiety and depression that complicated Mr. A's recuperation and persisted even after his physical recovery), a behavioral disturbance (e.g., compulsive eating or substance abuse), or impaired interpersonal relationships. As discussed in preceding chapters, there may also be neurobiologic correlates to the inability to work through feelings precipitated by ill health. Severe stress, such as physical illness and other circumstances involving loss of control, influences the neurochemistry by endogenous opioids, catecholamines, indoleamines, and pituitary functioning. Van der Kolk (Chapter 9) suggests that these changes promote heightened anxiety, difficulties modulating aggression, and depression—affective disturbances characteristic of unresolved grief—which may represent adult responses to the effects of earlier trauma and stress. Similarly, immunologic and neuroendocrinologic data highlight the correlation between grief and discrete physiologic changes (Irwin et al, 1987). Consequently, a patient's ability to come to terms with the loss of health is a comprehensive psychobiologic response. One's illness dynamics facilitate or impede this grief process; in the latter circumstance, the person is likely to develop one of the following pathologic reactions.

ABNORMAL ILLNESS RESPONSES

Persons unable to acknowledge and put into perspective the disturbing feelings brought on by disease are prone to abnormal illness responses, which significantly detract from physical and/or mental health. In these circumstances, one may deny his or her feelings or, more often, strongly experience one emotion while significantly minimizing all others. In essence, the patient becomes mired in one stage of the grief process, promoting a preoccupation with feelings characteristic of that phase, thereby preventing resolution of the varied emotions precipitated by loss of health; the situation is analogous to pathologic grief. Because of the interdependence between emotional and somatic functioning, abnormal illness responses often aggravate organic pathology (e.g., increased cardiac irritability due to heightened anxiety following a heart attack), often promoting psychologic and biologic distress more disabling than the initial illness. The most common abnormal illness responses include the following.

The Denial Response

Denial is a common ego mechanism that enables one to reject cognitive and emotional aspects of anxiety-provoking unpleasant external reality. Despite this function, denial usually serves an adaptive role (Vaillant, 1977), such as facilitating continued functioning by moderating the impact of an overwhelming stressor that might otherwise threaten one's psychologic health (e.g., the massive anxiety that precedes battle or other potentially life-threatening situations). Denial becomes maladaptive only when it is exclusively defensive, causing significant distortions in the assessment and acceptance of life's realities. For example, persons who never recognize their contribution to many failed relationships will probably perpetuate the pattern and increasingly become isolated as life progresses.

Pathologic denial may be present throughout the course of a medical or surgical illness. A common example of denial during an acute medical emergency is seen in cardiac patients who dismiss severe precordial pain as "heartburn." Persistent denial is often reflected in noncompliance with a therapeutic regimen, which may commence immediately after a medical crisis (e.g., refusal to maintain bedrest while recuperating from a myocardial infarction) and continue throughout a chronic illness (e.g., continued smoking in a patient with chronic obstructive pulmonary disease). Denial is seen in terminal patients who refuse to acknowledge impending death. In sum, the denial, if extreme, may interfere with accurate diagnosis, impede definitive treatment, and, consequently, perpetuate the disease state.

The Anxiety Response

Anxiety is an adaptive feeling that signals danger, prompting one toward purposeful action. The fight–flight behavior of animals confronted by a predator illustrates how this affect spurs self-protective behavior. In relation to illness, anxiety promotes preventive behaviors (e.g., scheduled immunizations, healthy diet) and timely medical attention following the onset of symptoms. And its persistence during an episode of ill health, secondary to patients' concern about a multitude of diverse issues (e.g., the discomfort of diagnostic and therapeutic procedures, long-term limitations to daily functioning), further motivates compliance with treatment. However, anxiety can become excessive, prompting an irrational preoccupation with health issues that evolves into a pathologic illness response.

Anxiety is maladaptive when the concern it causes the person exceeds its protective function. In this circumstance, patients may become hypersensitive to all aspects of an illness (e.g., ruminating about casual remarks passed by caretakers, obsessing to the point of indecision about therapeutic options). Such absorption with one's physical status greatly detracts from all other aspects of life, progressively displacing former pleasures with a debilitating angst. Paradoxically, this also interferes with medical care. Heightened anxiety compromises objectivity and, consequently, one's ability to provide an accurate history, tolerate diagnostic procedures (e.g., colonoscopy, an MRI scan), or even cooperate in a routine physical examination. Should such pervasive apprehension progress into a chronic anxiety, the patient is then burdened with an unpleasant, counterproductive affective state, in addition to the limitations caused by his/her physical pathology. Finally, continued demands for reassurance from friends, family, and healthcare personnel may progressively alienate those support systems. The anxiety response compromises diverse aspects of medical treatment and, consequently, diminishes the patient's potential for returning to premorbid or optimal functioning.

The Anger Response

All medical and surgical patients become frustrated, resentful, or overtly hostile about their plight, and vent those feelings in several directions. The anger is directed globally and specifically. Patients may curse the fates, God, the unfairness of life, or, alternatively, castigate themselves for being ill whether such self-criticism is warranted (e.g., cirrhosis secondary to alcohol abuse) or unreasonable (e.g., the result of an uncontrollable infectious disease). They may lash out at family members and friends for varied reasons—condemning ancestors for passing on a defective gene, blaming friends or family for causing exacerbations of an illness (e.g., the impact of marital discord on labile hypertension), or basically resenting the reality of heightened dependency on people in their social network who enjoy continued good health. Medical personnel are often primary and direct targets for patients' hostility because of the restrictions they impose (e.g., constraints on diet and physical activity), the discomfort they may cause (e.g., performing painful diagnostic procedures, prescribing medications with unpleasant side effects), the limitations of the profession (e.g., the inability to cure some diseases), and their role as bearers of grim news about patients' welfare and mortality.

Patients who fail to work through these angry feelings may develop an illness response that is often characterized by severe interpersonal conflicts. They engage in overt and covert struggles with the people in their lives, which fosters a progressive isolation from necessary support and undermines their medical care. Patients may angrily refuse to submit to important diagnostic tests, comply with rehabilitative programs, or take prescribed medications, behaviors that frustrate family members, control caretakers, and also reflect a self-directed anger because all these actions are ultimately detrimental to the patient. Struggles may also occur in subtle, unstated ways, by passive–aggressive behaviors (e.g., failing to adhere to a prescribed diet or medication regimen), which afford the pleasure of secret control over persons. In this manner, the anger response progressively transforms the patient's supportive alliances into adversarial relationships, with widespread negative effects on treatment and day-to-day life.

The Depression Response

This illness response is characterized by the common cognitive, affective, and behavioral signs and symptoms that constitute a clinical depression. These include changes in mood, most commonly a sustained sadness with tearfulness and anhedonia, although irritability and agitation may also be present. The patient also manifests physiologic sequelae of depression, which span the spectrum from the usual neurovegetative complaints (e.g., insomnia, anorexia, fatigue, decreased libido) to somatic disturbances of any organ system (Lindemann, 1944). The most prominent behavioral manifestation of this illness response is a change in established daily patterns, which most often takes the form of generalized withdrawal from one's environment. Patients can manifest more specific behaviors, such as neglecting professional responsibilities or avoiding family interactions, reactions influenced by the particular illness and/or its treatment (e.g., one may be inclined to retreat from social committments, and rely more on family support, following a disfiguring surgical procedure). Behavioral changes also include radical departures from usual routines of life, such as quitting a satisfying job, preciptiously moving, or ending a long-term marriage. Finally, diminished self-esteem is a prominent feature of this illness response. Already stressed by the effects of a physical impairment that may prevent one from returning to a healthy premorbid level of functioning, the psychologic reaction to that reality can provoke a negativistic spiral of self-criticism and self-reproach that ultimately leaves the patient feeling helpless and worthless. Each of these four areas of objective and subjective signs and symptoms can vary in intensity, with the result that the depression response may range from a relatively mild adjustment disorder to a major depression.

The depression response detracts from medical care by direct effects on patients and its impact on their relationships with healthcare personnel. Diverse psychophysiologic symptoms are often mistaken as primary manifestations of serious underlying medical illness, which complicates accurate diagnosis and, consequently, treatment. The differentiation becomes even more difficult when depression causes such withdrawal that the patient is unwilling or unable to provide an adequate medical history or report objective and subjective responses to a therapeutic regimen. Depression also interferes with normative healing processes by debilitating neurovegetative symptoms (e.g., anorexia), a diminished immunologic response (Stein et al, 1985), the passive abandonment of a will to live (Engel, 1968), or even purposeful self-destructive behaviors (Slaby and Glicksman, 1985). In sum, depression may become so severe that it becomes a greater threat to one's welfare and survival than the original underlying physical pathology.

The Dependency Response

As discussed in Chapters 3 and 6, behavioral regression is common to all illness, the result of factors endemic to patients (e.g., general preoccupation with one's illness, restrictions caused by specific symptoms) and external issues (e.g., limitations of a structured hospital routine, constraints of the treatment regimen, like a controlled diet). Such adaptive regression forms the basis of effective medical care; reversion to more passive behaviors, characteristic of early developmental stages, allows a patient the comfort and familiarity of diminished responsibility while simultaneously enabling caretakers to assume a necessary degree of control over the treatment. Diminished autonomy also serves the defensive purpose of helping a patient deal with distressing emotions by assigning accountability for one's welfare to others and readily accepting their concern and support.

As previously mentioned in Chapter 1, Parsons (1951) discusses these aspects of regression in his description of the dynamics of the sick role, emphasizing the *collaborative* nature of medical treatment. He outlines the usual course of enhanced dependency on healthcare personnel during the early stages of illness, but emphasizes the importance of patients assuming increased responsibility for their welfare as they progress toward wellness. For example, the stable postmyocardial infarction patient is expected to adhere to a prescribed diet and exercise regimen, important steps toward recovery and maintenance of healthy, independent functioning. Some persons, however, are so gratified by the ministrations of others they refuse to cooperate in their treatment. Warmed by the concern and constant attention of healthcare providers and, consequently, disinclined to strive for the autonomy of premorbid life, they abdicate increasing responsibility to family, friends, and caretakers. This can lead to an increasing dependency, which may ultimately culminate in a semi-helplessness that endangers one's physical and emotional well-being.

Treatment noncompliance is a common manifestation of excessive dependency, as patients haphazardly adhere to prescribed therapies (e.g., a medication regimen, physical rehabilitation following a traumatic injury). Although the motivation for such behavior may be purposeful or unconscious, it yields the same end point: prolonged dependence on health personnel who must then compensate for the patient's self-neglect by providing an even greater degree of care. At a minimum, this slows one's return to optimal functioning; at worst, it aggravates the illness by intensifying its pathophysiologic effects.

Individuals' interpersonal relationships also suffer when illness spawns excessive dependency. Established family patterns must adapt to the patient's prolonged regression, sometimes causing considerable disruption to relatives who now tend to matters usually managed by the patient. Growing resentments may, in turn, detract from their supportive efforts. A parallel situation occurs when healthcare providers develop a negative reaction to so-called "hateful" patients (Groves, 1978), fostering conscious or unconscious neglect of their care. The dependency response signals the evolution of an individual into a professional patient who is more concerned with being cared for than achieving an optimal level of coping. When physicians fail to recognize this illness response, which may be hidden by a patient's stated desire to get well quickly, there is greater risk that the collaborative doctor–patient relationship will steadily degenerate into an adversarial association harmful to both parties.

THE DOCTOR-PATIENT RELATIONSHIP IN THE PSYCHOLOGIC CARE OF THE MEDICALLY ILL

The preceding pages demonstrate that comprehensive medical care requires an accurate appreciation of the emotions spawned by ill health in addition to a thorough knowledge of the patient's physical disease. This biopsychosocial approach, which reflects the inextricable link between mind and body, applies to all healthcare providers regardless of specialty or professional discipline. All medical personnel facilitate patients' psychologic accommodation to the loss of health: primary care providers (e.g., nonpsychiatrists, nursing staff, rehabilitation therapists) can help prevent the onset of pathologic illness responses, while mental health personnel usually attend to persons already manifesting those symptoms. (Discussion of the latter treatment is beyond the scope of this chapter; see Green, 1985.) This comprehensive approach, which respectively parallels the public health models of primary and secondary prevention, requires an understanding of one's illness dynamics and the application of standard psychotherapeutic principles to medical management (Reichard, 1964; Kahana and Bibring, 1964).

Psychotherapy may be broadly classified as supportive (anxiety-suppressing) or introspective (which at times is actually anxiety-provoking). The former seeks to preserve the patient's psychologic status quo; the latter attempts to heighten insight by obliging the patient to explore distinctively painful emotional experiences and memories. The role of general medical physicians in ministering to the psychologic needs of patients is predominantly a supportive one. The basic goal is to help patients identify and ventilate the intense feelings precipitated by ill health, thereby enabling them to contain emotional distress within limits that were acceptable premorbidly. As discussed by Frank (1961) in his classic study concerning the process of healing, this type of treatment is highly dependent on the personal influence exerted by caretakers. For example, a positive relationship can yield favorable effects even with *symbolic* interventions, such as the administration of an inert medication. Alexander and French (1946) specifically exploit the doctor–patient interaction in this manner by the technique of manipulating the transference during psychotherapy.

The psychotherapeutic care of the medically ill patient deserves special consideration in this context. Cohen-Cole and Bird (1986) discuss common supportive technical interventions used with the medically ill; Buckley (1986) explores their theoretical basis. In general, physicians must present themselves as available and empathically concerned, which requires "giving of self" as a real person, as opposed to being neutral, objective, and analytic. The essence of empathy is transiently identifying with the plight and painful feelings of the patient and verbally communicating to the patient your understanding of how difficult his or her situation must be. The nature of the physician's communication should be in a personable, conversational tone to offer advice and reassurance (e.g., commenting on the patient's response to a treatment regimen), praise when warranted (e.g., when the patient progresses in a rehabilitative program), and didactic instruction about the illness (e.g., identifying normal emotional and behavioral aspects of the sick role). The physician should consistently attempt to involve patients in the treatment (e.g., inviting input into decisions concerning therapeutic options) in order to strengthen the working alliance. This overall posture helps to limit a patient's regression by retaining focus on the here-and-now, to improve their compromised ego functioning by supporting usual defense, and methods of coping, and to enhance the person's self-esteem by acknowledging inherent strengths and therapeutic gains. Hollis (1964) broadly categorizes aspects of the supportive approach as follows: (1) sustaining procedures (e.g., demonstration of a desire to help); (2) procedures of direct influence (e.g., offering suggestions and advice); (3) facilitation of catharsis (e.g., sanctioning the expression of emotions); and (4) guidance concerning the day-to-day implications of illness (e.g., urging the return to work or a change in one's living situation).

Finally, effective psychologic care of medical patients is ultimately predicated on the ability of healthcare providers to maintain perspective on their own emotions. Frequent exposure to severely ill persons may cause considerable distress to caretakers frustrated by their patients' marginal improvement or continued decline. Clinicians' own heightened anxiety or mounting depression may cause them to minimize unconsciously the seriousness of symptoms or illness of their patients. Clinicians may also grow increasingly distant by spending less time with the patient or becoming increasingly aloof, cynical, or callously mechanical by generally neglecting the patient's psychologic needs and simply ignoring signs and symptoms of obvious emotional distress. Because patients are perennial targets for the conscious and unconscious prejudices of those ministering to them, antitherapeutic reactions are not always dependent on the patient's actual clinical status. Some patients are esteemed by healthcare providers, and others are ignored, because of a regard for such arbitrary factors as intelligence, physical appearance, cultural background, and personality traits.

Because medical illness triggers emotional responses that are part and parcel to the disease process, it is imperative that clinicians understand patients' illness dynamics and use that knowledge to facilitate psychologic adjustment to their medical condition. The biopsychosocial approach is the only acceptable medical model if "one is to treat the whole patient and not merely characterize the nature of an illness and impede biologic deterioration" (Slaby and Glicksman, 1985). Excellent, integrated, and compassionate treatment of each patient as a unique individual is the ultimate goal of the compleat physician—and the goal of this text.

ANNOTATED BIBLIOGRAPHY

Engel G: The need for a new medical model: A challenge for biomedicine. Science 196:129–136, 1977

In this article, Engel carefully articulates the shortcomings of the biomedical model, which he feels leaves no room within its framework for the social, psychologic, and behavioral dimensions of illness. He demonstrates a need for the biopsychosocial approach as a "blueprint for research, a framework for teaching, and a design for action in the real world of health care."

Engel G: The clinical application of the biopsychosocial model. Am J Psychiatry 137:535–544, 1980

An excellent complement to the above, this article employs the biopsychosocial model to describe the impact of an acute myocardial infarction on a middle-aged man. It explores the effect of relevant psychosocial issues (e.g., the role of family members, healthcare providers, and coworkers) on the onset, treatment, and course of his illness.

Frank J: Persuasion and Healing. Baltimore, Johns Hopkins University Press, 1961

In this classic study of psychotherapy, the author explores the relationship between healer and sufferer, stressing the fundamental importance of the clinician's personal influence. Frank's observations concerning general attitudes and specific procedures that facilitate communication with patients constitute the basis of all forms of psychotherapy, including the supportive care of the medically ill.

Green S: Mind and Body: The Psychology of Physical Illness. Washington, American Psychiatric Press, 1985

This text expands on the basic principles discussed in this chapter, including the clinical applications of the biopsychosocial model and psychodynamic factors in the doctor–patient relationship.

Lipowski Z: Psychiatry of somatic disease: Epidemiology, pathogenesis, classification. Compr Psychiatry 16:105–124, 1975

In this comprehensive article, the author presents a wealth of information concerning the linkage between psychiatric and physical illness. It is particularly notable for discussion of psychologic responses to disease and injury, and the psychosocial determinants influencing those responses.

Lindemann E: Symptomatology and management of acute grief. Am J Psychiatry 101:141–146, 1944

This landmark paper discusses the psychologic and widespread psychophysiologic manifestations of acute grief. Although subsequent investigations of bereavement modify Lindemann's initial conclusions (e.g., Rynearson E: Psychotherapy of pathologic grief: Revisions and limitations. Psychiatr Clin North Am 10(3):487–500, 1987), the work remains a standard in the field.

Parsons T: The Social System. Glencoe, IL, The Free Press, 1951

Part of this lengthy sociologic text is devoted to study of medical practice, including a sophisticated discussion of the dynamics of the sick role. Emphasizing the collaborative nature of medical care, Parsons details distinctive roles for patient and clinician during the various stages of illness. Of particular importance is his description of the changing levels of dependency and autonomy required of the patient by different aspects of the treatment.

REFERENCES

Alexander F, French T: Psychoanalytic Therapy. New York, Ronald Press, 1946

Brown J, Stoudemire G: Normal and pathological grief. JAMA 250:378–382, 1983

Buckley P: Supportive Psychotherapy: A neglected treatment. Psych Ann 16:515–521, 1986

Cohen-Cole S, Bird J: Interviewing the cardiac patient. II: A practical guide for helping patients cope with their emotions. Quality of Life and Cardiovascular Care 3:53–65, 1986

Engel G: The clinical application of the biopsychosocial model. Am J Psychiatry 137:535–544, 1980

Engel G: The need for a new medical model: A challenge for biomedicine. Science 196:129–136, 1977

Engel G: A life-setting conductive to illness: The giving-up–given-up complex. Ann Intern Med 69:293–298, 1968

Frank J: Persuasion and Healing. Baltimore, Johns Hopkins University Press, 1961

Green S: Mind and Body: The Psychology of Physical Illness. Washington, American Psychiatric Press, 1985

Groves J: Taking care of the hateful patient. N Engl J Med 298:883–887, 1978

Hollis F: Casework: A Psychosocial Therapy. New York, Random House, 1964

Irwin M, Daniels M, Weiner H: Immune and neorendocrine changes during bereavement. Psychiatr Clin North Am 10:449–466, 1987

Kahana R, Bibring G: Personality types in medical management. In N Zinberg (ed): Psychiatry and Medical Practice in a General Hospital. New York, International Universities Press, 1964

Lindemann E: Symptomatology and management of acute grief. Am J Psychiatry 101:141–146, 1944

Lipowski Z: Psychiatry of somatic disease: Epidemiology, pathogenesis, classification. Compr Psychiatry 16:105–124, 1975

Parsons T: The Social System. Glencoe, IL, The Free Press, 1951

Rahe R: Subjects' recent life changes and their near future illness reports. Ann Clin Res 4:1–16, 1973

Reich P, DeSilva R, Lown B et al: Acute psychological disturbances preceding life-threatening ventricular arrhythmias. JAMA 246:233–235, 1981

Reichard J: Teaching principles of medical psychology to medical house officers: Methods and problems. In N Zinberg (ed): Psychiatry and Medical Practice in a General Hospital. New York, International Universities Press, 1964

Slaby A, Glicksman A: Adapting to Life-Threatening Illness. New York, Praeger, 1985

Stein M, Keller S, Schleifers: Stress and immunomodulation: The role of depression and neuroendocrine function. J Immunol 135(Suppl 2):827–833, 1985

Vaillant G: Adaptation to Life. Boston, Little, Brown & Co, 1977

Zola I: Socio-cultural factors in the seeking of medical aid: A progress report. Transcultural Psychiatric Research 14:62–65, 1963

Appendix 1:
A Problem-Oriented Method for Teaching Human Behavior

Donald C. Fidler
and Mark G. Fuller

This section will briefly present a practical approach to developing a problem-oriented course in clinical psychiatry. Since the traditional lecture-based course has received extensive criticism (GPEP report, 1984; Resnick, 1987; Strayhorn, 1973), curricula that stimulate thinking and higher-order reasoning have been recommended by several sources (Wales, et al., 1987; Browne, 1989; Brinton, et al., 1988). One of the barriers to the more traditional approaches to problem-oriented learning, however, has been the large number of faculty members required to staff small group sessions. Our method requires little (if any) additional faculty commitment, yet stimulates students to become active participants in learning. Problem-oriented class sessions may be intermixed with periodic traditional didactic lectures. This overview presents the basic model we have implemented at the West Virginia University School of Medicine, which may be used in conjunction with this textbook.

METHODS

We have eliminated the use of lectures in our preclinical behavior science courses. In most cases, we believed that lectures simply repeated the material presented in the reading and did not promote the use of critical reasoning or problem solving. In the place of lectures, we have substituted textbook chapters, clinical problem-solving case discussions in the classroom setting, and other relevant material. The availability of the text in which this chapter appears has decreased the need for ancillary formal didactic lectures because pertinent background information can be derived during the students' reading time.

339

The purpose of the clinical problem-solving approach is to encourage students to actively apply didactic knowledge. We believe that simple memorization of facts does not adequately prepare students for the complexities of clinical medicine and the management of problematic behavior. The clinical problems should be designed so that certain aspects can be solved by applying information found in the assigned chapters. Other parts of the problems should require critical thinking and higher level judgments that exercise students' ethical, philosophical, and emotional reasoning. Ideally, the cases presented throughout the course also should be designed to interconnect so that students can learn about continuity and relationships in illness and health rather than be limited to learning about isolated cross-sectional concepts.

Preparing for this type of class format requires that students work alone or in groups before the lecture. The basic classroom experience can be divided into the following four sections:

1. The class beings with a student presenting the case, along with his or her understanding of it.

2. The presenting student is encouraged to call on colleagues to comment, agree, disagree, or question.

3. The teacher summarizes the discoveries and questions of the class. The teacher or an invited expert can then conclude discussion of the more straightforward aspects of the material and address any points of the case that were overlooked.

4. The students are challenged to explore more complex aspects of the case, which enhances the learning process.

The role of the teacher is crucial to the successful outcome of this method. It is essential that the instructor make the conceptual shift from deliverer of information to facilitator of learning. We recommend the use of a course coordinator, who is present at all class sessions. This provides a sense of continuity to the class and guidance to invited experts who may be present. These experts are usually faculty members who may formerly have served as guest lecturers on topics of special interest. In our program, with assistance from the course coordinator, all the experts found participating enjoyable, although many of them were apprehensive at first.

During the first two sections of the class, we recommend that the instructor be attentive and somewhat reserved while encouraging the students to explore the clinical problems. If there are too many comments from the instructor early on, the students may shift into a more passive "lecture mode" and it may be difficult to re-engaged them. The exception to this would be correcting students who present erroneous information, but even this may be handled best by questioning the student about the information or asking other students to express their opinion.

The third and fourth sections of a given class should be approached by the judicious use of questions (along the lines of the Socratic method). We recommend that students be challenged to examine the cases from various viewpoints and asked to support their reasoning. Questioning the students about the assigned readings as they apply to the cases may be useful in ascertaining if they have learned the information accurately and can apply it appropriately. Teachers should be reminded that multiple perspective solutions may exist and that the correct answer may be elusive.

Presenting a case to the class understandably may cause anxiety for some students. Instructors should try to be as helpful as possible in assisting students with this. Medical students and physicians are called on to answer questions about clinical material throughout their careers and this can be an excellent opportunity to practice. If students feel overwhelmed by this task, they should seek assistance from their instructors and be encouraged to work through their apprehensions. Teachers should be gentle but firm as they introduce this learning technique, which may be new to some students.

Our experience is that although students may be more comfortable initially with the traditional lecture and memorization format, given the opportunity, they are willing to explore alternative methods.

The Genogram

We have included a genogram of two fictional families used in developing clinical cases. Use of a genogram brings a sense of continuity to the course. Students also have the opportunity to see how an individual's problem can affect other family members; thus, the students' understanding of the interrelatedness of human behavior is supported. In our course, we designated several of the family members as physicians and one as a medical student. Their interactions with patients were the basis for the development of many educational situations. Various clinical situations and interrelationships between the family members in this genogram can be created as needed.

The Audiovisual Guide

Videotapes are used in our classes to enhance the students' appreciation of various concepts. Whether they are assigned as resource material to be viewed and interpreted before class or shown as a short segment during class, videotapes provide an alternative medium for illustrating some concepts further. In the audiovisual guide of this text, you will find a listing of tapes arranged by topic.

Evaluations

We use several methods to evaluate our students and enhance their learning. First, we evaluate the students on their participation in class. In larger classes, this may be problematic and should account for only a small part of the grade. In addition, we give four quizzes, evenly spaced throughout the semester. This encourages the students to stay up to date with their readings and provides them with regular feedback. At the suggestion of our students, we use questions modeled on the national boards to assess whether the students are acquiring the necessary factual material. This also allows the students to practice for their licensing exams. Our final exam is a comprehensive "take-home test" consisting of two essay questions that require a broad understanding of major course principles and how they interconnect. We believe this more closely simulates the type of problem-solving the students will be faced with in their clinical years and can be an excellent learning experience.

CLINICAL CASES

The following case is an example of one of the clinical problems used in our courses. We encourage the use of this text, the genogram, and the audiovisual guide to develop a problem-solving-oriented course based on the didactic information contained in this text.

A CASE STUDY

(Relevant chapter: The Biopsychosocial Model [Chapter 1])

    Vince Sammartino (see genogram), a fourth-year medical student, is rotating through the emergency room service and presents a patient to you, his attending physician. He tells you that Ernest Simpson is 62 and has been widowed for 2 years. He was brought in by the police because he was violent and confused and tried to attack an apartment manager. Mr. Simpson claims he has had mild memory problems for several years, and is being treated by his local physician. Mr. Simpson was agitated and cursing in the emergency room and needed to be sedated with a low dose of haloperidol (an anti-psychotic medication). He yelled that he was "tired of people screwing him over." A social worker who recognized him informed you that Mr. Simpson's wife was killed 2 years ago when a police car engaged in a high-speed chase of drug dealers hit her as she sat on a park bench in front of their high-rise apartment building. The social worker also reported that the city is trying to condemn the apartment building to build a parking deck to accompany an already planned indoor sports arena. Many of Mr. Simpson's neighbors of 42 years have already moved out, and the majority of the building is now a haven for drug dealers and "shooting galleries." Most of Mr. Simpson's best friends have moved out recently. After Mrs. Simpson's death, and until several weeks ago, his friends used to have Mr. Simpson over for dinner and accompanied him on walks before the park was cleared for the sports arena. The apartment manager had come by to discuss Mr. Simpson's need to move when he noticed that the apartment was in disarray, there were several dogs and cats present, and there was very little food in the kitchen.

    You ask Vincent about his evaluation. He tells you that the patient was oriented to person, place, and year but not the day of the week. "When I asked him what he was going to do he cursed at me. He refused to do serial sevens or any other calculations and just continued to yell at me. When I asked him about his wife, he was tearful but refused to discuss it." Vincent goes on to tell you that the patient has poor judgment and insight, but this can be attributed to his confusion. "In summary, I believe he is suffering from senile dementia and he needs a CT scan, EEG LP, and maybe a PET scan before he is transferred to a nursing home."

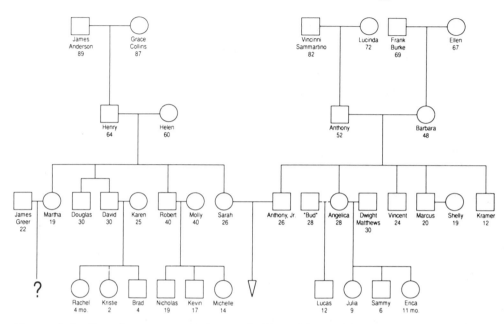

Figure A–1. *Sample genogram to be used with problem-solving oriented case discussion.*

QUESTIONS

1. As Vincent's supervisor, do you agree with his assessment? Why or why not?

2. What model of patient care does Vincent Sammartino seem to be using? Describe it.

3. In developing a case formulation of Mr. Simpson, what are the relevant variables (biologic, psychologic, and social)?

4. In developing a plan of management of Mr. Simpson's problems, use the biopsychosocial model to explain how you would intervene.

5. Do psychological and behavioral factors predispose people to physical illness? Explain.

6. Do psychosocial factors affect the course and outcome of illness? Explain.

7. Is Mr. Simpson's case unique or do psychiatric and social problems show up in a general medical practice? Explain.

8. What is social epidemiology and how does it relate to Mr. Simpson?

9. What factors impact on the use of medical care in this case, or why did Mr. Simpson really come to the emergency room?

SUGGESTED READING

Dornhorst AC: Information overload: Why medical student education needs a shake-up. Lancet 2:513–514, 1981

Eichna L: Medical school education, 1975–1979: A student's perspective. N Engl J Med 303:727–734, 1980

West DA, Moore-West M: Problem-based learning of behavioral science in a traditional medical school curriculum. J Psych Ed 12:111–116, 1988

REFERENCES

Brinton DA, Jarvis JQ, Harris DL: A small group instruction experiment in medical education. J Med Ed 59:13–18, 1988

Browne MN: Necessary tensions in assignments that stimulate critical thinking. Connexions 2:1–2, 1989

GPEP report: Physicians for the Twenty-first Century. Report of the Panel on the General Professional Education of the Physician and College Preparation for Medicine. Washington, DC, Association of American Medical Colleges, 1984

Resnick LB: Education and Learning to Think. Washington, DC, The National Academy Press, 1987

Strayhorn J: Aspects of motivation in preclinical medical training: A student's viewpoint. J Med Ed 48:1104–1110, 1973

Wales CE, Nardi AH, Stager RA: Thinking Skills: Making a Choice. Morgantown, WV, Center for Guided Design, 1987

Appendix 2: Audiovisual Guide

Donald C. Fidler

The following notes about videotapes are based on my reviews of videotapes for the American Psychiatric Association and the Association for Academic Psychiatry, and the experiences of myself and other psychiatric educators in using videotapes with medical students, psychiatry and internal medicine residents, nursing students, and audiences comprised of a variety of health professionals. Many of the videotapes are programs that I helped design and programs that my friends and colleagues, Ed Mason and Jim Lurie, helped design specifically for medical student education. I attempted to be as objective in reporting about our programs as I was with the other programs, having compiled data from other instructors as well as my own data about successes and failures.

I did not attempt to simplify my choices by considering programs to be "bad" or "good" in the fashion that many film and theatre critics choose to review productions for entertainment value, but instead, I attempted to approach the reviews with a knowledge of the great complexity of what makes teaching with a videotape a success or a failure. One must always ask the following questions and understand the multiple factors influencing the answers:

1. How large is the audience?
2. What is the philosophy of the instructor presenting the videotape? Does the instructor introduce the program with enthusiasm or disdain?
3. What is the admission philosophy of the school of the students who form this particular audience? Did they select students who enjoy learning about abstract issues such as emotions, ethics, and conflict, or did they select students who are fascinated only by hard data?
4. What are the developmental learning levels of the students? Are they just beginning to master a subject and therefore need simple, concrete facts? Are they further advanced in their training and need emotional stimulation to enhance them to dwell more on the

truths of how difficult decisions are made? Are they so far along in their development to be thinking about thinking itself?

5. How much time does the instructor have to cover the topic? Will the topic be covered in one teaching event? Will the instructor and students have the luxury to spread the topic over multiple sessions with time to ponder the topic between sessions?

6. What ratio of media to discussion time will the instructor use? Most media need about a 3:1 ratio of discussing to viewing time.

7. How much exposure do the students get to videotape and film? Is this a new or overused format? Are the instructors and students "media-sophisticated" enough to attend to the content without being distracted by the technology? Do they suffer from media burnout and starve for real human interaction?

Occasionally in my notes I address the above questions, but more often I describe the tapes in a manner that instructors and students can hopefully decide the usefulness of a particular tape by asking the above questions.

SPECIAL NOTES

Many of the reviews are followed by the caption *trigger.* This means that there is no didactic teaching in the production, and the tape can be used to enhance lecture material, much like a case presentation is a trigger that is then followed by a didactic presentation or discussion. Reviews that are not followed by this caption have narration or graphics that allow the tape to stand alone without supplementary reading or lectures.

It is our strong bias that it is best to use all tapes as triggers and unfailingly have teachers present to be involved with the audience and students. Assigning tapes for students to watch without arranging time for teachers to teach is an abuse.

Many of these productions use real patients and should be restricted to audiences of health professionals. Health professionals and health professional students should be cautioned to observe proper conduct of confidentiality. Patients and physicians were kind enough to consent to sharing themselves for our learning, and there have been horror stories of students and teachers not respecting videotapes of patients, leading to embarrassment, bad feelings, and mistrust. Please insist on confidentiality and respect.

Many of the productions are simulations, often using actors who are also trained in psychiatry or psychology. Often these are portrayals of actual case histories or recreations of previously videotaped patient interviews, but have changed names and localities to protect confidentiality. These tapes can thus be shared with nonprofessional audiences, but should be used with the respect that was intended by the producers, that of furthering our knowledge and understanding of the thinking, behaviors, feelings, growth, and suffering of people. They should not be used for entertainment or for any exploitive reasons. Although these tapes are listed here as useful for medical students, they are often helpful in college and high school classes.

Because many of the performances are performed by health professionals, they too should be treated with respect and thanked for their contributions to education rather than ridiculed for their courage of performing the roles of people who are in pain or are in helplessly compromising circumstances.

When simulated videotapes are used, audiences and teachers require a certain "TV" or "film" sophistication. They must understand that one of the advantages of using scripted material is that we can make lengthy material into concise, summarizing material. Rather than watch 1 hour of material to focus on five specific events out of the hundreds of events, we can shorten the material to show only the five specific points. What would have required hours to watch may then be viewed in a matter of minutes or even seconds. This helps us focus what we learn, much like during medical rounds we summarize our patients histories, or in writing journal articles we summarize our patients by including only what we wish to focus on, excluding much other material. This process is the same for scripting videotapes and for editing documentaries. The process of editing is enormously helpful, but helpful only as long as we understand it for what it is and remind ourselves frequently that we are seeing only a segment of truth rather than an all-encompassing truth. If we fail to remember this, then we start to believe that interviews can be brief, that every question or interpretation can be right on the mark, and that every patient can quickly reveal what we need to know. If we can rise above this kind of simplistic thinking, then simulated interviews, dramas, and edited documentaries can add enormous value to our learning.

I also include some commercial entertainment movies (noted "*") as suggestions for films that can be used with medical students outside of class, perhaps in psychiatry clubs or in electives, as triggers for further discussions about human growth or psychopathology. Although there are numerous films useful for this, I include only my favorites that I have already used with students and only those that are currently available on videotape format. Use of these films for public viewing may be restricted.

All programs are available in 3/4 inch and VHS videotape formats unless otherwise noted.

SECTION 1: THE BIOPSYCHOSOCIAL MODEL

Chapter 2: Culture, Ethnicity, and Behavior and the Practice of Medicine

American Tongues (color, 57 min). Louis Alvarex and Andrew Kolker, producers; Center for New American Media.

What makes a Texas accent different from an Ohio one? How does talking with a Brooklyn accent affect people's opinions of you? American society is examined through the prism of language.

The War Between the Classes (color, 32 min). Learning Corporation of American, producer; Coronet/MTI Film & Video, distributor.

Dramatization of the Color Game in which high school students are arbitrarily assigned to one of three socioeconomic classes, giving them different degrees of power, wealth, and privilege.

Ethnic Notions (color, 58 min). California Newsreel.

Ester Rolle narrates during this award-winning artistic blend of folklore, theatre music, animation, interviews, film clips, commentaries by historic scholars, and animation as the tape examines black racial stereotyping in the last 100 years in the United States.

Slaying the Dragon (color, 60 min). NAATA, CrossCurrent Media.

Examines the stereotyping roles and images of Asian women in film and television over the past 50 years.

Crosscultural Psychiatry

Cultural Issues in Psychotherapy: Patients' Requests for Therapists (color, 15 min). UNC-CH, producer; HSC, distributor.

Simulated patients made statements to the camera, thus putting the viewer in the role of therapist. Each statement has to do with issues that are cultural, racial, or sexual and would influence the therapist–patient relationship and the dynamics of the therapy. (Trigger)

Houses of the Spirit (color, 42 min). American Friends Service Committee.

Examines the Cambodian perceptions of health and well-being and those natural and supernatural forces held responsible for illness and mental disorder. Explores many of the tensions and misunderstandings faced by Western health practioners when treating Cambodian patients who are unfamiliar with Western procedures and treatments.

A Healing Faith (color, 25 min). UNC-CH, producer; HSC, distributor.

A documentary of people interviewed at a North Carolina faith-healing convention. People talk about their religious beliefs, and how these impact on whether or not they seek medical help.

The Honour of All (color, 56 min). Department of Health, Indian Health Service.

> *A docudrama reenacted by the actual Indians of a Canadian Indian community in which the inhabitants had an almost 100% population problem with alcoholism. Excellent production that also includes discussion by the Indians about making the tape as part of the process of recovery.*

A Biographical Interview with Dr. Robert Coles (color, 60 min). Harvard University Press.

> *The teacher and psychiatrist Dr. Coles focuses on literature being important to understanding psychology.*

SECTION 2: TWO FUNDAMENTAL PSYCHOLOGIC THEORIES OF HUMAN BEHAVIOR

Chapter 3: Psychoanalytic Psychology

Young Doctor Sigmund Freud (film, black and white, 96 min, German and French with English subtitles). Films for the Humanities, Inc.

> *With a splendid screenplay by George Stefan Troller, we are carried back to Freiberg, Vienna, and Paris during the life of young Sigmund Freud. This is a lengthy show, but it makes superb teaching material to show the beginnings of psychoanalytic theory.*

The Psychological Birth of the Human Infant: The Separation Individuation Process (black and white, 50 min, film-to-videotape transfer. Film and 3/4" videotape formats). The Margaret S. Mahler Psychiatric Research Foundation.

> *Dr. Mahler and two of her colleagues (all with German and Austrian accents) briefly introduce separation individuation and the four subphases: (1) differentiation, (2) practicing, (3) rapprochement, and (4) on the way to object and self constancy.*

Ego Defense Mechanisms and Character Formation

Psychiatry Learning System: Psychodynamic Considerations and Defense Mechanisms (color, 23 min). University of South Carolina, producer; HSC, distributor.

This tape of excerpts from patient interviews is excellent in teaching about defenses; it does not limit itself to one or two sentences but shows long enough excerpts to show how some people use a particular defense as their primary solution of dealing with their world.

*Harold and Maude (color, 91 min).

Strange black humor about an 18-year-old boy who has difficulty separating from his mother and continually and desperately attempts to do so by staging fake suicides. (Trigger)

*Amazing Grace and Chuck (color, 96 min).

A beautifully touching movie about a boy who becomes aware of world-wide issues outside his own family and community. (Trigger)

*Who's Afraid of Virginia Woolf? (black and white, 129 min).

In contrast to Chuck's positive development of character in the above movie, Richard Burton and Elizabeth Taylor use and twist every ego defense in the book to survive aging in a small college town in this multiple award-winning film based on the stunning Broadway play.

Chapter 4: Behavioral and Social Learning Psychology

Behavior (black and white, 30 min, 16 mm film only). University of Southern California.

Dr. Thomas Eisner of Cornell University illustrates differences between instinctive and learned behavior; relationship between instinct, intelligence, and learning; and advantages and disadvantages of these characteristics. Includes experiments with nerve cells. (Not reviewed)

As Man Behaves: Behavior Modification (color, 30 min, also in 16 mm film). KOCE-TV 50.

One of a 30-part series. Illustrates principles of classic conditioning, operant conditioning, modeling, aversive conditioning, and in vivo desensitization. Produced on film and transferred to videotape. Filmed at the Center for Behavior Therapy in Beverly Hills. (Not reviewed)

Pavlov: The Conditioned Reflex (25 min, also in 16 mm film). Films for the Humanities.

Intimate view of the Russian physiologist in his research center in Leningrad, with rare documentary shots of Pavlov at work, including his pioneer work with dogs. Shows the conditioned reflex. (Not reviewed)

SECTION 3: HUMAN DEVELOPMENT

Chapter 5: Human Sexual Development and Physiology

The Sexually Mature Adult (color, 16 min). John Wiley & Sons, producers; Media Guild, distributor.

A tasteful blend of interviews, discussion, art, subtle music, and films of couples loving one another and engaging in sexual stimulation and sexual intercourse.

Human Sexuality Videotape Series: Loving and Caring: Self Loving (color, 11 min). Sheldon Kule, DD, and Med-Pro Productions, producers; HSC, distributor.

Dr. Kule begins the introduction by quoting religious phrases that condemn masturbation. He then discusses the more contemporary viewpoint that masturbation is natural and that many couples include parallel or mutual masturbation with fantasy as an important part of their overall sexual relationship.

Human Sexuality Videotape Series: Loving Better (color, 21 min). Sheldon Kule, DD, and Med-Pro Productions, producers; HSC, distributor.

Dr. Kule very briefly introduces the tape and then immediately we see a young couple successfully demonstrate intimacy and sexual intercourse using techniques they learned in sexual therapy.

Human Sexuality Videotape Series.

Several other tapes by the same producers are offered in this series. They cover areas that may be of interest in normal human sexuality.

Chapter 6: Childhood and Adolescent Development

See "Everybody Rides the Carousel" reviewed below, Chapter 7.

Development (color, 60 min). WNET, New York, producer; PBS Video, distributor.

Part of the 9-part series, "The Mind," tracing particular brain cells, this program features the development of the human brain from a single cell to a 6-year-old brain. Computer graphics, time-lapse microphotography and in utero footage provide viewers with a detailed picture of the development of the human fetus.

Cognitive-Intellectual Development

A Good Beginning Has No End (color, 55 min). Les Anderson and Russell McCullough, producers; Mississippi Educational Television, distributor.

Narrated by Bob Keeshan, this production shows children learning at various ages, laying the foundations for intellectual development: learning to recognize the shape of the mouth, to classify by color or shape, to explore and question, to comprehend time, and to count. The examples are not from clinical settings, but from schools, playgrounds, and homes, and are excellent examples for thinking about the impact of the environment as we clinically evaluate children.

Psychiatry Learning System: Disorders of Infancy, Childhood, and Adolescence. Part 1 (color, 42 min). University of South Carolina, producer; HSC, distributor.

Although entitled "disorders," this tape begins with scenes of babies and children playing and interacting with parents and evaluators, with a narrator frequently describing what we are observing in terms of developmental milestones.

Beginning Pieces (color). Alfred Guzzett, producer; Filmakers Library, Inc., distributor.

The producer, a Harvard film maker, made a wonderful documentary about the growth of his daughter, Sarah, from age 2 to 5.

Development of Stable Emotional Bonding

Right from the Start (color, 55 min). Scott Craig Productions, producers; Prime Time School Television, distributor.

Sada Thompson narrates this superb PBS program that shows the Harry Harlow monkey and the Rene Spitz orphanage studies. The visual results are almost overwhelming and are extremely persuasive about the effects of bonding and the devastating effects of the lack of bonding.

NOVA: Life's First Feelings (color, 55 min). James Lipscomb Inc., and WGBH, producers; Coronet Films & Video, distributor.

This wonderful tape overlaps some with "Right from the Start," but mostly includes material that shows and discusses later emotional development of the child and is therefore almost like a "part two." Researchers show how biologic and learned experiences contribute to overall ability to express specific emotions.

Adolescent Development

Soapbox with Tom Cottle (color, series of 38 tapes that are 30 min each).
WGBY-TV, Springfield, MA, producer; PBS Video, distributor.

*Psychologist and author Tom Cottle is the host for a 38-program series
made between 1985 and 1987. Each program covers one topic on which
Dr. Cottle encourages teenagers to speak candidly. The series covers
adoption, drugs, college pressures, coping with death, young father-
hood and motherhood, physical disabilities, homosexuality, high
school dropouts, stress, anorexia, alcohol, legal rights, sex, intelligence,
depression, pregnancy, abortion, body image, being raised by divorced
parents, racism, religion, gender roles, nuclear arms, incarceration,
future dreams, suicide, finances and working, and overprotection.
(Not reviewed)*

Snowdream (color, 112 min). UNC-CH, producer; HSC, distributor.

*Very unusual tape for teaching about development. It is more about
what may be in the head of an adolescent, which is more in the feelings
and inner experiences of thoughts and dreams, than what is merely
observable. (Trigger)*

Tender Places (color, 25 min) Coronet/MTI Film & Video.

*Adapted by WBZ-TV in Boston from the play by the 13-year-old winner
of the Young Playwright's Award. A child's view of the anger, guilt,
loneliness, frustration, confusion, sadness, fear of abandonment, and
loss of innocence that develop when parents divorce. Stars Jean Sta-
pleton.*

*Stand By Me (color, 87 min).

*Recent, but already a classic. Two days in the lives of four 12-year-old
boys who set out on a journey to find a dead body and, along the way,
discuss everything from joking about the size of their genitals to what
species is Disney's Goofy to why people judge them by their families to
why parents do not love them, to what memories are so special as to
keep secret unto themselves.*

*Summer of '42 (color, 102 min).

*A little later in adolescent development than "Stand By Me," 15-year-
old Hermie comes of age sexually as he develops a crush on a 22-year-
old woman.*

*Racing with the Moon (color, 108 min).

*A good follow-up to the above two movies, this movie is about later
adolescence and early adulthood.*

Chapter 7: Adult Development

Everybody Rides the Carousel (color, 72 min). John Hubley, producer; Pyramid Films, distributor.

To appreciate Erikson's psychosocial approach in psychotherapy, one should first appreciate the eight stages of life that Erik Erikson suggested. This videotape (also film) is brilliant in its animation, animation that is playful and abstract enough to make us feel we are going through each of the stages, cueing early memories in the audience by blending clever animation and music with actual audio of children and families.

An Alzheimer's Story (color, 28 min). Ken Rosenberg, MD, Albert Einstein College of Medicine, producer; First Phase Video, distributor.

A moving documentary as Dr. Rosenberg and his camera crew capture the intimate feelings of one Bronx family as the elderly mother, Anna, slowly deteriorates from Alzheimer's disease.

*The Four Seasons (color, 117 min).

Comedy about four couples, one recently divorced and remarried, who live in the suburbs and vacation together. They play, argue, examine themselves, and grow through middle-age crises.

* East of Eden.

Film adaptation of Steinbeck's novel. James Dean as the prodigal son.

* Cat on a Hot Tin Roof.

Intergenerational and marital strife in a disturbed Southern family.

Marriage, Pregnancy, and Parenting

Things Your Mother Never Told You (color, 58 min). Filmakers Library, Inc.

Women of many ages and from different cultures talk about issues having to do with being women: pregnancy, raising children, working, loving, and so forth.

*Bill Cosby Himself (color, 99 min).

All about parenting. The famous Bill Cosby monologue that was the trigger for the Cosby TV show. Brilliant. Presented at the Academy of Child and Adolescent Psychiatry.

Single Parenthood and Divorce

After the Sexual Revolution (color, 60 min). ABC News.

Documentary about women who have deferred marriage and having children for career opportunities; and about women who based their lives around bearing children and being homemakers and are now single and must work to revise their identities.

Divorce: A Better Means to an End? (color, 30 min). KCTS-Seattle.

PBS documentary showing the new mental health specialty of divorce mediation to help couples negotiate their differences in a manner that is in contrast to the usual courtroom approach, thus making the transition easier for the couples and their children.

Divorce Wars (color, 58 min). PBS Video.

The couples, the lawyers, the judges, and the children who are caught in the middle are the subjects of this compelling documentary. Unique access to mediation and court proceedings shows the financial and emotional costs of divorce. (Not reviewed)

*To Kill a Mockingbird (black and white, 129 min).

Gregory Peck stars as the Alabama small-town lawyer who is a widower during the depression and must raise his 6- and 8-year-old daughter and son while dealing with poor race relations in the community.

*Alice Doesn't Live Here Anymore (color, 112 min).

No matter what you or I may think about the TV series spun off from this movie, the movie was fantastic and Ellen Burstyn won an Academy award for her leading role as the widow who had to survive by balancing supporting her 12-year-old son, learning to hold a job for the first time, and searching for a new identity.

Aging and Retirement

The Older Adults Series: In Sickness and Health (color, 16 min). Sheldon Retchin, MD, and Davis Stillson, producers; UNC-CH, distributor.

Many interviews from a rural North Carolina senior citizens' center and from the members at home are edited together as they discuss aging, activity, sex, medicines, and fun. (Trigger)

Issues and Attitudes Toward the Elderly Person (color, 9 min). Jim Lurie, MD, University of Washington Instructional Media Services, Carolyn Rabinowitz, MD, Barbara Lipkin, MA, and Jayne Kasarda, MAT, producers; American Psychiatry Association Office of Education, distributor.

Presents 17 brief simulated scenes of common problems presented to and by elderly people. (Trigger)

*The Trip to Bountiful (color, 106 min).

Adaptation of Horton Foote's Broadway play with Geraldine Page in her Oscar-winning role.

*On Golden Pond (color, 109 min).

Henry Fonda and Katherine Hepburn deal with aging, memory lapses, failing hearts, and two younger generations of people including a daughter, her boyfriend, and the boyfriend's son. While fishing, picking strawberries, and watching the loons, they seem to review their rich lives and make their peace.

Grief and Death

Some Babies Die (color, 54 min). University of California Extension Media Center.

Australian documentary shows a counseling team help grief-stricken families as they deal with depression and guilt after stillbirths and neonatal deaths.

Riding the Gale (color, 45 min). Filmakers Library, Inc.

Documentary about New Zealand woman struggling with multiple sclerosis.

Julie and Bob: A 36-year-old Woman Dying of Cancer (color, 35 min). Adult Program.

Covers from 1983 to 1986 in the life of a woman dying from cancer up to 6 days before her death. Invites much discussion.

The Older Adults Series: The Loss of a Spouse (color, 21 min). Sheldon Retchin, MD, and Davis Stillson, UNC-CH, producers; UNC-CH, HSC, distributor.

Two elderly women discuss the effect of their husbands' deaths. Their economic statuses and family supports are very different, and, thus, we hear them adapt with quite different solutions.

The Older Adults Series: Looking Back (color, 10 min). Sheldon Retchin, MD, and Davis Stillson, UNC-CH, producers; HSC, distributor.

The elderly husband (from "In Sickness and Health" reviewed above) talks about optimistic views toward aging.

The Last Right (color, 29 min). New Dimension Films.

Canadian actor Ed McNamara reenacts a true story of a 79-year-old man who moves with his wife into his grandson's home.

*Ordinary People (color, 123 min).

A classic motion picture depicting an unresolved grief reaction in an adolescent boy over the death of his brother and how it affected both him and the family.

Chapter 8: The Family in Human Development and Medical Practice

Patterns of Family Interaction (color, 25 min). UNC-CH, producer; HSC, distributor.

Introduces viewers to eight families, all played by the same four actors, and all consisting of the two parents living with their two biologic children (in contrast to videotapes listed below). Families shown are disengaged, enmeshed, gender-coalition, opposite gender-coalition, competing parents, distant father, exaggerated boundary, and more flexible structured families). (Trigger)

Can You Love Two Moms? (color, 29 min). Ed Mason, producer; Documentaries for Learning, distributor.

Seven children, adopted after infancy and now ages 8 to 13 years old, attend a special summer treatment camp. They tell their thoughts about their parents, the process of adoption, and the effect on their emotional lives.

We Are Family (color, 30 min). Filmakers Library, Inc.

Looks at families in which a parent, or both caretakers are homosexual.

Stepdancing: Portrait of a Remarried Family (color, 27 min). Pyramid Films and Video.

Oliver Johnson is 11 years old and shares a fact in common with millions of other children in the United states. We see his trials and joys in this candid and encouraging documentary.

*My Life as a Dog (color, 101 min, Swedish with English subtitles).

Memories of childhood, showing mostly the development of a young boy but has a major focus on a young girl who has everyone fooled into thinking she is a boy as she plays soccer. She has to examine her sexual identity as she becomes attracted to the boy. Delightful. A favorite among my medical students.

*Quarterback Princess (color, 104 min).

Based on the true story of a Canadian girl who moved with her family to a small town in Oregon for 1 year. The girl wanted to play football on the boys' team and made the tryouts and even becomes the quarterback. Interesting questions arise about gender identity and about relating to the opposite sex and relating to the same sex when people step out of stereotyped roles. Goose-bumpy film when the boys on the team can cheer her football talents and also lovingly buy her a dress for the homecoming dance.

*Breaking Away (color, 99 min).

> *Academy award-winning screenplay about a high school boy search-
> ing for his identity. Although he is the son of a Bloomington, Indiana,
> stone cutter, he decides to take on an Italian accent, shave his legs like
> the Italian bike racers do, and win the heart of a college woman. His
> parents, understandably, are upset. (Trigger)*

SECTION 4: BIOLOGIC ASPECTS OF BEHAVIOR

Chapter 11: Neurobiologic Aspects of Behavior

Addictions (color, 60 min). WNET, New York, producer; PBS Video,
distributor.

> *Part of the nine-part series, "The Mind." Experiments with persons
> suffering from addiction to heroin, alcohol, nicotine, food, or gambling
> give unusual insight into the nature of the mind. Viewers learn that the
> brain has natural receptors for certain kinds of chemicals that are
> activated in addictive behavior. Scientists also reveal the reasons for
> the pain of withdrawal.*

The Anatomical Basis of Brain Function Series (color, 14 to 23 min each).
The Altschul Group.

> *Twenty videotapes varying from 14 to 23 minutes. Human neuroana-
> tomy presented by Wendell J. S. Kreig, PhD, former professor of anat-
> omy at Northwestern University Medical School in Chicago, presented
> in didactic and laboratory formats. Topics deal with such areas as
> movements of the eyes and tongue, auditory system, visual system,
> bodily sensation, the pyramidal system, intellect and organization of
> reaction, muscular coordination, analysis and synthesis of sensation,
> prediction initiative, smell and ancient cortex, and visceral reflexes
> and taste.*

The Addicted Brain (color, 26 min). Films for the Humanities and
Sciences, Inc.

> *A documentary that tours the brain with colorful Disneyland Visual
> Media models of the brain and electron microscope photographs. An
> intoxicated man shows slow responses to a policeman's testing. How
> synapses and neurotransmitters work is shown with models.*

Brain Stimulation in the Monkey: Technique and Results (color and black
and white, 19 min, 16 mm film only). Psychological Cinema Register.

Surface and depth electrodes are surgically implanted in monkeys. Stimulation of area 4 evokes extension of contralateral arm and contralateral rotation of body.

ADDRESSES

ABC News
7 West 66th Street
New York, NY 10023

Adult Program
Mt. Airy Psychiatric Center
4455 East 12th Avenue
Denver, CO 80220

The Altschul Group
930 Pitner Avenue
Evanston, IL 60202
312-328-6700

American Friends Service Committee
NY Metropolitan Region
16 Rutherford Place
New York, NY 10003

Appleton-Century-Crofts
292 Madison Avenue
New York, NY 10017
212-532-1700

California Newsreel
630 Natoma Street
San Francisco, CA 94103

Carousel Film & Video
241 East 34th Street
New York, NY 10016
212-683-1660

Center for New American Media
524 Broadway, 2–4
New York, NY 10012
212-925-5665

Coronet Films & Video
108 Wilmot Road
Deerfield, IL 60015
800-621-2131
(in IL or AK, 312-940-1260)

Department of Health
Indian Health Service
5600 Fishers Lane, Room 6–22
Rockville, MD 20857

Extension Media Center
2176 Shattuck Avenue
Berkeley, CA 94704

Films for the Humanities & Sciences, Inc.
Box 2053
Princeton, NJ 08543
800-257-5126
(In NJ call 609-452-1128)

First Phase Video
Ruth Neuwald
553 Midvale Avenue
West Los Angeles, CA 90024
213-824-4206

Harvard University Press
79 Garden Street
Cambridge, MA 02138

Health Science Consortium (HSC)
201 Silver Cedar Court
Chapel Hill, NC 27514
919-942-8731

KCTS Channel 9
Seattle, WA 98105

KOCE-TV 50
Mr. Harry Ratner
Coast Community College District
157 Golden West Street
Huntington Beach, CA 92647

Mahler Research Foundation Film
  Library
P.O. Box 315
Franklin Lakes, NY 07417
201-891-8240

Media Build
P.O. Box 88
Solana Beach, CA 92075
714-755-9195

Mississippi Authority for Educational
  Television
Sandra Randell
P.O. Box 1101
Jackson, Mississippi 39215
601-982-6565

NAATA
CrossCurrent Media
346 Ninth Street, Second Floor
San Francisco, CA 94103
415-552-9550 or 414-863-0814

New Dimension Films
85895 Lorane Highway
Eugene, OR 97405

PBS Video
1320 Braddock Place
Alexandria, VA 22314-1698
800-344-3337

Prime Time School Television
40 East Huron
Chicago, IL 60611
312-329-0185

Psychological Cinema Register
Audio Visual Services
Pennsylvania State University
University Park, PA 16802

Pyramid Film & Video
Box 1048
Santa Monica, CA 90406
213-828-7577

University of California
University of Nevada School of
  Medicine
Department of Psychiatry
Reno, NV 98557

University of Southern California
Film Distribution Section
University Park
Los Angeles, CA 90007

Students, course directors and instructors interested in obtaining an updated version of this annotated audiovisual bibliography may contact:

Donald C. Fidler, MD
Chestnut Ridge Psychiatric Hospital
930 Chestnut Ridge Road
Morgantown WV 26505
Telephone 304-293-4000

RECOMMENDED TEXTBOOKS
FOR ADDITIONAL READING

1. Psychiatry, Volumes I through III, editor R. Michels. J. B. Lippincott Company, Philadelphia, 1987.

   This is an excellent and comprehensive textbook of clinical psychiatry. The chapters are lucid, well edited, and kept fresh by a subscription process that periodically updates the material.

2. Comprehensive Textbook of Psychiatry, 5th Edition, Volumes 1 and 2, editors H. I. Kaplan and B. J. Sadock. Williams & Wilkins, Baltimore, 1989.

   This is an encyclopedic textbook that covers all areas of psychiatry. Detailed and comprehensive, it should be primarily used as a reference source.

3. Textbook of Psychiatry, edited by J. Talbott, R. E. Hales, and S. Yudofsky. American Psychiatric Press, Inc., Washington DC, 1987

   This is an excellent textbook of clincial psychiatry that is eminently readable and practical. The chapters will provide a somewhat more expanded discussion of the psychopathological syndromes contained in this text.

4. Textbook of Neuropsychiatry, edited by R. E. Hales, S. C. Yudofsky. American Psychiatric Press, Inc., Washington DC, 1987.

   This is a clearly written and practical guide to neuropsychiatric disorders.

5. Principles of Medical Psychiatry, edited by A. Stoudemire and B. S. Fogel. Grune & Stratton, Orlando, 1987.

   This textbook is a detailed reference on the psychiatric disorders as encountered in medically ill patients. It contains detailed information regarding diagnosis, psychotherapy, and psychopharmacologic modifications that are required in treating psychiatric disorders in the medically ill.

6. Diagnostic and Statistical Manual of Mental Disorders, Third Edition, Revised. Washington DC, American Psychiatric Association, 1987.

   This is the "bible" of descriptive psychiatry. It contains epidemiological and descriptive data of the major psychiatric disorders.

7. The Medical Basis of Psychiatry, George Winokur and Paula Claton. Philadelphia, W. B. Saunders, 1986.

For students interested in basic descriptive and epidemiological data relative to psychiatric disorders this text provides a state of the art review.

8. New Harvard Guide to Psychiatry, 2nd Edition. Edited by A. M. Nicholi, Jr., M. D. Cambridge MA, Belknap Press of Harvard University Press, 1988.

This is an excellent overview of clinical psychiatry that is very readable and practical for a medical student audience. Chapters that are especially strong are those on biological aspects of depression, genetic aspects of schizophrenia, and the chapters on psychodynamic and psychoanalytic theory by Meissner, Vaillant, and Nemiah.

Index

Page numbers followed by f indicate figures;
those followed by t indicate tabular material

A

Accommodation, 137
Acetylcholine (ACH), 275–276
Ackerknecht, Erwin, 31
Acting out, 69
Adaptation, 137, 214
Adaptive point of view, 53, 59
Adolescence
  development in, 166–170
    affective, 167
    cognitive, 167
    physical, 166
  family during, 172–173
  response to illness in, 170
  sexuality in, 117–118
Adoption studies, 307, 308t
  of psychoses, 313–315
Adulthood, 178–204
  consolidation of, 189–190
  early, 185
  precocious, 188–189
  sexuality in, 118–119
  stages of
    bereavement, 200–202
    courtship, marriage and marital
      crisis, 190–195
    late life, 202–204

midlife transition, 199–200
pregnancy, childhood and parenting, 195–199
transition to, 185–189
Affect, neural substrate of, 264
Affective development
  adolescent, 167–169
  in early childhood, 157–159
  in infancy, 143-148
  in middle childhood, 163–164
  of toddlers, 152–154
Affiliation
  brain and, 233–234
  neuroanatomical
    correlates of, 234–235
Age, 20–21
  utilization and, 24–25
Age correction procedure, 306–307
Aggression
  ethological view of, 249–254
  neurobiology of, 293–296
Aggressive drives, 59, 61
Ainsworth, Mary, 145
Alcohol abuse
  fetal effects of, 138
  parental, 174
Alexander, F., 335

Alternation, 252
Altruism, 69
Ambivalence, 252
Anaclitic depression, 145
Anal stage, 53, 60–62
Anger, 329, 332–333
Animism, 156
Antecedents, 97–99
Anticipation, 69
Anxiety, 329, 331–332
  in psychoanalytic theory, 67–68
  separation, 230–231
  social deprivation and, 228
  stranger, 146
Anxious avoidant attachment, 145
Anxious resistant attachment, 145
Applied behavior analysis, 99
Appropriate stimulus control, 102
Arousal, neural substrate of, 262
Assimilation, 137
Associative play, 154
At-risk children, 173–174
Attachment, 51, 143–145
  effects of deprivation on, 145–146
  psychobiology of, 227–233
Attention, neural substrate of, 262
Attentional processes, 100
Autonomy, 184
  family and development of, 208–209
Avoidance behavior, 91

B

Baer, D. M., 99
Backup reinforcers, 92
Bandura, Albert, 87, 93, 100–101
Basic trust, 145, 183, 184
Bechterev, Vladimir, 86
Beck, A. T., 101
Beck, J. G., 127
Becker, 39
Behavior
  illness-related, 22–26
  and predisposition to physical illness,
    11–12
  reasons for study of, 3–4
Behavioral medicine, 103

Behavioral theory, 51, 85–108
  applications of, 101–103, 104t
  cognitivist, 100–101
  criticisms of, 106–108
  fundamental concepts in
    antecedents, 97–99
    classic conditioning, 88–90
    extinction, 93–94
    imitation, 93
    operant conditioning, 90, 91t
    punishment, 94–97
    reinforcement, 91–92, 94
  major contributions to, 86–87
  misconceptions about, 107t
  psychoanalytic theory compared
    with, 105–106
  reciprocal inhibition and, 99–100
Bereavement, 200–202, 328–330
Berlin, E. O., 46
Biofeedback, 103
Biologic interventions, 8
Biologic variables, 6
Biopsychosocial model, 3–27
  case formulation in, 6–11
  in general medical practice, 11–17,
    323–336
    abnormal illness responses,
      330–334
    doctor-patient relationship,
      323–325
    grief process and illness, 328–330
    illness dynamics, 325–328
    psychotherapy, 335–336
  for psychiatric patients, 27
Bird, J., 335
Black Americans, 41–42
Blum, G., 64
Boelens, W., 102
Bonding, 143, 246–248. *See also*
    Attachment
Borderline personality disorders, 74
Boundaries
  in family, 209, 215–216
  generational, 171
Bowen, Murray, 211–213
Bowlby, John, 143, 146, 230

Bradshaw, W. H., 41
Brain
    affiliation and, 233–234
    location of steroid binding in, 281
    in regulation of reproductive behavior, 291
    social environment as mediator of development of, 235–236
Brenner, C., 68
Buckley, P., 335

C

Castration anxiety, 67
Central nervous system, development of
    social environment and, 233–236
    thyroid hormone and, 283–284
Character disorders, 53
Character neurosis, 70
Chess, Stella, 147, 148
Childbirth, 196–197
Childhood, development in. *See* Development, childhood
Chromosomal abnormalities, 114t
Circadian rhythms, 302
Circular reactions, 142–143, 151
Classic conditioning, 88–90, 286–287
Clinical cases, study of, 342
Cognitive development, 133, 137
    in adolescence, 167
    in early childhood, 155–157
    in infancy, 142–143
    in middle childhood, 162–163
    of toddlers, 151
Cognitive psychology, 51
Cognitivists, 100–101
Cohen-Cole, S., 335
Communication
    cross-cultural, 46
    in family, 208
    in infancy, 143
    psychiatric disorders in, 17–19
Competence, family and development of, 208–209
Compromise formation, 53, 70, 252
Concrete operations stage, 162

Concrete thinking, 156
Condensation, 58
Conditioned punishers, 97
Conditioned reinforcers, 92
Conditioned response, 88
Conditioned stimulus, 88
Conditioning
    classical, 88–90, 286–287
    operant, 90, 91t
    respondent, 88t
Conflict avoidance in family, 216
Conflict behaviors, 249–254
Conflict-free aspect of ego, 71
Conflict resolution in family, 208
Conscience, 163–164
Conscious processes, 53, 57
Consolidation of adulthood, 189
Consumptive behavior, 292–293
Contingency contracting, 102
Contingency management, 102
Continuous reinforcement, 94
Cooperative play, 160
Core morphologic identity, 153
Counseling for marital crises, 193–194
Countertransference, 54, 79
Courtship, 190–191
Crises
    familial, 171
    marital, 192–193
    normative, 181, 182
Cross-cultural communication, 46
Cultural influences on development, 170
Culture, 31–37
    and explanatory models of illness, 33–34
    normality defined by, 34–35
    personality development and, 35–37

D

Danger, increased attachment in face of, 229
Day care, 157–158
Day residue, 57
Decision time, 23–24
Declarative memory, 286

Deductive reasoning, 156
Defense mechanisms, 54, 66, 68–70
  in adolescence, 168
  development of, 153
Delay, developmental, 182
Delusional projection, 68
Demographic variables, 20–21
  in utilization, 24–25
Denial, 168, 329, 331
  psychotic, 68
Denver Developmental Screening Test,
    133, 134–135f
Dependency
  forced, 80
  in response to illness, 334
Depression, 329, 333
  anaclitic, 145
Deprivation
  attachment behavior and, 145–146
  social, 228
Desensitization, systematic, 99
Desire, sexual, 125
Despair, ego integrity versus, 185
Determinism, 105
  psychic, 55, 57
  reciprocal, 100
Development, 131–175
  adolescent, 166–170
  adult. *See* Adulthood
  childhood, 141–166
    early, 155–161
    elementary school age, 161–166
    infancy, 141–149
    risk factors, 173–174
    toddler, 149–155
  cognitive, 133, 137
  and eight ages of man, 183–184
  normal, 132
  prenatal, 137–141
    mental retardation, 139–141
    risks to fetus, 137–138
  risks of disturbances of, 173–174
  role of family in, 170–173
  of self, 76–77
  sexual, 114–118

theories of, 132–137
trauma of. *See* Trauma, developmental
triad of stage, transition and normative crisis in, 180–183
Developmental point of view, 54, 59
Diagnostic and Statistical Manual of
    Mental Disorders, Third Edition
    (DSM-III-R), 35
Diathesis, 173
Differential reinforcement, 93
Differentiation, scale of, 211–213
Differentiation subphase, 74
Discrimination, 88, 97–98
Disease, definition of, 22
Disengaged family, 215
Displacement, 58, 69
Displacement activity, 251
Display, 254
Dissociation, 69
Distortion, 69
Divorce, 173–174
  parenting and, 198–199
Doctor-patient relationship, 323–325,
    335–336
  genograms and, 217
  psychoanalysis and, 78–80
Dopamine, 274–275
Dreams, 57–58
  in early childhood, 159
Dream work, 58
Drug abuse
  in adolescence, 168–169
  fetal effects of, 138
Dunham, H. W., 37
Dyads, 213
Dynamic-motivational point of view, 54,
    58–60
Dynamic unconscious, 54, 57

E

Early adulthood, 185
  failures in, 187–188
Early childhood development, 155–161
  affective, 157–159

cognitive, 155–157
family and, 172
physical, 155
and response to illness, 161
Echolalia, 151
Edelman, G. M., 233
Ego, 54
development of, 65–67
mechanisms of defense of, 68–70
Egocentrism, 155
Ego ideal, 54, 66
Ego integrity versus despair, 185
Ego psychology, 71
Ego-syntonic behavior, 53, 70
Eight ages of man, 183–184
Elderly, 202–204
sexuality of, 119
Elementary school age children. *See*
Middle childhood
Elliott, G. R., 264, 265
Ellis, Albert, 101
Ellis, Havelock, 125
Emde, R. N., 152
Emotional boundaries, 209
Emotional stress. *See* Stress
Emotions
development of, 153
neural substrate of, 264
reasons for study of, 3–4
Empathy, 54, 153
Enactive information processing, 231
Enculturation, 171
Endocrine system in middle childhood,
166
Engel, G., 324
Enmeshment, 215, 216
Environment
CNS development and, 233–236
genes and, 313
Epidemiology
of psychiatric disorders, 17–20
social, 20–22
Epigenetic approach, 184
Episodic memory, 284
Epistemology, 133

Equilibrium, 133
Erikson, Erik, 51, 71, 145, 178, 180,
183–185
Escape behavior, 91, 92
Ethnicity, 25, 31, 41–44
Ethnocentrism, 32
Ethnomedical systems, 33
Ethology, 241–259
aims of, 242–244
concepts and phenomena in,
245–259
bonding, 246–248
conflict behaviors, 249–254
fixed action patterns, 248–249
imprinting, 245–246
innate releasing mechanisms,
256–259
ritualization, 254–256
definition of, 242
history of, 242–244
Excitement, sexual, 125
Experimental analysis of behavior, 90
Explanatory models of illness, 33–34
Externalization, 168
Extinction, 88, 93–94
resistance to, 94

F

Failures, 184
in early childhood, 187–188
Family, 206–209
basic functions of, 208–209
definition of, 206–208
genograms and, 215–221
referrals and, 221–222
role in development of, 170–173
Family risk studies, 306–307
of psychoses, 313–314
Family romance, 159
Family systems theory, 51, 210
Family therapy
family of origin, 211–214
schools of, 210
historic background of, 210
structural, 214–216

Fantasy, schizoid, 69
Faris, R. E. L., 37
Favassa, A. E., 32, 34
Fears
   in early childhood, 158
   in middle childhood, 164
   of toddlers, 153
Feeding behavior, 292–293
Female genital anatomy, 120, 122–123
Femininity, primary, 64
Fenichel, Otto, 64
Fetal development. *See* Prenatal
   development
Field, T., 229
Fine motor development
   in early childhood, 155
   in middle childhood, 162
   of toddlers, 149
Fixation, 60
Fixed action patterns, 248–249
Fleck, S., 170, 208
Flooding, 103
Forced dependency, 80
Formal operations stage, 167
Foster, G. M., 33
Fowkes, W. C., 46
Frank, J., 333
Free association, 54
Freedman, D., 36
French, T., 335
Freud, Anna, 68, 178
Freud, Sigmund, 52, 54–67, 71,
   77–80, 133, 178, 180, 210, 229,
   241, 245
Friedman, E., 212

G

Gamma-aminobutyric acid, 276, 277f
Gender identity, development of,
   153–154
Gender role behavior, 153, 158
Gene markers, 310
   in psychoses, 315–316
Generalization, 88, 98
Generalized punishers, 97

Generalized reinforcers, 92
Generativity, 185
Genetic abnormality, 137–138
Genetic point of view, 59
Genetics, 306–318
   environment and, 313
   human development and, 237
   methods of investigation, 306–312
      family, twin, and adoption studies,
         306–307, 308t
      molecular biology, 310–312
      pedigree analysis, 308–309
      phenotype classification, 312
      susceptibility traits and gene
         markers, 309–310
   psychiatric, 313–318
      major psychoses, 313–316
      personality, 317–318
Genital anatomy, 120–123
Genital damage, fear of, 67
Genograms, 216–222, 341, 343f
   data for, 217–218
   role between patient and doctor of,
      217
Gerson, R., 217
Gesell, Arnold, 133
Goldberg, S., 144–145
Green, M., 149
Grief process, 200–202
   illness and, 328–330
Gross motor development
   in early childhood, 155
   in infancy, 142
   in middle childhood, 162
   of toddlers, 149
Guilt, 67

H

Habituation, 286, 288f
Handicap in newborn, parental
   response to, 141
Harlow, Harry, 228, 234
Hartmann, Heinz, 59, 71
Harwood, A., 43–44
Hatching process, 74

Hauri, P., 299
Head Start, 160
Health belief model, 39–40
Hertzig, M., 168
Hispanics, 42–44
Hollingshead, A. B., 37
Hollis, F., 336
Holmes, H., 13
Hormones
  steroid, 279–283
  thyroid, 283–284
Horney, Karen, 64
Hospitalism, 145
Hospitalization
  in early childhood, 161
  of toddlers, 154–155
Hostility. *See also* Aggression
  separation anxiety and, 230–231
Hubel, David, 236
Humor as defense mechanism, 69
Hunt, M., 117–118
Hypochondriasis, 69
Hypothalamus, 264

I

Iconic information processing, 231
Id, 54, 66
Identification, 63, 66, 168
  with aggressor, 230–231
Identity
  family and development of, 208–209
  gender, 153–154
  lifecycle, 184–185
Identity consolidation versus role diffu-
    sion, 185
Illness
  abnormal responses to, 330–334
  in adolescence, 170
  in childhood
    toddlers, 154-155
    middle, 166
    early, 161
  definition of, 22
  dynamics of, 325–328, 329f
  grief process and, 328–330

  in infancy, 148–149
  normative crisis in, 182
  onset, 12–14
Illness behavior, 22–26
Imaginal flooding, 103
Imaginary companions, 159
Imitation, 93
Immune system, stress response and,
    298
Imprinting, 245–246
Independence, promotion of, 171
Inductive reasoning, 156
Industry, 184
Infancy
  development in, 141–149
    affective, 143–148
    cognitive, 142–143
    communication, 143
    physical, 142
    sexual, 115–116
  family during, 172
  response of child and family to ill-
    ness in, 148–149
Information processing, 231–232
Inhibition, reciprocal, 99–100
Initiative, 184
Innate releasing mechanisms, 256–259
Insecure attachment, 145
Insight, 54
Instinctual drives, 55, 58–59
Integrity in older adults, 204
Intellectualization, 69
Intelligence tests, 139t
Intention movement, 249
Intermittent reinforcement, 94
Internalization, 66
Interpretation, 55, 81
Interventions
  biologic, 8
  early, 160–161
  psychotic, 8–10
  psychosocial outcome and, 15
  social, 10
Intrauterine growth retardation, 137
In vivo exposure, 103

J

Jacklin, C., 115
Jacobson, Edith, 72
Johnson, William H., 125
Jones, Ernest, 64
Jouvet, M., 303

K

Kagan, Jerome, 36, 230
Kandel, E. R., 233
Kaplan, H. S., 125
Kardiner, A., 36
Kernberg, Otto, 72
Kerr, M. E., 211, 212
Kleeman, J., 64
Klein, Melanie, 247
Kleinman, A., 44
Kling, A., 234
Kohut, Heinz, 77
Kraemer, G. W., 235

L

Language development
  in early childhood, 157
  in middle childhood, 163
  of toddlers, 151–152
Late life, 202–204
Latency, 55. *See also* Middle childhood
Latent dream content, 57
Leadership patterns of family, 208
Learning, neurobiology of, 285–289
Learning theory. *See* Behavioral theory
Leighton, A. H., 39, 45
Lifecycle, 51, 178, 180
  and eight ages of man, 183
  identity and, 184–185
  psychologic stages of, 179t
    postinfancy aspects, 186t
  sleep and, 301
Life events, impact on sexuality of, 119
Lines, developmental, 183
Localization of learning and memory,
  286–289
Locus ceruleus, 260
Lorenz, Konrad, 242, 243f, 245, 246,
  249, 257

M

McGoldrick, M., 217
MacLean, P. D., 227
Maccoby, E., 115
Magical thinking, 156
Mahler, Margaret, 71, 72, 75, 147, 152,
  178
Male genital anatomy, 120, 121f
Malinowski, Bronislaw, 36
Management, biopsychosocial, 8–11
Manifest dream, 57
Marital coalition, 170
Marriage, 191–192
  alternatives to, 194–195
  counseling in, 193–194
  crisis in, 192–193
Masters, Virginia E., 125
Maternal behavior, neurobiology of,
  289–292
Mead, Margaret, 36
Meichenbaum, D. H., 101
Memory, 71, 231–232
  neurobiology of, 285–289
  stress and, 232–233
Mental illness. *See* Psychiatric disorders
Mental retardation, 139–141
  causes of, 140t
Metacognitive abilities, 163
Metapsychology, 55
Middle childhood
  affective development in, 163–164
  cognitive development in, 163–164
  family during, 172
  physical development in, 161–162
  response to illness in, 166
  social development in, 165
Midlife transition, 199–200
Midtown Manhattan study, 39
Milestones, developmental
  in early childhood, 156–157
  in middle childhood, 163
  of toddlers, 151
Minsky, Marvin, 233–234
Minuchin, Salvador, 214–216
Modeling, 93, 100

Molecular biology, 310–312
Monoamine-containing pathways, 262
Monotropism, 227
Mood, neural substrate of, 264
Mood disorders, genetic factors in, 313–316
Moral development, 156, 162
Moral realism, 156
Moratorium, 185
More, Sir Thomas, 245
Mothering, neurobiology of, 289–292
Motility, 71
Motivation
  neural substrate of, 263
  process of, 101
Motor development
  in early childhood, 155
  in infancy, 142
  in middle childhood, 162
  of toddlers, 149
Motor performance, neural substrate of, 263
Motor reproduction processes, 100–101
Multifactorial-polygenic effects, 308
Murillo, N., 43

N

Narcissism, 77
Naturalistic medical systems, 33
Negative reinforcement, 91, 92
Neurobiology, 261–303
  of affect, mood, and emotions, 264
  of aggression, 293–296
  of arousal and attention, 262
  chemistry of
    neuropeptides, 276–279
    neurotransmitters, 264–276
    steroid hormones, 279–283
    thyroid hormone, 283–284
  of consumptive behavior, 292–293
  of learning and memory, 285–289
  of motivation, 263
  of motor performance, 263
  of reproductive behaviors, 289–292
  of sleep, 302–303
  of stress, 296–298
Neurologic development
  in adolescence, 166
  in infancy, 142
  in middle childhood, 161–162
Neuropeptides, 276–279
Neurosis, 55
  psychoanalytic theory of, 70
Neurotransmitters, 264–276
  criteria for, 265t
  discovery of, 264–265
  in learning and memory, 289
  linking behavior to, 265t
  neuropeptide, 277t
  receptors relevant to psychopharmacology, 267t–268t
  release of, 270f, 271f
  representative, 266–276
  in reproductive behavior, 291–292
Newborn
  medical complications in, 138
  parental response to illness or handicap in, 141
New York Longitudinal Study, 147
Night terrors, 151, 159
Noncompliance, 39–40
Nonadrenergic pathways, 262
Norepinephrine (NE), 266–267, 270–271, 272f, 273
Normal autistic phase, 72
Normality
  cultural definitions of, 34–35
  in development, 132
Normal symbiosis, 72
Normative crisis, 181
  in health and illness, 182
Nurturing, 171

O

Object constancy, 75–76, 157
Objective morality, 156
Object permanence, 76, 143, 151
Object relations
  development and, 152, 157
  theory of, 71–76

Objects, 55, 58, 71
  loss of, 67
  transitional, 147
Obsessive-compulsive personalities, 62
Oedipus complex, 36, 62–64, 159
  resolution of, 64–65
Offer, D., 167
Older adults, 202–204
  sexuality of, 119
Onset of illness, 12–14
Operant conditioning, 90, 91t
  antecedents in, 98t
Oral stage, 55, 60–61
Organization, 133
Orgasm, 125
Outcome
  impact of health attitudes on, 23–24
  interventions and, 15
Overprotectiveness, 216
Ovesey, L., 36

P

Parallel play, 154, 159
Parental coalition, 170–171
Parenting, 197–198
  alternatives to traditional, 194–195
  divorce and, 198–199
  styles of, 171–172
Parsons, Talcott, 26
Passive-aggressive behavior, 69
Part-object, 72
Pavlov, Ivan, 86–88
Pavor nocturnus, 151, 159
Pedigree analysis, 308–309
  of psychoses, 315
Penis envy, 64
Perception, 71
Personalistic medical systems, 33
Personality development
  cultural influences in, 35–37
  genetics of, 317–318
Phallic-oedipal stage, 55, 60, 62–65
Phenocopies, 308
Phenotype classification, 312
Physical development

in adolescence, 166
in early childhood, 155
in infancy, 142
in middle childhood, 161–162
of toddlers, 149, 151
Physiologic reactivity, influence of early
  experience on, 229
Piaget, Jean, 51, 76, 133, 137, 142, 151,
  155–156, 162, 167
Play
  associative, 154
  cooperative, 160
  parallel, 154, 159
  solitary, 159
  symbolic, 154
Pleasure-unpleasure principle, 55, 66
Positive reinforcement, 91
Practicing subphase, 74–75, 152
Precocious adulthood, 188–189
Preconscious, 55, 57
Precosity, 182
Prediction studies, 307
Predisposition to physical illness,
  11–12
Pregnancy, 195–196. *See also* Prenatal
  development
Prematurity, 137
Prenatal development, 137–141
  sexual, 114–115
Preoperational stage, 151, 155
Preschool children, 160
Primary care, epidemiology in, 19–20
Primary process, 55, 57
Primary punishers, 97
Primary reinforcers, 92
Problem-oriented method, 339–342
Procedural memory, 286
Productivity of family, 208
Projection, 69, 168
Pseudo-adults, 188
Pseudo-self, 212–213
Psychiatric disorders. *See also* Neu-
  rosis
  biopsychosocial model of, 27
  developmental trauma and, 236–237

epidemiology of, 17–20
genetics of, 313–317
parental, 174
Psychobiologic mechanisms, 15–16
Psychic determinism, 55, 57
Psychoanalytic theory, 51–81
anxiety in, 67–68
behavioral theory compared with,
105–106
defense mechanisms in, 68–70
ego development in, 65–67
fundamental concepts of, 56–60
dreams, 57–58
dynamic point of view, 58–60
glossary, 53–56t
neurosis in, 70
physician-patient relationship and,
78–80
psychosexual development in, 59–65
therapy based on, 80–81
Psychologic intervention, 8–10
Psychologic variables, 6–7
in decision time, 23–24
in predisposition to illness, 11–12
in utilization, 25–26
Psychoneuroimmunology, 298
Psychopharmacology, neurotransmitter
receptors relevant to,
267t–268t
Psychoses, genetics of, 313–316
Psychosexual development, 56, 59–65
Psychosocial interventions, 15
Psychotherapy for medically ill,
335–336
Psychotic denial, 68
Puberty, 116–118, 162, 166
Punishment, 90, 94–97

R

Race, 21. *See also* Ethnicity
Rahe, R. H., 13
Rapprochement subphase, 75, 152
Rationalization, 168
Reaction formation, 69, 153, 168
Reciprocal determinism, 100

Reciprocal inhibition, 99–100
Reconstituted family, 173
Redirection, 249–250
Redlich, F. C., 37
Reduced penetrance, 308
Referral process, 222–224
Regression, 59–60, 183
Reinforcement, 90–92
differential, 93
schedules of, 94, 95t
Relaxation techniques, 103
Releasing mechanisms, innate,
256–259
Repetition, 183
Repetition compulsion, 56
Repression, 68, 69, 168
Reproductive behavior.
See Sexuality
Resilient children, 174
Resistance, 56
Respondent conditioning, 88–90
Response prevention, 103
Retention process, 100
Reticular formation, 262
Retirement, 202–203
Rigidity in family, 216
Risk-taking behavior, 168–169
Ritualization, 254–256
Rituals, family, 209
Robertson, James, 143
Role diffusion, identity consolidation
versus, 185
Roles
boundaries of, 209
gender, 158
Rosen, R. C., 127

S

Sadistic-anal stage, 61
St. Cuthbert, 245
Satiation, 92
Scale of differentiation, 211–212
Satir, V., 208
Scheper-Hughes, N., 37
Schizoid fantasy, 69

Schizophrenia, genetic factors in,
    313–316
Sechenov, Ivan, 86
Secondary elaboration, 58
Secondary process, 56, 57
Secure attachment, 145
Self
    development of, 76–77
    pseudo-, 212–213
    solid, 212–213
Self-esteem, family and development
    of, 208–209
Self theory, 76–77
Selye, Hans, 16, 266
Semantic memory, 286
Separation
    psychobiology of, 227–233
    psychophysiologic and biochemical
        responses to, 235
Separation-individuation, 72–75, 147
Sensitization, 286, 288f
Sensorimotor stage, 142, 151
Serotonin (5-HT), 273–274
Sex differences, 21
    in utilization, 24–25
Sexual drives, 59
Sexual history, 128t
Sexuality, 113–129
    in adulthood, 118–119
    development of, 114–118
        in infancy, 115–116
        prenatal, 114–115
        in puberty, 116–118
    in early childhood, 158–159
    of elderly, 119
    human sexual response, 119–127
    impact of life events on, 119
    in middle childhood, 164
    neurobiology of, 289–292
Shaping, 93
Shapiro, T., 168
Sick role, 26
Signal anxiety, 67
Simple schedule of reinforcement, 94
Single parent families, 207

Skinner, B. F., 87, 89–90, 100
Sleep, 298–303
    architecture of, 299–301
    in infancy, 142
    lifecycle and, 301
    in middle childhood, 162
    neurobiology of, 302–303
    of toddlers, 151
Snow, L., 42
Social aggression, 294–295
Social class, 22, 31, 37, 39
    utilization and, 25
Social deprivation, 228
Social development
    in early childhood, 159–160
    in middle childhood, 165
    of toddlers, 154
Social environment, CNS development
    and, 233–236
Social epidemiology, 20–22
Social intervention, 10
Social learning theory, 100–101
Social networks, 25
Social processes, reasons for study of,
    3–4
Social Readjustment Rating Scale,
    13–14
Social selection, 39
Social skills training, 102
Social stress, 39
Social variables, 7
    in decision time, 24
    in predisposition to illness, 11–12
    in utilization, 25–26
Solid self, 212–213
Solitary play, 159
Solnit, A. J., 149
Speech
    in early childhood, 157
    in middle childhood, 163
    of toddlers, 151–152
Spiro, M., 36
Spitz, Rene, 71–72, 145, 228
"Spoiling," 230
Spontaneous recovery, 88

Spurlock, J., 41
Srole, L., 39
Stages, developmental, 180
Stereotyping, 40
Steroid hormones, 279–283
    location in brain of binding of, 281
    mechanisms of effect of, 280–281
    metabolism of, 281–282
    regulatory effects of, 282–283
Stoller, Robert, 64
Stranger anxiety, 146
Stress, 12–14, 222
    fetal effects of, 138
    memory and, 232–233
    mechanisms of, 15–16
    neurobiology of, 296–298
    physiologic disorganization in face of, 231
    social, 39
    thyroid hormone and, 284
Structural model, 56, 57, 65–67
Stuttering, 151–152
Subjective morality, 162
Sublimation, 69, 168
Subsystems, 215
Successive approximations, method of, 93
Superego, 56, 66–67, 163–164
Suppression, 69
Susceptibility traits, 309
    in psychoses, 315–316
Symbolic/linguistic information processing, 231
Symbolic play, 155
Symbolism, 58
Symptom neurosis, 70
Systematic desensitization, 99

T

Taxon system, 232, 233
Taylor, C. B., 102
Temperament, 147–148
    differences in, 230
Teratology, 138
Therapeutic alliance, 56

Thomas, A., 147, 148
Thorndike, Edward L., 87, 89
Thyroid hormone, 283–284
Timing of development, 182–183
Tinbergen, Nikolaas, 242, 243f, 257
Toddlers
    affective development in, 152–154
    cognitive development in, 151
    families of, 172
    physical development in, 149, 151
    response to illness of, 154–155
    social development of, 154
Toilet training, 149, 151
Tokens, 92
Tolman, Edward C., 87, 89
Topographic model, 56, 57
Transactional patterns, 214
Transductive reasoning, 156
Transference, 56, 77–79
Transitional object, 147
Transitions, 180–181
    to adulthood, 185–189
    to late life, 202–204
    midlife, 199–200
Trauma, developmental, 226–227
    attachment and separation, 227–233
    psychiatric illness and, 236–237
    social environment and CNS development, 233–236
Treatment alliance, 79–80
Triangles, 213–214
Trust, basic, 145, 183, 184
Turmoil, adolescent, 167–168
Twin studies, 307
    of psychoses, 313–315
Type A behavior, 12, 15

U

Unconditioned response, 88
Unconditioned stimulus, 88
Unconscious, 56, 57
    dynamic, 54, 57
Utilization, 22–26

V

Vacuum activity, 251
Variables, psychosocial, 6–7
  influence on course and outcome of
    illness of, 14–15
  in predisposition to illness, 11–12
Violence, 296
von Frisch, Karl, 242, 243f

W

Watson, John B., 86, 89, 100

Weiss, H. D., 124
Whiting, Beatrice, 35
Whiting, John, 35
Winnicott, D. W., 147
Wish-fulfillment, 57
Wolf, N. M., 93
Wolpe, Joseph, 87, 99–100

Z

Zborowski, M., 40